DATE DUE

WITHDRAWN

Brodart Co.   Cat. # 55 137 001   Printed in USA

SIMONE DE BEAUVOIR

Also by Margaret Crosland

Colette: The Difficulty of Loving
Women of Iron and Velvet
Beyond the Lighthouse
Piaf

MARGARET CROSLAND

Simone de Beauvoir

The woman and her work

HEINEMANN : LONDON

First published in Great Britain 1992
by William Heinemann Ltd
an imprint of Reed Consumer Books Ltd
Michelin House, 81 Fulham Road, London SW3 6RB
and Auckland, Melbourne, Singapore and Toronto

ISBN 0 434 149020

A CIP catalogue record for this book
is available at the British Library

Typeset by Deltatype Ltd, Ellesmere Port
Printed in Great Britain by
Mackays of Chatham PLC

For Rita Lüdecke Hodge
as promised

CONTENTS

PHOTOGRAPH CREDITS

1. Courtesy of Hélène de Beauvoir
2. Courtesy of Hélène de Beauvoir
3. Courtesy of Hélène de Beauvoir
4. Courtesy of Sylvie Le Bon de Beauvoir
5. Centre Audio-Visuel Simone de Beauvoir, Paris
6. Courtesy of Sylvie Le Bon de Beauvoir
7. Courtesy of Sylvie Le Bon de Beauvoir
8. Bob McCullough, courtesy of Bloomsbury Publishing Ltd
9. Courtesy of Peter Owen Ltd
10. Simone de Beauvoir, courtesy of Sylvie Le Bon de Beauvoir
11. Magnum Photos Ltd
12. Simone de Beauvoir, courtesy of Sylvie Le Bon de Beauvoir
13. Rex Features Ltd
14. Rex Features Ltd

ACKNOWLEDGMENTS

Simone de Beauvoir was her own first and tireless biographer, writing over a million words about herself, her life and work. Later biographers therefore must know their place and remember the words of Stendhal, a writer whom Beauvoir admired: 'Egotism, *provided it be sincere*, is one way of portraying the human heart.'

Energy and patience have been needed to write her life and link its avatars to the development of her work and reputation, apparently full of contradiction and paradox. The time I have spent on this book has been extended by two principal factors, Beauvoir's death in the spring of 1986 and the later decision by her adopted daughter Sylvie Le Bon de Beauvoir to publish, in 1990, two volumes of Beauvoir's letters to Sartre, covering the years 1930–1963 and the *Journal de Guerre*, September 1939 to January 1941. If Beauvoir's death was an irreparable loss, these posthumous publications have allowed deeper insight into her personality and relationships.

The cooperation of Hélène de Beauvoir, Simone's younger sister, and of Sylvie Le Bon de Beauvoir has been essential. I am also much indebted to the detailed compilation by Claude Francis and Fernande Gontier, *Les Ecrits de Simone de Beauvoir*, published in 1978, with its 'unpublished or rediscovered texts', and I thank the editors, early biographers of Simone de Beauvoir, for their research and advice.

Many other people have helped me with encouragement, research and memories. They include Bruce Hunter of David Higham Associates, Amanda Conquy, Elspeth Sinclair, Jane Carr, the editorial staff of William Heinemann Ltd, Stephanie

Darnill and Henry Maas. In Paris Denise Merlin gave reliable support, François Jonquet carried out interviews and extensive research both in Paris and New York, while Paul Webster continually gave me valuable advice. I am indebted to many others, especially to my friend the late Richard N. Coe, who first stimulated my interest in Beauvoir's thought and writing method. The list of helpful people is long: Neville Armstrong, Madame Simone d'Auvigny, Jean Cau, Claudine Chonez, Lawrence Daly, Lily Denis, Mademoiselle Du Moulin de Labarthète, the Queen of Denmark, André Deutsch, Dr Peter Dupré, Robert Gallimard, Dr George Gaskell, Sabrina Izzard, the late Dr Marthe Lamy, Monique Lange, Jan Le Witt, Patrick Marnham, Jean Mauldon, the late George Mikes, Marcel Mouloudji, Nicholas Powell, Diana Quick, Robert A. Tibbetts, Curator of Rare Books and Manuscripts, Ohio State University Libraries, Thomas J. Watson, W.J. Weatherby, Michael Williams, the late Sir Angus Wilson, Ellen Wright.

The London Library was as helpful to me as ever, while the staff of the Centre Audio-Visuel Simone de Beauvoir and the Bibliothèque Marguerite Durand in Paris supplied me with information, documents and photographs.

I have had invaluable help with word processing and typing from Christopher Crofton-Sleigh, Wendy Mackenzie, Diana Phillips, Rosemary Riley and Ann Sharp.

M.C.

INTRODUCTION

In 1978 Beauvoir encouraged two of her friends, Josée Dayan and Malka Ribowska, to make a documentary film about herself, her life and her work. When asked why she wanted it, she replied that her wish was due partly to vanity; in this way people who did not read her would come to know her, while people who had misconstrued her would come to understand her. A film, she thought, was a way of putting the record straight, 'a kind of vanity and a desire for truth'.

When asked how she would define the unity and continuity of her life she said that in one way it was due to Montparnasse. Her 'long march' from the old-fashioned but comfortable bourgeois apartment at the Carrefour Vavin, where she spent the first ten years of her life, to the classless intellectual ambiance of her last home, the studio in the rue Schoelcher, covered many decades but only a few kilometres of streets. She had begun to write in Montparnasse and had made only a few brief excursions outside it. The other constant themes in her life had been her long relationship with Sartre and her close friendship with a few other people. She and her 'family', as she called them, rarely deserted Montparnasse.

The area, which lies across the 6th and 14th *arrondissements* of Paris, has a long and picturesque history, its name recalling the mountain in Greece that was the haunt of the muses. A small hill where the students of Paris used to gather several centuries ago,

1

Montparnasse never lacked personalities of all kinds, ranging from *Bubu de Montparnasse* in the moving novel by Charles-Louis Philippe[1] to Kiki de Montparnasse, the extraordinary artists' model who lived and outlived herself until after World War II. Trotsky frequented La Rotonde, while the Restaurant La Coupole still lives nostalgically on its past. Montparnasse has been described as the Greenwich Village or the Chelsea of Paris, and between the wars it was the most international area of an international city. Ideas were always in the air and you could have a good time there for not much money. There were probably more painters and writers per hectare than in any other *quartier*, especially after Montmartre had declined into a cheap tourist attraction. The inhabitants of Montparnasse always accepted foreigners and they are so tolerant that they have even accepted the gigantic Tour de Montparnasse, built to a height of 209 metres in the late 1960s when it generated as much hatred as the Eiffel Tower had done a century earlier.

Saint-Germain-des-Prés, despite its so-called existentialist years after World War II, has not lasted so well. Gone are the days of Le Tabou and Le Méphisto, the days when Boris Vian would refer to the 'Comtesse de Beauvouard'. Gone is the Café de Flore of *les temps héroïques*, although the establishment itself is indeed still there. In 1987 one Paris correspondent for a London newspaper looked in vain for traces of Sartre, 'Mrs Sartre and all the little Sartres'. These latter, the students, he decided, could only afford the latest fast food counter. In fact all that remains of the historical Saint-Germain-des-Prés, apart from the books written in it and about it, together with a few songs, is the church itself; Saint Germanus, the sixth-century Bishop of Paris who founded a monastery here, has outlasted them all.

In the Montparnasse Cemetery Beauvoir's grave, which she shares with Sartre, looks like concrete, but probably isn't. It is conveniently sited near the entrance, and students, with textbooks in their hands, can often be seen standing there. As with the cemetery of Père-Lachaise, the administrators provide a list of

---

[1] Charles-Louis Philippe (1874–1909): novelist. His first success, *Bubu de Montparnasse* (1901), a study of the destitutes of Paris, was influenced by Tolstoy and Dostoevsky.

the celebrities buried there. They include very few women: Cécile Sorel, the actress, Clara Haskil, the pianist, and only one writer – Simone de Beauvoir. Her name and dates, following those of Sartre, have been added to the grave without any further embellishment. If no one can dissuade French admirers from offering plastic flowers, at least, in the April of the following year her death, there was one appropriate tribute, a single red rose, emblem of the 'true socialism' she had always wanted, the ideal socialism in which no individual or minority would be oppressed and in which half the citizens of the world – women – would be free to make their own personal contribution to life.

ONE

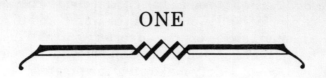

I was a
good little girl

In late June, 1970, a group of French intellectuals were walking along the Paris boulevards towards the east of the city. They were handing out copies of a left-wing newspaper called *La Cause du Peuple* which the conservative government, led by Jacques Chaban-Delmas, disliked. The paper was not illegal, but copies had been confiscated by the authorities and the editors had been arrested. The demonstrators wanted to make the French public aware of a serious double threat: the freedom of the press, the freedom of the individual, were in danger.

Simone de Beauvoir had helped to form an association in support of *La Cause du Peuple* and was joint president. She, along with Jean-Paul Sartre, had organized and led this demonstration. Now aged sixty-two, her whole life was dedicated to the defence of individual freedom; any attack on it attracted her anger, criticism and action. The personal progress that led to this protest against government repression had been long. She had begun life as a 'good little girl' among the old-fashioned, traditionalist middle class. The study of philosophy led to various teaching posts and a distancing from her bourgeois background. Since publishing her first novel, *L'Invitée* (*She Came to Stay*), during the German Occupation of France, she had never stopped writing and she became first the radical theorist, and gradually later the active supporter, of many causes which were all the 'cause of the people'. One cause, with which she will always be associated, was the most radical of all. Her long-term plan, formulated as far back as 1949 in *The Second Sex*, was to end a basic social divide existing within all kinds of people in all countries of the world, and to integrate within the human race an oppressed caste: women. When women and men had acquired equal status and personal freedom, then, and only then, could society make any true progress.

The writer had been born in Paris on January 9th, 1908, and christened Simone Lucie Ernestine Marie Bertrand de Beauvoir. Two years earlier her parents-to-be, Georges de Beauvoir and Françoise Brasseur, had met at Houlgate-sur-Mer, a seaside resort to the west of Deauville on the French Normandy coast. The meeting followed careful family negotiations about a possible marriage. The two young people belonged to two different spheres of the French middle class and their respective families came from two different regions of the country. The Bertrand de Beauvoirs belonged originally to Burgundy in the central eastern area, while the Brasseurs lived in the extreme north-east, near the frontiers of Belgium and Luxemburg.

The known history of the de Beauvoir family stretches back to the eighteenth century, and at least one member lost his head during the excesses of the French Revolution. In the following century however Simone's great-grandfather, François-Narcisse Bertrand de Beauvoir, moved further west and settled in the Limousin region. He was a Contrôleur de Contributions, a kind of tax inspector, in Argenton-sur-Creuse in the Indre, situated between the large town of Poitiers and the Berri area, associated with the writer George Sand. By chance, when the inspector was travelling still further south, in the neighbourhood of Uzerche in the Corrèze, he discovered the hamlet of Meyrignac and the small but welcoming house of the same name. It was an attractive property, surrounded by five hundred acres of land, which included two farms, a wide stream and many different kinds of trees. The tax inspector had found a bargain, for the area was poor and the price of property low. He bought Meyrignac and began to develop the estate.

His son, Ernest-Narcisse, Simone's grandfather, inherited this romantic country home. He planted more trees, many of them rare. Meyrignac became even more attractive, and by the early 1900s the façade of the house, with its white shutters, was festooned with wistaria and decorative climbing plants; there were peacocks, exotic bignonias. Waterfalls had been built in the stream, there were goldfish and waterlilies, the air was scented with magnolia and honeysuckle. Meyrignac still stands, although much changed and enlarged, and has remained within the family.

From early childhood Simone de Beauvoir knew and loved this house, with all the richness and mystery of its gardens and woodlands. Her grandfather, however, had not always been a country-dweller; he spent his professional life working in Paris for the Préfecture de la Seine. He had married a rich wife, a member of the Wartelle family from Arras in the northern department of the Pas de Calais. Simone's father, Georges de Beauvoir, was the youngest of their three children and his mother's favourite. Unfortunately for him this loving mother died when he was still a schoolboy of thirteen at the Lycée Stanislas in Paris. His mother had directed her family and household with loving and ordered care, but her widowed husband could not continue in the same way. He so disliked arguments that he gave up any attempt at discipline and his children did as they pleased. Despite his academic successes at school, Georges seems never to have developed any true sense of responsibility. Neither country life nor urban professional life attracted him greatly. He decided that since he had an aristocratic name he would spend his adult existence living as an aristocrat. There were problems however. It was a good name, but not a great one, and although he had a private income it was unfortunately limited.

In order to augment this income he made up his mind to study law, and his intelligence allowed him to earn some qualifications with a minimum amount of effort. He was then employed by one of his father's friends, a well-known lawyer. However, Georges de Beauvoir had no ambition to rise within the legal profession because he wanted not the drama of the courtroom but the drama of the theatre; he wanted only to be an actor and please an audience.

The reason he did not become an actor was simple, at least in social terms. In France, in the early 1900s, the time of the 'sacred monsters' such as Mounet-Sully[1] and Sarah Bernhardt,[2] a

---

[1] Jean Sully Mounet, known as Mounet-Sully (1841–1916): famous tragic actor associated with the Comédie Française.
[2] Sarah Bernhardt (1844–1923): world-famous actress, renowned for her magical voice. Her roles included Phèdre, Marguerite in *La Dame aux Camélias*, L'Aiglon in Rostand's play of the same name and Cordelia in *King Lear*.

member of the de Beauvoir family did not tread the boards. It was not done. Actors nearly always came from a different, that is, a lower class, or they were *déclassés* for one reason or another. Women, of course, if they persisted in acting, could become immensely popular, but they were often regarded as near-prostitutes, however high-class. For a member of the respectable middle class to become a professional actor, more single-minded ambition was needed than Georges de Beauvoir appears to have possessed. He did the next best thing, he did what many of his friends were doing: he became a dedicated amateur actor.

At this period the French amateurs, even more so than their Edwardian counterparts in Britain, were almost a class within a class, each one having a private income of sorts, and if this was insufficient to allow them to escape a profession altogether one was chosen which did not make too many demands on them, leaving sufficient time to visit the professional theatre, read plays, write plays of their own, study the critics and generally spend their time very pleasantly indeed. Paris already had a long history as a centre of entertainment and its citizens lived in a kind of social complacency which prevented any serious intrusion of reality. International crises tended to take place far away: the Russo-Japanese war of 1904–5 and the formation of the first soviet in St Petersburg did not disturb the life of *petit bourgeois* society in France. The most serious domestic upset had been the long-running case of Alfred Dreyfus,[1] accused of giving military secrets to the German government. When, in 1906, he was at last rehabilitated, after twelve years spent in exile and imprisoned, the middle- and upper-class French, who had remained, as many still do, unwaveringly anti-semitic, could hardly rejoice. France itself, backed by a solid agricultural economy, was prosperous, the Exposition Universelle held in Paris in 1900 had spread French

[1] Alfred Dreyfus was born in Alsace, the son of a Jewish manufacturer. He entered the army and in 1894, then a captain on the general staff, he was charged with selling documents of value to the German government. He was court-martialled, found guilty and sent into exile on Devil's Island. A re-trial in Rennes sentenced Dreyfus to ten years' imprisonment. He was pardoned by the President and in 1906 a higher court found him innocent. He was restored to the army and later made an officer of the Legion of Honour. The case aroused bitter controversy in France, which rippled throughout Europe, enflaming anti-semitic sentiments.

influence abroad and brought many exotic influences into the country, leading to an expansion in the arts and entertainment. The French middle class, regarded as the most rigid and conservative in Europe, had little to worry about.

Georges de Beauvoir did not worry, because he knew he could solve many problems, such as a possible lack of money, by making a good marriage. He had inherited some money from his mother but was spending it fast since he had expensive tastes, and when not watching plays or acting in them with his friends he enjoyed going to the races or playing bridge. He does not appear to have spent any time looking for a wife, for one was very soon offered to him.

His father knew a banker, who had a friend, also a banker, in Verdun, an old and prosperous town in the north-eastern Meuse area. Gustave Brasseur was of partly Belgian origin and had devoted his life to commercial success, which he achieved, building up, in addition to other business interests, the Banque de la Meuse. He had a son, Hubert, and two daughters, Françoise and Lili. The family were sufficiently rich to spend at least part of each winter in Paris, while Françoise, the eldest child, was sent as a day-girl to the Verdun branch of the old-established and expensive Couvent des Oiseaux. The education dispensed there was less concerned with learning than with a judicious mixture of high moral standards and social graces. Françoise Brasseur enjoyed her time there: the girls were taught in such small groups that they could hardly be called classes, and she never questioned the intense and exclusive Catholicism of the establishment, which influenced her for the rest of her life. She learnt to play the piano, she sang charmingly. She enjoyed the convent all the more because she had already realized that, despite their affluence, the home life of the Brasseur family was far from ideal: the sad fact was that her father preferred her younger sister to herself, while her mother was more devoted to her husband than to any of her children.

Françoise knew she could not escape the marriage market; she had been educated for it. She was a handsome girl and was to keep her looks well past middle age. Apparently she would have liked to be an explorer but she had not been brought up for such an adventurous future. Her father would not have tolerated a daughter who had even thought of a career, let alone one so outlandish. The time had come for her to go on display, but her convent education did not prevent her from developing romantic ideas of her own: she fell in love with a cousin, Charles Champigneulles, who was due to inherit a successful stained-glass factory in Paris. She fell in love at the wrong moment, because her ambitious father had recently expanded his business interests too far and had begun to make his first mistakes. He suddenly ran out of luck, for he had relied, in his merchant venturing, on support from a politician who held power locally. At a crucial election this man did not please the voters and lost his seat. There could be no question now of Françoise Brasseur marrying someone of her own choosing, and at this juncture Charles Champigneulles decided not to suggest any marriage arrangement with Françoise: he married her cousin instead. Gustave Brasseur condemned the young man as a cad and detested the Champigneulles family for the rest of his life. More than ever he was forced to regard Françoise as a commodity rather than as a daughter. He was still able to offer a dowry, which was an essential part of a marriage settlement, and the future husband had still to be well vetted. An alliance with the de Beauvoir family was interesting – at least from his point of view.

The Banque de la Meuse did not collapse at once, the family still took seaside holidays, and diplomatic negotiations with the de Beauvoir family were taken a stage further. When the two young people met, in 1906, Georges de Beauvoir was twenty-eight, Françoise Brasseur nineteen. Georges fell in love with the shy, attractive girl who, despite her recent disappointment – indeed, perhaps because of it – responded to the handsome, cheerful Georges. Soon afterwards he came to the splendid house in Verdun – which still stands – to claim her. His younger daughter, Hélène de Beauvoir, has told how he reacted when he found his fiancée seated with a group of other young ladies in the drawing-room. The chairs were arranged with stiff formality.

'*Mesdemoiselles*,' he asked, 'do you always sit round in a circle like this?'

Apparently Françoise Brasseur was deeply shocked. She had not expected a fiancé to be so amused, so casual.

Deep trouble was looming for Gustave Brasseur, but no legal proceedings were yet imminent and his elder daughter was married in Verdun that autumn from the family home. She had hoped to spend a romantic honeymoon among the Italian lakes, but since she had known her fiancé only for a few months she had not realized how far his passion for social life and entertainment could go. Their stay in Nice – the first stage of the honeymoon – was prolonged, because 'everyone who was anyone' was there for the racing season; Georges de Beauvoir could not tear himself away. It was then too late to go to Italy. The bride, of course, had no say in the matter. The young couple returned directly to the Paris apartment at 103 boulevard Montparnasse where they would live for the next twelve years, until the end of World War I.

Simone de Beauvoir was nearly fifty when she began to evoke her life as a 'good little girl', in her *Mémoires d'une jeune fille rangée*, the *Memoirs of a Dutiful Daughter*, as the first volume of her autobiography is known in its English translation of 1959. It is the only volume in the eventual series of four to which she added no explanatory introduction, but she made her purpose clear a few years later: this was to be no mere egocentric talk, no object lesson for young girls. She wanted to describe in detail how she had become a writer. She believed that the experiences of any one person, especially a writer, could benefit others: 'If any individual, an outstanding character or an ordinary one, Samuel Pepys or Jean-Jacques Rousseau, reveals himself honestly, everyone, more or less, becomes involved.' At the same time she wanted to preserve the image of her vanished younger self.

Thus she plunged into the story of her early life. Her beginning is direct, physical, with the date, time and precise place of her birth two years and some months after her parents' marriage. She then evoked the colour and atmosphere of her first home in Montparnasse.

> The apartment was red, red too the moquette, the Renaissance-style dining room and the embossed silk hangings over the glass-panelled doors; in my father's study the velvet curtains were red too; the furniture in this sacred haunt was made from black-stained pear-wood; I would crouch down in the hollow space under the desk, I would curl up within the gloom; it was dark, it was warm, and the red moquette was bright. This is how my first years passed. From my sheltered place I looked at the world, I touched it, I learnt about it.

It was not only the pear-wood desk but the entire life-style of the de Beauvoir family that provided 'a sheltered place' for the little girl. The apartment was comfortable, there was sufficient money for a resident maid, Louise, who was close to Simone and gave her 'a feeling of constant security. She would dress me in the morning, undress me at night and she slept in the same room as I did.' Louise was kind and protective, told stories and only scolded her young charge when it was essential. In this typically bourgeois setting Simone's parents were present but not too close. She loved her mother, but she saw her as 'more distant and more capricious' than the ever-stable Louise. She dreaded her mother's anger, especially because it spoilt the beauty she admired so much. Simone's early recollections fit a pattern that recurs in French autobiographical writing about middle-class family life during this period: both Proust and Cocteau recorded similar memories of their mothers' goodnight visits as they left on their way to a dinner-party, or an evening at the theatre. Simone described her mother as a near-theatrical figure, 'as pretty as a picture in her frothy green dress enhanced with a single mauve flower, in her black gown shimmering with jet'. Such elegance was no more dramatic than was usual in this kind of family at this time, just as domestic life would have been unthinkable without Louise in the background.

Home was secure enough, but as she looked back from middle age Beauvoir remembered how little she saw of her handsome, cheerful father. 'He amused me, and I was pleased when he took an interest in me; but he did not play a well-defined role in my life.' At the same time she remembered how he would read to her and teach her how to recite poetry. When she was a little older he would give her lessons in literature. Simone's parents were both traditionalists in their different ways and automatically brought up their daughter and her younger sister Hélène in the same nineteenth-century style that their parents had followed. Despite the fundamental differences between husband and wife – his penchant for good times contrasted sharply with her adherence to the rules of convent morality – their arranged marriage was at first an emotional success, unmarred by any shadows. The parents loved one another and loved their daughters. It was too early to see the story of Françoise de Brasseur as an object lesson for feminists.

In later volumes about herself Beauvoir tended to stress the stifling, bourgeois nature of her early life and upbringing. She condemned it, she questioned, reflected and speculated. However, when she began this long and detailed autobiography any criticism was implied rather than emphasized. She was preoccupied with external facts and remembered images, trying to describe herself honestly.

In her response to the outside world the young Beauvoir foreshadowed the woman. She hated anyone who considered her as 'a child', as though she were a member of a large anonymous group. 'I was not a child, I was me', she felt – an assertion of individuality that she was to repeat, with suitable amendments, at different stages of her life. At the same time she wanted her rights. 'I took advantage passionately of that privilege of childhood which allows beauty, luxury and happiness to be edible.' The colours of sweets in the shop windows were as exciting as the anticipation of their taste. She also considered, like all children, that she had the right to do what she wanted to do. Since beauty and happiness were edible, anything that was dull and insipid, such as milk puddings, must be rejected. Just as her enjoyment was intense, her hatred was ferocious. In certain situations she would become immediately violent: 'In order to upset me someone only had to treat me as a baby.' When corrected or scolded she would yell, howl, kick and scream so violently that the grown-ups would be alarmed, and she herself pondered over her behaviour later. She decided that the fits of rage could be 'partly explained by a fierce vitality and by an extremism which I have never entirely renounced'.

Another privilege sought by the young Simone was permission to hold the centre stage. The de Beauvoir parents were not tyrannical, they cherished their daughters but were determined not to spoil them. That treatment was left to visiting friends, who must surely have noticed Simone's vanity. She herself admitted that she was pleased by the reflection of her face in the mirror as Louise curled her hair. She was pleased with herself generally and set out to please others, enjoying any social occasion at the same time. When she could not eat beauty she wanted to touch it: 'I would stroke the ladies' furs and their satin-clad bosoms; I had more respect for the gentlemen, their moustaches, the way they smelt of tobacco, their deep voices, their arms which lifted me up from the floor.' Sight, touch, sound and scent; she was aware of all kinds of sensuous pleasure, she learnt about the world, she sought out happiness. She learnt, inevitably, that even if she could attract attention she could not always hope to keep it. She made a wry, dry comment: 'I discovered, with resentment, the short-lived nature of fame.'

There were few moments of disappointment and unhappiness, however, for there was a good deal of love and care. 'My heaven,' she wrote, 'was studded with a myriad benevolent eyes.' She knew her parents loved her, each in their own way. Like Colette before her, who had made Sido and Le Capitaine[1] into two of the most famous parents in twentieth-century French writing, Beauvoir expressed her love for her parents in similar style: she presented them with clear-sighted reality, without sentimentality, or nostalgia.

Her father was both present and absent. He liked the old-fashioned, unchanging but now unreal world of the nineteenth century and saw no reason for modifying his conservative views. When Simone was young he still went to his office every day but his professional career held little interest for him. In his social life he was gregarious, whereas his wife was shy. He would take her to the theatre and bring the theatre into the apartment through his fascination with amateur acting. His tastes in drama, as in literature, were predictable. He liked what was conservative and safe, he liked plays that were graceful and pleasing, suited to his own style of acting. When he had been in his early twenties, at the turn of the century, the Parisian theatre was concerned almost exclusively with entertainment. The brave experiment of the Théâtre Antoine[2] had barely lasted ten years and was over by 1896, when the money ran out. Of Sardou,[3] Scribe,[4] Brieux,[5] little

[1] Colette (1873–1954): Sido and Le Capitaine were Colette's own parents, immortalized in *La Maison de Claudine* (1922) and *Sido* (1929).

[2] Théâtre Antoine: known as Le Théâtre Libre, it was an experimental venture producing plays by unknown authors and using new methods of production. Founded by André-Léonard Antoine (1858–1943), it lasted from 1887 to 1896, when it closed, having accumulated 1 million francs of debts. In its brief life it revolutionized stage conventions and was a landmark in the evolution of modern theatre.

[3] Victorien Sardou (1831–1908): author of comedies and historical dramas characterized by complex, though skilfully constructed plots. Bernhardt took the title role in *Fédora* and Puccini used *Tosca* for his opera.

[4] Eugène Scribe (1791–1861): prolific dramatist of over 300 plays, mainly light-hearted pictures of bourgeois life.

[5] Eugène Brieux (1858–1932): dramatist. His first play was produced by the Théâtre Libre, his work reflected his preoccupation with moral and social reform.

has survived beyond their names, but Labiche,[1] Feydeau[2] and Courteline[3] can still make audiences laugh. Georges de Beauvoir was particularly happy with romance, allegory and poetry: *Cyrano de Bergerac* by Edmond Rostand[4] and Maurice Maeterlinck's *L'Oiseau bleu*.[5]

Simone's father liked to instruct his family. He had read to his wife such serious historians as Taine[6] and also too from *L'Essai sur l'inégalité des races humaines* by the Comte de Gobineau.[7] This had been published in the mid-nineteenth century and was one of the earliest books to develop the theory of the superman and the super-race, the idea that appealed so strongly to the leaders of Nazi Germany in the 1930s. Georges de Beauvoir was convinced that Dreyfus was guilty of the crimes of which he was accused and saw little wrong with the sinister if muddled right-wing ideas of Charles Maurras[8] whose newspaper, *L'Action française*, promoting monarchism, nationalism, anti-semitism and

[1] Eugène Labiche (1815–88): wrote successful farces which are still performed. He is best known for *Un Chapeau de paille d'Italie*.
[2] Georges Feydeau (1862–1921): the author of many brilliant farces.
[3] Georges Courteline (1861–1929): probably the greatest humorous writer of modern French literature, his work is based on the caustic observation of the small happenings of daily life.
[4] Edmond Rostand (1868–1918): poetic dramatist who won fame with *Cyrano de Bergerac* (1897), which was followed by *L'Aiglon* (1900), a historical drama based on the life of Napoleon's son.
[5] Maurice Maeterlinck (1862–1949): Belgian poet and dramatist, prominent in the symbolist movement. He is best remembered for his play *Pelléas et Mélisande* (1892), doubly successful because of Debussy's music. *L'Oiseau bleu* (1909) was a play for children.
[6] Hippolyte Taine (1828–93): influential philosopher, critic and historian. He outlined theories on the interdependence of the physical and psychological factors which influence human development, identifying dominant characteristics conditioned by racial inheritance and physical, social and political development.
[7] Joseph-Arthur, Comte de Gobineau (1816–82): diplomat, novelist and historian. His philosophy of racial aristocracy led to the doctrine of Gobinism popular with propagandists of the pan-Germanic movement.
[8] Charles Maurras (1868–1852): essayist and political writer. He was born and brought up in Aix-en-Provence and came to Paris, aged seventeen, in search of literary success. The Dreyfus affair sparked off within him a passionate political commitment based on anti-semitism. In 1898 a small group of writers founded the Comité de l'Action Française, which became prominent with the publication ten years later of its journal, *L'Action française*, serving as an outlet for Maurras's propaganda, under the clever editorship of the unscrupulous Léon Daudet.

intense Catholicism, lasted from 1908 until 1944. In 1926 Pope
Pius XI tried to stem the influence of the movement on Catholics
and two years later episcopal regulations prohibited adherents to
Action Française from receiving religious rites such as those for
marriage or burial. The readers and supporters of Maurras
became as aggressive as their leader and his success in making
L'Action française a force to be reckoned with is an indication of
the decadence and decay that were to overtake the country,
culminating in 1940. Georges de Beauvoir neither subscribed to
L'Action française nor took part in political life, but he supported
the right wing as a matter of course. Virtually all his class took the
same attitude. They were comfortable, they had few worries.
They devoted a good part of their lives to literature and the arts,
but were much more concerned with aspects of style than with
any practical application of ideas to the problems of everyday life.

Simone's father was in fact more serious-minded than many of
his contempories. He had found it necessary to supplement the
convent education of his wife , and she herself was aware all her
life that she was a provincial, not a Parisian. The distinction
between the capital and the rest of the country has always been
greater in France than, say, in Britain. According to her
daughter, Françoise de Beauvoir felt particularly aware of this,
especially because she was nine years younger than her husband.
As she was also pretty, he soon coaxed her into becoming a
successful amateur actress and appearing on the stage with him.
Often in summer the two children would be sent to relatives in the
country while their parents went to Divonne-les-Bains, near the
Swiss border; there, along with other amateur actors from Paris,
they entertained holidaymakers, and, of course, themselves.

Georges de Beauvoir put together an anthology of poems which
he considered good background for a little girl. They were
nineteenth-century poems by writers who produced sentimental,
moral messages in well-turned stanzas, but their fame has faded:
François Coppée, Théodore de Banville, Hégésippe Moreau.
Simone was taught how to recite them, and she listened while her
father read to her from the romantic classics of the early and later
nineteenth century. She soon came to appreciate the effort he
made to educate her without becoming the fierce schoolmaster.
He was unpretentious and proud of knowing his limitations; he

helped her with writing and spelling and she apparently did not resent the fact that when she wrote to him he would send back her letters with corrections. He would also dictate to her, choosing difficult passages from Victor Hugo, and was pleased that she was a 'natural speller'. He sounds like the ideal father, delighted with his intelligent daughter. She wrote a few significant sentences about their relationship, emphasizing that it was a distant one, for she felt she communicated with only one aspect of her father: 'He did not intimidate me, in the sense that I never felt uneasy when I was with him; but I did not try to cross the gap which separated him from me; there were many subjects that I could not even imagine mentioning to him; for him I was neither a body nor a soul, but a mind. Our relationship was situated in a limpid atmosphere where nothing unpleasant could happen. He did not come down to my level but raised me up to his and I was proud then to feel I was a grown-up person.' Much later she came to the conclusion that the quality of this particular relationship was to influence her when she first encountered Sartre.

Later too she was to realize the extent to which her father had been unable to cope with the real world. He had been a dandy and a social success when young, but none of this satisfied him. He could not have become a writer:

> Literature [wrote his daughter] allows revenge on reality by subjugating it to fiction; but if my father was a passionate reader, he knew that writing demands harsh virtues, effort and patience. It is a solitary activity in which the public exists only in hopeful imagination. The theatre, on the contrary, brought a privileged solution to his problems. The actor avoids the horrors of creation. . . . On the stage, he reigns supreme, and he truly exists: he feels he is really the king. My father took a particular delight in making up: as he adjusted his wig and his whiskers, he escaped from himself; in this way he avoided all confrontation.

He also escaped from the particular sphere of the middle class into which he had been born. 'Thanks to his talents as an amateur actor he in fact gained access to circles more elegant and less austere than the milieu into which he had been born.'

Through his social success the milieu into which his daughter had been born provided the growing, observant child with

17

privileged and magical moments. Her descriptions of them symbolize the happiest years of the de Beauvoir marriage. One particular soirée described by Simone was probably little different from many others but she relished it deeply. The figure of her mother appears briefly, but it is she who holds together a scene which combines family entertainment and private theatre. 'My mother would sit down at the grand piano to accompany a lady clad in tulle who played the violin, and a cousin who played the cello.' Simone is no mere spectator, she assimilates the scene to herself. 'I cracked between my teeth the skin of a candied fruit, a bubble of light burst against my palate with the taste of blackcurrant or pineapple; I possessed all the colours and all the lights, the gauzy scarves, the diamonds, the lace; I possessed the whole evening.' All her life Beauvoir retained this talent for visual gourmandise; she had been lucky enough to learn it at home.

Family and social life formed a kind of well-constructed drama in which everyone played their part. Her 'provincial' mother had become a good hostess, thanks in part to her husband, for he believed it was a husband's responsibility to make his wife into 'somebody', to use his word, and he had obviously been successful, at least superficially. However, where practical matters and moral issues were concerned it was his wife who took all responsibility. Women's work was clearly defined; Louise and other servants carried out all domestic duties, supervised by Simone's mother. One of *her* most important duties was the religious education of her children. Françoise de Beauvoir was a devoted believer and therefore her daughters were taken regularly to Mass practically as soon as they could walk. Their father, and all their male relatives, were never seen to enter a church. As she began to grow up Simone wondered about this: was religious practice somehow connected with women's role in life? For the time being, she, who was incapable of half-truths and half-beliefs, gave her small self to God. She was wary of her mother, whom she described as 'distant', because she was a mother who was always *present*, if not physically so. 'At every moment, even within the secret places of my heart, she watched me, and I saw hardly any difference between a glance from her and the gaze of God.'

Her mother's rigid code of ethics meant that the moral dimension of life was presented to Simone in simple, straightforward terms: 'The two major categories which ordered my universe were Good and Evil. I inhabited the region of the Good, where happiness and virtue reigned in indissoluble unity.' Later in life Beauvoir often spoke of her vocation for happiness, which she considered a rare talent. She had learnt it early, thanks no doubt to the love and security which surrounded her and also to her mother's teaching that 'a sword of fire separated Good from Evil'. She did not know what Evil was, it 'remained at a distance. I imagined its myrmidons only as mythical figures: the Devil, the fairy Carabosse, and Cinderella's two sisters . . .' However, her sojourn in the region of the Good did not mean that Simone herself was good all the time. She would sometimes disobey for the sake of being disobedient and when the grown-ups merely laughed at her she considered she had won. She learnt something then that remained with her always: 'These minor victories encouraged me to believe that rules, orthodox behaviour, accepted routine, are not insurmountable: they are at the root of a certain optimism that was to survive all attempts to tame me.'

If all moral teaching came to Simone from her mother the child, as she grew up, became aware that none of this involved her father, at least not directly. Her mother believed in God, her father did not. Yet her mother accepted *his* attitude. Her father was 'never wrong'. He could not be wrong, her mother could not be wrong. Although he respected the church her father was a pagan and when young had thrown away his own mother's 'moral conventionalism'. He had now encountered it again in his wife. His daughter saw two aspects to life: the intellectual aspect, dominated by her father, and the spiritual, moral aspect, controlled by her mother. 'My family situation,' said Simone, 'echoed that of my father . . . In my case also his individualism and his pagan ethical outlook contrasted with the severe, traditional morality that my mother taught me. This lack of balance led me into constant argument and is the principal reason why I became an intellectual.'

Despite her father's part in her education Simone was aware of how deeply she was influenced by her mother. She insisted that this devoted and seriously Catholic woman was no tyrant, although late in life her sister Hélène said that she was. Both girls were terrified of earning her disapproval, which often took the form of mocking derision. Simone decided later that this fear was the cause of her own timidity, for both girls felt it was unsafe to take any initiatives: 'Prudence counselled us to remain silent.' At the same time Simone loved her mother and did not want to upset her. She was especially aware that if she had told a lie the upset would have been intolerable to both of them, so 'I always told the truth.' She described the relationship with her mother as 'a kind of symbiosis, and without attempting to imitate her, I was shaped by her. She implanted within me a sense of duty and she also taught me unselfishness and austerity.' The foundations of Beauvoir's character were laid in this way, and although he taught her more, in the end she learnt more from her mother than from her father. He 'was not averse to putting himself forward, but I learnt from mama to stay in the background, to control my tongue, to limit my desires, to say and do exactly what had to be said and done. I made no demands and I was not very daring.' It is not difficult to see why, in later life, it took Beauvoir a long time to learn audacity and why, though enjoying admiration, she never favoured personal publicity for its own sake. Eventually she was to become very daring indeed, but in her own special way.

Françoise de Beauvoir accepted without question the traditional role of the respectable married woman. She would not have contemplated any infidelity to her husband but understood very well, like all the women of her class, that he had had sexual adventures before marriage. He apparently kept a photograph of his last mistress in his desk, and accused his wife, not uncheerfully, of having thrown it away. The former mistress, now married, was received as a guest in the apartment. A bachelor friend of Georges de Beauvoir who lived in sin was also received, but not his mistress. As the years passed there were quarrels between Simone's parents and even Louise, the maid who represented cosy security to the girls, remarked upon her mistress 'screaming her head off'. She would gossip to other servants about Madame's 'eccentric' clothes and say that she was going out too much. Simone would be deeply upset, but only temporarily, for she noticed that if there was a quarrel one day it was all over by next morning.

Like so many Parisian children Simone and her sister would leave the Montparnasse apartment every summer for a long country holiday, going to Meyrignac, some 250 miles from Paris, where their grandfather and his family lived an entirely different kind of existence. Georges de Beauvoir himself was not particularly interested in country life, because it lacked the sophistication he enjoyed so much. The young Simone, however, enjoyed every moment she spent in the Limousin village, describing not the rooms in the Meyrignac house so much as the gardens. Their richness was astonishing, there was an aviary, stepping-stones to an island in the river, trees and flowers of every possible kind. There was no running water, no electricity. The family would also stay at the nearby Château de La Grillère, about twelve miles away, the home of Georges de Beauvoir's married sister. Here there was much heavy bourgeois splendour including a billiard room though without a billiard table, but still no running water, no electricity and, even years later, no telephone. The château was only about fifty years old but it was surmounted with little turrets which reminded Hélène de Beauvoir of the châteaux in the fairy tales of Charles Perrault. There were no flowers in the vast wild park but the children were fascinated by something else – the basement kitchens with their huge array of *batterie de cuisine*, and a cast iron stove that threw out flames.

The girls' aunt Hélène had married Maurice de Bisschop, a local squire, and they lived at the château with their children Madeleine and Robert. Robert hardly encouraged his girl cousins to the admiration of the masculine, for he stayed in bed all morning, cared only for trout-fishing and not at all for lessons, which were provided by elderly tutors paid at very low rates. His sister Madeleine, a few years older than Simone, was the only member of the family who ever read a book, and her reading was never censored. She became important in the life of the Beauvoir girls when they were a little older: it was she who explained to them all the things that grown-ups kept secret from children, in particular the contents of forbidden books and the facts of life.

Meyrignac and La Grillère completed Simone's education in other important ways. 'I was allowed to run freely over the lawns and I could touch everything. Scraping in the soil, digging in the mud, crushing flowers and corollas, polishing horse-chestnuts, stamping on hollow seed-pods, I learnt things that were taught neither by books nor by teachers . . . I learnt that holly berries are redder than the fruit of the rose laurel or the mountain ash, that autumn gilds the peaches and burnishes the leaves with copper . . .' It was a far cry from Montparnasse, where children had to be taken to the Luxembourg Gardens or allowed to make sand-pies in neighbouring squares.

It was at Meyrignac, that Simone, aged about six or seven, decided for the first time to make a bid for freedom. She, her sister and her cousin had been punished for some misbehaviour and were not allowed to have any dessert at lunchtime. Hélène recounted how Simone reacted. ' "I've had enough," she said. "This can't go on, we're going to leave." ' With the other two girls she put aside biscuits and bread for a few days and when the food store was considered sufficient all the children climbed into a toy pedal car. They 'drove' off, down to the end of the garden drive. Simone then considered that they had gone far enough and had made their gesture of independence. Her sister told this story because she believed it was the first example of Simone's natural leadership. 'If she said "we're leaving", we left . . . People followed her.'

The relationship between Simone and Hélène was one of heartening closeness. When the second child had been expected, the family believed they deserved a son. One of the grandfathers had even written a letter saying, 'We are awaiting so impatiently the birth of our little boy.' On hearing of the birth of Hélène he had to add a postscript: 'I have just learnt that a little girl has been born. God's will be done.' And, added that little girl when telling this story, 'he was not even a believer'. Simone was only briefly jealous of the new daughter, who had to struggle until the end of her adolescence with the problem of being the younger girl. The sisters were treated fairly and dressed alike, but Hélène always knew that Simone was more 'interesting' to her parents while she was more 'affectionate'. Simone, to the very end of her life, loved her sister with all her heart and as a child, whenever she herself learnt something, she at once passed on her knowledge to Hélène. Having learned these skills very early she taught 'Poupette', as Hélène was called, to read and count. She, like her father, loved teaching.

Soon it was time to learn in a more organized way. It was a sad moment for Hélène when Simone, with great enthusiasm, began to go to school, for the two girls had never been separated. In 1913, when she was five and a half, Simone started to attend the Cours Désir, or, to cite its correct name, the Institut Adeline Désir, situated then at 39 rue Jacob. It was a private school, patronized mainly by children from well-off, even aristocratic families, and although Simone's father was not rich he had decided that his intelligent daughter deserved serious education. She has described this establishment, where the twentieth century had not yet begun to exist, and other details came to light from women who were her contemporaries. It was not precisely a school, for the students attended for lessons only on three days a week. For the rest of the time they worked at home under the supervision of their governesses. Since the de Beauvoirs could not afford such a person Simone studied on her own with help from her mother. Governesses or mothers actually attended the Cours, sitting in the background, while the students themselves sat round big tables covered in green.

One former schoolgirl remembers that when the pile of compositions was placed on the table everyone knew that the top one, the best one, would inevitably be that of Simone de Beauvoir. According to Madame Simone d'Auvigny, who attended the Cours Désir for three years along with Simone, 'she composed essays which were always interesting. She was very much in advance of her age.' She did not linger on the premises after lessons were over and tended to be somewhat distant with the other girls.

Years later the girl who was always top of the class admitted one of the reasons why she enjoyed school work so much: it compensated for what she was beginning to see as the inadequacy of home. The first shadow had fallen, the marriage dowry had not been paid. The de Beauvoir home was not uncomfortable but the life-style could no longer be lavish. With an unambitious father, who lacked success in the business world, and a mother whose rigidly conventional morality led her close to tyranny, the atmosphere was not always cheerful. However, such was the positive nature of Simone that she made the best of it. Learning and teaching kept her thoroughly occupied, for when not teaching her sister she would teach her dolls. Though she did play with dolls, she did not show them obvious affection. She liked to keep

23

them in order, whereas her sister loved them, although not, she maintained, in any maternal way.

Simone had glimpses of the outside world, which was close at hand but must have seemed very far away. From the apartment balcony the children could see people who belonged to the other and much more glamorous world of Montparnasse, the men and women who laughed in the street (which was apparently forbidden to middle-class children) as they came out of La Rotonde, the new café which had opened at ground level in the street below them.

Simone was growing up fast. She claimed that even at the age of four she questioned the 'familiar miracle of Christmas', and became even more sceptical when she found the grown-ups only pretended to believe it. By the time she was eight she decided that she was too old to play with dolls. She was six in 1914, when World War I broke out. There were still dolls in the apartment, and at least one of them had been made in Germany. So she stamped on it, crushing its celluloid body. Her patriotism, like her religious belief, was total and energetic. In her enthusiasm she had forgotten that the doll belonged to her sister.

When her early memoirs were published in 1958 the name of Simone de Beauvoir was still associated with the existentialist movement, by then part of recent history, with her Goncourt Prize novel of 1954, *Les Mandarins* (*The Mandarins*), and with radical thinking close to the left wing, although not in any way connected with party politics. In 1949 she had brought out her most controversial book, *Le Deuxième Sexe* (*The Second Sex*), which was to retain its reputation as a key work of the feminist movement. Hers was the leading name among serious contemporary French women writers, and now, unexpectedly, came the revelation of how she had lived as a little girl. No young children had appeared in her fiction and though she had drawn heavily on her own experience as an adult she had never referred to her childhood. Her novels and polemical essays had been so deeply concerned with philosophical and abstract themes that it was hard to imagine that she had been a happy child in an orthodox, middle-class environment.

Childhood, Beauvoir came to recognize, was the key to

personality, and in describing the early years of the child Simone she had traced, even if remotely, the predominating characteristics of the future writer. She looked at everyone and everything round about her with a loving yet dispassionate eye, her tendency to analysis often masking the emotional intensity of her memories. The differences between her parents and the differences in her own attitude towards them were to colour the rest of her life and work. Her mother, simultaneously loved and feared, who guided her into the region of the Good with moral attitudes she was never to forget: her father, admired, appreciated, loved in a different way. She had explained how their contrasting personalities had led her towards the intellectual life. The insistence that she was 'not a child', but her own individual self, a trait apparent so early, was to lead her down the road to her own individual radical beliefs, including feminism. The road was a long one, for she had far to travel, in metaphorical terms, from the safe hiding-place under the black pear-wood desk.

If feminism still seemed remote, femininity was ever-present in this first volume of autobiography, and Beauvoir never denied it within herself. She recorded the image of the 'good little girl' who was so pleased with her own reflection in the mirror, so impressed by her mother's beauty and the charm of women's clothes. The child was feminine, a feminine individual. By the age of fifty Beauvoir knew very well how her early life had influenced her. Even if her account reads like fiction, she maintained that she had left nothing out of the story. Except, perhaps, the emotional depth of her own persona.

In the meantime the nineteenth century ended at last, in 1914.

TWO

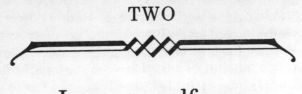

I saw myself as a character in a novel

Before 1914 few European leaders, let alone the general public, had foreseen the certainty of war. The warnings had been ignored: Germany was increasingly jealous of France's growing colonial power acknowledged by the international community at a conference in Algeciras in 1906 which recognized the primary role of France in Morocco. The progressive military occupation of Morocco by French troops continued, provoking the sending of a German gunboat to Agadir in 1911 to strengthen German demands for territorial compensation in the French Congo. The threat of war was averted with a compromise, when the French Prime Minister, Joseph Caillaux, agreed with the German Foreign Minister that France would cede part of the Cameroons in West Africa to Germany, while Germany, in turn, would recognize the French protectorate in Morocco. Caillaux fell from office early in 1912, when the nationalist right wing refused to accept this compromise solution. The following year, under the presidency of Raymond Poincaré, a law was passed making three years of national service obligatory for all Frenchmen.

The intense political struggle between left and right within France overshadowed the increasingly darkening international situation. In mid-July 1914 the President and his Prime Minister, René Viviani, paid a five-day visit to Russia without realizing the significance of what had already taken place at Sarajevo in Bosnia: anti-Austrian nationalism culminated in the assassination of the

26

Austrian Archduke Francis Ferdinand and his wife. On July 23rd
Poincaré and Viviani left Russia, unaware that Austria had sent
an ultimatum to Serbia that very day. Within a few days Austria
declared war on Serbia. French mobilization followed and
Germany declared war on France on August 3rd, 1914. This
ended what some historians saw as a potentially good period in
French history, even if the previous hundred years have been
described as 'the bourgeois century'.

In some ways the two Beauvoir girls were not greatly affected
by the war. Simone still went to the Cours Désir and Hélène
followed her there in 1915. Every summer they were still able to
go to Meyrignac, though all the horses there had been comman-
deered by the army. Their parents, however, knew change
enough, for Georges de Beauvoir was called up. If he had not
suffered from some heart trouble he would have left for the war as
soon as it broke out, for he was only thirty-six. However, as the
military situation worsened the army needed every man it could
find. It was surely a strange idea to draft this not too healthy
recruit into a regiment of Zouaves, for, as carefully selected
troops, they were expected to fight a tough war, and that is exactly
what they did. The Zouaves, who had come originally from
Algeria, were well known for their picturesque uniform, with its
red tarboosh and baggy trousers. No doubt this 'costume'
appealed to the actor in Georges de Beauvoir; he grew a vast
moustache and his daughters thought he looked magnificent.
Hélène, not Simone, as the latter stated in her memoirs, played a
game called 'the brave Zouave', dressing up in one of her father's
tarbooshes and something she imagined to be baggy trousers. The
best part of the game was to hit out at everything within reach
and Hélène did so with such enthusiasm that she hurt her lip and
had to have a stitch put in it. She recalled that her father often
wrote home from the front and that during his absence the girls
felt closer to their mother. Françoise de Beauvoir made an effort
to maintain some social life of her own and at the same time left
her daughters a little more liberty.

In 1916 Georges de Beauvoir suffered a heart attack and was
sent to hospital at Coulommiers. He used his time there in
producing a revue for the patients and staff. After convalescence
he was sent to work at the Ministry of War in Paris. His illness

27

saved his life, for the Zouave regiment was almost wiped out at Verdun.

Verdun was a town well known to the Beauvoirs, and if the soldiers were massacred, the houses remained. The Brasseur family, after the sufferings and disgrace following the collapse of the Banque de la Meuse, had left Verdun. They were living in Paris, not too far from the Beauvoirs, although in an area much less chic. The ex-banker Gustave Brasseur had been in prison and seen all his possessions sold, but he survived because he was an eternal optimist. Since he was incapable of doing nothing he was now running a boot and shoe factory. The war had brought him large orders from the army, so the family could survive, although everyone kept a firm watch on Gustave Brasseur in order to prevent any more speculations. This was achieved by a constant refusal on all sides to lend him any money.

The war also brought fuel shortages and freezing cold winters, but in any case Françoise de Beauvoir had always thought it wicked to heat bedrooms. There was ersatz food, so-called wine made from fermented figs and omelettes without eggs. The Beauvoirs offered shelter from bombing to the tenants of apartments situated higher than their own, which was on the second floor. Simone was encouraged to contribute to the war effort: she knitted a balaclava helmet and saved food for the Belgian refugees, although it had usually gone bad by the time they received it. Some attempts were made to teach her those domestic, 'feminine' accomplishments which were *de rigueur* for all young girls, or had been so when her mother was young. Françoise de Beauvoir was fond of quoting the somewhat sickening nineteenth-century author Marcel Prévost,[1] who had said that a young girl had two friends, her mother and her needle. Simone did not take easily to most forms of needlework. 'I could not tolerate boredom . . . I detested idleness; but tasks which paralysed my body without occupying my mind left me with the same feeling of emptiness.' She tried to sew, and she received help. 'My grandmother succeeded in interesting me in tapestry work and embroidered filet lace . . . I put together a dozen antimacassars and

[1]Marcel Prévost (1862–1940): author of popular 'society' novels specializing in feminine psychology.

28

covered one of the chairs in my bedroom with hideous tapestry. But I would make a mess of hems, overcast seams, darning, scalloping, cross-stitch, raised satin stitch and macramé work.' She admitted to failure in other ways: she enjoyed the challenge of anything new but was not interested in following it through to the end. 'In every sphere I was keen to learn but just as unwilling to apply myself to detail.' Her handwriting was 'formless'. When it came to music lessons she liked sight-reading but never learnt to play from memory and could not sing in tune. Neither could she draw a simple flower, and as for tracing the outlines of a map the future intellectual 'was so clumsy that people could not bring themselves to criticize me. This characteristic was to remain with me for ever. I came to grief over all practical tasks and careful precision was never my strong point.'

However, there were compensations. Her time was filled with omnivorous reading and, despite the bad handwriting, she began to write. When she was about seven she wrote two stories: *Les Malheurs de Marguerite* was about children trying to escape from Germany to France, led by an orphan elder sister. The young author was, however, frustrated by reality: the River Rhine turned out to be in the wrong place. Simone gave up the story and went briskly on to another. It was based on a well-known children's tale, *La Famille Fenouillard*, by 'Christophe', popular in the Beauvoir household because it concerned a family with two young daughters. The author called her story *La Famille Cornichon* but gave no details of the plot. The adult Beauvoir described her early stories as the kind of *bêtises* that all children write, but her parents were amused by them and her Aunt Lili copied them into a blank book presented by her grandfather Brasseur. Simone admitted that she could only write pastiche. It did not occur to her to write down her own experiences or her dreams. Books, she said, were her only models.

When she was a little older Simone began to write on a different level, for she had learnt to relish the act of creation. 'I admired any act that brought something real and new into the world. I could only attempt to do this in one area: literature . . . I knew how to use language . . . I had a spontaneous tendency to recount everything that happened to me; I talked a lot, I enjoyed writing.' She believed that if she described an episode from her own life 'it would escape from oblivion, it would interest other people, it was saved for ever'. She invented some stories, although they were still based on her own experience, and in addition 'I wrote my "French compositions" with great care, so much so that I copied some of them into the *livre d'or*', the blank book reserved for 'special' pieces of writing.

However, this was not the precocious start to a long, unbroken career as a writer, for reading was still more important. There were increasing opportunities for it all the time, especially when Simone was old enough to go with her mother to the circulating library. When very small, at Meyrignac, she had played at being a bookseller, offering her 'customers' leaves endowed with imaginative titles from trees and shrubs.

Books were even more fascinating than the theatre, where she was taken occasionally. The trouble with the theatre was its failure to appeal truly to the imagination: Simone found the actors were 'too real, and at the same time not real enough'. Her elders considered the cinema either 'vulgar' or unsuitable for children. Simone preferred to be alone with her books, and temporarily she gave up her attempts at writing. In any case life was so well filled with school work, teaching her sister, playing games with her and participating in Catholic activities that there was little free time. She found teaching so creative that she announced she would be a teacher when she grew up. This horrified her parents, who saw her as a poor governess with servant-like status in her employers' house.

Simone was determined to control her own destiny and although she hated being classed as 'a child' along with other children, she had no objection to being classed as a girl: 'I resented passionately my childhood state, but never my femininity.' She saw nothing remarkable about boys of her own age, although she did admit that the men in her own family appeared to her to be 'superior to their wives'. She also noticed that men did not play important roles in many famous children's books, and fathers, like her own, often tended to be out of the house or apartment, or somehow absent from family activities. One aspect of her 'destiny' however was more important than any other, and her early view of herself must not be forgotten: 'In my games and day-dreaming I never transformed myself into a man; my entire imagination was directed towards the anticipation of my destiny as a woman.' She was realistic about her sex: 'In particular I did not regret that I was a girl ... I wasted no time in vain desires, I accepted cheerfully what had been given to me. Moreover, I saw no positive reason for thinking I had had a bad deal.'

As a girl and as the daughter of Françoise de Beauvoir Simone was involved in one aspect of life from which her father was exempt: the practice of the Catholic faith. The Gospel stories had impressed her early, for she had been told they were *true*. Her imagination had been touched by the external, legendary horrors to which the early believers had been subjected. She would devise games which her sister Hélène described as 'Catholico-sadico-masochistico'. The best game was to play at being Christian martyrs persecuted by Nero, and the girls would try hard to hurt each other, rubbing their skins with a pumice-stone or pinching each other with sugar-tongs. Hélène remembers that only Simone, because she was the elder, had the right to die and go to heaven. Simone wrote that she cheated in any case. She went into great detail about the tortures she inflicted upon herself after she had been impressed by the sufferings of the saints, especially the female ones. 'I would convert into challenge the passivity to which my sex condemned me,' she wrote, but at the same time admitted that 'my piety disposed me towards masochism'.

It is hard to think of Beauvoir, even as a child, being 'passive', or to remember that she spent so much time playing games, but it is easy to understand that she took play, like everything else in life, very seriously. She realized later how far she must have irritated other children by turning games into a kind of reality and making no allowances for anyone who broke the rules. She herself, as she approached adolescence, obeyed the rules of Catholic living. After she had taken her First Communion she accompanied her mother three times a week to Mass at the church of Notre Dame des Champs in the boulevard du Montparnasse and soon entered a phase of emotional religious fantasy: 'In the darkness of the confessional, facing the suave Abbé Martin, I would feel faint with ecstasy.' There were other intense moments: 'I often imagined that I was Mary Magdalen and that I was drying the feet of Christ with my long hair.' Her fervour became obsessive and she would even go into the chapel at the Cours Désir and offer up prayers between lessons. She wrote honestly about her feelings for God and explained her attitude: 'I loved Him with all the passion that I brought to life.' Belief was all or nothing, and for the time being it was all.

Nevertheless, within the religious setting some of her thoughts were concerned with the secular life and they were happily self-satisfied. 'Despite my timidity . . . I aspired . . . to be a star. On the day of my First Communion I was triumphant . . . I had no scruples about enjoying the profane delights of the celebration.' Her dress had been lent by a cousin, 'but the pupils of the Cours Désir wore not the usual tulle cap but a wreath of roses; this detail showed that I did not belong to the common herd of parish children'. To complete her stardom, it was Simone who was chosen to make the responses on behalf of all the other girls in her group. After a lunch party and a later tea party she laid aside her finery with regret. 'In order to console myself I thought about marriage for a moment: a day would come when, clad in white satin, among a blaze of candles and loud peals of organ music, I would once again be transformed into a queen.' The following year she was a bridesmaid at her Aunt Lili's wedding. 'I loved the silky feel of my blue foulard dress; my curly hair was held in place by a black velvet ribbon and I wore a wide-brimmed hat of natural straw trimmed with poppies and cornflowers.' She enjoyed the company of the *garçon d'honneur*, 'a good-looking boy of nineteen who talked to me as though I were grown-up: I was convinced he found me delightful.'

Simone and her sister thought about marriage occasionally, because it was the orthodox future for any young girl. But what was the reality? Simone could not understand how anyone could tolerate what she called the 'promiscuity of marriage'; how could she live if she could not be alone at night and cry if she wanted to? Late in life she told a journalist friend that for one reason or another she had spent half her life in tears.

Marriage, together with the secrets of sexuality and childbirth, had been explained to Simone by her cousin Madeleine, who based her physiology lessons on the behaviour of her dogs. When Simone's mother was asked if babies arrived through the navel she accused her daughters of knowing everything already. Then she told them that babies came from the anus, painlessly. This inherited, evasive system of telling nothing, with the excuse that such things were improper, had far-reaching effects on Simone. In 1972, when she concluded the last volume of her memoirs, she expressed herself firmly about the problem. 'To dispel mystifications and tell the truth, this is one of the aims I have pursued most persistently throughout my books. This obstinacy has its roots in my childhood; I hated what my sister and I called *la bêtise*, stupidity: a way of stifling existence and its pleasures beneath prejudice, set ways, pretence and hollow phrases. I wanted to escape from this oppression, I promised myself that I would denounce it.'

The 'mystifications' caused an over-reaction in some ways. So much had been kept secret from the young Beauvoir and from all of her sex that she looked for any possible way to change attitudes. When, as a child, she was given books to read, Simone would find sometimes that certain pages had been pinned together; they contained 'unsuitable' details. As a result, in later life, she would never, ever tolerate censorship in any form. Perhaps she went to the opposite extreme. Nothing must be kept secret, and as a result everything, literally everything, every object, every person, every thought, every feeling, every experience must be described, analysed and explained. No emotional or physical disturbance caused by the inescapable onset of adolescence was to remain secret. She was soon to record how deeply it affected her.

Writing as an experienced novelist, she presented remembered incidents from her childhood as though they were episodes in fiction. She imagined the child Simone thinking about her own future and saw herself as someone more interesting than a little girl who liked attention. 'I saw myself as a character in a novel. Since the plot of a novel demanded obstacles and setbacks, I invented them.' The setting was a game of croquet at Meyrignac or La Grillère; the players were Simone with her sister and her girl cousins. 'We were wearing beige linen pinafores with red scalloping and embroidered with cherries. The clumps of laurel shone in the sunshine, the earth smelt good. Suddenly I stood still: I was living through the first chapter of a novel in which I was the heroine . . . we were going to grow up; my sister and my cousins were prettier, more graceful, more pleasing than I was. I decided they would find husbands: I wouldn't.' She would not resent this, 'but something would happen which would raise me up beyond all preference; I didn't know in what way this would happen, or through whom, but I would be appreciated.' She was convinced that she was *hors série*, an exceptional person, but she added at once that 'Only rarely did I allow myself these conceited claims: the esteem in which I was held made them unnecessary.' However, she had recorded what may have been an unconscious glimpse of her own future.

Simone began to notice the world about her, the people outside her own family and the books excluded from the family bookshelves. She knew that her family's social status kept her in the world of private schools, but the status of the Beauvoirs was uneasy and brought its own problems. The young Simone was invited to lavish children's parties where all the guests of her own age were decked out in silk and lace while the Beauvoir girls wore plain woollen dresses in 'dead colours'. Yet the family maintained certain standards in various minor ways. Though Françoise de Beauvoir economized over her daughters' clothes she would still insist on buying her *pâtisserie* from certain expensive shops only. She protected her children in the ways she considered important. The girls' magazine she chose for Simone to read expressed a higher moral tone than its more popular competitors. Simone was forbidden to use the metal cups attached to public drinking fountains and her grandmother gave her a special one in the shape of a mother-of-pearl shell. Nobody else would drink from it. Simone was also forbidden to play with unknown girls encountered in the parks. She did not yet complain about her treatment, and she did not envy the rich. 'My entire upbringing convinced me that virtue and culture were more important than riches: my own tastes led me to believe this; I therefore accepted calmly the modest nature of our life.' It was her natural optimism, she thought, that allowed her to see their 'mediocrity' as a kind of *juste milieu*, a 'golden mean' from which both rich and poor were excluded. She herself had no contact with 'the highest and lowest spheres of society; in reality the former were closed to me and I was completely cut off from the latter'.

How then was she to make friends? When in the country she was satisfied by the world of nature, but in Paris she felt differently: 'I was hungry for human presences; the reality of a city is in its inhabitants.' Suddenly she wanted to break out of the narrow family circle. 'I would be moved by someone's way of walking, a gesture, a smile. I wanted to run after some unknown person met at the corner of the street, never to be seen again.' Beauvoir preserved one image from these fleeting encounters. 'In the Luxembourg Gardens, one afternoon, a tall girl in an apple green suit was with some children, skipping; she had pink cheeks, a glowing gentle smile. That evening, I said to my sister "I know what love is!" In fact I had had a glimpse of something new . . . I felt for the first time that one can be deeply touched by a radiance from *outside*.'

The boys in this outside world did not strike Simone as particularly interesting. However, she came to admire one of them, who was to remain in her life for a long time. He did not truly belong to the outside world, for he was her cousin Jacques Champigneulles, son of the man who had considered marrying her mother, before marrying her cousin instead. Jacques's father had been killed in a motoring accident when the boy was very young. Simone admired her cousin as someone very clever, assured and mature, although he was only six months older than herself. He looked down on girls as a lower form of life but approved of her, because she was 'precocious'. Simone was flattered. The two cousins decided they were engaged and would get married when they grew up. But, in 1917, just before she was ten, she fell in love.

Elisabeth Lacoin, daughter of a senior railway engineer with strong Catholic beliefs and a large family, came to the Cours Désir after her education had been interrupted by an accident. She was placed next to Simone for lessons and immediately fascinated her. After the two girls had taken part in a play – Simone acted Madame de Sévigné as a little girl, Elisabeth played a boy – they had talked so much together 'in the glow of the footlights' that they became inseparable. For over ten years this small, dark-haired, thin-faced brilliant girl was to play a vital part in Simone's life. Her image never faded. Elisabeth, known to all readers of Beauvoir as 'Zaza', occupied a major part of the early memoirs and returned as a very real ghost in the later and fourth volume, *Tout compte fait (All Said and Done)* in which the author reassessed herself and her relationship with her friend. Zaza also made brief appearances, not always easily recognized, in Beauvoir's early fiction.

There were many strands to this deep friendship, so deep in fact that it could be characterized as an *amitié amoureuse*, a little more than friendship, a little less than love as generally understood. For the young Simone Zaza was the first person outside the family with whom she formed a close and lasting relationship. Soon after introducing her into the early memoirs Simone set out her straightforward attitudes towards emotional relationships of all types – affection for the outer fringes of her family, love for her parents and her sister. Zaza was her 'best friend'. She added the phrase 'there was nothing more to say', going on to differentiate between friendship, 'the mysterious splendour of love' and 'the sacred dignity of filial devotion'.

These abstract phrases seem to have no relevance to the Simone–Zaza relationship. It became so intense on Simone's side that it went beyond the set of emotional rules she had worked out for herself. She admitted that she idolized Zaza. What would she do if Zaza were to die? Her whole life seemed to depend on what Zaza said and did. In many ways Zaza was more sophisticated and grown up, while her sarcasm and irony, which are remembered by everyone who knew her, gave her personality an 'edge' which was new to Simone. She was accustomed to her own mother's critical attitudes, but after all she belonged to the older generation. Zaza was everything that Simone was not, she seemed worldly-wise and independent when she was barely a teenager. Simone appears to have relished their 'grown up' discussions more than anything else in their friendship, and the two of them did not always behave like average schoolgirls. At this stage they would talk about school work, about books and teachers but never apparently about themselves. Despite Simone's passionate attachment to Zaza there was no exchange of 'girlish confidences'. They addressed each other as *vous*, not *tu*, there were no kisses, except at the end of letters.

Beauvoir devoted many pages to Zaza in her writings. She could sense in Zaza 'a presence, pouring out like a spring of water, a presence as strong as a block of marble, as firmly drawn as a portrait by Dürer'. As a result Simone felt that she herself had no personality at all. Everything about Zaza seemed to cancel *her* out, while Zaza herself would make sarcastic comparisons between the two of them, at least affecting to praise Simone's perfections. Every facet of this friendship is evoked in the early memoirs. It was no *amitié particulière*, no quasi-sexual relationship such as, for example, the obsessive love of a schoolgirl for a young teacher, but it was intense enough.

In the midst of this exclusive, all-absorbing friendship Simone was overtaken by the inevitable problems of adolescence, and surely no writer has described with more intensity the early sexual awareness, bewilderment and fears of an imaginative girl. 'I had nightmares. A man would jump onto my bed, he would thrust his knee into my stomach, I felt I was suffocating . . .' As she became more aware of sexuality she made other discoveries:

> forbidden books frightened me less than in the past; I would often glance at the scraps of newspaper hanging up in the lavatory. In this way I read a fragment of a novelette in which the hero kissed the heroine's white breasts with his ardent lips. This kiss scorched my flesh; I was man, woman and *voyeur* all at the same time, I bestowed the kiss, I received it and I watched it. . . . I would toss and turn in bed, my throat was dry, I yearned for a man's body against my body, a man's hands on my skin.

She realized desperately that girls were not allowed to marry until they were fifteen, her nightdress turned into 'a poisoned tunic', and no man came near her. She described in detail the first day of menstruation, emphasizing, as she was to do on later occasions, that like so many girls she had been given no warning beyond vague words from her cousin Madeleine. She noticed that her mother's friends were told about this development and her father even made jokes about it. One day, when she wore a new beige crêpe-de-chine dress at a cousin's wedding it was found to be too tight above the waist, so her newly-visible breasts were bandaged and flattened for the day, otherwise she would have looked indecent. She knew only too well what the wedding photographs revealed: 'I was badly got up, I looked clumsy and plain, I was hovering between girlhood and womanhood.'

She wanted to be a grown-up woman, but as she experienced fantasy sex-life and real-life weddings, she came to realize that marriage was a bad bargain. She had often felt sorry that so many adult women lived such boring lives: 'Every day, lunch and dinner; every day washing up; all those hours that began over and over again and led nowhere: could I live like that?' She had quickly grown beyond those romantic daydreams when she saw herself as a bride. In her early admiration of Louisa May Alcott's *Little Women* she had already identified herself with Jo March, the 'intellectual', the girl who loved books and knowledge, who was not interested in being 'good' and 'feminine' in the orthodox way. Simone was then angry when she learned from *Good Wives* that Laurie, the young man whom Jo had loved, had actually married her sister Amy, who was 'blond, vain and stupid'. Later, however, she realized that Jo had already rejected him and in the end she found a 'teacher, older than she was, endowed with the highest qualities' whom she married. The young Simone was not entirely satisfied all the same; she found the husband figure a kind of intruder: 'I did not want the future to impose any breaks: I wanted it to embrace my past as well.' In some ways she had not yet emerged from the safe darkness below the pear-wood desk.

Of Zaza's attitude towards Simone little can be known. Sadly, she was to die in 1929 of an undiagnosed illness after the deep emotional disappointment of a thwarted love-affair, as will become evident later. Beauvoir immortalized her in the early memoirs which were published some thirty years later. After thirty further years had passed, and Beauvoir had died a world-renowned writer, one of Zaza's cousins, Mademoiselle Du Moulin de Labarthète, could not find a good word to say about the young Simone. She had been reluctant to speak about her because she felt she could only find 'unpleasant' things to say. She admitted that Simone worked hard at her studies, but she was not outstanding, she was arrogant, she was *une brute pompière*, coarse and pretentious, while Zaza was much more brilliant. The success of Simone de Beauvoir as a writer obviously rankled. Simone experienced a 'violent passion for Zaza, admiration which was not reciprocated'. Simone was not likeable, added Mademoiselle Du Moulin, she was not affectionate, 'she thought only about culture, the one sphere in which she could shine'. The opinions of this lady might seem to represent the classic attitude of the materialistic French bourgeoisie: culture was far less valuable than money and good social standing. There are many social strata within the bourgeoisie and Zaza's cousin, as she looked back, also looked down on the de Beauvoir family. She condescended to say that Simone's mother was *une très brave femme, une petite bourgeoise*, but her father, whom Simone had admired greatly, was *un sauteur*, unreliable. Mademoiselle Du Moulin attempted to take her family's revenge for Beauvoir's criticism of their 'bourgeois' attitude. She said that the young Simone was ugly and dirty, for she did not wash her hair. She was also covered with spots and 'was not the kind of girl capable of making conquests'.

The personal aspect of the friendship between the two girls cannot be isolated from the social background. The Lacoins were a large and prosperous family, especially after Zaza's father left the railway and became secretary-general of Citroën. The family then moved from the rue de Varenne to the rue de Berri near the Champs-Elysées and could be regarded as even more socially superior to the de Beauvoirs. Simone's mother was conventional and Catholic in an old-fashioned way, Madame Lacoin was also conventional and Catholic but in a newer and more subtle way, ostensibly allowing her children more liberty but in effect conditioning them firmly. Zaza loved her mother but maintained she had been too much occupied with Catholic good works to love her children fully in return. This was apparently the origin of Zaza's sarcasm and cynical, 'adult' outlook on life. But the two girls responded differently to the demands of home. Zaza was the truly 'dutiful daughter', for if she did not enjoy domesticity she at least put up a good pretence. She would help her mother with interminable entertaining, seemingly with good grace, and would even look happy, wearing a perpetual smile. Simone disliked this aspect of bourgeois life and hated any sign of hypocrisy.

Zaza would go shopping for her mother when required, she would spend time crystallizing dried fruit, she played the piano and violin, she could turn cartwheels: what could she not do? In fact she was too good to be true. Simone flourished in her shadow and even said that she was the negative to Zaza's positive. Her obsession was such that her sister felt neglected, although she did not make any serious complaint. Later on Hélène came to know Zaza better and liked her. The two of them even started and circulated a secret and subversive magazine at the Cours Désir. This must have needed great ingenuity because if they had been found out they would certainly have been expelled. It is hard to think of Simone taking part in such an enterprise, but she did so occasionally.

If much of her life was dominated by Zaza, Simone still belonged to her family, where developments were hardly cheerful. After the war her father had little to look forward to, his health would never be good again and he did not feel able to return to legal work. His wife was unhappy and frustrated as a result. By 1918 they had been married for twelve years and although the payment of a dowry could be delayed, it was now clear that it would never be paid. Simone only learnt of this situation much later in life, but when she and her sister visited their Brasseur grandparents the children sensed that the atmosphere was 'grey'. Georges de Beauvoir was also beginning to encounter real difficulties, although his landlord had not asked for any rent while he had been in the army.

By 1919 there was no longer any choice. The family exchanged their second-floor apartment at the Carrefour Vavin – where the boulevard du Montparnasse and the boulevard Raspail meet – for the fifth floor of a house at 71 rue de Rennes, not too far away, not so roomy, but cheaper. There was a sunny balcony, together with a view of the Eiffel Tower, which was illuminated at night by Citroën advertising. Everything about the apartment was slightly smaller, there was no central heating, no elevator, no real bathroom, although this was not unusual at the time. Simone recorded the fact that there was 'only a *cabinet de toilette*, without running water': she also remembered that her father had to empty the washing bowl every day, but her sister Hélène has said that this was 'fantasy'. Simone shared a bedroom with her sister and did her homework in the study which was also a sitting-room.

She admitted the fact that her family had joined the ranks of the *nouveaux pauvres*. Louise left to marry a slater, a girl came from Meyrignac to replace her but was quickly dismissed for 'running after men'. Françoise de Beauvoir decided she would do the domestic work herself but according to Hélène she still invited women friends to tea and occasionally gave dinner parties. One form of economy might have been possible: Georges de Beauvoir considered taking his daughters away from the expensive Cours Désir and sending them to a lycée, where the education was free of charge and much better. But Simone yearned to stay at the Cours, for she could not bear the thought of separation from Zaza. Her father's attitude to this friendship is not known but he was presumably aware that the two girls talked and corresponded about serious subjects, including literature. He must have listened to Simone's pleading and he gave in to her, assuming perhaps that if she was personally happy and in close touch with her friend, she would work better. Hélène has confirmed that the sisters remained at the Cours Désir because of Zaza, but she thought their parents had made the wrong decision. 'It would have been preferable,' she said, 'to send us to the lycée and give us slightly prettier dresses to wear. We suffered all our childhood and youth from this lack of elegance, although we had been warned about the sin of coquetry.' The Beauvoir family was not alone in this, for Hélène also pointed out that the 'right-thinking' middle class did not dress their daughters well, because they were afraid that elegance would have a bad effect on them. But Hélène also thought that if her mother had been less concerned about 'what will people say' 'we should not have presented the image of what was called at the time "genteel poverty" '. One girl who studied with Simone both at the Cours Désir and later summed up the situation: 'At the Cours Désir all the girls, the younger ones and the older ones, were badly dressed, but Simone de Beauvoir was even worse dressed than the others.'

Simone, as she helped her mother to wash up and put the plates away, was convinced that she would never tolerate the drudgery of married life. Professional work, which her father considered socially degrading for a woman, was far preferable. Her father had serious work problems himself. Even his father-in-law's boot and shoe factory, where he had worked as an administrator for some time, was now in difficulties. Simone remembered years later how calmly he accepted his changed, reduced life, and she came to admire him more than ever. He still believed that culture was more valuable than money, but he believed also in the theories of the inherent superiority of some races over others put forward by Gobineau. Having read them earlier to his wife he now read them to his daughters. Hélène de Beauvoir said later that he

41

had carefully brought up his children as 'good little racists', but the results were not what he had expected.

Those results became obvious only much later. In the meantime Simone adopted his ideas about class without much question, but she rarely met anyone outside her own immediate circle and the élitist atmosphere of the Cours Désir. Her father believed that 'enlightenment is the prerogative of the bourgeoisie' and she agreed with him. However, she did not see why poor people should not have the vote, and her father had to explain the situation: administration should be carried out by people who owned property. Simone honestly recorded her acceptance of his attitude: 'It seemed obvious to me, in a moral and therefore an absolute sense: the class to which I belonged was far superior to the rest of society.' She did not enjoy visiting the tenant farmers at Meyrignac: 'The smell of manure and the hens running through the dirty rooms seemed to me to reflect the coarseness of their souls.' She sounded like a typical bourgeois girl and she judged the peasants by her father's criteria: 'They did not read, they had no ideals.'

As she accompanied her Aunt Lili on charitable visits to deprived families she observed that 'the poor did not seem unhappy'. She learnt more about the lives of the poor from books, including novels by Dickens. She was also told about *les faux pauvres*, *les mauvais pauvres*, those who were lazy or dishonest and those who could eat well because they did not have to keep up appearances. 'If the workers hated the bourgeoisie,' she was informed, 'it was because they were conscious of their superiority. Communism and socialism were merely the result of envy.' Georges de Beauvoir had an answer for everything and continued to support *L'Action française*.

Simone admitted she knew nothing about industrial workers and the way they lived. Only once was she moved by poverty when she saw it at first hand, visiting their former maid Louise, who now lived in a garret with her husband and baby. 'Here I had a glimpse of a universe in which the air you breathed tasted of soot, in which no ray of light ever penetrated the filth: existence here was a slow death.' Soon after this visit Louise's baby did in fact die, and Simone wept for hours. It was the first time that she had seen true suffering, the first of many occasions when the case of an individual, especially a woman, moved her deeply. She began to consider the possible implications. ' "It's too unfair," I said to myself. I was thinking not only of the dead child but also of that sixth-floor corridor.' However, she was still too young to question a situation that everyone else seemed to accept. 'But in the end I dried my tears without having called society in question.'

At the age of fourteen she realized that she could not truly think for herself, for 'brought up as I was on the morals of the Couvent des Oiseaux and my father's nationalism I was perpetually caught up in contradictions'. She had been taught that the Gospel exalted poverty, but in this bourgeois Catholic milieu material values always triumphed over moral ones: 'Caesar always defeated God.' In the constant controversy between the right-wing supporters of Charles Maurras and his opponents her father naturally supported the Maurras faction, and she followed his lead. Zaza's father believed Maurras to be wrong, and Zaza assumed the same attitude. Slowly the schoolgirl Simone began to learn about the problems of the real world and recognized that 'it was possible not to share my father's opinion. Not even truth was guaranteed now.'

The truth: throughout all her later life she was to defend it, but for the time being she was still in the same bewildering situation as that caused by her parents' differing attitude towards religion and the church. Instinctively, though, she perceived certain aspects of 'truth' for herself and questioned some of the social 'rules' she was expected to obey. She was shocked by her cousin's attitude towards people below her own class: 'I was indignant when my cousin Madeleine refused to say good morning to the bakers . . . who delivered the bread to La Grillère: "It's for them to address me first," she declared.' Simone could not share this attitude. 'I believed in the absolute equality of human beings.' Despite her faith in her own class she refused to believe that 'riches could . . . endow anyone with rights or merit'. She valued the individual in his or her own right, an attitude she maintained for the rest of her life. 'I had much more respect for Louise than for many well-off ladies.'

Simone had to face other aspects of truth. Her father, for instance, played bridge often and sometimes even stayed away from the apartment all night. Also, during the most disturbed moments of her adolescence she had to accept her plainness which was sufficiently marked to irritate her father. He warned her he could give her no dowry, a social disaster in itself, but a plain girl with no dowry had virtually no chance of marriage, and marriage, at least in the conventional view of her parents, was the future. Simone, of course, still saw herself as a teacher, or possibly a writer, an idea which grew stronger as her reading increased. Her sister Hélène was lucky enough to keep her looks and her father thought that she might succeed in finding a husband. He had failed to notice that she was already an unconscious feminist, well before Simone began to express such subversive beliefs. Hélène planned her career early: she would go to art school, where she anticipated no shortage of competition from men, and somehow she would become a painter. In the meantime both girls had to pass their *baccalauréat* examination. Whenever higher education was discussed their mother had one deep concern, especially on Simone's behalf: she would have to spend at least some time at the Sorbonne and there she would not be able to avoid contact with that ever-growing species, the unbelievers; she would surely lose her faith.

In fact it was already lost. It was inevitable perhaps that Simone's early, intense and unquestioning belief would undergo some change as she moved through adolescence, studied more and saw new aspects of the outside world. At the Cours Désir the older students went into religious retreat once a year and during this time they were required to keep a notebook in which they recorded their meditations and prayers. By chance the notebook kept by Simone in 1922, when she was fourteen, has survived, and in 1980 it was acquired by an antiquarian bookseller in Caen. These seventy-four well-written pages reflect her struggles. *Tiédeur*, half-heartedness, was a dangerous slippery slope which led to mortal sin, for if one became half-hearted then sin was no longer horrifying. Simone was aware of this *tiédeur* within herself and asked God for help: 'Give me the strength to persevere, the desire to begin.'

But God did not help, and neither did her religious supervisors.

> One evening, at Meyrignac, I was leaning . . . out of my
> window . . . my prayer began to rise feebly, then fell back to

earth. I had spent my day eating forbidden apples and reading, in a forbidden Balzac novel, the strange idyll of a man and a fiendish woman; before falling asleep I was going to tell myself some strange stories which would put me in strange states of mind. 'These are sins,' I said to myself. It was impossible to cheat any longer; continuous and systematic disobedience, lying and impure fantasies were not innocent. I plunged my hands into the cool cherry laurels, I listened to the gurgling of the stream and I realized that nothing would make me give up these earthly delights. 'I no longer believe in God,' I said to myself, with no great surprise. This was the proof. If I had believed in Him, I would not cheerfully have decided to offend Him.

It was a crucial admission. She thought the situation through in a logical manner. 'His perfection excluded His reality. That is why I felt so little surprise when I realized He was absent from my heart and from heaven ... I saw that He no longer intervened in my life and I concluded from this fact that He had ceased to exist for me.' There was to be no bargaining, no compromise. She knew she was too much of an extremist for that. 'As soon as I had seen the light I made a clean break.' She knew too that her father's scepticism had shown her the way, but the way was not easy. She was aware not so much of freedom, but of intense loneliness, she felt 'with anguish the emptiness of heaven. Previously I had stood at the centre of a living tableau where the colours and the light had been chosen by God Himself. ... Suddenly, everything was silent.' During one of these crisis moments at Meyrignac she was forced to join her mother and her aunt in the garden because she needed so desperately to hear human voices.

Worse still, the loss of God occasioned another form of anguish, one that became obsessive and dominated one aspect of Beauvoir's thought for the rest of her life: the fear of death. It came upon her suddenly. 'One afternoon, in Paris, I realized that I was condemned to death, I was alone in the apartment and I did not hold back my despair; I screamed, I tore at the red carpet ... I asked myself: "What do other people do? What shall I do?" It seemed impossible to live all my life with such horror wringing my heart.' She thought that the end might come 'at thirty or forty and you say to yourself: "It will be tomorrow"; how can anyone bear it?' As she wrote these lines she knew that her fear would never be forgotten: 'More than death itself I dreaded that terror which would soon be my lot, and for ever.' She was to make several attempts to exorcize the terror, notably in her novel *Tous les hommes sont mortels* (*All Men are Mortal*), published in 1946, but she never described it more graphically than in these early memoirs.

Although Simone felt she had been 'freed from my childhood and my sex' she also found that she had entered a phase of behaviour which she disliked more than any other, for she was now living the life of a hypocrite. She told her parents nothing, for her father would have been embarrassed and her mother deeply upset. Simone was no longer concerned about the possible 'supernatural' source of her mother's authority, 'it was my respect for her which endowed her orders with a sacred character. I continued to obey her.' Nothing was more important than the decrees issued by Françoise de Beauvoir: 'Concepts of duty, merit, sexual taboos: everything was preserved.' However, Simone could not merely limit herself to these moral attitudes, she also had to deal with religious practice. For some two years she lived as a lonely hypocrite, still attending Mass and taking the sacraments. Her confessor refused to believe that she had lost her faith. If she had told Zaza about the change within her she would also have lost her best friend. So she remained silent. After two years or so she was able to share her secret with her sister, who had also lived through the same crisis and told nobody.

When she was seventeen the time had come for Simone to leave the Cours Désir. She had made the best of the old-fashioned establishment where academic standards were rated less highly than prudery. Students had been encouraged to pronounce the name De-sir, eliminating the *accent aigu*, in case anyone had been led into wicked thoughts about 'desire'. Simone had succeeded in taking her *baccalauréat* and clung to the friendship with Zaza which had enriched her life, complementing what she had learnt from books. When Georges de Beauvoir attended the leaving ceremony at the school he noticed that all the girls looked sad. No doubt, like Simone, they had longed for the real and adult world; now it awaited them at last, but they were not ready for it. Many, like Zaza, dreaded the future with its inevitable threat of a 'suitable' marriage.

Simone's main enthusiasm now was her programme for higher education, linked to her possible future career. Her parents had agreed to her following courses at two establishments: she would study general mathematics at the Institut Catholique and take a *licence ès lettres*, roughly equivalent to a British B.A. degree in literature, at the Institut Sainte-Marie at Neuilly. In this way contact with the dreaded Sorbonne and its atheists would be reduced to a minimum and deferred until later, when she progressed to the study of philosophy. Even though God had disappeared from her universe, Simone was prepared to accept higher education under the aegis of the Catholic church; because she was still financially dependent on her parents she could hardly have done otherwise.

Since God no longer existed, He had to be replaced, especially as Simone, even while rejecting Him, admitted that 'religion had accustomed me to mysteries', and she was intrigued by 'enigmas'. She was drawn to the mysteries of abstract thought and stated that 'what attracted me most about philosophy was my feeling that it went straight to essentials'. Her enthusiasm led to extremism, as it so often did, and philosophy became a passion. Zaza's cousin, Mademoiselle Du Moulin de Labarthète, complained years later that the earnest teenager would bore and irritate people by talking continually about philosophy. However, at the Institut Sainte-Marie Simone formed a good, if complex relationship with her philosophy teacher, Mademoiselle Lambert. This lady was in no way surprised that her new student – for whom she prophesied a brilliant future – had become an atheist. At the same time she seemed uncertain about the girl's future from an emotional point of view. Simone asked her 'if one should resign oneself to love and happiness', assuming that one might have to give up a career and live the life of a 'normal' woman. 'She looked at me with a kind of anxiety: "Do you believe, Simone, that a woman can fulfil herself without love and marriage?"' Her student had already decided that her eminent teacher did not 'live her life. She took her classes and was working on a thesis: I found this existence very arid.' Simone wanted a full life, she wanted a much richer life, with professional success and independence, all

47

enhanced with emotional happiness. She hoped she might have a future like that of a certain Mademoiselle Zanta, whom she had read about in a magazine. This lady had become a doctor of philosophy, which was comparatively rare in the mid-1920s, and lived with a young niece, whom she had adopted: 'In this way she had succeeded in reconciling her intellectual life with the demands of her feminine sensibility.' Years later the adult Beauvoir was to live in a similar way.

However, as she moved out of adolescence, Simone continued to identify herself not with a real but a fictional heroine and her creator. Earlier she had seen herself as Jo in *Little Women*, now she had come close to Maggie Tulliver in *The Mill on the Floss*. 'She was dark-haired, she loved nature, reading and life. She was too impulsive to follow the conventions observed by her entourage, but sensitive to the criticisms of a brother she adored. Maggie Tulliver was like me, divided between others and herself: I recognized myself in her.' When she first read the novel Simone was not old enough to understand all Maggie's feelings, but 'when she took refuge in the old mill, misunderstood, reviled and abandoned by everyone, I was consumed with love for her. When she died I wept for hours.' She had seen herself again as 'a character in a novel' and was still romantic enough to daydream about her own vague ambitions. 'I was like her, and I saw in my future isolation not a mark of infamy but a sign that I had been singled out.' She was not tragic about the fate she imagined for herself, for through Maggie Tulliver she saw George Eliot. 'I did not think I would die of solitude. Through the heroine I identified myself with the author: one day some adolescent, someone like me, would drench with her tears a novel in which I would tell my own story.'

She began to see writing, rather than teaching in itself, as her way to true independence. If she could become a writer many problems would be solved: 'Literature would ensure immortality for me which would compensate for the loss of eternity; there was no longer any God to love me but I would burn like a flame in millions of hearts.' These sentences may sound like the fantasies of an ambitious adolescent but the older Beauvoir was to repeat these assertions, with little basic variation, at different stages of her life. 'In writing works based on my own story I would re-create myself again and I would justify my existence. At the same time I would serve humanity.' Her preoccupation with herself and her delight in communicating were closely connected, for she enjoyed talking about herself and sharing her opinions.

Like most teenagers Simone began to think about adult relationships. Zaza was still her best friend. She had decided that marriage seemed inseparable from drudgery, but she could not refrain from thinking about it. While remembering Maggie Tulliver she had written that 'I could conceive only *amour-amitié*, love-friendship; to me the exchange and discussion of books created eternal bonds between a boy and a girl'. At the same time she had made up her mind about the ideal man–woman partnership. She thought about a possible future husband and worked out a 'precise notion about our relationship: I would feel for him a passionate admiration'. In this she sounded old-style feminine; far from feminist. The man she chose 'would have to impose himself, as Zaza had imposed herself, by proving himself the right one ... The day when a man would dominate me by his intelligence, his culture and his authority, I should be in love.'

She longed to break away from home but she insisted that she did not want a father-figure, she wanted independence. 'I never thought of myself as the female companion to a man', but when she found her partner, 'we would be two comrades'. This concept, she realized, 'was influenced indirectly by the feelings I had had for my father. My upbringing, my culture, and my vision of society all convinced me that women belong to an inferior caste.' Men were privileged, she saw, but in the *absolute* sense their value was no greater than hers. She decided that in a *relative* sense their value was less: 'In order to recognize [a man] as my equal, he would have to be superior to me.' There could be only one solution: 'I would only marry if I met my equal, my double, more accomplished than myself.'

As Beauvoir remembered and re-created the young Simone, she presented that earlier self as someone who had made up her mind early about man–woman relationships. She had thought about the problems involved and discussed them with Zaza. As she set out on her two-fold adventure, intellectual and emotional, she was optimistic: 'Four or five years of study, and then an existence which I would shape with my own hands. My life would be a beautiful story, as I told it to myself it would come true.' She behaved in accordance with her chosen pattern. When she was about eighteen she experienced her first 'passionate admiration' for a man, a serious-minded teacher of literature at the Institut Sainte-Marie, a fervent Catholic named Robert Garric.

THREE

I was no longer alone

Simone's early admiration for Garric, the only male teacher who impressed her during her first year as a student, was not entirely straightforward. Her interest was sparked by her feelings for her cousin Jacques, who also knew Garric. 'If I could succeed in making myself noticed by my new teacher,' Simone wrote, 'if he praised my merits to Jacques, then Jacques might stop regarding me as a mere schoolgirl.' Her cousin was still the only young man she could claim to know, but he seemed elusive and their relationship was static. Though Simone's first attempt to write an essay for Garric was a failure, she was overwhelmed by his teaching: 'His commentaries on Ronsard dazzled me.' Her teacher was fairly young but not handsome. He was 'just over thirty, he was fair but starting to go bald, he spoke in a cheerful voice with a slight Auvergne accent'. However, Garric was much more than a teacher of literature; his heart was in the particular kind of socio-educational work that he had initiated. His academic career had been interrupted by the war but 'in the trenches he had discovered the delights of a comradeship which broke down social barriers'. He did not want to lose this new-found type of friendship when he returned to his studies. He believed that 'everyone had a right to culture'. He wanted 'to create between students and working people a system of exchange which would remove the former from their selfish solitude and the latter from their ignorance'. Garric often sounded like a socialist. However, when

51

he gave lectures to bourgeois audiences seated on gilded chairs he was applauded. He believed that 'no social progress could result from a struggle fired by hate: it can only be accomplished through friendship'. To Simone, these ideals seemed to coincide with those she had half-formulated to herself. 'I drank in his words; they did not overturn my own universe, I did not contest them, and yet to me they sounded absolutely new.'

Garric was no mere theorist. He had given up personal academic ambitions and devoted himself to organizing his 'Equipes sociales', teams of student teachers who now operated all over France and aimed to bring education and culture to working people. Jacques himself took part in the work. Although Garric was a devoted Catholic he did not see his work as a religious mission and his ten thousand supporters included unbelievers. He maintained that 'the working class are good when they are well treated; if the bourgeoisie refused to befriend them they would be committing a serious error and would suffer the consequences'. Garric himself lived an 'ascetic life' in the working-class *faubourg* of Belleville. Simone had been brought up to think that working people were a race 'just as dangerously foreign as the Boches or the Bolsheviks'. She was carried away, she was electrified, she would emerge from her class, from her own self, she would join the Equipes and serve humanity.

She was looking urgently for something new. Superficially, she was grown up. She had told her mother that there was no need to explain the facts of life to her, she already knew them. She was even able to tell her that she was no longer a believer; she was sad to see her mother's eyes fill with tears but felt relieved that she was no longer a hypocrite. Although in some ways Simone had entered a new world, she still had to live in the rue de Rennes, there could be no question of living anywhere else. Her family, who had given her so much early happiness, were now a problem to her. 'I had made the best of living in a cage, for I knew that one day, which came closer with every day that passed, the door would open; now I had gone through it, but I was still imprisoned.' She felt disappointed: 'This prison had no bars, but I couldn't find the way out. Perhaps there was one, but where?'

At the end of the twentieth century it is hard to imagine the restrictive atmosphere in which Simone was living, although it was not exceptional at the time. She was not allowed to go out with Jacques in the evening, she was even in trouble if the two of them remained alone in the drawing-room before dinner, talking of modern literature. When she went to a dancing class she was chaperoned. Simone's mother opened and read any letters addressed to her daughter, adding commentaries of her own. A kind of domestic warfare developed: 'My parents did not find me to their liking, and so I deliberately made myself unpleasant.' She hardly ever brushed her teeth and never cleaned her nails. 'My mother dressed me badly and my father was always reproaching me for being badly dressed: so I became a slut', as Mademoiselle Du Moulin de Labarthète had remembered. She admitted to being stubbornly silent and rude. She would read books during meals and refuse to speak to her mother's friends.

She felt she had lost touch with her mother, who spent a great amount of time praying for her, and she was forced to change her mind about her father. He had not, after all, resigned himself to his reduced financial situation. He would make a scene whenever his wife asked for housekeeping money, he had been soured by the failure of his life and as a result became aggressive while at the same time masochistic; he even 'took a bitter pleasure in being looked down upon by his inferiors'. All this was upsetting for Simone. Although she felt no deprivation at being a girl she would often hear her parents say 'if only she had been a boy', for it was easier for a boy to receive higher education. If she had been a rare and outstanding prodigy her father would have been pleased, but he disliked 'pedagogues' and 'intellectuals'. The intellectuals, after all, had supported Dreyfus. Nothing was easy for Simone: although her father appreciated witty women, he had no time for bluestockings. Any hint of feminism drew his wrath, but that was not the worst of his resentment: 'I was not just a burden . . . I was going to be the living incarnation of his own failure.' Again Simone found herself caught up in contradictions: 'He had destined me to a life of study, and yet I was being reproached with having my nose in my books all the time.'

Her unhappiness at home did not help Simone in the outside world, for she had not yet outgrown the timidity caused by her mother's domination when she was younger. She still found it hard to make friends, for 'I didn't dare speak to anyone, and nobody spoke to me'. She compensated for this isolation by allowing her 'passionate admiration' for Garric to become a kind of adoration. She felt that his example would help her break away from 'the ghastly banality of everyday life'. She exhausted herself in study until this very exhaustion gave her 'an impression of fulfilment'. But this was not enough, she needed Garric's inspiration, and as usual her extremism took over. Other students were not excited by their literature teacher. Zaza, who had reluctantly been allowed to continue her studies, would complain that he was always late, and even Simone noticed that he sat down so casually that he revealed his mauve sock-suspenders. Although Zaza did not realize the extent of Simone's hero-worship she regarded it as 'excessive'. Simone had even begun to wonder if Garric was to be the man in her life: she now considered that 'his merits eclipsed the charm of Jacques: had I encountered my destiny?' However, she still could not face the reality of sex: 'I felt shy as I toyed with this thought. It was shocking to think of Garric as married.' She wanted only to 'exist' for him, and in the end she won his praise for literary essays.

It was the moral dimension to Garric's teaching, as well as the literary appreciation, that fascinated Simone. Intent on following his precepts and on breaking away from home influence she applied to join one of the Equipes sociales. Garric's teaching had however expanded her universe through literature. She wondered why he talked about Péguy,[1] of whom she had never heard, and why he mentioned another obscure name, André Gide,[2] with a kind of apologetic bravado. She achieved one personal ambition: Garric and Jacques *did* talk about her, and she, who admitted she yearned to be 'someone', felt elated, not because Garric had asked how she saw the future but because Jacques, who was as

[1] Charles Péguy (1873–1914): essayist and poet. At first an ardent socialist with strong anti-clerical convictions, he was by the end of his life a keen patriot and nationalist. He died leading his company at the Battle of the Marne.
[2] André Gide (1869–1951): novelist and critic, author of a number of short novels including *L'Immoraliste* (1902), *La Porte étroite* (1909), *La Symphonie pastorale* (1919), *Thérèse* (1946) and two longer novels, *Les Caves du Vatican* (1914) and *Les Faux-Monnayeurs* (1926). Gide insisted on sincerity in life, without any fixed or moral beliefs. An autobiography of his early years, *Si le grain ne meurt* (1926) describes his revolt against his Protestant upbringing. *Les Nourritures*

important to her as ever, invited her to go for a drive round the Bois de Boulogne. There was no emotional progress between them, but Jacques listened to Simone's problems. He told her that *on peut être très bien, même licenciée*: even if she had a degree she could live in a happy and comfortable state. Did he imply that one could be something of a bluestocking *and* a bourgeois *and* an accepted person all at once? In any case he lent her books by all the celebrated French twentieth-century authors – Barrès, Montherlant, Claudel, Valéry, Cocteau, Alain-Fournier, Giraudoux, Proust – and they led her on to omnivorous library borrowing. If Jacques wasted emotional time for Simone he enriched her intellectual life. Books were no longer 'historical monuments', she found; they were written by living people who spoke to her directly, personally. God had been replaced and the dreary antagonism of home life made bearable. 'I lost myself in reading as I had once done in prayer. Literature assumed in my life the place that had once been occupied by religion: it over-whelmed and transfigured my whole existence.' If books had been important earlier, they were now life itself. 'For months I drew my nourishment from literature: but it was the only reality at that time to which I had access.' Her parents, seeing all these strange books in the house – 'pretentious, decadent, immoral', her father said – were not pleased. But the days of censorship were over.

However, reading is a solitary occupation, and never did Simone feel more solitary than at this period. She began a journal and wrote in it: 'I am alone. One is always alone.' Her mother continued to pray for her, her father saw her moving inevitably away from the bourgeois élite into which she had been born. Many of her new-found authors were bourgeois like herself, they were critical of their class, but they were not rebels and did not know where they were going. 'They limited themselves to studying in minute detail their states of mind', and they preached *inquiétude*, 'disquiet', while some professed 'a scornful aestheticism; others devoted themselves to immoralism'. She herself would have felt less solitary if she had been interested in any group or communal movement apart from the Equipes sociales. But 'only the

Terrestres (1897) and his *Journal*, covering the years 1885 to 1949 in various volumes, have been much quoted.

individual seemed to me real and important', and she gave the origin of her belief: 'Catholicism had persuaded me that no individual, however much disinherited, was to be neglected. . . . My path was clearly marked out: I must perfect myself, enrich myself and express myself in a work which would help others to live.' She was sickened by the orthodox bourgeois attitude towards girls and women but at the end of her teens she had no wish to share her beliefs with any movement: she was as indifferent about feminism as she was about Mussolini[1] and the League of Nations,[2] and said bluntly that 'I didn't care a damn about the right to vote'. (Frenchwomen in fact did not win it until 1944.)

How was she to find other people who felt as she did? She wanted only the individuals whom she could choose. She began to write a novel about herself, called 'Eliane'. Its purpose was to express her 'most obsessive worry: how to defend myself against other people'. She complained about her solitude but even more about her parents' attempts to break into it, for she could no longer share her feelings with them. She clung to the image of Garric: 'He was alone, he was free.' She tried to think as he thought, to adopt the 'group spirit', which she found so difficult. She found it easier to continue her admiration of the individual, Garric the man. She progressed beyond his literature classes but not beyond her own hero-worship. One day she went to the suburb of Belleville, which she had never seen before. 'I walked down the main street where Garric lived; I knew the number of the house; keeping close to the walls I came up to it; if he were to surprise me there I was ready to collapse with shame. For a moment I stopped in front of his house, I gazed at the dreary brick façade . . . What had I come for? In any case I went away empty-handed.'

This sentimental pilgrimage brought the end of her 'passionate

[1] Benito Mussolini (1883–1945): founder of the Fascismo Institution of Italy, dictator from 1922. Through the fascist system Mussolini put down all opposition with the aim of leading a revitalized Italy into the forefront of progress.
[2] The League of Nations, founded in 1920 as part of the treaty that followed World War I, aimed to promote international cooperation and achieve international peace and security. The League aimed to settle disputes between nations and called several conferences on disarmament. The United States, Russia, Mexico and Brazil were not members.

admiration' for Garric and was followed by an even greater disappointment. Her wish to be of service seemed to come near fulfilment when she was appointed leader of the educational group in the same Belleville district, but she found none of the satisfaction for which she had hoped. Her students, after their day spent working in the clothing or fashion business, were unlikely to assimilate Balzac or Victor Hugo. Simone realized that they had not the educational background necessary to learn further from Garric's programme. It was impossible to establish any genuine friendships with the students, and how could an inexperienced young teacher talk to these girls and young women about 'human dignity or the value of suffering'? Simone decided that they met 'to pass the time together, nothing more'. When Garric himself came to her centre his former admirer realized that she could no longer take his themes seriously: he kept on repeating himself, his ideas about saving 'human value in every man' were unworkable. She could find no link between Garric's idealism and the real world, with its real people. The young Beauvoir decided that 'action was a disappointing solution: people who imagined they were devoting themselves to others were deceiving themselves'. Later she thought her condemnation of 'action' was the result of her inexperience: 'I did not realize that action could take forms far different from the kind I was condemning.' She regarded her attempts to carry out Garric's precepts as 'fake experience' which left her more ignorant of *le peuple*, the working class, than she had been before.

She was much happier when asked to supervise a correspondence course for patients in the sanatorium at Berck. This work was more satisfactory because it was 'less ambitious' and it probably suited her better because it was *written* work: in carrying it out she could deal with individuals on a personal basis but without the awkwardness of personal contact, which she still found difficult. She did not meet the young patients because Berck was a long way away on the northern coast.

The visits to Belleville at least provided her with an excuse for going out in the evening, and she made the best of the situation, sometimes inventing classes when none existed. She did not know what to do with herself, for nothing really gripped her. She would hear her father and his friends talking endlessly about the serious problems of the moment – 'the recovery of the franc, the evacuation of the Rhineland, the Utopian ideas of the League of Nations' – but these were no concern of hers, she thought, and she compared them to 'family quarrels and money troubles'. In any case Jacques and Zaza did not worry about them, and her teacher Mademoiselle Mercier never mentioned them. Philosophy no longer fascinated her, lectures bored her. She felt that death was eating her life away, while at the same time she 'loved life passionately'. She was so torn between the positive and negative aspects of her own outlook on the world that on the day she was nineteen, in January 1927, she tried to express them by writing 'a dialogue for two voices, both of which were mine'. She walked round Paris in tears. She would eat a brioche in a pâtisserie and try to calm herself by quoting ironically a remark by Heine: 'However many tears you shed you always blow your nose in the end.' There was one last form of escape: 'I would take refuge in the side aisles of a church in order to cry in peace.'

She needed friends of her own age, intelligent friends. She was the first to realize that her lack of friends was due at least in part to her own attitude: 'I continued to rate social questions lower than metaphysics and morals.' This meant that she did not become close to students who were politically involved and her ideas about politics in general remained 'nebulous'. She could not put her mind to the tedious 'moderation' of socialism and if she preferred the extremism of the Communists she suspected they were 'as dogmatic and stereotyped as seminarists'. She asked a crucial question: 'What was the point of worrying about the happiness of humanity if humanity had no *raison d'être*?'

Her obstinacy in taking this approach robbed her, she admitted, of any friendship with the brilliant Simone Weil,[1] who was a year younger but following the same syllabus at the Sorbonne. When Weil heard about a famine in China she had wept, and Beauvoir envied her: 'I envied her for possessing a heart that could beat

---

[1] Simone Weil (1909–43): writer on religion, sociology and philosophy. Her desire for first-hand experience led her to spend a year as a factory hand at the Renault works in Paris. Her last known works are posthumous: *La Pesanteur et la Grâce* (1947) and *L'Attente de Dieu* (1949). She always tried to identify with the oppressed and died as a refugee in Britain, having attempted to exist on the 'official' food rations allowed to the French during the Occupation.

across the whole world.' The two young women had a single brief conversation. Weil wanted Revolution and food for everyone, while Beauvoir had other priorities: 'The problem was not to make men happy, but to find a meaning for their existence.' 'It's obvious you've never been hungry,' Weil said. This was the beginning and end of their relationship. 'I realized that she had classified me as "a high-minded little bourgeoise", and this annoyed me.' In the first place she thought she was struggling out of the bourgeoisie and secondly she always reacted with fury when anyone attempted to apply any label to her.

In the summer of 1927 Simone Weil was placed first in the general philosophy examination, with Simone de Beauvoir second. Her family and her teachers were pleased at her success but after the first excitement she herself became tearful again. 'I was bitterly aware that my heart was empty. I continued to desire passionately something else that I could not define because I refused to give it the only name that was right for it: happiness.'

She had made a few acquaintances among the students, women and men, but she at last found a good friend in the young man who had come third in the summer examination, someone whose name was later to become well known: Maurice Merleau-Ponty.[1] In her memoirs she called him 'Jean Pradelle' and used his real name only once, when she referred to their meeting during teaching practice at the Lycée Janson-de-Sailly. She liked him in particular because they found they could discuss endless topics, philosophical and religious, as freely as they wished. They did not always agree, especially when it came to religion. Merleau-Ponty maintained that he was no longer a believer but continued to go to Mass in order to avoid upsetting his family. Later he regained his faith after a visit to the famous Abbaye de Solesmes where Simone Weil also discovered her spiritual path, although she never actually became a member of the Catholic church.

Merleau-Ponty was a most attractive man; Simone described in much detail his handsome face, his thick, dark eyelashes, his schoolboy laugh. He had nothing of her extremism, and was

[1] Maurice Merleau-Ponty (1909–61): philosopher. He based his philosophy on the phenomenology of Edmund Husserl. He disliked absolutes and conclusions, regarding his philosophy more as a vision of reality than as a system. He was for a time closely associated with existentialism.

prepared to accommodate, to compromise. At the same time he believed most people were rational and he had confidence in them. She later remembered their many long discussions and realized how much he had helped her to become aware of a basic fault in herself: he was totally impartial and did not confuse feelings with ideas. She realized she had a tendency to do precisely that: her 'states of mind', she wrote, had very often been 'substitutes for thought'. This is hardly surprising in someone as exceptionally emotional as she was, although she was perhaps not aware how clearly this aspect of her personality appeared later in her writing.

The range of their discussions was stimulating and through their disagreements Simone came to see herself more clearly. She could not accept that Merleau-Ponty, 'an intellectual like me', felt no hostility towards his class. She compared his 'happy optimism' with Jacques's 'nihilism' and realized that both men, although they were so different, found her somewhat alarming. This led her to ponder the disturbing question: 'Do men marry women like me?' She was concerned because 'at that time I made no distinction between love and marriage'. More than ever she saw herself 'destined to solitude', for she had come to a pessimistic conclusion: 'What separated me from everyone else was a certain violence that I encountered only in myself.' She did not think that she would ever meet someone like herself. 'I'm so certain he does not exist, the man who would really be everything, would understand everything, the man who would be truly my brother and my equal.'

The violence within herself led her to seek it in the world outside. Books, theatres, films, exhibitions, even the discovery of surrealism failed to satisfy her: she wanted colour, action, danger in fact, for she needed now to express something which fascinated and frightened her at the same time – sexuality. At the age of eighteen or so she knew that her bourgeois upbringing had left her *une oie blanche*, innocent, naive. When she was younger she had felt that her mother, despite her early married happiness, had identified sexuality with vice, and did not want to talk about it. She herself had had two unpleasant experiences when still a schoolgirl: a man in a cinema had pawed her through her clothes, despite the presence of her aunt, and one day, in a religious bookshop, a young assistant had exposed himself to her in a dark corner. She had ever stopped going to a dancing class because she was too disturbed by the proximity with young men. 'When my partner held me in his arms and clasped me against his chest, I felt an odd sensation, like butterflies in the stomach, but I didn't forget it so easily.' On returning home she would feel 'an indefinable languor which made me want to cry'. A little later she thought her fellow students were immoral, and when they talked about flirting she did not know what they meant. She was upset when students were described as 'going together' and shuddered at the mention of *ces moeurs*, homosexuality, in men or women.

Just as she had felt alternately positive and negative about her future when she was wandering round the city in tears, she now seemed torn between her self-confessed prudery and her reckless attempts to break out of it. Her social timidity prevented her from encountering 'life' in any natural way, so she attempted the unnatural way, trying to force herself into those aspects of reality which eluded her. She went to bars by herself, using the pretext of her work at Belleville. When she tried La Rotonde, below her former home, and ordered an aperitif, the barman refused to take her money. Once she went out, with permission, with her cousin Madeleine, who applied a little rouge to Simone's cheeks. Her mother instructed her to remove it, and when Simone protested, she slapped her. The girls eventually went to a sordid dive in Montmartre. Two male prostitutes sat down at the same table and 'were surprised to find us there, for we were obviously not offering any competition'. It was apparently not easy for the girls to lose their bourgeois aura. The visit was hardly a success for they were not only bored but Simone was also sickened by the place.

She went to Le Jockey, a famous bar in the boulevard Montparnasse which she knew by reputation through Jacques. There she was fascinated by the colours, the atmosphere, the smell, 'voices, laughter, the saxophone'. Most of all, she was intrigued by the women. She could find no words to describe 'the fabric of their dresses, the colour of their hair'. She noticed their sheer silk stockings, their high-heeled shoes, their lipstick, and could not imagine any shop where such things could be bought. She overheard the women discussing with their pimps details of pay and clients' requirements, but she remained at a distance. 'My imagination did not react: I had blocked it.' She thought of

61

these people not as real human beings, but as abstractions, allegories: 'disquiet, futility, stupidity, despair, genius perhaps, and certainly the many faces of vice'. She would make naive attempts to take part in the scenes she was observing, she would claim to be an artists' model or a tart. But still her bourgeois appearance, *petit bourgeois*, poverty-stricken even, was against her: 'With my faded old dress, my thick stockings, my flat-heeled shoes, my un-made up face, I deceived no one.' One man saw through her very clearly: ' "You're a little bourgeoise trying to play at being bohemian", he said.'

Another man showed her a crude sexual sketch. When she said it was badly drawn he unfastened his trousers and she turned away. Everybody laughed.

Though she had found the door to the invisible cage of home she had not found the door to sexuality, and when she was nineteen, twenty or even twenty-one this was her insuperable problem. Men sensed she was a virgin, she admitted that she had a virgin's fear of men, but though they fascinated her she realized that she was in no danger: 'People would offer me a drink, or invite me to dance, nothing more; it was obvious that I discouraged lubricity.'

She herself was not discouraged. Sometimes she would go out with her sister; they would pretend not to know each other and start a sensational scene in a bar, anything to attract attention. Simone had embarked on a life of minor deception, explaining the disappearance of money – which she spent on drink – as a contribution to Garric's centre at Belleville. She became a regular at Le Jockey, she even began to accept harmless advances from men: 'I would find it consoling that an unknown hand touching the back of my neck could bring a warmth and gentleness that resembled affection.' She did not understand this world that was so foreign to her, but she felt that at last she was in touch with freedom. She was proud of the progress she had made since she was a schoolgirl but it was the defiance of convention that really appealed to her. 'The attraction that bars and dance-halls held for me was based largely on their illegal character. My mother would never have set foot in such places; my father would have been horrified to find me there.' Even her friend Merleau-Ponty, who was admittedly accepted and liked by her parents, would have been upset. 'I felt a deep satisfaction at knowing that I was totally *hors la loi*, outside authority.'

Simone was determined to explore the forbidden aspects of life as far as she could. She allowed men to accost her in the street and in bars, remembering later what Gide had said: 'Live dangerously. Refuse nothing.' She had several lucky escapes. After climbing boldly into a strange man's car she later ran away when he tried to kiss her. When a group of thugs wanted to 'teach her a lesson' she handed over all her money and was really frightened.

Her escapades were a far cry from the holidays she spent with Zaza, still her best friend, at the Lacoin country house in the south-east. Despite her attachment to her friend, which knew its own ups and downs, these weeks could hardly have been comfortable for her. She did not see enough of Zaza, very much the 'dutiful daughter' still, busy with domestic tasks and acting as junior hostess. She had to be lent dresses, for she had nothing smart to wear; she knew that Madame Lacoin hated intellectuals and said so openly; she had to listen to the right-wing Du Moulin cousins talking about *L'Action française* and the Pope's attitude to Maurras and his supporters. She also had to listen to Zaza's sister Lili announcing that it would be dangerous if women were allowed to vote: she insisted that in the poor districts the women were more 'red than the men', and nobody disagreed. Simone decided that it was prudent to say nothing, 'but within the chorus of approval this silence was subversive'.

However, it was at the Lacoin country house that she met someone whose influence on her was to be more important than she might have guessed. This was Stépha Avdicovitch, a Polish girl who was studying in Paris and had been employed by Madame Lacoin as *gouvernante* to look after the youngest group of her nine children. Stépha's father owned a large sweet factory in Lwow and had already sent his daughter to Berlin for two years or so of study. Everything about her life was new to Simone. The Polish girl had an early history of political protest, for she had taken part in demonstrations in support of Ukrainian independence and spent a few days in prison. In the Lacoin house she shared a bedroom with Simone, who learnt for the first time that a young woman could wear pyjamas if she wanted to – a nightdress was not obligatory. She found Stépha delightful, they talked freely and Simone realized that her new friend possessed something she dared not even name: sex-appeal. Stépha herself had been astonished by the old-fashioned orthodoxy of the Lacoin household. She had found it natural to sit down at the piano and sing Ukrainian folk-songs, but her employer thought she was abusing her position. The girl had a graceful, feminine charm and a social ease that made both Zaza and Simone look immature, like 'young nuns', Simone remembered. Stépha told everyone's fortune with playing-cards and flirted discreetly with the young Xavier Du Moulin, a relative of the Lacoin family who was studying for the priesthood. She remained 'indifferent to his cassock'. Madame Lacoin did not remain indifferent to Stépha's behaviour. She reprimanded her daughter for being too close to the girl who, she decided, was not *une vraie jeune fille*, implying that she was not a virgin.

Stépha was the friend whom Simone needed. She was foreign, feminine and free, free of French bourgeois conventions, intelligent but not an intellectual, she was adult, sophisticated. In Paris, after the holidays, the girls met often, and Stépha undertook to educate the *oie blanche* in some of the harder facts of life. People did not always mean what they said, she told her, and going to Mass regularly did not in itself make people 'good'. One night in Montmartre the two girls saw by accident a violent scene in the street when the police were arresting a pimp. Simone was upset and wanted to go away. Stépha was not upset at all: *C'est la vie*, she explained. She went into more detail: 'Physical love is very important, especially for men.' She added that it was all 'rather unpleasant, but it existed, and it meant a lot, for everybody'. Simone was shocked, shocked too when Stépha's principal boyfriend, Fernando, a painter whom she later married, said casually that Stépha had posed for the portrait of a nude woman. Simone was subjected to endless shocks: Stépha had seen Zaza's cousins, the young Du Moulin men, in Montparnasse, in what she called 'unmistakable company'. Simone was also told that even among strict Catholics young men were not virgins when they married. She began to question herself further on the cause of her resistance to reality. Was her attitude a hangover from Catholic teaching, or was it pride? she asked herself. She felt she was 'a soul, a pure spirit'. Her 'other-worldliness' had been exploded by the intrusion of reality and she admitted to being terrified by the horizons which now opened up before her.

Stépha found time in Paris, despite her many admirers, to undertake the 'feminization' of Simone, the girl who was deeply emotional but so far had no chance to express her feelings, especially since the relationship with Jacques was so patently one-sided. Stépha wanted Simone to exteriorize the femininity which she, so feminine herself, could easily see. One of her attendant young men had said that Simone, at twenty, was too young to be a *femme savante*. Stépha had her own personal reasons for improving Simone's appearance: she didn't want her best friend to look like 'an ugly blue-stocking'. Simone herself remembered that Jacques had once said she was pretty, and she was gradually becoming more confident about herself in all ways. Her constant self-examination was no longer restricted to emotional or philosophical problems; she had taken a liking to her own image: 'I enjoyed looking at myself in mirrors: I liked what I saw.' She felt she could compete with other women, and she acknowledged she took women's opinions seriously: 'In many ways I placed Zaza, my sister, Stépha . . . above my men friends: these young women seemed more sensitive, more generous, more gifted for dreaming, for tears, for love.' In one self-assessment she was more confident than ever, while at the same time accepting, ironically perhaps, one traditional view of women: 'I flattered myself that I united within me "a woman's heart, a man's brain". I considered myself unique.' At the same time, she listened to Stépha and took her advice: 'I began to go to the hairdresser regularly and took an interest in buying a hat or having a dress made.'

The next sentence in her memoirs seems to follow logically from her extrovert decision: 'I made friends.' She needed friends more than ever after Madame Lacoin had resolved to send Zaza to Berlin for a year, after deciding that the Sorbonne contained more hated intellectual unbelievers than she had feared. Zaza had even been forbidden to go to tennis parties in Paris because her mother did not know the families of all the young men invited. While Simone was separated from her friend they wrote long letters to each other but Simone, though working harder than ever now for the competitive *agrégation* examination, was finding it much easier to meet and like her fellow students. Sometimes she would feel depressed, but gradually, with help, especially from Stépha, she was entering the real, adult world. The time for quoting Gide's famous remark, 'Families! I hate you,' was over. In January 1929 she was twenty-one, after all. By the beginning of the summer term that year, her last term, she realized that she knew nearly all the students in her own year. However, one small group, a trio of men, remained 'hermetic' to her. These men were Jean-Paul Sartre, Paul Nizan and René Maheu, the latter described in the memoirs as 'André Herbaud'. The three of them had studied together at the Ecole Normale Supérieure, where they had all behaved badly. They were particularly remembered for having thrown water-bombs at distinguished members of the E.N.S. returning from a reception one night. Nizan, whose grandparents had been illiterate peasants, was in some ways the most sophisticated of the three: he had travelled, he was a member of the Communist Party and he was writing a book. Simone found his gaze, from behind his big horn-rimmed spectacles, 'very intimidating'. He was married, as was his friend, René Maheu, the son of a provincial schoolmaster. Sartre's reputation was particularly bad: he was said to be the 'worst of the three and he was even accused of drinking'. However, he was not married.

Simone thought that Maheu was the most approachable of the three. He would even talk to her a little when he was alone but when he was with the others he remained as stand-offish as they were and ignored her. She wanted to meet men, she decided she was tired of being a 'disembodied spirit', tired of being half-alive. 'I want life,' she wrote in her journal, 'the whole of life.' After a day of hard study she could find relaxation only in the cafés of Montparnasse. She still responded to *la séduction des mauvais lieux*, and she was no longer horrified by what she saw along the streets. She even envied the pimps and prostitutes because they were living the life they had chosen. She realized with surprise that she yearned for 'noise, struggle, savagery', and most of all she wanted to be 'dragged down', to enter this other world. She was shocked by her own 'perversion', but refused to deny her instincts. She knew what was happening to her: 'I was very close to admitting the truth to myself . . . I was not tormented by desire, as I had been just before puberty. But I guessed that the violence of the flesh, its raw crudity, would have saved me from this vague, insipid atmosphere in which I was living so feebly.' Honest admissions to herself and her journal were in order, but practical action was not. She knew very well she could not yet escape the taboos with which she had been brought up, however much she now 'detested' Roman Catholicism. She had no plans for sexual experiment and 'I did not even think of *libertinage*'.

She was more than ready to make experiments in friendship, and René Maheu became the second of her adult friends among men. He was 'safe', he was married and 'very far away, I would never exist for him'. He amused and charmed her. There was an undercurrent of sexuality in the camaraderie with Maheu and once, when she saw him walking in the Latin Quarter arm in arm with a woman, she felt excluded. She was quick to notice that he did not treat her as other students did, his attitude was entirely different, it was personal and physical. This friendship was crucial: he would make remarks about her clothes, her hairstyle, her husky voice, and she felt he treated her as a woman, not an abstraction. She confided her feelings to her journal again: 'Meeting with André Herbaud [i.e. Maheu]: or with myself?' She realized that 'something had happened' to her, 'something which indirectly shaped my whole life; but I was not to learn that until later'.

Maheu also felt that something had happened; he had not met anyone like Simone de Beauvoir before. One brief conversation between the two of them expresses the atmosphere of this friendship and gives a concise picture of Beauvoir as she then was. In some ways she would never change.

' "Our relationship is strange. At least for me: I've never had a feminine friendship."

"Perhaps that's because I'm not very feminine."

"You?" He laughed in a way I found flattering. "No. It's rather because you accept everything so easily: we're on an equal footing at once." '

Maheu become proprietorial. He was even displeased one day when Simone greeted Merleau-Ponty as an old friend. It was Maheu who christened her 'Le Castor', the nickname that she never lost, and he wrote in her notebook, 'BEAUVOIR = BEAVER', adding, ' "You're a Beaver," he said. "Beavers operate together and have a constructive attitude." ' He was obviously very much preoccupied with his new friend. He talked to his fellow students about her, for there was a common bond between them: their study of the philosopher Leibniz, whom the men regarded as profoundly boring. As directed by her supervisor, the well-known philosopher Léon Brunschwig, Simone had already written her thesis on 'The Concept in Leibniz'. Surely, therefore, if the four of them pooled their knowledge they could only improve their grasp of the subject. She knew from Maheu that Sartre wanted to meet her. He would have introduced them one day in the Luxembourg Gardens, he said, but she was with another student at the time, and he did not want to disturb her 'meditations'. Sartre tried an indirect approach. He hoped to interest and amuse her by dedicating a drawing to her: he called it 'Leibniz bathing with the Monads'.[1] He did not send it but gave it to Maheu to give to her. She did not record her response. She remembered that Sartre and Nizan had issued a 'cordial invitation' to her, hoping that all four of them could meet. However, Maheu was leaving Paris for ten days or so to join his wife in Normandy, and the study group could not take place immediately. Sartre made another suggestion. 'He wanted to meet me: he suggested a meeting one evening soon. But [Maheu] asked me not to go: Sartre would take advantage of his absence to take me over. "I don't want anyone to tamper with my most cherished feelings," he said to me in a conspiratorial tone.' He insisted that the meeting should take place only on his return, in his presence.

Simone agreed. However, since there was not enough time to cancel the appointment with Sartre, she decided to send her sister, now an art student, to take her place. Poupette, as she was still called, asked how she would recognize Sartre. Simone gave her a rapid description: 'He wears glasses and he's very ugly.'

When Poupette entered the crêmerie in the rue de Médicis – *plutôt lugubre*, she said – she saw two men, both wearing glasses. She went up to the more ugly of the two and asked: ' "Are you Monsieur Sartre?" '

' "How did you recognize me?" '

She replied that she was Simone de Beauvoir's sister, but this did not satisfy him.

---

[1] Monads: according to Leibniz's theory, put forward in the *Monadology*, monads are the ultimate units of being.

' "How did you know that I was Sartre?" '

' "Because . . . because you wear glasses." '

When Sartre pointed out that there was another man in the restaurant wearing glasses Poupette adroitly answered that she had one chance out of two of being wrong. Was he taken in? She thought not. She told the prepared lie, that Simone had been summoned at very short notice to attend to some family business in the country. Sartre politely invited her to the cinema and they found very little to talk about. As a result Poupette told her sister that Sartre was not amusing at all. Many years later she remembered how soon she changed her opinion.

In 1978 Beauvoir gave a slightly different version of the story. In replying to a question from Malka Ribowska during the film made about her she said that it was she, and not Maheu, who had decided that this first meeting with Sartre had to be put off. 'I didn't want to [meet him] straightaway because I had a fairly exclusive friendship with Maheu and I sent my sister instead to see Sartre, who was furious.'

Sartre was three years older than Beauvoir and just as glad at the time to struggle out of a bourgeois family as she was. His early life had not been too happy. His father, a naval officer, had died when this only son, known as 'Poulou', was six months old. His mother, who was a cousin of Albert Schweitzer, re-married when the boy was twelve and he never forgave her. Sartre was educated at various lycées, mainly in Paris, and went to the Ecole Normale Supérieure in 1924 when he was nineteen. When Beauvoir met him, five years later, he was a much talked-about student who, according to Maheu, never stopped thinking. He seemed to have read all possible books and yet found time for melodramatic thrillers as well. He was addicted to the cinema, especially Hollywood comedies and cowboy films. He was absorbed by his ambition to become a writer but had so far published nothing. He was five feet two inches tall; he suffered from a squint and ten per cent vision in one eye, caused by a cold caught when he was about three years old.

Maheu returned to Paris in early July 1929 and Beauvoir was summoned to Sartre's room in the Cité Universitaire. 'The air was thick with smoke. Sartre greeted me politely; he was smoking a pipe.' Nizan looked at the girl student critically and said nothing.

'All day, petrified with shyness, I commented on "the metaphysical treatise".' She came back each day and quickly 'thawed out'. The group soon decided that they knew enough about Leibniz and instead, Sartre, the unquestioned leader of the four, undertook to talk to the others about Rousseau's *Social Contract*,[1] interpreting it in his own individual way. Beauvoir reacted to him as his listeners and readers did for the rest of his life and continue to do so as the years pass after his death. Beauvoir enjoyed the challenge he represented, she would try 'ingenuity and obstinacy' in these discussions, but Sartre always won. He was a superb teacher and essentially generous, in her view, for he poured out facts, analysis and commentary, while his superiority was such that he learned nothing in return.

These sessions took place mainly in the mornings and there was plenty of time later in the day for the students to enjoy themselves. Their diversions were the very reverse of intellectual: funfairs, pin-tables and shooting-galleries, interspersed with singing, usually led by Sartre, who had a good tenor voice and enjoyed every aspect of music: the classical composers, romantic operettas, the latest imported jazz or negro spirituals. How sad that nobody was able to record the motet composed by Sartre and Maheu to words by Descartes. The words were the chapter headings to two of the *Méditations métaphysiques*, concerning the existence and essence of God. A ritual student adventure in which Beauvoir also participated was a climb over the roofs of the Ecole Normale Supérieure.

A few days of philosophical discussion in a smoke-filled room had changed the world for her. The comrades, as Maheu called them, were determined to undertake the re-education of this girl who may have known a good deal about Leibniz but nothing of what they at least regarded as the real world. If Beauvoir thought she had made some progress during the last year, as she escaped from the invisible cage of her bourgeois home, her friends were not impressed. The Beaver was now subjected to a devastating culture shock. She must forget all talk about ideals, high-

[1] Jean-Jacques Rousseau (1712–78): *Du Contrat social* (1762), a treatise on political philosophy, maintained that since man is free, and force cannot be the

mindedness, the 'inner life', anything that was 'unreal' or unexplained. Everything could and should be explained, for only one thing mattered; reality: 'They demonstrated that men were not spirits but bodies, a prey to physical needs and thrown into a brutal adventure.' The adventure was life. Only a year earlier she would have been terrified. Now the young men asked her to do only one thing – 'to look reality in the face'. She knew that so far she had lacked courage, but now she was determined to find it.

To say that her personal life changed with her conversion to 'reality' would be an understatement. 'I was ecstatic,' she wrote. Any past loneliness was utterly forgotten. René Maheu was obviously very much attracted to her, and if he had been possessive earlier he was now jealous and eager to assert his 'rights'. In the street he took her arm, and the other men allowed him to take her out on her own. But things changed. 'I found Sartre more amusing than [Maheu].' The latter became more affectionate than ever, asking her to think of him when she spent any time with the others. But very quickly Sartre was winning. 'I felt that any time I didn't spend with him was time wasted.' She had met Sartre in the last few weeks of her last term at the Sorbonne, and during the period of the oral examinations, which went on for a fortnight, 'we hardly left each other except to sleep'.

Her native intelligence, her beaver-like study and the added stimulus of this last-minute excitement brought her success in the oral examination. In the *agrégation* results Sartre was placed first, Simone was second. Nizan passed too, but Maheu failed. Sartre's wider background, due to his time at the Ecole Normale Supérieure, had gained him first place, but some members of the examining jury thought that in some ways *she* was the true thinker, *la philosophe, the* philosopher. The jury had apparently even considered giving the first place to Beauvoir. If she herself had heard these rumours she did not mention them, but since her sister certainly knew about them it is likely that the 'mere Sorbonnarde', as she called herself at least once, heard them too. In July 1929, at the age of twenty-one and six months, she became the youngest *agrégée de philosophie* in France. Her father, who

source of right, his subjection to the authority of government must be based on a compact.

had wanted her to be a prodigy, must have declared himself satisfied. For her it had been a formidable challenge, the first of many in her life, for she had been told by at least one teacher that women students usually had to compete in the *agrégation* five or six times before they were likely to win a place.

What now? Personal life was evolving at a dizzying pace. Maheu, soon aware that Beauvoir and Sartre were becoming inseparable, regretfully moved out of her existence. They had a nostalgic meeting in a café, and when they said goodbye, she cried, which annoyed him. He may have been hopeful that she would consent to an affair with him, despite the fact that he was married. Later in life she said that she eventually did so, but this was after she had embarked on a liaison with Sartre. Maheu, prepared to act in some ways like a member of the despised bourgeoisie, believed that all women should marry, and even advised Beauvoir to marry her cousin Jacques, with whom she had earlier imagined herself in love. Her cousin also had behaved in the accepted bourgeois manner, taking a mistress and then treating her badly. Beauvoir was upset when she heard about his conduct, and cried. If she had felt, during her depressed moments, that marriage to Jacques would 'save' her, any such desperate hopes were now gone. Jacques was exorcized. Soon afterwards he married and had several children. He told Beauvoir later that he wished he had married her. He became an alcoholic and died at the age of forty-six.

While preparing for her final examinations and accepting in her life the dominating presence of Sartre, Beauvoir was disconcerted by the parallel developments in the life of Zaza, still her best friend. At first it looked as though her story would have a happy ending, for she returned from Berlin a changed person: she was happy, extrovert, adult, she had even recovered from a sentimental adolescent love-affair with a cousin that had taken place several years earlier. Before her temporary banishment Beauvoir had introduced her to her friend Maurice Merleau-Ponty and they now met again. It was soon obvious that he was attracted to Zaza, and they fell in love. Beauvoir did not feel excluded when she was with them, she was pleased that two of her friends should respond to each other so fully. She used the language of romantic fiction: her two friends were 'made for each other' and she herself thought that one of her dreams would come true: Zaza would be happy at last.

The next chapter in the story could have been anticipated: Zaza's mother hovered in the background like a dark storm cloud and quickly discovered why her daughter was refusing to show any interest in a prospective husband who had been found for her. When the girl said she did not love him she received the stock answer offered on behalf of bourgeois society: it was the man who loved, not the woman, and Zaza should remember how well her sister Lili had behaved, agreeing obediently to marry a man much less intelligent than herself.

However, when the Lacoin parents realized that Merleau-Ponty seriously wished to marry their daughter they followed the usual procedure adopted by middle-class families at the time: they arranged for secret enquiries to be made about his parents, who lived near La Rochelle. The results were surprising. Merleau-Ponty's father had been a naval officer and during his many absences his wife had taken a lover, whose existence was concealed from no one. She had two children by him and the family situation was well known in La Rochelle.

The children were given the family name, everybody accepted the affair, but unfortunately nobody explained it to the illegitimate son, Maurice Merleau-Ponty.

Now he had to be told, and it was Zaza's father who took the young man into the Bois de Boulogne to break the news. There could be no question of marriage. Zaza suffered the most because she was told the truth but could not share her dismay with anyone. She could not tell the young man that she knew, and for that reason presumably did not tell her friend Simone. Merleau-Ponty appeared to hesitate, using family problems as an excuse. Zaza, who was to be sent to Berlin again, seemed temporarily to recover her spirits, then suddenly began to behave oddly: she called on Madame Merleau-Ponty, flushed and hatless, she entered the family drawing-room with no clothes on. Suddenly she was ill, and just as suddenly she was dead. The cause may have been meningitis, encephalitis, but Beauvoir was convinced that there was a deeper cause – the lack of love, the belief that rigid social convention was more important than human feeling.

Beauvoir herself did not know the whole story until years later, when the Lacoin family, after reading her early memoirs, thought they should put the record straight. She wrote later that 'Madame Mabille' had thanked her for making Zaza live again, but her friend's cousin, Mademoiselle Du Moulin de Labarthète, maintained even in 1986, nearly sixty years afterwards, that Simone had behaved badly following her friend's death. She did not explain precisely how, but Mademoiselle Du Moulin de Labarthète could not have relished Beauvoir's attack on the class to which the Lacoins and their relatives belonged. The social background, the contrast between the way in which their two families lived and thought, was meaningful. Yet Zaza was one of the first people to bring out Beauvoir's capacity for friendship, especially friendship with women.

Zaza, idol for a time, friend and symbol, never died for Beauvoir. Her attempt to write at least one novel about her failed, but she succeeded in introducing aspects of Zaza's character and incidents from her life into some of her fiction, notably in *Quand prime le spirituel* (*When Things of the Spirit Come First*). Beauvoir has been accused of describing her friend's tragic death in a cold, unemotional way, but her straightforward, slightly laconic treatment of this drama surely reflected her own drained emotional state. In *Tout compte fait*, published in 1972, she thought further, and finally, about her lost friend.

The girls had met in 1917, their friendship lasted for twelve years and marked Beauvoir for the rest of her life. However, so much else had happened in this year, 1929, that her mourning, if not her memory, was cut short. Now, she was 'no longer alone'. The reason was that over the last two months the cheerful student camaraderie with Sartre had developed rapidly into a much deeper relationship. After the *agrégation* results were announced, reported Beauvoir in her memoirs, Sartre told her that he would now 'take her in hand'. Not long before she died, she told two joint French biographers, Claude Francis and Fernande Gontier, that she did not want this phrase quoted. Did she decide that she had misinterpreted Sartre, or that readers would misinterpret her? The biographers added her request in a footnote to the U.S. edition. Whatever the reason, Sartre now dominated her life. As she and her sister were going to spend at least part of the summer at Meyrignac Sartre decided that he would go to the Limousin too, in the hope that they could meet there.

His presence led to some of the funniest incidents in the early Beauvoir–Sartre story. He took a hotel room in the neighbouring *chef-lieu* of Saint-Germain-les-Belles and every day he would walk over two miles to join Simone at the edge of the Meyrignac estate. He disliked walking, especially in the country, and used to say he was 'allergic to chlorophyll'. The two ex-students would talk endlessly. The Beauvoir parents were told that they were working together on a book which would attack Marxism. When Simone dutifully went back for the family lunch her sister and her cousin Madeleine would arrange picnic lunches for Sartre, usually consisting of bread rolls and *fromage blanc*, which were hidden in an empty dovecote. In order to explain away the disappearance of the food the girls would pretend they were *very* hungry.

The young couple were not always alone, for Hélène and Madeleine often joined them. Sartre's ability to amuse was undiminished. He would improvise plays so brilliantly, said Hélène, that he stimulated the others into collaboration. He would also sing, especially in the evening, when it began to grow dark. His repertoire was varied, including the *Chanson indienne*, an aria by Rimsky-Korsakov, and a romantic ballad about moths flying towards the light, irresistibly drawn to it like people in love. He amused the girls, just as he had amused Simone in Paris, he had a talent for entertaining a small audience. He liked irony: he would render in highly comic style a song about a young man who committed suicide and another about a soldier whose job it was to fight for France.

Simone's parents were not taken in by the story about the anti-Marx book and one day Georges and Françoise de Beauvoir suddenly appeared to confront the two young people. It was also the day when Sartre happened to be wearing a red shirt, described by Simone as *rose vif.* Georges de Beauvoir played the bourgeois father, told Sartre he was compromising his daughter, that gossip would make it difficult to carry through wedding plans for Madeleine. Would he please leave? Sartre said he would do so, did nothing of the sort and continued to meet Simone a little further away from the estate. Their father was appalled to think that his two daughters should have grown up in the way they had, one a would-be writer, the other a painter. He even told a visiting friend, in their presence, that he wished they had never been born. The girls replied that he should have thought of that earlier, but this was the last holiday the girls from Paris spent at Meyrignac.

The holidays over, Beauvoir and Sartre – who was to start his already much delayed military service shortly – met again in Paris in October. By now they had exchanged endless ideas, literary and philosophical, and told each other something of their experiences so far. On the personal side Beauvoir had little to relate, although Sartre teased her about her earlier admiration for Garric. When she told him about her relationship with Jacques he listened, predictably enough, 'without enthusiasm', and, unlike René Maheu, 'he hadn't a good word to say for marriage'. He realized however that after her bourgeois upbringing it was perhaps hard to avoid it. Although he too came from a bourgeois background his personal life had been very different, for as a man he had been able to escape family life more easily.

By the age of twenty-one Beauvoir had acquired an intensely emotional but non-sexual past, but Sartre, who was now twenty-four, had been enjoying varied amorous adventures for several years. If Zaza possessed charisma for both women and men, Sartre fascinated women as much as they intrigued him. His early love-affair with another Simone (Simone-Camille Sans, who later called herself Simone Jolivet), was almost too comic to be true, although presumably neither of them found it funny at the time. At the age of twenty he had met her at a cousin's funeral in Thiviers in the Dordogne. She was a good-looking provincial girl whose talent for sexual melodrama was obviously wasted on Toulouse, where her father was a chemist. Sartre could hardly afford the railway fare from Paris, but somehow he managed to travel down to see and sleep with her; she would let him into the house secretly, keep him awake all night, usually talking about literature or philosophy, preferably Nietzsche, and he would then attempt to sleep on a park bench before catching the train back to Paris. In 1926, when he was twenty-one, he wrote a revealing letter to her, explaining that he was extremely ambitious, that fame temped him but above all his ambition was to create, to construct, it didn't matter what. His creations so far varied from philosophical systems – silly ones, he said, because he had been sixteen at the time of their creation – to symphonies, and he had written his first novel when he was eight. He added that he could not 'see a sheet of blank paper without wanting to write something on it'. The details of his relationship with this bizarre woman could form a book on their own; she remained in his life and soon entered that of Beauvoir.

Beauvoir herself was still intent on becoming a writer, having decided that she had no wish to be a kind of 'female Bergson', though she had abandoned or torn up her various attempts at fiction-writing. She had not yet become an inventive writer: all of her attempted novels, as she was the first to acknowledge, had been about herself. However, she had achieved her *agrégation* success only two years after leaving the glorified dame school of the Cours Désir, while Sartre, who was three years older than she was, had taken twice as long. He had put most of his effort into creative writing of various kinds and acting in student revues, which brought him much *succès de scandale*. Stimulated by the excitement of his love-affair with Simone Jolivet, Sartre had actually covered many sheets of blank paper. He embarked on a novel which he at first called *Une Défaite*, based on the life of Wagner and his relationships with his second wife Cosima and the philosopher Nietzsche. The Germanic background came easily to him, for his mother's cousin, Albert Schweitzer, had once known and corresponded with the ageing Cosima in Bayreuth. The themes foreshadowed most of those in the Sartrian *oeuvre* to come, while both the heroes in the book are not far from the writer; Sartre planned that one of them would state, 'Only one man is alive for me, myself.' Later Sartre changed the title to *Empédocle* but the novel remained unfinished. He found time to write his thesis on the theme *L'Image dans la vie psychologique: rôle et nature*. The thesis fared better than the novel; it was completed, submitted and the examiners found it *très bien*. (Later, after revision, it became his first published book in 1936, entitled *L'Imagination*.)

In 1927 he wanted to be accepted personally, especially by women, and even wanted to get married, perhaps because several of his good friends, including Maheu and Nizan, were either married or engaged. He was so keen on the idea that he became unofficially engaged to a girl from Lyon whom he had met while on holiday with a friend in Usson-en-Forez. Her parents acted as the

Lacoins had done in the case of their daughter and Merleau-Ponty. A private detective was sent to observe Sartre's behaviour in Paris and alleged that he had been heard to say 'unpleasant and even crude' things about the girl and the engagement was broken off.

By the autumn of 1929 Beauvoir had disentangled herself from Jacques and, more importantly, she disentangled herself from her family. By giving private lessons and teaching part-time at a lycée she was able to earn a little money, and this enabled her to live on her own in a studio apartment owned by her grandmother in the rue Denfert-Rochereau. Her ideas about the décor were clear but not too original: she modelled it on the room of a mythical English schoolgirl she had seen pictured in a magazine. There were bookshelves and a divan bed, her sister helped her to paint deal furniture dark brown, the walls became bright orange and heating was provided by a paraffin stove which smelt horrible, but Simone was so excited by her new freedom that she even enjoyed the stink.

Beauvoir felt she was permanently on holiday now and expressed the feeling in a typically 'feminine' way; she bought new clothes and used make-up, which had been forbidden when she was living at home. She made a point of telling the readers of her memoirs – the second volume, *La Force de l'âge* (*The Prime of Life*), was published in 1960 – that she had never been much interested in clothes and cosmetics, and had never taken her personal appearance seriously. At the same time she went into great detail, thirty years after the event, about the clothes and make-up she now wore: crêpe de chine and embossed velvet instead of the wool or cotton she had been forced to wear when younger, as well as powder, rouge and lipstick.

Beauvoir gave herself a holiday of two years; it was her reaction to her cabined, cribbed adolescence and the hard work at the Sorbonne. At the same time she needed all her energy for one thing: the formation of an ever-closer, ever-deeper intellectual and emotional relationship with Sartre. The dozen or so pages in the memoirs which describe the formation of these two people as a couple deserve detailed reading, for they are crucial in understanding how the partnership was established. It is absurd to regard the two of them as Great Lovers, for Sartre made his own position quite clear: he loved Simone but he was 'polygamous'. Does love mean fidelity? Only, presumably, if one observed Christian and/or bourgeois morality. Does love imply marriage? The answer no doubt is the same. Apart from the weeks spent at Meyrignac Beauvoir and Sartre had already spent most of the summer of 1929 writing to each other, but these letters were subsequently lost, or so Beauvoir claimed. During October they spent most of the days together and would part late at night, when Sartre returned to his grandparents' home in the rue Saint-Jacques.

One letter from him to his *petit charmant Castor* has survived from this year and sums up in a few lines a good deal of what they felt about each other at the start of their relationship. In the first sentence he treats her as any old-fashioned husband might have treated a wife in the traditional rôle of housekeeper: would she please give his washing to the laundrywoman? The key was in the lock. Then the tone improved. He went on, using the formal *vous* as they did somewhat unexpectedly all their lives: 'I love you tenderly, my love. You looked delightful yesterday when you said: "Ah, you looked at me, you looked at me" and when I think of that my heart breaks with tenderness.' This was the very first letter addressed to her that she chose to publish in the *Lettres au Castor et à quelques autres* which appeared in France in 1983, three years after Sartre's death.

Presumably, during the intensive autumn courtship of 1929, he told her something of his sexual history, but the details did not appear in print until 1981, a year after his death. When he was eighteen a doctor's wife he had met in Thiviers talked him into his first sexual encounter. He claimed not to have enjoyed it though he had managed fairly well, he thought, while admitting he had never understood the incident.

Before the first *grande histoire*, the long intermittent relationship with Camille, or 'Toulouse', as she was often called, there had been several casual sexual affairs during his time at the Ecole Normale Supérieure. When in 1974 Beauvoir recorded his reminiscences about them she was quick to point out that these male students had been thinking and behaving in a totally bourgeois sexist fashion, for they operated a set of double standards: they disapproved of the girls who slept around, and they would not have considered any more developed relationship with them. As men however, they could do as they liked.

This was the early sexual history of Jean-Paul Sartre, to whom Simone de Beauvoir committed herself in the autumn of 1929. She had no doubt told him her own, infinitely less complicated, story. Despite the time and effort they spent in analysing the meaning of love and freedom they lived through the heady excitement of what one might call an old-fashioned love-affair.

On October 6th, 1939 Sartre, who was then in the army, wrote several letters to his dear Castor dwelling on their 'anniversary', a sad anniversary, he said, because they could not celebrate it together. He was no doubt recalling their first sexual encounter and the not so old-fashioned and much publicized two-year contract they had made, by which they would allow each other minor, subsidiary love affairs, known as 'contingent', and they would tell each other everything. In one way such a high-minded agreement might seem based on some form of superhuman idealism, in another way it could have been interpreted as unemotional and realistic, based on reason alone. It was surely Sartre who set the tone here: he appreciated women so deeply that he could not even have pretended to limit himself to one. He was not so much concerned with continual sexual experiment, but with the deep sensibility which he believed women possessed. Relations with women were richer than friendship between men. At the same time he liked women to be pretty, beautiful even. He noticed, when Beauvoir came to join him and his friends in their discussions about Leibniz, that she was badly dressed and wearing a hideous hat. But in Beauvoir he had been exceptionally lucky, he had found a woman who corresponded to all his needs, someone who could be an intelligent, understanding friend as well as a lover. He did not believe it was easy for a man to be friendly with a woman on a non-sexual basis and he admitted that in his own case it was practically impossible.

As an only son who had lost his father when very young he had grown up surrounded with women and used to say that he recognized feminine elements within himself. But there was also a considerable masculine element and it was he who initiated any relationship with a woman. As a self-confessed polygamist any search he might have made for an ideal woman would surely have been short-lived. Beauvoir, however, as she had watched her parents' marriage cool, before it began to disintegrate, had dreamed about marriage when she imagined herself in love with Jacques. She had formulated her ideal – a man who was like herself, she thought, but 'superior', more intelligent. Presumably she did not invent her aspirations years afterwards, when she wrote the memoirs; they were surely in her mind, if only half-formulated, by the time she was twenty. On the other hand she might not have written so much about them had they not actually come true. Sartre was about as unlike any fairy prince as any man could be, but his intelligence, wit and charisma were irresistible. Beauvoir had made up her mind when very young that she was destined for happiness; over several decades, whenever she wrote or spoke about her finding of it she seemed so exultant over her good fortune as to appear smug.

The themes of their contract were those of freedom and equality, but it has never been possible to assume that women and men are identical beings. Beauvoir may have been content to agree to the two-year contract, but how could she be certain that a 'contingent' love affair would remain contingent? Only a super-human trust in Sartre could convince her that she would never lose her own privileged position. This trust she possessed, but she could never let it weaken, for Sartre appeared to be continually testing her. For instance his first adult love, the Simone from Toulouse, had not disappeared. This extraordinary woman did not wish to waste her life in the provinces, where she would probably not find many brilliant young men ready to join in her orgies of intellectualized sex. She came to Paris increasingly and succeeded in her ambitions of writing and acting, becoming, en route, the mistress of Charles Dullin, the actor and theatrical innovator. She also saw Sartre, who made no attempt to avoid her, and Beauvoir became aware that she was feeling timidly jealous.

Eventually she saw the other Simone for the first time on the stage at the Atelier in 1930, taking part in a play by Armand Salacrou.[1] He was unknown at the time but was later to become a very successful playwright. *Patchouli* was an odd play about a

[1] Armand Salacrou (1899–1989): surrealist and a Communist journalist, well known later as a successful writer of plays ranging from tragedy to comedy and farce.

young man who preferred the past to the present; he was in love with a virtuous girl who lived during the time of the Franco-Prussian war. Simone Jolivet, although she was already Dullin's mistress, did not have a major rôle. Beauvour identified her after some time in a group of five *femmes légères*. Beauvoir realized that she could only understand her, and at the same time Sartre's feelings for her, if she actually met her. She went to the apartment in the rue Gabrielle, where Dullin had installed Simone, and found her wearing theatrical clothes, as she usually did. She talked about Japanese Nō plays and a play she herself was adapting. Yet Beauvoir was upset because she could not understand why Sartre had been so impressed by her: she only recovered when, in the company of her sister and a friend, she went to see her in the next Atelier play. They all found her acting and dancing 'quite grotesque'. Beauvoir had seriously tried to be understanding both of Sartre and his girl friend. She could hardly admit to herself that the man who 'thought all the time', as Maheu said, could have been interested in someone who hardly seemed capable of 'thought' at all, despite her pseudo-intellectual interests and her ambitions to write plays in addition to acting in them. Eventually Beauvoir admitted her jealousy openly, for she always tried to be honest with herself. She had not suppressed her own earlier feelings of intense loneliness, she was not only cerebral and analytical but she was also given to primitive emotions.

Despite all her reading, all the confidences and 'education' she had received from Stépha, Beauvoir's previous knowledge of sexuality had gone no further than sublimated emotional response. At seventeen, she had believed that 'all is well if the body obeys the head and the heart, but it should not take the lead'. Later, when she began to pick up men in bars, she still thought the same way. She also realized that her cousin Jacques never inspired within her 'the slightest disturbance nor a hint of desire'. Now there was no escaping the body. Yet Sartre, despite his obvious love for Beauvoir, was not too much interested in 'the right true end of love', however much he was fascinated by women. Late in life he admitted that sexual relationships with women had to take place because 'classic relationships implied that these had to occur at a certain moment. But I didn't attach much importance to them. And, to be precise, that didn't interest me as much as caresses. In other words, *j'étais plutôt un masturbateur de femmes qu'un coïteur.*' He went on to say that the 'essential and affective relationship implied that I would kiss and caress and touch a woman's body with my lips'. He was honest. 'But, the sexual act – it existed also, and I carried it out, I even carried it out often – but with a certain indifference.' Desire in its crude state was not for him, and he wondered if men did not feel obliged to demand something back from women – the sensitivity which they themselves had lost, in their hope perhaps of developing their intelligence in compensation. The complexities of his attitude were to become clearer in his fiction.

Beauvoir, now twenty-one, might have expected her own sexual life to begin in a simpler, more straightforward way. However, since she had agreed to tell Sartre everything she, in her turn, and from personal choice, also told her readers what at least appeared to be everything. There was a good sex life at the beginning of this relationship, which makes it sound like a normal love-affair, for she wrote of 'feverish caresses and love-making'. It is touching all the same to think that when she and Sartre stayed in the country they were 'too shy to go up to a hotel bedroom in broad daylight'. She believed that love-making should be spontaneous but she was frightened when she found a discrepancy between her 'physical emotions' and her 'conscious will'. She had been delighted to emerge from her state of 'pure spirit', but she had not expected to feel sexual hunger during separation from Sartre. She learnt that physical separation could produce physical pain and she was upset that she could not control her hunger. 'I had shaken off my puritanical upbringing just enough to allow myself unconstrained delight in my own body, but not enough to permit any inconvenience it might cause me.' She wrote of her sexual problems with her usual honesty. When she returned by the night train to Paris, after visiting Sartre on military service in Tours, 'an anonymous hand could awaken in my leg a disturbance that overwhelmed me with frustration'. She made these admissions in her second book of memoirs, and she was rarely more explicit than she was here. She had felt shocked when observing how Simone Jolivet expressed herself so casually through her body, but now she was beginning to see, after the years of self-confessed prudery, that the body could indeed tyrannize the mind. She admitted that during this phase of her life she was not a militant feminist, and that 'the sex-war meant nothing' to her. Her own femininity could not be ignored, and even if she still hated being classified as 'a woman', preferring always to be just herself, she was discovering, every day, more about femininity, especially her own.

Paris offered a vast range of enjoyment and entertainment, whether Sartre was there or not. Sometimes she joined in, sometimes she would merely watch and listen, as though in training, on the way to becoming the good reporter she eventually was. When Blaise Cendrars[1] and other flamboyant characters would dominate evenings in the Montparnasse cafés she would keep quiet, enjoying the atmosphere, the clink of glasses and the music that penetrated the smoke. She once followed a group of men into the ground-floor bar of the famous brothel, Le Sphinx, also in Montparnasse, and found the half-nude girls in their setting of incredible bad taste fascinating. Some of the girls were prostitutes, some were there merely to enhance the décor. This expedition had a double attraction for Beauvoir: she could enjoy the men's conversation and look at the women at the same time. Any romantic ideas she had about the place were rapidly dispelled.

Now she had truly escaped from home, she could do as she wished. However, she missed her women friends. Zaza was dead, the others were scattered or out of France. Through one of Sartre's students she met a sales-girl from the famous 'Burma' jewellery shop. The two of them would apply thick make-up and go round the dance-halls in the rue de Lappe, former haunt of the legendary apache dancers. The women danced with any likely young men they could pick up. Beauvoir's favourite partner was a butcher's boy who tried to entice her into 'contingent' sex. But she remained faithful to Sartre.

There were two reasons for the obvious pleasure she took in these incidents and in recounting them so many years later: the first, probably unconscious, was her wish to prove that she had a life of her own, independent of Sartre, however close to him she felt. The second reason was different. She was still drawn to the

[1] Blaise Cendrars (Frédéric Sauser) (1887–1961): novelist and poet. Of Swiss birth, he travelled a great deal before World War I, during which he lost an arm fighting in the Foreign Legion. He was associated with cubism and wrote novels of travel and epic adventure.

violent, dramatic, sordid side of life, the scenes she had sought out when a student. She had admitted earlier that she relished the 'illegal' nature of the forbidden bars. They were 'illegal' no longer, but years were to pass before she lost her curiosity for aspects of life outside the bourgeois scene. She visited them as though sight-seeing in a foreign country.

Sartre took her back to the days of student jokes, in which he was very experienced. They invented their own version of a 'morganatic marriage'. Such a marriage is normally one between persons of unequal rank, but Beauvoir said that they chose the description 'before we had even defined our relationship'. They called themselves 'Monsieur et Madame M. Organatique', or 'Monsieur et Madame Morgan Hattick'. The 'Organatiques' were a *petit bourgeois* couple with little ambition. The 'Hatticks' were American millionaires. Beauvoir and Sartre were acting out 'a parody which confirmed our disdain for *la grande vie*'. The aim was to assert their own odd social status and at the same time show they could escape from it.

Sartre's obligatory military service began in early November 1929, and did not cause him much suffering, apart from boredom and the separation from Beauvoir and Paris. His poor eyesight meant that he was not involved in active service and was allocated, as he had hoped, to the meteorological unit. He spent some time at the Saint-Cyr military academy where the sergeant responsible for his training was none other than his former colleague from the Ecole Normale Supérieure, Raymond Aron, later to become the well-known sociologist. After two months Sartre was transferred to a training centre at Saint-Symphorien, near Tours, close enough to Paris for Beauvoir to visit him on Sundays or for him to come to Paris to see her. His training allowed him some free time, all of which he used for creative writing. Beauvoir was usually the first person now to see anything he wrote, and it would be her life-long role to offer him her careful editorial advice. She was impeccably honest and at first, despite her admiration of Sartre, she did not always like what he wrote. 'Just as Sartre's thought had struck me through its maturity, I was disconcerted by the clumsiness of his attempts to express it.' She had not lost her intellectual independence, although she regarded Sartre as her 'superior' in thought.

For her, his two years of military service supplied a kind of holiday. She spent a vast amount of time reading, accompanied by English cigarettes and by Sartre himself whenever he could escape the army. This reading, the second stage in her intellectual development, was fairly predictable but also somewhat snobbish and mainly foreign, for she found that France had very little to offer during the late 1920s and early 1930s. The many-volume sagas such as *Les Thibault* by Roger Martin du Gard[1] were presumably too much concerned with a mere portrait of the hated or boring middle class. Catholic writers such as Mauriac[2] or Bernanos[3] held little interest for atheists, but Beauvoir grudgingly admitted that she enjoyed Claudel's drama *Le Soulier de satin*.[4] Yet literature was to be taken seriously, for apart from Sartre and a little part-time teaching it was the centre of life, her entire future. There could be no more half-serious admiration for the second-rate, such as *The Constant Nymph* by Margaret Kennedy or *The Green Hat* by Michael Arlen. There could be reading for relaxation, but it had to be kitsch of a special kind, usually thrillers selected by Sartre. The literary reviews, notably the *Nouvelle Revue Française*, kept Beauvoir up to date, but there is no mention in her remembered reading of Gide or Giono,[5] and no names of French poets. William Blake, however, is listed. It seems odd that the supercerebral Beauvoir and Sartre should have been impressed by Saint-Exupéry[1] but not so odd perhaps that they found it 'hard to swallow D. H. Lawrence and his phallic

[1] Roger Martin du Gard (1881–1958): novelist. His novel cycle *Les Thibault*, written between 1922 and 1940, won the Nobel Prize in 1937.
[2] François Mauriac (1885–1970): novelist. A passionate Roman Catholic, he wrote short psychological studies set in his native Bordeaux. Conflict between sensuality and religion forms the dramatic interest in his novels.
[3] Georges Bernanos (1888–1948): novelist of Spanish descent, at first active in L'Action Française, he later broke with them and was to denounce the atrocities committed by Franco's side in the Spanish Civil War. The main theme of his novels is the struggle between the forces of good and evil.
[4] Paul Louis Charles Marie Claudel (1868–1955): diplomat, poet and dramatist. *Le Soulier de satin* (1925–28), a drama set in Spain, Bohemia and at sea off the Balearics in the late sixteenth century, is a treatment of his recurring theme: man clinging to his earthly desires and denying God's love.
[5] Jean Giono (1895–1970): novelist of Italian origin, he made his name with tales of pastoral life set in Provence, depicting in rich poetic language a way of life that is simple but hard and close to Nature, which is seen as a healing force. His pacifism, the outcome of service in World War I, led to his imprisonment for some months early in World War II.

cosmology'. They were however privileged: they could read *Lady Chatterley's Lover* thirty years before the British could.

Beauvoir read a great deal of British and Irish writing, from classics such as *Wuthering Heights* to twentieth-century novels including Arnold Bennett, Mary Webb, Aldous Huxley and plays by Synge and O'Casey. Soviet fiction, Babel, Zamyatin and Ehrenburg, made a great impact, but apart from *My Life* by Trotsky, non-fiction was found to be dull. Kierkegaard did not warrant close attention. She was anxious to fathom Marx and Engels, who had been neglected by her teachers at the Sorbonne. She was not successful with Marx, for she 'made no distinction between Marxism and the philosophies to which I was accustomed'. She thought he was easy to understand but realized later that she had grasped practically nothing. However, 'new light was shed on the world when I saw work as the source and substance of all values', and nothing changed her opinion on this point.

There was still little sign of the future feminist. At this period of her life, when she was still in her early twenties, it had not occurred to her to take any special interest in women writers as such, or in their presentation of women's problems, even if this was unconscious on their part. She thought of herself as a writer-to-be, and reacted to women writers as writers, not as women. She read the whole of Virginia Woolf but concluded that her experimental fiction was disappointing. She never forgot Rosamond Lehmann's *Dusty Answer*,[2] which had been part of her teenage life, and it was to influence one of her early attempts to write fiction. Beauvoir was reading, but not yet writing. She had first to come to terms with her own changed and changing life.

[1] Antoine de Saint-Exupéry (1900–44): aviator and author. His works are a direct transmutation into literature of his physical and spiritual experiences in the air. Best known for *Courrier-Sud* (1928); *Vol de nuit* (1931), which made his name; *Terre des hommes* (1939). He served as a pilot at the start of World War II and went to North Africa at the fall of France. He published *Pilote de guerre* in 1942 and *Le Petit Prince* a year later. He was lost in a reconnaissance mission in North Africa in 1944.

[2] Rosamond Lehmann (1903–1990): *Dusty Answer* (1927) describes the awakening into womanhood of an eighteen-year-old girl. Other novels include *A Note in Music* (1930), *Invitation to the Waltz* (1932), *The Weather in the Streets* (1936), *The Ballad and the Source* (1944) and *The Echoing Grove* (1953). The insistence on emotional and sensuous aspects of life in the novels has been described as romantic and female and their pioneering frankness points to an assumption that women's lives are as interesting and important as men's.

FOUR

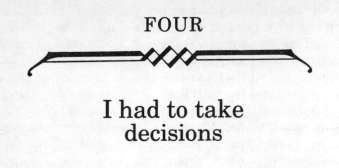

I had to take decisions

By moving out of the family apartment in the rue de Rennes, Beauvoir had won a battle – she had moved out of the stifling and oppressive middle-class into a free and individual life, a whole world of liberty which had been inaccessible to her earlier and might even have remained so, had she not achieved high academic success. During her intensive work for the *agrégation* she had developed from student into intellectual, she had joined that élite group which in France more than in any other country still constitutes a form of social class. Ever since the time of Diderot, when the eighteenth-century *encyclopédistes* had finally supplanted the clerics in the exercise of ideological power, intellectuals had maintained and even improved their status. During the watershed revolution of 1789 and those that followed in the nineteenth century they had put forward theories and opinions, they had argued long and hard about the beliefs they supported or attacked. These theories and opinions were usually expressed in writing, and it was left to younger activists, who tended to see things in simpler, more dramatic terms, to translate the theories into slogans, to desert the study and take to the streets. In modern France intellectuals participated in the long-drawn-out Dreyfus case; later they were to lead the attack on the French government during the bitter Algerian war of 1954–62 and there can be no reference to the events of May 1968 without recalling their participation.

French intellectuals, it has been said, are 'very intellectual', implying that they are preoccupied with abstractions, usually preferring to leave any action, let alone violence, to others. As the 1920s moved into the 1930s there was little talk in Beauvoir's circle of violence or revolution, or action of any kind. She and Sartre considered themselves anarchists, convinced that creative activity on their part would be more radical than any orthodox or superficial moves, such as joining a political party. Though their friend Paul Nizan had proved his commitment by joining the Communist party, that was his way, not theirs. In later life Beauvoir often remembered her 'anarchism', but during the years immediately following her *agrégation* she was concerned with her personal relationships and the establishment of her own individual self, which was not yet clearly defined. In this new and central partnership with Sartre many of her attitudes were so dependent on his that as she remembered them she did not often say 'I', she said 'we'. As a schoolgirl she had hoped to link her life with someone who was like her, but 'superior', and this is what she had done. Other girls may have looked for a Prince Charming, she had found Sartre, whose nickname among friends and students was 'le Kobra': ugly enough, fierce enough, likely to fascinate and to win whenever challenged.

Beauvoir had earned the freedom to live in the way she had chosen, supporting herself financially with teaching work, and indulging that capacity for happiness, that rare gift she was so convinced she possessed. The agonizing uncertainties of adolescence were over and her life with Sartre, close but not too close, was in its own way idyllic. 'We would meet in the morning in the grey and gold Luxembourg Gardens, beneath the blank stone gaze of the statues of queens. We would walk across Paris, and we went on talking . . . about ourselves, our relationships, our future lives and books.' After which they parted late at night. They felt they had no problems: 'We had confidence in the world and in each other.' For Beauvoir it was a time of euphoria, the April of her life. How could anything possibly go wrong? The unending talk was life itself to her, but later, much later, she made a confession: 'What seems to me today to have been the most important thing about these conversations was not so much the things we said as the things we took for granted: but we were wrong about

89

practically everything.' She was referring, in general terms, to politics and public morality. They regarded themselves as writers, it was their destiny, but they saw only 'one kind of reality – that of our own situation'. Sartre, who 'lived for writing', told her that she must write 'in order to open her conscience to the multiple splendour of life', she must write 'in order to snatch it from time and nothingness'. Writing was to be the present and the future.

What were they going to write about? How were they going to communicate, and to whom? Beauvoir's descriptions of the contribution that she and Sartre would make to society was ambitious enough: 'Man had to be re-created and this invention would be partly our work.' The programme was grandiose but it would be implemented in one precise way, 'only through books'. Beauvoir described their view of the world: 'We were against society in its current form; but there was nothing gloomy about this hostility, it implied firm optimism.' In one sense she and Sartre were still behaving like the most unrealistic of students, looking at the world – despite their atheism – with the eyes of Voltaire's Dr Pangloss: 'God's in his heaven, all's right with the world.'

In order to believe that, Beauvoir had indeed to be optimistic. The autumn of 1929 had brought the Wall Street crash in New York and its international repercussions, but the two Paris intellectuals remained starry-eyed: 'The exceptionally severe crisis that shook the capitalist world allowed us to think that this society would not survive for long. We felt we were already living in that golden age which for us constituted the hidden truth of History.' Later in life Beauvoir looked back and saw the situation more clearly, analysing the reasons for their mistakes. 'At every level we were unaware of the weight of reality. We boasted about our radical liberty. We believed so long and so tenaciously in this word that I have to look closely at the way we interpreted it.' Liberty was more important to her than anything else in life but she also realized that there was more than one way of defining the concept. She claimed that 'a kind of liberty can be found in all activity, and particularly in intellectual liberty because it is little concerned with repetition'. Liberty implied development, evolution, the possibility of change. She believed that the 'intensity of their work', i.e. study, thinking and some writing, had forced Sartre and herself 'to understand and invent things anew; we had a practical, undeniable notion of liberty . . .' Understandably enough, however, there were flaws in their vision: 'Our mistake was our failure to contain it within its limits.' They did not relate their intellectual ambitions to the world in which they were living, and that world was no golden age. In fact Beauvoir and Sartre did not look beyond the accepted opinions within their small if lively circle. They saw themselves as 'sharing the euphoria of the French left wing' and they were convinced that any minor problems would soon fade away. 'Peace seemed definitely assured; the expansion of the Nazi party in Germany represented only a minor phenomenon that was not serious. Colonialism would soon disappear; this was guaranteed by the campaign launched by Gandhi in India[1] and the communist agitation in Indo-China.' How easy everything seemed! No direct action was needed, and if they found public affairs 'boring', as Beauvoir admitted, there was no need to feel guilty, for many intellectuals of the period reacted in the same way. They believed there were sound reasons for their attitude, and they had planned no easy escapist life for themselves. The serious projects they had devised needed concentration and self-analysis. 'Our political blindness,' said Beauvoir, 'that spiritualist pride, can be explained in the first place by the violence of our plans.' She returned to their shared ambition and the way in which they hoped to achieve it: 'To write, to create: one could hardly embark on this adventure without assuming one was absolute master of oneself, one's ends, one's means.' They had already made that assumption. Their audacity, she felt, 'was inseparable from the illusions which fed it and circumstances favoured it'.

This optimistic and brilliant young woman saw no obstacle to her existence as an intellectual. Beauvoir and Sartre have been attacked by later critics for their complacency, but when they were young they accepted neither one another's nor other people's ideas without argument. 'We did not hesitate to contest everything and ourselves whenever the occasion demanded it: we criticized ourselves, we condemned ourselves readily, for every

[1] Gandhi's campaign of civil disobedience against the British colonial government in India started in the 1920s. Punctuated by periods of imprisonment and fasts unto death, the campaign continued, supported by an increasing number of activists, during the 1930s.

change seemed to be progress.' The older Beauvoir again condemned her younger self, realizing she had taken a limited view of
the world. With hindsight she gave a straightforward explanation: 'Since our ignorance concealed from us most of the problems
which should have worried us, we contented ourselves with these
reappraisals and believed we were intrepid.' Eventually she was
to become truly intrepid in her examination of fundamental
problems, both individual and universal, but that lay far ahead.

As for the realities and problems of everyday life, she and Sartre
made the best of things. They were poor, but for what would they
have needed money? After the crisis of 1929 many people were
poorer than they were. 'Why regret that we did not drive about in
a car when we could make so many discoveries walking beside the
Canal Saint-Martin or along the quais de Bercy?' These were two
of the old-fashioned picturesque spots in the city. Beauvoir
admitted a weakness for 'cocktails made with honey at the Bar
des Vikings, for apricot cocktails at the Bec de Gaz in the rue de
Montparnasse'. These were the popular cheap drinks of the
period. 'How could the Ritz bar have offered us anything better?'
The partners did not envy the rich: their 'puritanical upbringing'
and 'the firmness of their intellectual commitment' left them
uninterested in 'the habitués of luxury hotels, men in Hispanos,
women in mink, dukes, millionaires; and since this *beau monde*
profited from a regime we condemned, we considered them to be
the dregs of the earth'. Beauvoir felt sorry for such people; they
were excluded by their wealth from the exciting reality of the
outside world. She missed their 'privileges and refinements no
more than the fifth-century Greeks missed the cinema and the
radio'.

Her optimism helped her to dismiss all possible problems in
daily existence, to crush envy by reversing any potentially unfair
situations. However, just as she was not prepared to examine
political or social reality, she was not ready to deal with various
personal problems of her own. She could not accept *les
contrariétés*, she was upset when she could not have her own way.
'My face changed, I withdrew into myself, I became obstinate.'
Sartre, like others who observed Beauvoir closely, especially in
later life, decided that she had 'a double personality; as a rule I
was the Beaver; but at certain moments this creature was

supplanted by a somewhat unpleasant young woman, Mademoiselle de Beauvoir'. For the rest of her life she could, if she chose, be obstinate, she could be distant, she could display reminders of her bourgeois upbringing, varying from formal manners to cold brusquerie. She became aware, about the time of her twenty-second birthday, early in 1930, that there was a good deal of unreality in her attitude: she considered herself detached from humdrum occupations, including her teaching work, and thus her exterior life became a kind of 'masquerade'. Sartre was in the same situation. She realized later that these lofty ideas did not help them at the time, for the partners had failed to stand back and look at themselves from a distance: 'We did not want to.' In some ways they were still adolescent. Beauvoir had already noticed that Sartre did not want to grow up, she had seen him unhappy at the thought of entering the 'detestable world of adults'. He had made up his mind how a writer should live: he should be like J. M. Synge's 'playboy of the western world' and never settle down anywhere. The two of them could have come to terms with reality, said Beauvoir, if they had been interested in the disciplines of Marxism or psychology, but they knew little about either and did not really want to know more. There was another problem: they looked down on the bourgeoisie, they despised them, but were they not in their debt? Beauvoir freely admitted the fact: 'We owed our openmindedness to a culture and to a set of projects accessible only to our class. It was our status as petit bourgeois intellectuals which led us to believe we had no status at all.'

She came to see that life in the so-called free adult world was not as simple as she had imgined it to be, for the legacy of the bourgeoisie was inescapable. She and Sartre were so pleased at their escape from childhood and family life that they did not realize at the time one strange way in which their early existence had affected them. Later, in remembering how she and Sartre were 'indifferent' about and contemptuous of the importance attached to childhood by the Freudians Beauvoir realized the crucial mistake they themselves had made. The emotional detachment, of which they were so proud, 'could be explained by that very childhood itself'. Eventually she did accept that 'childhood was the key to personality', but in her twenties, when she was still relatively close to it, she preferred not to think about her early life.

This early life had been dominated by reading, and by all the dreams and ideas that grew from books. Now there was a new attraction, especially for Sartre: the cinema. Beauvoir's parents had found many films 'unsuitable' for children and she was not very experienced in this bright world. 'I was less fascinated than he was,' she said, 'but I still followed him eagerly to see new releases or to small local cinemas where he had discovered tempting programmes.' She was ready to obey Sartre in most things. He persuaded her to give up 'artistic' films in favour of westerns and thrillers from the U.S., an intellectual fashion of the time. Beauvoir felt now that films, like books, needed earnest attention. 'We did not go [to the cinema] merely for entertainment; we went there just as seriously as young devotees today [1960] go to see classic films.' An additional reason for this interest in the cinema was the lack of good theatre, for according to the two filmgoers the plays of the period, and their presentation, were 'mediocre'. They enjoyed the French version of *The Threepenny Opera*, even if they admitted to knowing nothing about Brecht. They believed the work embodied 'the purest anarchism . . . Sartre knew by heart all Kurt Weill's songs and later we often repeated the slogan *Erst kommt das Fressen, dann kommt die Moral*'.[1] Politics may have been boring but if they found their way into the theatre they became relevant. The same was true of social problems. The brilliant Marie Dubas, the singer and music-hall artist who made everyone laugh, pleased them greatly: 'We saw in [her] parodies a satire on the bourgeoisie.' She also included in her repertoire 'some splendid songs, crude songs which seemed to us to challenge the protected classes: we saw her too as an anarchist'.

There was one major problem at this time: Beauvoir still preferred 'living', Sartre still preferred writing, and during his time as a conscript, always found time 'to write, to create'. She, so lively in so many ways, so optimistic, relishing everything from café gossip to long country walks, from the Paris music-hall to

[1] *Die Dreigroschenoper*: by Bertolt Brecht, music by Kurt Weill (1928).

American thrillers, was not enjoying the sight of blank sheets of paper. Unfortunately she could not think of anything to put on them. Sartre constantly reminded her that she had always wanted to write, or so she had said, she *must* write now, she must join him in this crucial aspect of their life together. Beauvoir had begun to see that her happy partnership was not helping the career which she had seen as the true purpose of her existence. She realized that her earlier insistent need to become a famous author had been her 'one recourse against solitude . . . Now I had no need to express myself.' She had begun to understand why so many people wanted to become writers, and tried so hard: 'A book is an appeal for help: to whom should I appeal, and why? *J'étais comblée*, I had found fulfilment.' So she was in a difficulty: she could not admit that the potential writer had been silenced by the young woman who was now so happy in the old-fashioned 'feminine' way, in the shadow of Sartre. Part of her was aware that she was playing truant from the career she had chosen for herself, and she came close to admitting that she had chosen it on false pretences. She became confused and depressed, achieving no more than pastiche. Under the eye of le Kobra, she struggled on, aware of her failure.

She made life harder for herself by choosing unassailable models, two novels she had admired passionately when she was a schoolgirl: *Le Grand Meaulnes* by Alain-Fournier[1] and Rosamond Lehmann's *Dusty Answer*, both stories about a disappointed search for love. Perhaps she was unconsciously looking for a corrective to her own situation of requited and unquestioning love. At the same time she had always related books, those she read and those she attempted to write, to the one subject that preoccupied her deeply: herself. As a student she had not enjoyed Alfred Jarry's famous play *Ubu roi*[2] because she could find no

The slogan is from Macheath's song, 'What keeps a man alive': 'First comes the grub, then come the morals.'

[1] Alain-Fournier (Henri-Alban Fournier) (1886–1914): *Le Grand Meaulnes* (1913) is remarkable for its sensitive treatment in terms of a childlike dream world of events which all the time have a rational explanation.

[2] Alfred Jarry (1873–1907): author of the satirical farce *Ubu roi* (1896). Ubu, who makes himself King of Poland, is a grotesque, puppet-like figure, the embodiment of cowardice and cruelty and bourgeois avarice. Jarry's preoccupation with absurdity places him among the precursors of surrealism.

trace of her own obsessions in it. Her new attempt at a book did not gather momentum and she gave up after three chapters. Her heroine, who was modelled on herself, was due to experience 'poetic adventures, but I didn't know which ones'. Worst of all, she had to admit that there was always *un petit côté Delly*, something of 'Delly' about her first drafts. 'Dely' was the name used by a prolific brother and sister team whose romantic fiction, written in the first part of this century, is still available in France.

Her current troubles were due at least in part to her extremism. As a schoolgirl and young student she had loved Zaza totally; she had felt 'subjugated' by her friend, and realized she had been in danger of losing her own individuality. Now she was in danger of being 'subjugated' by Sartre. She had begun to behave like the traditional 'little woman', dominated by a brilliant, adored man. At first she could not see how she was going to emerge from this state; she knew Sartre did not want an idle companion, he wanted her to concentrate, as he was doing, on a writer's career. Yet she had begun, unconsciously, to 'dwindle into a wife'. Sartre himself had applied for a lectureship in Japan and was fairly certain of winning it. So, other considerations apart, Beauvoir might have to spend two years or so in Paris on her own, and she must have something to do. He nagged her gently: ' "But, Castor, you used to have lots of ideas" ', he told her. He reminded her seriously of the destiny that might be awaiting her, the destiny she had sworn never to accept: ' "Take care not to become *une femme d'intérieur*, a housewife." '

Beauvoir saved herself, with much help from Sartre, just in time. For two years, ever since he had said he would 'take her in hand', there had been no problems. 'When I met Sartre I believed all was well; with him, I could not fail to fulfil myself.' But there had been a reaction, not against Sartre, but against her own attitude. 'I told myself now that expecting salvation through someone other than oneself is the surest way to self-destruction.' She remembered that when she was a young schoolgirl, she had hated being described as ' "a child", now I did not think of myself as "a woman": I was me'. When God had disappeared from her universe she had retained the idea of salvation: 'The first of my convictions was that each person should ensure his/her own salvation.' She could not accept life as 'a secondary being, a relative being'; this would be 'degradation'. She realized that this problem arose 'only because I was a woman. But I tried to solve it as an individual.' She had been living so close to Sartre, that unconsciously perhaps she had lost something of herself. She had been puzzled and uncreative because she had also lost sight, temporarily, of her own convictions. Now she must re-establish herself as a person, forget that she ever came close to that 'secondary' status: 'The contradiction from which I was suffering was not social, but moral and almost religious.'

Beauvoir saw the danger of 'subjugation' but at this stage of her life she did not relate it to the problems of women as a group. 'Feminism made no sense to me,' she stated. Isolated as she was within a small coterie of intellectual friends she saw relatively little of the lives of ordinary people in the world about her. In the 1920s, some women, notably those from the middle and upper classes, were working on behalf of other women, doing their best through journalism, meetings and demonstrations to draw attention to some of the most obvious social injustices, such as intolerably long working hours and abysmally low pay. So far the young Simone de Beauvoir had worried little about other women's earnings and hardly at all about her own. When seriously short of money she had survived by selling some of her books and even her jewellery, which upset her mother. Sartre had inherited a small legacy from his grandmother and spent it with rapid enjoyment. Both partners were convinced he was now practically on his way to Japan and Beauvoir, still young enough to see his two-year absence as lasting 'for ever', now moved, in her extremist way, from euphoria to fits of despair. Whatever would she do without him? In the end she did not have to deal with that problem for in February 1931 Sartre learnt that he had failed to get the post. By April he had taken a replacement teaching job at the Lycée François Ier in Le Havre.

Beauvoir realized that she must at last think about a job and a salary; she must 'take decisions'. She was determined to stay in Paris, where Sartre would join her as often as he could, but she did not see herself as a serious lycée teacher; she wanted some new and stimulating experience. With this aim she allowed herself to take up an introduction offered by her family. 'The rich influential cousin who had helped my father in the past recommended me to one of the co-directors of *L'Europe nouvelle*', a periodical founded in 1921 which published articles on current affairs. The co-director, Madame Le Verrier, explained the way in which the magazine was run and the type of work the editors preferred. The more active editor was Louise Weiss, a name well known at the time, a woman with many worthwhile achievements behind her. She was an *agrégée*, like Beauvoir, and in 1921, while working in the U.S.S.R. for the newspaper *Le Petit Parisien*, she had encountered a group of Frenchwomen who were in severe difficulties. They had originally come to Tsarist Russia as governesses to the aristocracy. In the aftermath of the revolution, these women were stranded. It was through the efforts of Louise Weiss, who brought the matter to the attention of the French Foreign Office, that the former governesses were repatriated.

Back in Paris Weiss was determined that Frenchwomen should be granted the right to vote and she founded the Association for the Equality of Political Rights of Frenchmen and Women. In the long wait for women's suffrage she, and other women with similar interests, gave their attention to the question of paid holidays and working hours for women, especially those with babies and young children. Some of the more activist women would climb lamp-posts or onto the roofs of department stores in an effort to ban the sale of warlike toys for children. This kind of behaviour made no appeal to Beauvoir. She was interested in more abstract problems. She was not ready for encounters, social or intellectual, outside her immediate circle of café-haunting acquaintances. When she was invited to a cocktail party to meet the staff and contributors attached to *L'Europe nouvelle* she remembered it as her 'first appearance in *le beau monde*'. She herself, who had drunk endless cocktails in the bars of Montparnasse, had never been to a cocktail party before. Beauvoir admitted that she 'did not shine'. She felt self-conscious because she was unsuitably dressed, just as she had been when she was a young adolescent. 'All the ladies of *L'Europe nouvelle* were dressed by the couturiers; Louise Weiss, in black satin, was talking, surrounded by a circle of admirers.' Beauvoir had chosen to wear 'a red woollen dress with a wide collar in white piqué, much too modest for the occasion'. She could not muster any conversation. Madame Le Verrier explained to her young friend that if she wanted to make a good start in journalism she would have to contribute ideas: 'Did I have any? No.' It is hard to think of Beauvoir without ideas but those she had were more likely to be concerned with philosophy, literature and the arts than with social problems. She lost no time in making up her mind: 'I realized I could never get on with these people and I decided to go and teach in the provinces.'

She was not inexperienced as a teacher, even if she had not taken the work seriously. She had tried, not very successfully, to work as an adult education teacher for Robert Garric. She had given lessons in psychology to older girls when she herself was studying at the Institut Sainte-Marie in Neuilly. When she had accepted part-time work at the Lycée Victor Duruy in the 7th *arrondissement* one of her assignments had been to teach Latin to girls of ten, the youngest class in the school. She was not well suited to this kind of work, for though adolescents interested her, younger children did not. They in their turn were not much interested in Latin but enjoyed examining her jewellery and clothes. 'I tried to harden my voice, to look at them in a threatening way . . . I decided to be severe and gave a bad mark to the worst behaved girl.' The child screamed: ' "My father will beat me!" The entire class repeated in a reproachful voice: "Her father will beat her!" ' Any inexperienced teacher will sympathize with Beauvoir; she could not handle a group like this. 'I found only one solution and that was to drown their racket by shouting.' She consoled herself by deciding that the girls who wanted to listen did listen and learnt as much Latin as those in any other class. 'But I was summoned to the headmistress more than once and my appointment was not renewed.'

Hardly surprising, therefore, that Beauvoir tried to find some teaching work which would take her abroad for a time. The suggestion that she should join a cultural institute in Morocco alarmed her. She reacted in the same way when a young Hungarian friend thought she might teach at the University of Budapest. Beauvoir herself asked Stépha's friend Fernando, who was Spanish, if he could find her a post in Madrid, which she wanted to see, but he couldn't.

So there was no escaping a post in France. She was qualified by her *agrégation* to teach in a lycée, but under the current system she could not apply for a specific post; she would be treated as a civil servant within the sphere of higher education. Because she had not previously worked as a full-time teacher she knew that she would not be given an assignment in Paris. When she finally applied for a posting in spring, 1931, she was appointed to a large city but one so far away that she considered it Ultima Thule – Marseille, the old-established port on the Mediterranean coast and three times as far from Paris as Le Havre.

The word she used was 'panic' – the thought of being far away from Sartre and from Paris upset Beauvoir so deeply that he in his turn was reduced to panic suggestions. Perhaps they should get married after all? Married teachers were given posts in the same lycée, so surely this was the right thing to do. Beauvoir knew that Sartre was no marrying man. She said later that she 'saw how much it cost Sartre to bid goodbye to his travelling, his freedom, his youth, to become a teacher in the provinces and to become, for ever, grown up'. Although she knew he would bear no grudge against her she did not wish her future to be 'poisoned' by remorse. She was no marrying woman. 'I did not even have to think it over, I didn't hesitate, I didn't calculate, my decision was taken without me.' In any case, the whole concept of marriage offended them both, it brought out all their feelings of anarchy, and it was this anarchy 'which incited us . . . to reject the interference of society in our private lives'. They were hostile to marriage because it was one of the institutions which 'emanated from the bourgeoisie'. They were hostile to the bourgeosie, and they believed that conviction should be matched by behaviour, so 'celibacy for us was normal'.

Beauvoir knew that if she had wanted children her decision might have been different. She had nothing against motherhood as such, although she admitted that babies did not interest her. 'I had thought of having children when I was contemplating marrying my cousin Jacques', but now the circumstances were different: 'my happiness was so complete that no novelty could attract me. A child would not have strengthened the links which bound Sartre and me together; I did not wish Sartre's existence to be reflected and prolonged in that of another being: *il se suffisait, il me suffisait.* And I was sufficient to myself.' Marriage would increase social obligations, which she disliked in any case, and she sensed the most dangerous result of all: 'By modifying our relationships with other people, it would inevitably have changed for the worse those that existed between the two of us.' Beauvoir was strongly influenced by memories of her own childhood, which at this stage of her life were depressingly negative: 'I felt so little affinity with my parents that any sons or daughters that I might have appeared to me in advance as strangers. I imagined they could feel indifference or hostility, so great was my aversion to family life.' As a student she had already been depressed at the sight of the Nizans pushing a baby carriage for she believed (like Eloïse in the eleventh century) that the only bond between lovers should be love. Children, thought Beauvoir, impeded not only personal life but professional ambitions. 'I knew that in order to become a writer I needed a great amount of time and a great amount of freedom.' A writer had at least two reasons for writing: 'Through literature, I thought, one justifies the world by creating it anew, in the purity of the imagination, and at the same time one preserves one's own existence.' Later in life Beauvoir could recall no emotional struggle: 'I did not have the impression that I was refusing motherhood: it was not my lot; by remaining childless, I was assuming my natural condition.'

Yet during the 1970s a retired French gynaecologist revealed that Simone de Beauvoir had come to see her, asking whether she should have a child with Sartre. After examining her the consultant told her that for physiological reasons she was unlikely to have a child in any case. However, it was rumoured in Paris that the young Beauvoir had in fact become pregnant and undergone an abortion. It was also rumoured later that Sartre introduced the episode into his novel *The Age of Reason* in 1945. The 'hero', Mathieu, on learning that his girl-friend Marcelle is pregnant, tries desperately to borrow the money needed for an abortion, which in fact she does not want. During the 1930s Sartre's friend Madame Morel, with whom the couple often stayed in the Maine et Loire district near Angers, suggested, perhaps not too seriously, that they should have a child, whom she would bring up. The novelist Françoise Sagan was to sum up the situation concerning Sartre in 1984, after his death: 'Sartre a father? What a ridiculous idea! Sartre a husband? Just as unthinkable! A lover? Perhaps.'

In any case the lovers revised their pact in 1931, for their relationship had become more complicated, more demanding. Short separations were in order, but not large-scale one-sided adventures. They decided too that *des éventuelles dissipations*, any possible lifting of the agreement, could be put off until they were thirty, which in Beauvoir's case lay seven years ahead. Since Sartre was three years older, would he have had permission to escape sooner, if he so wished? This not irrelevant point was ignored.

That summer, despite the firmness of the decisions she had taken, she still needed to escape from the anxieties of the coming separation from Sartre and the fear that her work in Marseille would take her into an unknown and solitary world. So, with Sartre, she went to Spain on holiday. There was not much money for travel, but Stépha's friend Fernando told Beauvoir that she and Sartre could stay in his apartment in Madrid. Ever since the time of Victor Hugo and Prosper Mérimée Spain has fascinated the French, in particular its writers. The country, so close geographically, seemed so different from their own, so full of drama and mystery. The terror of the Inquisition contrasted strongly with the unique individuals of the past such as Saint Teresa of Avila, Cervantes, Philip II, builder of the forbidding Escorial, and the impressive contemporaries such as Miguel de Unamuno, whose famous book *The Tragic Sense of Life* (1913) has been seen as a presage of existentialism. Spain had produced the two painters, Picasso and Dali, who dominated modern art. How different from the country of Versailles, Voltaire, Renoir!

Partly financed by the remains of Sartre's legacy, the eager travellers entered Spain through its north-east corner, and 'when we saw at Port de Bou [a small town on the Mediterranean coast] the civil guard officers with their patent leather cocked hats we felt', Beauvoir remembered, 'that we had been thrust into the midst of exoticism'. Beauvoir took charge of the travel details, the train tickets and the country bus routes, an arrangement which suited Sartre very well. They could just afford cheap hotels and meals, and Beauvoir had no interest in luxury. They stayed in Figueras on their way to Barcelona where they were able to see Hélène de Beauvoir, who was on holiday there briefly.

The Spanish republic had been proclaimed only a few months earlier, the King had gone into exile without renouncing his rights to the throne, and so far Spain had experienced only a patchy form of democracy. In Barcelona the two French tourists, who did not speak the language, were mystified by a strange atmosphere along the Ramblas. The next day some streets were deserted, some full of 'unusual agitation', and there were no buses. The French visitors noticed that the police had handcuffed a man, while small groups were talking earnestly among themselves. Beauvoir and Sartre, who were looking for an elusive church they wanted to visit, approached one of the 'effervescent' groups and attempted to ask their way. 'We were answered by a smile and one man, with grace and charm, indicated our route with gestures; as soon as we had thanked him the men returned to their discussion.' Later the visitors succeeded in deciphering a newspaper: trade unionists, they learnt, were on strike against the edicts of the provincial government. The 'agitation' and 'effervescence' reflected the discussion among the workers as to whether they should fight to defend their comrade who had been arrested. The French tourists, so apathetic about politics in their own country, wished now they had understood what was happening in the streets of Barcelona. 'We felt very mortified: we were there, and we had seen nothing.' Beauvoir recalled the experience of Stendhal's hero Fabrice del Dongo in *La Chartreuse de Parme*, unaware that he had taken part, if only on the sidelines, in the battle of Waterloo.

If Barcelona had produced a strike incident Madrid, she found, was still celebrating the establishment of the republic. She had a glimpse of Ramón del Valle-Inclán, the revolutionary writer who was now nearing the end of his life but still drew admiring audiences round him on the café *terrasses*. Literature formed the background to Beauvoir's holiday. She had learnt from books by literary travellers that the visitor to any foreign land must seek out the secret soul of the country by mingling with the crowd, absorbing smells and tastes, not simply by walking round museums and galleries as over-organized tourists. Beauvoir had also read that she would see the truth of a town in the *bas-fonds*, the low-life districts. As a result she and Sartre, like literary critics analysing the technique of a book rather than enjoying it for its own sake, became more curious about spectators than about the spectacles themselves. In this way they felt they were assimilated into the crowd. They knew that officially the republic did not approve of bull-fighting but made no serious attempt to stop it. As a result the tourists went to the bullring every week and became *aficionados*. On this first trip abroad Beauvoir was essentially a literary-minded, intellectual tourist. She remembered what Gide had said when he drank Spanish hot chocolate: he felt that the whole of Spain was in his mouth, just as she herself, when a little girl, had absorbed the atmosphere of her mother's evening parties through the taste of crystallized fruit.

This first trip to Spain was very much a cultural exploration, and as she remembered the art galleries in Madrid Beauvoir later made a confession. She and Sartre had apparently seen very few paintings at home, astonishing in people who had spent so much of their time in Paris. As students they had worked very hard and for relaxation had preferred pin-tables and the cinema to the study of art. Together they had seen a few galleries in the Louvre but without a little tuition from her cousin Jacques, Beauvoir said that she would have been no more advanced in art appreciation than Sartre, who seemed to know little or nothing about the subject. 'I liked pure art,' she said, meaning presumably art without any subjective interference from the artist, its message, if any, implied perhaps but not emphasized. She enjoyed abstract art but could not convert Sartre, who reacted to subject matter. When this led him to admiration of the Bolognese painter Guido Reni (he lived from 1575–1642 and was often accused of sentimental religiosity) she talked him out of such an unsuitable taste. Sartre responded to her lecture by deciding to dislike Titian. *'C'est de l'Opéra,'* he said, not so much operatic as theatrical, presumably reminding him of the style of the Paris Opéra, in architecture rather than production. El Greco surpassed their expectations, while on a different level they were fascinated by the tortures and monsters depicted by Hieronymous Bosch, on show in the Prado.

Fernando complained at their over-enthusiasm about the mysterious Flemish painter, but in fact it was of a piece with their interest in monsters and larger-than-life villains.

The partners behaved on this first trip together much as they were to do during the many that followed. She was tireless, always ready to do something active, while Sartre, she realized, would sometimes have preferred to sit quietly on a bench and smoke his pipe. He rarely got the chance, for if he was always curious and ready to produce an opinion or a theory, she, as extremist as ever, described herself as 'gluttonous' about seeing things. This early glimpse of the couple shows her also in the role of quiet organizer, a role that was to strengthen as time went on. She did not tell Sartre precisely what to do, but she seems to have been the leader. Sometimes he refused to fall in with her plans, and did *not* want to see a mountain of salt at Lerida. They succeeded in visiting most of the important centres accessible from Madrid but did not go south.

The trip meant a great deal to Beauvoir: she would come back to Spain, she knew, but could hardly bear to wait even a year for further artistic and architectural 'revelations'. This first foreign holiday was the start of a life-long passion for travel. She was not influenced by friends who had told her that travel did not change the traveller, 'one never gets away from oneself'. She could not agree: 'I did get away from myself; I didn't become another person, but I disappeared.' She described, with a touch of poetry, an experience in Avila in which she felt herself merging with the landscape: 'In the morning I opened the shutters, I saw towers rising proudly against the blue of the sky; past, future, all vanished; there was only one glorious presence: my own, and that of the ramparts, mingled together and defied time.' She added that during her early travels such moments of happiness 'transfixed' her often. She had not 'disappeared', but she had entered into a new dimension, recovering perhaps something of the enchantment she had felt during her childhood stays in the Limousin.

On their way back to France Beauvoir and Sartre saw the principal towns and sites of central north-western Spain – Santillana, San Sebastian, Burgos (where the cathedral made a deep impression on Sartre), Pamplona and the caves of

Altamira. They had arrived in eastern Spain from the south of France and now returned through Hendaye on the French Atlantic coast. Sartre was going back to Paris but Beauvoir had to leave the train at Bayonne and join the mainline express running from Bordeaux to Marseille.

She remembered her arrival there as though she had reached another foreign country and in a sense this was so, for Provence, in 1931, must have seemed a strange and remote place to someone whose life had been dominated by Paris, the city she had left only for family holidays and brief stays in the south-east with the Lacoins. She was now literally alone; no family, no Sartre. She had not yet seen the Lycée Montgrand where she was to teach and knew not a single person in the town. In later life she said that she could not describe any moment in her life as 'decisive', 'but some of them, in retrospect, have become charged with such heavy meaning that they emerge from my past like outstanding great events. I remember my arrival in Marseille as if it had marked a completely new turning in my story.'

She recollected this moment as though she were still a tourist with a sense of the dramatic. She stood at the top of the vast modern stone staircase near the station. ' "Marseille," I said. Beneath the blue sky were tiled roofs in the sunshine, patches of shade, plane-trees tinged with autumn; distant hills and the blue of the sea; sounds rose from the city accompanied by the smell of charred herbs, while people came and went in the depths of the dark streets.' Beauvoir was deeply aware of her solitude. She realized that her future was her own responsibility and in retrospect she dwelt in a theatrical way on the degree to which she would have to manage her life: 'Nothing had been prepared for me, not even the bed in which I would be sleeping; it was for me to invent my occupations, my habits, my pleasures.' As she began to walk down the staircase she felt she was walking towards a new life. 'I stopped at each step, moved by those houses, those trees, those streams, [those] rocks and pavements which would gradually reveal themselves to me and reveal me to myself.'

Within a few hours she had begun her new life, arranged her timetable with her headmistress and found a furnished room. 'It was not a room after my own heart: a vast bed, chairs and a wardrobe; but I thought that the big table would be useful for work and the landlady offered me good terms.' Beauvoir's sister Hélène, who visited her twice during her time in Marseille, wondered how anyone could have tolerated this bedsitting room with its Henri II style buffet covered with family photographs. She emphasized that Simone was oblivious to her day-to-day surroundings, years would pass before she took any real interest in creating *une intérieur*, one of the somewhat frigid words that the French use for 'home'. Rented furnished rooms in hotels or *pensions*, basic and impersonal, were all she needed. Her life was held within her mind, her ideas, her relationships. A décor was not necessary.

However, for the time being, most of life would take place at the lycée, and there was nothing dull about that. Beauvoir now enjoyed her classes and preferred to talk to her senior students rather than to the other members of staff. She looked so young that she was sometimes mistaken for a student herself, but she did not sound like one when she talked her classes out of the conventional beliefs they had inherited from their parents. This was particularly the case when she had to deal with the question of morals, and the diffidence she had felt when trying to teach younger girls had now vanished. She made no attempt to be impartial. 'About work, capitalism, justice and colonialism I said, *avec feu*, what I thought.' At last she began work as a communicator, a task which she later carried out so brilliantly. She emerged from the apathy that had overtaken her in Paris, she was able to express to people who were ready to listen something of the strong anti-bourgeois, anti-capitalist feelings that had dominated her life for the last two years. In the classroom at least she was an activist. She was even *avant-garde* by Marseille standards in the early 1930s, for she would give lessons abut Proust and Gide and offer her girls works she called 'provocative', including the great poem by Lucretius written during the first century B.C., *De rerum natura*. Presumably her intention had been for her students to learn something of the Epicurean doctrines he described, how to free themselves from superstition and any idea of life after death, or interference from any form of deity. In fact she asked for trouble and got it, causing at least one student to go on classroom strike; parents complained and the bold teacher had to discuss the situation with the headmistress. She was able to stand her ground: 'We talked it over and things went no further.'

107

The town of Marseille was not yet the second city of France but it had a good deal to offer, old and new, which Beauvoir explored in detail. She found it 'inexhaustible' and the waterfront area intrigued her. 'I would lose myself in the sadness of the docks; I would wander round the Porte d'Aix in districts where sunburnt men bartered old shoes and rags.' She liked to look closely at the sort of life which she could never live herself. 'In view of my mythology the rue Bouterie [famous as a street of brothels] delighted me.' She was fascinated by its inhabitants: 'I would look at the painted women and the big coloured posters over the iron beds which could be seen through the half-open doors.' She remembered what she had seen at the famous Sphinx in Montparnasse, but this was 'much more poetic'.

The surrounding countryside enchanted her in a different way, and the herb-scented hills encouraged her to a lifelong passion for exploration and country walks. It so happened that the population of Marseille was devoted to these outings, and if Beauvoir caught the addiction from them she adapted it to her own personal taste; she joined no ramblers' groups or clubs, she wore no spiked shoes and carried no rucksack. She preferred espadrilles and took with her bananas and brioches in a shopping basket. At the same time she studied maps and guides and was soon walking twenty miles a day, usually alone. When Hélène de Beauvoir visited her sister in Provence, having borrowed the necessary money from Sartre, the two young women would go walking together. Years later Beauvoir remembered one incident from her sister's first visit, which proved her own extremism and at the same time the 'schizophrenia' that Sartre found in her. Hélène de Beauvoir was not in such good training as her elder sister: she developed blisters on her feet and then a high temperature. Simone told her to rest in a hostel and then take the bus back into the town, for she herself was determined to finish her walk. When Hélène developed flu Simone felt guilty and later she looked back on her own behaviour with horror. She loved her sister, but she loved her own plans more: 'Instead of adapting [them] to reality, I pursued them in the face of all opposition, regarding reality as merely accessory.' She explained why she had behaved as she did: 'I denied my sister's existence rather than give up what I had planned: she had always entered into my plans so faithfully that I did not even want to contemplate that on this occasion she was upsetting them.' She looked back at her younger self, the self who had refused to think that life could interfere with her own projects and she saw her alleged 'schizophrenia' as 'an extreme, absurd form of my optimism'.

As a child Beauvoir had dreamt of seeing the entire world and in the deserted areas of Provence nothing daunted her. Sometimes, climbing up steep hillsides with no other companions except the lizards, she found herself in difficulties. Once when she could not see how she was going to jump across a wide cleft in the rocks, she even called for help, which did not come. But she had already grown into the strong-minded young woman whose bravery, physical and mental, never left her. 'I summoned up my courage and landed safely.' She had been warned by school colleagues that walking alone in such remote places left her in danger of being raped, but she ignored this advice. One day she accepted a lift from two young men in a car. When she saw that they were driving her into a particularly deserted area she demanded to get out, and fortunately the car had to slow down at a level crossing. It was the kind of thing she had done as a naive schoolgirl. She was less naive now, but just as ready to take risks: 'Far from teaching me a lesson this episode strengthened my presumption: with a little care and decisiveness one can cope with everything.' In fact, she did, and made the best of it: 'I don't regret having cherished this illusion for a long time, for I drew from it a boldness which made existence easier for me.'

Life in and around Marseille was rich and exciting for Beauvoir, who wrote regularly to her sister all the time she was there, telling her about all her adventures. Later, when she began to write her autobiography, Simone would borrow the letters back from Hélène in order to refresh her memory, but Hélène did not allow them to be published until several years after her sister's death. In addition to her walks in Provence, Hélène also walked a great deal in Paris, for it had become her duty to console Sartre, who missed Simone badly and needed to talk about her. So Hélène and Sartre would walk about Paris, especially in the Gobelins area of the 13th *arrondissement*, of which he was very fond. These two were good friends now, and Sartre would write to Simone describing their meetings. Unfortunately many of the letters he wrote at this time were lost, but one long and fascinating one, written from Le Havre on October 9th, 1931, did survive: '*O partie de moi-même,*' he wrote, relating to her all the *petits faits vrais* of his daily existence, and explaining how he felt about her: 'My dear love, you can't know how much I think of you every hour of the day, in this place which is full of you. Sometimes I miss you and I'm a little unhappy (just a very very little) and sometimes I'm very happy to think that the Castor exists and buys herself chestnuts and goes for walks; the thought of you never leaves me and I carry on little conversations with you in my head.'

In this same letter he described how, in Le Havre, he had contemplated a tree for twenty minutes. 'Unfortunately I don't really know what tree it was.' He tried to describe the leaves and made a very bad drawing of one of them, but she could tell him it was a sweet chestnut, the tree which later occupied such an important place in his first novel, *La Nausée*. He hoped Beauvoir would make the best of the All Saints' Day holiday on November 1st and join him in Paris.

She, although enjoying Marseille, made no secret of the fact that Paris was the centre of her life, and the elderly spinsters who made up most of the staff obviously regarded her as 'fast'. She hardly fraternized with them and admitted that she was not always polite in the conventional sense. 'I would go into the staff room without saying good morning, I would put my things in my locker and sit down in a corner.' During the winter she had worn the 'classic skirt and pullover' which teachers were expected to wear 'but when in spring I began to play tennis I would sometimes arrive without having changed, in my white tussore dress'. She would receive disapproving looks.

One member of the staff, Madame Tourmelin, was not an elderly spinster but a married woman of thirty-five who taught English and to Beauvoir at least even looked English: she was plump, with chestnut brown hair, a fresh complexion that was beginning to look blotchy and 'flat' lips. She also wore tortoiseshell-rimmed spectacles. She lived in a splendid apartment overlooking the avenue du Prado which led down to the beach. When she offered Beauvoir a small studio, which had been converted from a maid's bedroom, the young teacher was only too glad to leave her furnished room with its vast bed and wardrobe for a place where she could look out over plane trees as she stood on the balcony. There were bookshelves and, of course, a table for work, her 'ideal' room, thought Beauvoir. Her colleague was married to an officer, who was often away, fortunately for her, for Madame Tourmelin had a physical horror of sex life with him. She could not bear the disgusting manifestations of heterosexual love-making, 'that sticky dampness on her stomach'. She preferred the near-lesbian 'crushes' and 'pashes' of her student years to the problems of marriage.

She liked women. In a restaurant one evening Beauvoir noticed that the good-looking young *patronne*, with her dark curly hair, sent Madame Tourmelin into ecstasies, but since her friend liked 'pretty things, nature, fantasy, poetry, impulsive behaviour' she saw nothing unusual in her reaction. The English teacher also affected 'extreme prudishness', she criticized 'vice, libertinage, anarchy', which restricted their subjects of conversation. Beauvoir tried to escape, but she did not try hard enough because she did not know how to go about it. Her friend said that she believed in the maintenance of high moral standards and between women expressions of love should not go beyond kisses on the mouth. Beauvoir made one cruel attempt to shake her off; when her hopeful friend asked if she could go for a long walk with her she led her off on a marathon expedition, making the poor plump lady walk so fast that she was soon worn out and had to retire to bed for a week. But she still persisted; she dyed her hair in the hope of pleasing Beauvoir, she bought a pink angora sweater which revealed too much of her flesh. One evening there was a drama. Madame Tourmelin threw her arms round Beauvoir. ' "*Ah, jetons les masques!*" ' she said, confessing that she had fallen in love at first sight. She begged Beauvoir to spend the night with her. Her young friend tried to extricate herself from the situation by saying that they would not feel very happy the following morning, but the aspiring lover asked if she should go down on her knees – and Beauvoir fled. Next day Madame Tourmelin tried to excuse herself by saying that of course it had all been a joke, but as they walked down the avenue du Prado towards the lycée she murmured tragically that she felt as though she were on the way to her own funeral. When Beauvoir later told this sad and funny story in detail she had become an experienced novelist. She referred to the episode more than once, remarking that her puritanical upbringing had not prepared her for this kind of behaviour.

Beauvoir met many people outside the lycée and was cheerfully invited into their homes. On one occasion her interest in the extremes of human behaviour was strongly revived, for through Madame Tourmelin she had met a doctor with whom she played tennis. One of his sisters had once been the wife of Doctor Bougrat, hero of a resounding scandal: the body of a murdered man had been found on top of a medicine cupboard in his dispensary. 'His wife had given evidence against him which led to his condemnation to life imprisonment. He had always denied the crime.' The 'murder' took place in 1925 and the doctor was tried in Aix-en-Provence. Beauvoir's doctor acquaintance described Bougrat as intelligent and of good character and she herself felt 'very flattered at knowing the family of a famous convict'. Bougrat's former wife was an unattractive character: 'Red-faced, loud-mouthed and quarrelsome [she] had taken a new husband and boasted that her son was illegitimate.' Beauvoir enjoyed the melodrama and was intrigued by this woman: 'I liked to imagine she had lied in order to ruin her husband; I saw Bougrat as a likeable adventurer, the victim of a detestable conspiracy.' She 'formed the vague project of using this story in a book'. Even though Dr Bougrat later escaped from the penal colony near Cayenne in French Guiana, set up a clinic on Margarita Island off Venezuela and became something of a folk-hero, the book was never written.

It would have been difficult for her to use a story that lay so far outside her own experience, although murder was to occur in several of her future novels. However, she made another serious attempt to write for she had 'too much [free] time not to work'. Although she enjoyed her life in Marseille she would sometimes feel a little sad as she left the lycée and bought her dinner on the way back 'through the dusk to my room where nothing awaited me'. She had come to terms with the absence of Sartre, whom she saw in Paris whenever a holiday allowed her to get there, and she was not above extending her time away by pretexting illness. From a physical point of view she found that a complete or longer separation was less upsetting than any 'incessant *va-et-vient* between presence and absence'. But the absent Sartre was never far from her thoughts: 'That year, I lapsed somewhat from the morality that I had adopted with Sartre, who condemned any form of narcissism: I filled my life by watching myself live.' She did this by reading and writing in cafés and brasseries where the decor pleased her – photographs of boxers on the walls, brass-ringed beer barrels, clients who whispered among themselves, 'the rattle of passing trams, rowdy voices peddling clams, mussels, sea-urchins, while others announced departures for the Château d'If, L'Estaque . . .' She began to enjoy being on her own because she had found or rather revived a literary identification for the state: Katherine Mansfield, who had so often written about 'the solitary woman'.[1] Beauvoir found the idea romantic and had made a special visit to Bandol, where the New Zealand writer had stayed.

So there was every incentive to work on a new novel, and she seems at least to have finished it. The content, predictably, was autobiographical and included one of her many attempts to exorcize the death of Zaza, the most important event, apart from the appearance of Sartre, that had occurred in her life so far. It was barely three years since Zaza had vanished, not long, considering the depth of Beauvoir's feeling for her. Zaza was named 'Anne' and married to a bourgeois husband who did not understand her. Beauvoir introduced herself in the character of 'Geneviève', 'giving her some of my characteristics, magnifying them', and for the first time concentrated on a theme which was to recur in later novels, notably *L'Invitée*, 'the mirage of the Other'. She explained further: 'I did not want this fascination to be confused with a banal love story and took as protagonists two women: in this way I thought – not without naïveté – I would avoid in their relationship any *équivoque sexuelle*.' The conflicting tendencies within herself were divided between them: 'my love of life and my desire to accomplish a literary work'. Qualities from friends and acquaintances, such as Madame Morel, were projected into the character of an older woman, Madame de Préliane, who lived, like the Katherine Mansfield heroines who so intrigued

[1] Katherine Mansfield (1888–1923): came to London from her native New Zealand in 1903, and spent nearly all her life in Europe, writing short stories, while at the same time battling with persistent bad health.

Beauvoir, as a 'solitary woman', independent of everyone. At the end of her book 'Anne', that is Zaza, fades and dies because the bourgeois milieu in which she lives does not allow her, through friendship with Madame de Préliane, to develop her talent as a musician. She imagines 'Geneviève', herself, as a woman of forty, successful in her search for her own identity. Through her novel Beauvoir was working towards the independence that she knew she must win, it was essential to her.

She was aware of all the faults in her novel, its artificiality, its lapses into conventional description. There is no evidence that she considered it fit for possible publication or that it was ever offered to a publisher or review editor. If Sartre had thought it publishable he would surely have helped the author as much as he could, although he himself had to rely on Nizan for advice in this field. So far he had published no more than part of a story in an obscure magazine.

During the Easter holidays of 1932 Sartre was persuaded by Beauvoir to visit Brittany, as different from Provence as any part of France could be. She was intent on seeing everything the region offered, from la Pointe du Raz, Morlaix, the Mont Saint-Michel, to Saint-Malo. Near here, on the Grand Bé, they saw the tomb of Chateaubriand, the early Romantic writer.[1] It is built from plain granite, bearing no name. The tourists found it 'so ridiculously pompous in its false simplicity that Sartre, in order to mark his disapproval, peed on it'. Brittany has never been renowned for good weather, and on this occasion the rain and mist drove the visitors away early, a rare defeat for Beauvoir. She had however won another kind of victory: public transport was not very good and she had persuaded Sartre to walk twenty miles to see a low hill in Finistère and even climb up it.

He did in fact join her in Marseille at the end of the summer term, when his own students were taking their examinations. She felt she had come a long way during the academic year 1931–32: she had explored an old large town and walked all round it, her sister had been to see her twice, even her parents had come. She

[1] François René de Chateaubriand (1768–1848): one of the pioneers of the French Romantic movement, best known for *Le Génie du Christianisme* (1802), a Christian apologetic, based on the appeal of religion to the deepest instincts in man's nature.

summed up her new life: 'I had not read much, my novel was no good; but I had exercised my profession without being bored . . . I was emerging victorious from the ordeal to which I had been submitted: absence and solitude had not reduced my happiness. It looked as though I could rely on myself.' She was particularly pleased with one aspect of the failed novel: no longer limited to writing solely about herself, she felt she was now capable of writing about the interaction of different people. She celebrated the fact in one sentence: 'I was beginning to have something to say.'

FIVE

I sank into
provincial boredom

After leaving Marseille Beauvoir spent a few weeks in Nice conducting oral examinations for the *baccalauréat* students and found the atmosphere of the town pleasantly informal. She did not begrudge a little more time in Provence because she had received some excellent news. Her friend Madame Morel knew the Minister of Education and had been able to exert some influence: as a result Beauvoir was to start work in the autumn term of 1932 at the girls' lycée in Rouen. The prospect of living in the busy Normandy town did not in itself excite her but two aspects of the new job were of vital importance to her: Rouen was only fifty-four miles from Le Havre, which meant that she could meet Sartre regularly without long and expensive train journeys, and it was also a mere eighty-seven miles from Paris. The journey to the capital was rapid, so she would also be able to visit her intellectual home easily.

Beauvoir left in exuberant mood for a long summer holiday, going first with Sartre to the Balearic Islands and Spanish Morocco. From there they went to Seville to join Madame Morel, who had invited them to join herself and her friend Pierre Guille, a graduate of ENS who had met Sartre on their assignment to the meteorological unit during their military service, on a tour of southern Spain by car. In Seville itself they witnessed the 'divertissement of a coup d'état', similar to the incident they had seen the previous year in Barcelona, but much more dramatic.

The mayor had been arrested and when fire broke out in a group of aristocratic homes the firemen did not operate their hoses until they were sure all the furniture had been destroyed.

The holiday *à quatre* was not always enjoyable, for Sartre and Guille could not avoid disagreements caused by their diverging political views. Guille was committed to 'bourgeois liberalism' while Sartre's anti-bourgeois anarchy was now turning into left-wing anger. Beauvoir realized that Sartre was in a weak position: he 'was travelling as a *petit bourgeois aisé* and did not complain about it', while he 'had not found the way to express the sympathy which inclined him towards the proletariat'. The two sets of partners did not always agree on which places they wanted to visit and one day in Cordova, when the temperature reached over one hundred degrees Fahrenheit, the two men only just avoided a bitter quarrel.

On the way back to Paris Beauvoir and Sartre visited 'Camille', Simone Jolivet, in her native city of Toulouse and found that she was writing a novel, starting work at midnight every night and working on until six a.m. This concentrated activity left both Beauvoir and Sartre feeling guilty: they decided that they too should be working equally hard. However, Beauvoir made one important discovery – though she wanted to work as hard as Camille she was no longer personally jealous of her.

For three and a half years Beauvoir taught philosophy at the Lycée Jeanne d'Arc in Rouen. During that time her life became highly complex and she lived it on various levels. She was a teacher, earning her living through fourteen hours spent in the classroom each week and remaining financially independent. She was still an aspiring writer, making slow progress because, despite her self-discoveries in Marseille, she was still searching for her own identity and for ways of relating to other people. Although she did not always relish her professional work, as she had done in Marseille, it led her to an extension of her own personal life and later to an awareness of a world she had not thought about in any conscious way – the world of women, the problems of femininity. Since it was axiomatic that her life remained indissolubly bound up with that of Sartre, she had to keep up with any developments in his life also. At the same time she began to make other discoveries, she began to open her eyes to the world of society and politics, with their clustering, apparently unsolvable problems.

The lycée in Rouen was not too different from the lycée in Marseille. Beauvoir looked round the staff room and realized that she was going to be bored. The English teacher was no Madame Tourmelin but she looked very odd, and dressed in girlish frocks, unwilling to relinquish her childhood. She detested her students, who responded in kind. One teacher, Simone Jahan, was a friend of Madame Morel and another, Colette Audry, was known to Paul Nizan, who had described her as 'dark, young and a Communist'. She was in fact a Trotskyite, a member of a splinter group consisting of five people only. Later her name was to become well known in France as a writer, journalist and editor. These three young women soon formed an avant-garde trio in the lycée, for they all took an anti-bourgeois, left-wing view of the world, even if Audry was the only one sufficiently committed to join a political party. Beauvoir retained her position as an anarchist.

The group attempted, in a small way, to demonstrate their subversive attitude, distinguishing themselves from their depressingly conventional, old-fashioned colleagues by dressing differently: Audry in a black suede jacket with white revers, teamed with an elegant shirt and tie, her friend Jahan in second-hand model clothes and Beauvoir in highly individual sweaters which were knitted by her mother after she herself had carefully chosen the patterns. These outfits were sufficiently 'different' to impress Beauvoir's students and some of them even knitted their own copies. The three teachers completed their efforts to make life superficially interesting by adopting unusual, striking hairstyles and applied a great deal of make-up.

Marseille had delighted Beauvoir because she found Provence very much to her taste and the people of the town were extrovert and welcoming. Rouen depressed her; it was old-fashioned, and the inhabitants could only be described as 'stuffy'. At the same time, like Marseille, it was a picturesque town with a long history, and again, like Marseille it contained enough *vieux quartiers* and *bas-fonds* to fascinate Beauvoir, but the novelty of working as a teacher in the provinces had worn off. She was quickly aware of 'provincial desolation' and could only think of herself as an exile, even if she was not in a state of 'panic' as she had been in 1931.

She was more like a new, intellectual version of Flaubert's Normandy heroine, Emma Bovary, longing for the unattainable, the one city in France, the one city in the world, where life could be full, satisfying, stimulating – namely Paris. All other cities or towns now existed for her only as holiday centres, while Rouen merely generated work and therefore money which paid for trips to Paris. The first thing Beauvoir did on arrival in Rouen had been to buy the kind of excursion railway ticket which would take her away from the town at the cheapest rate. She chose to live in a furnished room near the station, at the Hôtel La Rochefoucauld, she liked to sit in a café near the station and imagine she was in one of the suburbs of Paris. Sartre, in Le Havre, preferred to live near the station too. Beauvoir's frustration was completed by what she saw as the tame, wet and 'over-civilized' countryside of Normandy. She gave up the long and dramatic country walks and preferred to stay in the town, selecting as her home-from-home an old-fashioned quiet café where the elderly waiters were not likely to disturb her reading or writing and her long gossips with her few friends.

As Beauvoir had hoped, Sartre came to Rouen often and saved her from depression. She would also join him in Le Havre. He did not save her, nor himself, from what seems in some ways to have been an unrewarding way of passing the time. The bourgeois inhabitants of Rouen, unlike those of Marseille, extended no friendly invitations to the young teachers, so they had to make the best of their own small group. 'In Paris, Le Havre and Rouen the principal subject of our conversations was the people we knew . . . the slightly unpredictable, often surprising activities taking place within these unknown lives filled our days and saved them from monotony.' They discussed engagements, marriages, family quarrels, Colette Audry and Lionel de Roulet, one of Sartre's students who was later to marry Hélène de Beauvoir. Like Sartre, Beauvoir was ready to examine all these individuals, 'to take them to pieces, put them together again and re-make their images', but she admitted there was one thing she could not do: 'I could not see them as they really were: my experience with Madame Tourmelin proved my blindness.' She regretted the strange impersonal climate of near-alienation, a kind of coldness, in which she found herself living and attempted to analyse the faults she discerned in her own attitudes. 'I preferred to judge [people] rather than understand them. This moralism dated from a long time back. When I was a child the superior qualities of which my parents boasted had encouraged me to be arrogant; later, solitude had led me into an aggressive pride. Circumstances favoured even more my inclination towards severity.' The result was that her friends, Sartre included, would laugh at her 'lack of psychology'. She tried to explain it, listing all the elements which had combined to make her so detached, so wary when trying to deal with other people. 'Why did I not try to remedy this? I had also retained from my young days a taste for silence and mystery.' Was she thinking of the gardens of Meyrignac, the churches where she had spent so much time as a child, or even that dark hiding-place beneath her father's desk? She mentioned also another factor which might have influenced her attitude and kept her at a distance from the 'real' world: 'Surrealism had left its mark on me because I had found in it a kind of supernatural element.'

The results, as they affected her own behaviour and attitudes, were strange: 'I would allow myself to be charmed, amused and intrigued by dazzling surface appearances without wondering what lay beneath.' She was left with problems which for her seemed insuperable: 'The existence of other people remained for me a danger which I could not face in a straightforward way.' She remembered her father's ambition to transform her into a 'monster', a young woman so brilliant that she would become a freak of nature. She remained 'on the defensive' in case some other person would try to make her into a creature she was not. But what kind of a person was she? She had not found the whole answer in Marseille. Her uncertainty had left her in isolation and the basis of her indissoluble relationship with Sartre was unusual. She had come to terms with the situation by stating *'on ne fait qu'un'*, 'we are only one person', a phrase which was often to recur later in his letters to her. But she introduced it, implying that her relationship was less a relationship with him than with herself. She went further: 'I had installed us together at the centre of the world; round us there circled hateful, ridiculous or comical people, who could not see me; I was the only one who could see.' In fact Beauvoir often seemed distant from other people, as Colette

120

Audry remembered in later life. She would sometimes behave in an excessively well-mannered way, as though remembering the bourgeois politeness she had learnt as a child. On other occasions, she could be surprisingly off-hand.

As a rule, however, she did not care what other people thought, whereas Sartre did. One comical and illuminating story proves that if she and Sartre were in some ways fused into one person, they were very different too. He refused to take her into a smart Rouen hotel for a drink because she had such a big hole in her stocking. As he possessed at that time 'much respect for others' she assumed he did not wish to offend the other hotel clients through her unkempt appearance. Perhaps too he did not wish to be seen accompanying such an untidy person. On many occasions Beauvoir made a point of saying she had never been elegant and did not care about her appearance. This seems odd, and illustrates a paradox within her character, for she was inclined to mention her clothes in great detail as though they reflected her mental state at different moments throughout her life.

Beauvoir never accepted Rouen and the town did not accept her. She and Sartre had so few friends and acquaintances there that it was 'partly in order to mitigate this lack that we took a close interest in *faits divers*', minor items of news, preferably sensational. This interest had begun in Paris a few years earlier and Beauvoir would now read the magazine *Détective* which at that period maintained a subversive attitude towards the police and respectable society in general. The journal itself, started by the novelist Joseph Kessel and his brother, had at that time a respectable publisher, namely Gallimard, and its contributors were often well-known writers, not mere hacks. Beauvoir and Sartre also liked to study people suffering from neuroses and psychoses, believing that these did not contradict so-called 'normal' behaviour but indicated its extremes. Beauvoir, always aware of 'extremism' in herself, was at pains to point out her serious purpose in reading sensational stories in the press: 'Every kind of disturbance satisfied our anarchism, monstrous behaviour attracted us.' She was fascinated by criminals and also by the treatment these other 'extremists' received from society.

In the early thirties, in France, there was no shortage of 'monstrous behaviour'. In May 1932 Pavel Gorguloff, a Russian fanatic, living illegally in Paris and Monaco, went to a book fair in the rue Berryer, just off the avenue de Friedland, where he acquired an autographed copy of a book by the successful author Claude Farrère. A few moments later Paul Doumer, the seventy-five-year-old President of France, arrived and also acquired an autographed copy, in a de luxe binding, of an early novel by Farrère, *La Bataille*. A few moments later still Gorguloff produced a revolver and shot Doumer. Farrère, in an attempt to shield the President, was wounded. Gorguloff was recognized to be insane but still went to the guillotine. Beauvoir and her friends found this verdict inexcusably unfair: 'If he had killed an ordinary mortal he would certainly have been spared.' The intellectuals were 'amused' to find their own society so 'primitive', for 'the assassin was not tried: he was made a scapegoat'.

In February 1933 came another shocking crime. Christine and Léa Papin were resident maids who had spent seven years in the service of a retired lawyer in Le Mans, an old town to the south-west of Rouen. Unable to tolerate the scolding of their employer's wife any longer, the two girls, aged twenty-eight and twenty-two, murdered her and her daughter. They used blunt instruments, cut the corpses with knives and gouged out the eyes. Every detail of the crime and the ensuing trial produced a feast of grisly scandal. The whole of France took sides: 'It was not a murder,' wrote Janet Flanner,[1] 'but a revolution.' The girls were found guilty, evidence of mental abnormality was ignored, and Beauvoir, like many French intellectuals of the time, was outraged at the way these victims were treated by the bourgeois-based judicial system.

The following year, in Paris, the eighteen-year-old Violette Nozière, a mythomaniac and well-educated prostitute who wanted her parents' money, attempted to murder them through the skilful administration of veronal. Her father died, her mother survived. Violette was hardly an attractive character but Beauvoir and her group decided that this 'parricide' was more of a victim than a killer. Society was the guilty party, for in a bourgeois world the figure of the 'Father' was held to be sacred.

[1] Janet Flanner (Genêt) (1892–1978): American journalist, Paris correspondent from 1925 of *The New Yorker*.

The friends in Rouen found all murder trials particularly fascinating and 'most of the verdicts nourished our indignation, for through them society openly flaunted its class prejudice and obscurantism'. The crimes nourished literature, for Paul Eluard[1] wrote a poem about the trial of Violette Nozière and later, in 1947, Jean Genet based his play *Les Bonnes* (*The Maids*) on the story of the two sisters in Le Mans.

Moral issues fascinated Beauvoir. She still took only a cautious interest in professional psychology, preferring Adler to Freud because he allotted less importance to sexuality in his analyses of patients. Beauvoir complained that analysts took people to pieces instead of understanding them but forgot that she lived in a glass house; she and Sartre enjoyed 'dissecting' people too, but presumably regarded themselves merely as amateurs. They were shocked that friends of Colette Audry consulted psychoanalysts in their search for help in running their lives. The future existentialists both insisted on the importance of individual responsibility, believing that it was wrong to talk indiscriminately about the 'inferiority complex'. Beauvoir welcomed the inauguration of the Institute of Sexology in Berlin, for its director, Dr Hirschfeld, supported birth control and opposed any laws which attacked sexual freedom. She also approved of an international congress on sexual reform convened in Czechoslovakia.

Despite her interest in the more sensational events in the outside world – politics excluded – Beauvoir was still deeply and constantly preoccupied with her own personal 'alienation', her detachment and failure to face reality. She was impressed when she heard more from Colette Audry about Simone Weil, whom she had met so briefly at the Sorbonne. She admired her former fellow student for 'her intelligence, her extremism, her courage' and admitted that if Weil had known *her* she would not have reciprocated her own admiration. Beauvoir still felt so solitary that despite her admiration for Weil she 'could not add her to [her own] universe' and felt 'vaguely threatened' by her although Weil was many miles away in Le Puy. It was difficult for her to come close to other people: 'I hardly moved away from my caution; I

[1] Paul Eluard (1895–1952): lyric poet. He made his name as a love poet. The impact of political events turned him into an active Communist and he became a leader of the intellectual resistance in World War II.

avoided considering that other people could be like me a subject, a conscience; I refused to put myself in their place: that is why I practised irony.' Later Beauvoir became aware of her faults when young: 'On more than one occasion this prejudice and stupidity led me towards harshness, malevolence and mistakes.'

If she was 'cautious' about people she was, on her own admission, 'blind' about politics. She would complain when Sartre spent too long reading the newspaper, when, that is, he was reading something other than *faits divers*. She would defend herself by quoting her belief in the strength of the 'solitary man', a partner no doubt of that 'solitary woman' she had read about in Katherine Mansfield's stories. Sartre however countered by saying that if such a man 'thinks without the help of others that does not mean that he chooses to be unaware'. Beauvoir obstinately maintained that one should disdain the futile contingencies of daily life, 'like . . . Rimbaud, Lautréamont, Van Gogh'. She admitted that such attitudes did not really suit her, 'there was nothing of the lyric poet about me, nothing of the visionary or the solitary'. She felt bound to confess the true meaning of her attitude: 'In fact it was a question of running away; I was wearing blinkers in order to preserve my security.' She admitted that she was avoiding human contact, ordinary life: 'I liked landscapes from which people seemed absent, and the disguises which concealed their presence from me: the picturesque, local colour.' This explains the attraction of *les bas fonds, les vieux quartiers*. 'In Rouen the place I preferred was the rue Eau de Robec: the shapeless, unstable houses standing by filthy water seemed to be almost destined for some alien species. I was attracted by people who in one way or another rejected their humanity: madmen, prostitutes, tramps.'

Events in the outside world took a turn for the worse, causing Beauvoir to retain her blinkers even more firmly. Sartre took some interest in what was happening but she took virtually none. The two of them were only 'moderately affected by the war between China and Japan[1] or Gandhi's campaign in India'. They could hardly avoid developments closer to home, especially in

---

[1] China and Japan: Japan overran Manchuria in 1931, attacked Shanghai in 1932 and thereafter infiltrated North-East China.

Germany, but they were not too upset by them: 'Like the entire French left wing we surveyed them in a fairly serene fashion.' One drama followed another: Hitler became Chancellor, the Reichstag burnt down, from early May (this was 1933) 'the swastika flag flew over the German Embassy in Paris. Many German writers and scientists, especially the Jews, went into exile'. They included Einstein and also Kurt Weill, whose songs had so delighted Sartre. 'The Institute of Sexology was closed. The fate of intellectuals at the hands of the Hitler régime moved French opinion deeply.' Twenty thousand books were burnt in Berlin and Jews were prevented from earning a living.

'I am astonished,' Beauvoir said later, remembering this year, 'that we were able to observe these events with relative calm . . . the Nazi movement horrified the French left wing even more than the fascism of Mussolini, but it refused to face up to the threats that it posed to the world.' Beauvoir identified herself with the left wing because she needed to feel safe, and though she could not bring herself to join a party she realized that there could be no other ideological home for her. She did not forget her 'anarchy', but she remained passive. Not only the French, and not only the left wing, favoured inaction. In February 1933 the Oxford Union Society in Britain passed the motion that 'this House will in no circumstances fight for its King and Country'. The older French writers, notably Henri Barbusse, famous for his novel *Le Feu* (1916)[1] about World War I, made constant anti-war declarations. There was support from many intellectuals who opposed the developments in Italy and Germany but in a schizophrenic way refused to hear any talk of militarism. It was confusing, especially for the apolitical spectator. 'In short,' Beauvoir recalled later, 'the entire left, from the radicals to the Communists, cried simultaneously "Down with Fascism!" and "Disarmament!"'

Beauvoir and Sartre did not support any of the more active groups of intellectuals and in 1933 did not join the poet Louis Aragon[2] and their friend Paul Nizan on *Commune*, the organ of the newly created Association of Revolutionary Writers. In 1935,

[1] Henri Barbusse (1874–1935): novelist. *Le Feu* contained realistic descriptions of life in the trenches.
[2] Louis Aragon (1897–1982): poet, novelist and journalist. He became a Communist in 1927.

when André Malraux published his anti-Nazi novel *Le Temps du Mépris*[1] Beauvoir merely condemned it as the worst book he had written. In fact it was not good, but at least it was a gesture. Beauvoir regarded her generation as conditioned against the inevitability of war although Sartre, she said, 'had too much imagination to accept such a ban and some of the horrific visions' crept into the novel, eventually *La Nausée*, which he was currently writing. She herself was happy to accept the conditioning; it suited the person she was at the time. 'I pursued my schizophrenic dream with diligence,' she said. She wanted neither the practical world nor the present. She noted that the word 'technocracy' had just been invented but she was not impressed by technical progress in such areas as aviation or the study of the stratosphere. 'Economic and social problems interested me, but from a theoretical point of view; I paid attention to events only if they had taken place a year or several months earlier, if they had solidified into objects.' She was prepared to read Marx, Rosa Luxemburg, the Polish-born anarchist, Trotsky, 'studies on the life of the American worker, on the crisis in Britain'. This latter crisis was mainly financial. She could not move into the present and examine contemporary problems. The 'defeat of the ruling class', was the only way, she and Sartre thought, to abolish social 'alienation'. There was still no need for any action to hasten this defeat: capitalism was crumbling, bringing severe unemployment to Britain, Germany and the U.S.: 'starving mobs had marched on Washington' while coffee and wheat were being thrown into the sea. The ruling class could surely not last much longer. 'Political articles bored me,' she said. She realized she was only likely to understand any chaotic state of affairs if she could see ahead into the future, but she did not want to. She believed only in the distant future and hoped more than anything else that she could remain in control of her own life. She could not accept 'the fact that from day to day history . . . was in the making and that an unforeseen future would appear on the horizon without my consent'. It was

[1] André Malraux (1901–1976): left-wing novelist and essayist. A militant antifascist, he fought in the Spanish civil war and later in the Resistance. After the war he moved to the right and allied himself to de Gaulle. One of his best-known works, *La Condition humaine* (1933) is a powerful novel about the brutal suppression of the Communist revolutionaries in Shanghai.

her own personal happiness she cared about, she said, and she cared so much that she hoped to make time stand still if necessary.

Later in life Beauvoir was to become internationally famous as a radical thinker but as she moved into her later twenties there was little sign of this, preoccupied as she was in her optimistic, extremist yet unrealistic way with her own future. She saw herself as dedicated to the anti-bourgeois cause but, along with Sartre and her few other friends, she was uncertain about commitment to any action. However, she remembered two incidents which proved that she was becoming socially more aware. At a concert in Rouen she found herself surrounded with members of the opulent bourgeoisie and was overwhelmed. How could so many people be removed from power? 'For how long would they be allowed to believe that they incarnated the highest human values and could bring up their children to embody the same image?' On another occasion she saw a young docker, in his blue overalls, turned out of a restaurant.

The questions had to be asked: 'Can we limit ourselves to sympathizing with the struggle conducted by the working class? Should we not be sympathizing with the struggle conducted by the working class? Should we not take part in it?' Sartre, said Beauvoir, had been 'vaguely' tempted to join the Communist party. 'His ideas, his plans, his temperament were opposed to such a move; but if his taste for independence was no less than mine, he had a much stronger sense of his responsibilities.' The two of them were determined that the bourgeoisie must be eliminated, but they reached only a 'provisional' decision, as Beauvoir maintained they always did. 'We concluded . . . that if one belonged to the proletariat, one had to be a Communist, but this struggle, although it concerned us, was after all not our struggle.' They would always side with the workers, but that was all. 'We had our own enterprises to pursue and they did not fit in with membership of the party.' Any militant action among the left-wing opposition was against their principles: 'We had a very high regard for Trotsky and the idea of "permanent revolution" satisfied our anarchist tendencies much more than that of constructing socialism in one country only.' However, they believed that 'ideological dogmatism' would achieve nothing and repeated, with some additions, the plans they had formulated in Paris before either of them had taken up professional work: 'We wanted to exercise personal action through our conversations, our teaching, our books; this action would be more critical than constructive but in France, at that moment, we believed that criticism was extremely useful.' This was to be their action. They had not yet been able to embark on any programme in a positive way, for Beauvoir had no publishable work to show to anybody while Sartre so far had still only published part of one story in a small-circulation magazine. Paul Nizan, on the other hand, published author and Communist party member, had earned the disapproval of the educational authorities, forcing him to leave teaching. He had joined the Communist newspaper *L'Humanité* instead.

If Beauvoir complained about the boredom of Rouen she at least spent a good part of her time reading. 'We read everything that came out,' she said, as she searched partly for models and partly for something to dissect and criticize. She found few French writers deserving of her attention and looked to foreigners for something more stimulating. She admired the two Italian novelists Silone[1] and Moravia[2] but knew nothing of Kierkegaard,[3] despite the appearance of the first translations. She appreciated Lytton Strachey's *Eminent Victorians*, which has been described as 'a kind of "debagging" of public figures'. Beauvoir's older contemporaries in France, Gide, Valéry,[4] François Mauriac, the established and over-literary big names, could offer nothing new, while the self-conscious novelty of Cocteau[5] and André Breton[6]

[1] Ignazio Silone (1900–1978): novelist. He broke with the Communist party in 1931 and became an active member of the Social Democratic party of Italy.One of his best known novels was *Fontamara* (1933).

[2] Alberto Moravia (1907–1990): novelist. His first novel was published in 1929. He was a successful writer occasionally in difficulties with the fascist authorities in Italy.

[3] Søren Kierkegaard (1813–1855): Danish philosopher. Son of a Jewish merchant, he converted to Christianity in 1848 and bitterly denounced the Danish State Church. Kierkegaard held that the Individual Self is the ultimate and only human reality. This doctrine lies at the base of existentialism as a philosophical concept.

[4] Paul-Ambroise Valéry (1871–1945): poet, critic and essayist. His poems written between 1913 and 1922 made his name. He also studied philosophical and metaphysical problems in terms of Being and Nothingness.

[5] Jean Cocteau (1889–1963): a writer in all forms. His versatility made him a spearhead of literary and artistic movements between the wars. His later work in the cinema brought him international fame.

[6] André Breton (1896–1966): poet; a leader of the surrealist movement.

could not appeal for ever. There were plenty of other names. Giono, Marcel Pagnol,[1] Giraudoux,[2] Julien Green,[3] Bernanos, Jules Romains:[4] their books and plays were well written but still, to Beauvoir at least, in the inescapable bourgeois tradition. However, in 1932 there had been an important event for both her and Sartre: an unknown writer, a doctor who used his mother's Christian name as a pseudonym, published his first novel: *Voyage au bout de la nuit* (*Journey to the End of Night*). The two teachers who felt impelled to examine the *bas-fonds* in every town they visited now found someone who had lived and worked in these places before writing about them. They were deeply impressed. Céline's[5] book had all the qualities these two bourgeois would-be writers were looking for, the material was drawn from first-hand observation, the dialogue was 'real' and not literary. 'We knew many passages by heart,' Beauvoir remembered with enthusiasm. 'His anarchism seemed very close to ours. He attacked war, colonialism, mediocrity, platitudes and society in a style and tone which delighted us.' Céline had invented something that fascinated them: 'a new instrument, a way of writing as much alive as the spoken word'. At first Céline knew immense success with a large section of the French public. According to Beauvoir it was Céline who caused Sartre to revolutionize his early literary style, which was stiff and artificial. Unfortunately the name of Céline soon became associated with aspects of fascism, although he attempted to deny any such thing. When Beauvoir read *Mort à crédit* (*Death on the Instalment Plan*), in 1936, she understood at once the direction in which the author was moving and regretted that she could no longer admire him.

[1] Marcel Pagnol (1895–1974): dramatist and film writer, well known, too, for his autobiographical books, *La Gloire de mon père* (1957) and *Le Château de ma mère* (1958).
[2] Jean Giraudoux (1882–1944): novelist and playwright. His use of paradox and imagery lent themselves to the discipline of dramatic form and stylized dialogue.
[3] Julien Green (1900–): novelist of American parentage. Converted to Roman Catholicism in 1916, his novels are sombre with an acute apprehension of evil and an underlying spiritual presence.
[4] Jules Romains (1885–1972): poet, essayist and novelist. His work is characterized by irony and fine observation.
[5] Louis-Ferdinand Céline (1894–1961): novelist. He qualified and practised as a doctor and won fame with his first novel, *Voyage au bout de la nuit* (1932). His antisemitic views led to an involvement with the Vichy regime.

However, the principal influence on the early work of Beauvoir and Sartre was neither French nor even European, but American. 'On the whole', the critical Beauvoir remembered, after a lukewarm reaction to Malraux's *La Condition humaine* (*Man's Estate*) in 1933, 'we found the technique of the French novelists was very rudimentary compared to that of the great Americans.' Dos Passos[1] impressed them deeply but it was Hemingway[2] who changed their attitude to fiction writing, partly because they found him 'very close to us through his individualism and his conception of man'. The French partners hated Malraux's eroticism but enthused about Hemingway's treatment of love. His 'lovers loved each other body and soul the entire time; sexuality permeated their actions, their emotions, their words, and when it expressed itself freely in desire it united them totally'. Beauvoir liked Hemingway's gift for making man present in every small detail, his way of creating 'a romantic charm' by describing 'a walk, a lunch, a conversation'. In many ways she felt at home as she read Hemingway: 'Insignificant details suddenly acquired a meaning; behind the fine stories of love and death ... we recognized our familiar universe.' She had to admit however that 'the social implications of these novels escaped us since we were led astray by the idea we had about our liberty, we did not understand that individualism is the assumption of a position in relation to the whole world'. She admired other aspects of Hemingway's technique and acknowledged a heavy debt to the author of *The Sun also Rises*: 'Many of the rules we imposed on ourselves in our novels were inspired by Hemingway.'

If French writing during the first third of the twentieth century had been essentially literary, and not noted for its action content, American writing contained not only action, but violence; it was

---

[1] John Dos Passos (1896–1990): American novelist. He is best known for his novel *Manhattan Transfer* (1925), a collective portrait of life in New York, and *U.S.A.* (1939), a trilogy which tries to capture the variety and multiplicity of American life in the 20th century.
[2] Ernest Hemingway (1898–1961): American novelist and short story writer. He served with an ambulance unit in World War I and settled for a time in Paris. He made his name with *The Sun Also Rises* (1926). *A Farewell to Arms* followed three years later and *Death in the Afternoon* was published in 1932. He caught the post-war mood of disillusion with his economy of style and tough charac-

the reverse of precious and poetic. Henry James and Edith Wharton were excluded from Beauvoir's recollections of these formative influences because, perhaps, they may have seemed too 'European', and they wrote about the 'upper crust' of society. She found no women writers to admire and when she assessed creative work she did not differentiate between women and men.

Part of the admiration Beauvoir and Sartre felt for American fiction was due to an element they could not share, something outside their experience. If there is convincing action in a novel, there has probably been action in the life of the novelist. Malraux had known action, even if Beauvoir and Sartre did not like his writing. Dos Passos, Hemingway, Céline had all taken part in action of some sort. The two young teachers discussing literature or moral problems in the cafés of Rouen or Le Havre had seen no action at all. So far nothing had happened to them except their intellectual, emotional and sexual adventures. They had travelled a little, Beauvoir had gone for long walks, Sartre had done his military service.

They admired the ideological and political change from the old to the new Russia but reacted against the didactic tone of so much contemporary Soviet cultural output. While they disliked the political atmosphere of the U.S. they were still fascinated by the country. They were fascinated too by American films and jazz and also by the thriller writers such as Dashiel Hammett, who, despite the appearance of Simenon's 'Maigret' in 1931, had no equivalent in France. They shared this taste with such different writers as André Gide and Robert Graves. Such reading was a stimulating antidote to the classical, academic education that Beauvoir had received and was expected to pass on to her students.

Beauvoir was keener than ever on the stimulus of travel, and in the spring of 1933 she and Sartre spent their Easter vacation in London, where they did everything expected of conscientious, not too affluent tourists. They rode on the top of buses, walked the streets of London by the hour 'lunched in a Lyons [a once-popular, now vanished chain of teashops] or in one of the old taverns in the Strand or in a Soho restaurant'. They were disconcerted by the

terization. His active support for the republican cause in the Spanish civil war forms the background to *For Whom the Bell Tolls* (1940).

absence of French-type cafés and Sartre was annoyed by the snobbish manners of the undergraduates in Oxford. He announced that on their next visit he would make a point of seeing the industrial centres: Manchester and Birmingham. The partners found that some legends were true: men really did wear bowler hats, really carried rolled umbrellas. There were speakers at Hyde Park Corner, taxis were shabby, posters old-fashioned and shop windows unattractive. The National Gallery and the Tate Gallery had riches to offer, while Beauvoir was delighted by the conjurors and the popular magic shows at Maskelyne and Devant's, which sadly vanished during World War II. They saw one of their favourite film stars, Kay Francis, in *Cynara*, a film which took its name from the much anthologized poem by Ernest Dowson with its Latin title: *Non sum qualis eram bonae sub regno Cynarae*. The famous line in it, 'I have been faithful to thee, Cynara! in my fashion' became a useful motto for Beauvoir and Sartre, for there was no better evocation of their 'contract' and the meaning of the 'contingent' love affair.

Beauvoir again took charge of the tourist programme. Though Sartre disliked walking for walking's sake, she led him through all the London parks, Kew Gardens and Hampton Court. He then took his revenge by making her walk all round Whitechapel in the East End. He was looking for a small cinema which was showing another film with Kay Francis and William Powell, *Outward Bound*. Sartre liked to 'linger in the *faubourgs populeux*, trying to work out how the thousands of unemployed who lived in these dismal streets passed the time and what thoughts went through their heads'.

Sometimes Sartre would not behave as Beauvoir had expected and this kind of unpredictable behaviour upset her. When he refused to set foot in the British Museum she did not enjoy seeing 'the bas reliefs, statues and mummies' on her own. She was also disconcerted when they quarrelled over some intellectual topic, although this was rare. Their philosophical discussions were the central part of their relationship and followed a set pattern: 'As a rule Sartre put forward a "theory"; I put forward criticisms, modifications; sometimes I rejected the theory and succeeded in making him revise it.' They were happy 'only after we had reached agreement'. The quarrel in London took place on the first floor of a 'little restaurant near Euston station'. They were eating 'tasteless synthetic food' and watching the glow of a fire in the docks on the eastern horizon. Sartre had already amused Beauvoir by comparing 'English cooking and the empiricism of Locke, both based, he explained to me, on the analytical principle of juxtaposition'. But when he 'attempted to define London in its entirety' she was irritated by the false premise from which he started and complained 'that in twelve days Sartre had not understood London'.

In fact this was a new chapter in a near-perpetual quarrel between them about the way to deal with reality. She believed that 'reality goes beyond anything that can be said about it; rather than reduce it to meanings which can be explained in words we should confront it, complete with its ambiguities and its mysteries'. Sartre believed that observation and reaction were not enough: the essential thing was to grasp the meaning of everything observed and 'fix it in words'. Over the 'tasteless synthetic food' the philosophy teachers could not reconcile their points of view, mainly because this discussion illustrated a basic difference between them, a difference of which Beauvoir was always aware: she preferred life, 'in its immediate presence', while Sartre preferred literature. They survived together happily through a kind of compromise: 'However, since I wanted to write and he enjoyed living, we quarrelled only rarely.'

She now began a highly ambitious novel, in which she intended to 'put paid to society'. When she told Paul Nizan what she was doing he was ironic: *Un roman d'imagination?* He obviously believed she was incapable of inventing anything. Yet she saw herself now as a changed person. She felt she had learnt a good deal in Marseille, she had escaped from fear and remorse and 'was losing interest' in herself. At the same time 'I looked at other people from the outside, I did not feel involved with them; neither did I feel any need to talk about them.' She was no deprived person seeking attention through writing, her happiness could not be expressed in words and 'the minor episodes of my daily life deserved only to be forgotten'. She thought back to her adolescence and her early attempts at writing: 'As during my early youth, since I had nothing precise to say, I proposed to bring the whole world into my book.' At the end of her year in Marseille she had felt ready to say something, but now she could not organize her ideas. Her point of departure was still her 'hatred of the bourgeoisie', and it was sincere, she said. She intended to trace the history of the post-war years, that is the 1920s, through the experience of a brother and sister, and in so doing she would set out her ideas about morality. This time she chose for herself a model far grander than Alain-Fournier or Rosamond Lehmann; she chose Stendhal himself, that great if isolated figure of the early nineteenth century, the 'romantic realist' who wrote so much of his own life into his fiction.

Beauvoir did not fail to introduce herself into her new novel; she was Madeleine, the heroine, who had a brother, Pierre. She also introduced her own childhood memories and gave fascinating technical details about how she transposed relatives, friends, houses, social milieux into her story. Remembering too one of Stendhal's innovations, his attempt to understand women and go beyond mere male descriptions of them, Beauvoir attempted to understand her principal male character and endowed Pierre with some of her own current *'perplexités'*. She even remembered the story of Dr Bougrat in Marseille who, as a young man, like her own hero, had been deprived of education. Pierre, unthinkably, made a rich marriage in order to finance his own education but soon abandoned his 'cynical' plan. Beauvoir remembered in particular how she handled the bourgeois milieu that he had intended to 'use' – 'I attacked it with all the ferocity of which I was capable.' This was no simple story and the plot thickened: the brother-hero joins the Communists, then realizes that individualism supplies a surer set of values. The sister-heroine falls in love with a Communist and then, when she sees that he loves her, she decides to renounce him. It would be a far better thing to live a proud and independent life without him. Domination, subjugation, must be resisted. The inevitable Zaza figure reappears, again named Anne, as in the previous novel, and just as inevitably dies as a result of her bourgeois entourage.

Beauvoir had shown the first chapter of her novel to Sartre, who approved of it, while their friend Pierre Guille found the start of her book had 'the charm of certain English novels'. Although she persevered to the end and did not abandon any of her characters Beauvoir realized the novel was a failure. She was convinced her technique had improved in all ways but she admitted she had written without adequate knowledge of various backgrounds, in particular that of Pierre. Despite the 'solid construction' none of the personal relationships was convincing. Of all her 'lost' work, however, this is the book the modern admirer would most like to read, for it would surely tell us so much about Beauvoir herself. In describing the 'complicity' between Madeleine and her brother Pierre she unconsciously described at least one aspect of her relationship with Sartre. 'This couple,' she maintained, 'did not correspond to any experience or fantasy of mine; I used it in order to narrate the *années d'apprentissage* from a double point of view: masculine and feminine.' In saying this she looked back to her model Stendhal but she also looked forward, to *The Second Sex*, written some ten years later, and particularly to its ending. Before the 'reign of liberty' can be established in society, before the 'supreme victory' can be gained, 'it is necessary, for one thing, that by and through their natural differentiation men and women unequivocally affirm their brotherhood'. Beauvoir and Sartre were friends, they were still lovers, but in one sense they were so indivisibly close that it is not impossible to think of them as sister and brother. At the same time she knew that despite Madeleine's efforts to remain independent of the man she loved, she herself had failed in the same endeavour: 'I had not finally resolved the most serious of my problems: how to reconcile the concern I felt for my independence with the feelings that drove me impetuously towards another person.'

Writing this novel also taught her something else. While researching among old newspapers and magazines in order to fill out the historical background to her story, she was surprised to find that the same events, reported by the glossy magazine *L'Illustration* and the Communist newspaper *L'Humanité*, appeared to be entirely different. Little wonder she was unsuccessful with a fictional presentation of the previous decade, if she had not yet realized that there was more than one way of recounting and interpreting attitudes and events.

In the meantime that 'other person', namely Sartre, was embarking on an intellectual adventure which was to be crucial in his life as a thinker. In Le Havre he liked his students but found most of his colleagues and the lycée administration tedious. He was obsessed with a desire to write, and he wrote constantly. At the same time he was equally interested in any developments within philosophy which challenged him or seemed close to the ideas he was working out for himself. He was still rewriting the early drafts of what was to be his first novel, so far entitled *Melancholia*. He had developed a passion for phenomenology, which entailed the study of Edmund Husserl, the German philosopher, now in his seventies.[1] Sartre realized he could only study him with concentration, and in the right atmosphere, by actually going to Germany. In this plan he was helped by his former student friend and army instructor, Raymond Aron. Aron had been working at the French Institute in Berlin, which was attended by a small group of French post-graduate students wishing to specialize in the study of German culture. It had been Aron who had told Sartre, half-jokingly, over a drink, that his interest in 'contingency' proved him to be a 'phenomenologist' and suggested that they should change places, Sartre to take over Aron's post in Berlin and carry out his research for a year while Aron would replace Sartre at Le Havre.

These arrangements concluded, Beauvoir and Sartre spent their summer holiday of 1933 in Italy. They differed in their reactions to the country; she found everything beautiful, he found it 'dry', but Beauvoir knew the real reason for his attitude: 'He could not tolerate passing the little black-shirted fascists in the streets.' She had to admit that they had accepted Mussolini's offer of very cheap railway tickets – he wanted as many French tourists as possible to visit the big fascist exhibition in Rome. It was hard to escape the fascists, for the police would not allow the visitors any individualistic behaviour. When Beauvoir and Sartre tried to stay up all night in order to greet the dawn, they were told to go back to their hotel, but they didn't: 'It was moving to walk along the

[1] Edmund Husserl (1859–1938): German philosopher, creator of the modern school of phenomenology. His most important works included *Logical Investigations* (1900–1901) and *Ideas for a Pure Phenomenology* (1907). According to Anthony Quinton (*Fontana Dictionary of Modern Thought*, 1977), phenomenology 'takes philosophy to begin from an exact, attentive inspection of one's mental, particularly intellectual processes in which all assumptions about the causation, consequences, and wider significance of the mental process under inspection are eliminated ("bracketed")'. Husserl's best-known student was Heidegger.

neatly paved Roman streets and hear only the sound of our own footsteps: as though by some miracle we had arrived in one of those Mayan cities which the jungle protects from any gaze . . .' But at three a.m., in the Colosseum, they were again told to go to their hotel and this time they obeyed.

They saw Orvieto, Bologna and Venice, the latter visit marred by the sight of some German Brownshirts, and Sartre's realization that he would soon be living among them. Despite their cheap railway tickets the partners failed to manage their money, for by the time they reached Milan they had none left, and were forced to give up their plans of visiting the Italian lakes on their way home. The extremist Beauvoir shed 'tears of rage, the slightest sacrifice made me so angry'.

In Berlin Sartre set himself an intensive programme, dividing his time between the study of Husserl and his own writing. He liked German food, he enjoyed exploring the city, he was shocked by the behaviour of the Nazis but did not allow it to interfere with his intellectual or social life. He preferred the company of the French students to that of any Germans he might have met and, like the French at home, underestimated the consequences of Hitler's rise to power. His studies apart, Sartre was no hermit. One of the students at the French Institute was Jean-André Ville, a mathematics graduate, who was accompanied by his wife, Marie. They were a strange couple, so vague and out of touch with ordinary life that Sartre, who had in fact known them in Paris, christened them *les lunaires*, for they seemed to be living on the moon. Without Beauvoir at his side Sartre needed a feminine companion and his choice fell on this strange, remote young woman. He admitted that his need to talk to women was so great that he had to choose a Frenchwoman. Although his own spoken German was good it did not allow him the intimate conversation that was so essential to him. At this stage of his existence, and for many years afterwards, he also needed to tell Beauvoir everything that was happening in his life, and especially in his emotional and sexual life. Unfortunately the letters he wrote to her during his German stay were lost – or so Beauvoir maintained – and therefore few details about this relationship have reached an audience. However, in time, something of the story came to the surface.

In the meantime Beauvoir, in Rouen, found very little to enjoy or interest her. During the autumn of 1933 she again lapsed into a state dangerously close to that of the 'little woman', not this time because her partner was too close to her, but because he was too far away. 'Once Sartre had left for Berlin,' she remembered, 'I completely lost interest in public affairs.' These public affairs in Europe and also in France at the time were not so much interesting as tragic, for in Germany now there was no escape from Hitler. Would fascism spread to France? The left wing dreaded such a development, the right wing exploited the international situation 'and the economic depression in order to propagate an anti-democratic and bellicose nationalism'. It was surely hard for anyone living through the 1930s to ignore what was happening, but Beauvoir did not find it difficult. She later remembered how she reacted to the darkening international scene: 'All through Europe fascism was growing stronger, war was coming closer: I remained in a state of eternal peace.'

While maintaining that, unlike Sartre, she preferred life to literature, on her own admission that 'life' seems to have been restricted to her own, along with that of Sartre and her few friends in Rouen. She could hardly fail to take some interest in the Stavisky scandal,[1] although this Russian-born naturalized Frenchman was no 'monster' to be wondered at, merely a daring swindler whose luck eventually ran out. Each act of embezzlement became public knowledge during the winter of 1933–34, like a series of bombs exploding: there were political repercussions which appeared to show the left-wing government coalition in a bad light. When the mysterious and unfortunately Jewish Stavisky was found dead, the right wing, led by the infamous and indefatigable Charles Maurras, insisted that the government had planned it all: the Prime Minister, Camille Chautemps, was accused of having 'arranged' the death of Stavisky in order to suppress the truth.

Whatever that truth was, the population of France and in

---

[1] The Stavisky scandal: a financier, Stavisky, with something of a dubious reputation, floated a loan of a million francs' worth of bonds. He disappeared when the bonds started to come on the market and shot himself in January 1934. His long immunity from prosecution could only have been made possible by the connivance of influential associates, possibly including the police.

particular the citizens of Paris, suspected even more corruption in high places. In January 1934 there were demonstrations in the Place de l'Opéra. Chautemps resigned, but he had been slow in doing so. Worse was to come. If historians or commentators of any kind had shown any unanimity in describing the extraordinary events that occurred in Paris on February 6th, 1934, then the episode known as 'Bloody Tuesday' would be better known outside France. It involved a sudden coalition of the extreme right, notably the Croix de Feu, a league of ex-Servicemen, the Communists on the left and various centre parties. Their aim was a serious protest against the inept performance of the government and the high cost of living. Daladier had succeeded Chautemps but made if anything even worse mistakes. The protest was to be violent: there was a confused attempt to seize the Chamber of Deputies, but the bid collapsed. There were deaths and injuries, but next morning the newspapers offered a range of inquests and interpretations, sufficient to satisfy readers of every political colour. Nobody was ever sure precisely what happened, beyond the fact that the whole thing was a failure. The left–right confrontation was repeated in some provincial towns but soon faded away, except from the public memory. 'I followed all this from a distance,' said Beauvoir. 'I was convinced that it did not concern me. After the storm would come the calm.' That was a comforting way to look at the political scene. One of her visits to Paris, with a friend, Marc Zuorro, brought Beauvoir there the day after 'Bloody Tuesday', and as they walked round the Place de la Concorde after dinner they saw overturned, burnt-out cars, surrounded by sightseers. Beauvoir was not shocked: 'It seemed to me pointless to worry about these disturbances, about which, in any case, I could do nothing.'

She realized in retrospect that she needed 'a great deal of obstinacy' to maintain her indifferent attitude. Colette Audry, she felt, used her interest in politics as a way of justifying her existence while she, Beauvoir, had few problems: 'My enjoyment of life, my plans to be a writer, the guarantee supplied to me by Sartre' had spared her from any such problems. Now it was becoming harder to avoid politics. Not too many women in the early 1930s were prepared to join a political party, as Colette Audry had done, for British and American readers of Beauvoir

139

tend to forget that Frenchwomen could not vote. Ten or so more years were to pass before they could do so. Farsighted women maintained that by joining a party or a pressure group they might have helped to introduce or hasten women's suffrage, but Beauvoir did not see things that way. In any case, the left-wing leaders predicted that most women, if given the vote, would support the right, in which they were eventually proved near-correct. Three days after 'Bloody Tuesday', on February 9th, the Communist party organized an anti-fascist demonstration which again led to loss of life. Three days after that the Communists and socialists joined forces – a rare event – to declare a one-day general strike, and teachers were asked to join in. At the girls' lycée in Rouen only Colette Audry and two other colleagues did so. Beauvoir's explanation as to why she did not join the strike is revealing: 'I did not even consider joining them, for I was such a stranger to any political activity. There was another reason for my abstention. I disliked any action which would have made me take on my actual status; I refused, as I had done in the past, to coincide with the teacher that I was.' In Marseille she had enjoyed her work, but now her feelings had changed. 'I could no longer maintain that I was merely playing at giving lessons; I suffered my profession as a constraint; it forced me to live in Rouen, to come to the lycée at set hours . . .' She regarded her teaching as a role imposed upon her, she accepted it, but she kept her true feelings to herself. She needed to be independent, and in France, in the 1930s, only well established writers could earn useful money from their books. Beauvoir was ready to take action of a kind, the kind she chose. She would take action in the classroom, but only as an individual expressing her ideas to other indi-viduals: she would not take action as part of a group, as a member of the teaching body. Beauvoir's own personality and the years of discussion with Sartre had formed her attitude, one which she maintained until late in life. She kept it so long and so firmly that the change during her sixties was to be all the more surprising. For the moment however her belief in individual action was linked to her hope of becoming a writer with an authoritative voice: a voice to which people would listen.

It was as an individual that Beauvoir did in fact take action in the classroom on one aspect of the government's social policy, and at last there is a glimpse of the future feminist. Following the disturbances in February Daladier had resigned and the new government of Gaston Doumergue included as Minister of War someone whose name was to remain famous and infamous many years later: Marshal Pétain. He made a speech in which he urged closer links between the army and the schools, obviously hoping for increased recruitment to the army. There was an immediate follow-up: teachers received circulars encouraging them to include in their lessons propaganda for a higher birthrate. Beauvoir referred to this command in 'ironic' terms, for she had already told her students that women did not exist merely for the production of children. In 1934 her attitude was courageous and it earned her a bad report as an 'unworthy teacher'. She replied angrily and even accused many parents of being supporters of Hitler, who believed that woman's place was in the home. One schools inspector took her side, mainly because he had a low opinion of the bourgeois of Rouen, but the philosophy teacher at the boys' lycée never missed an opportunity to attack her in his classroom.

This incident hardly improved Beauvoir's opinion of the town where she was living so unwillingly, and she was far from popular with the parents of her students. These conventional, Catholic, bourgeois people were suspicious of her. She was a handsome, unmarried young woman who did not look or behave like a spinster, and she was frequently seen either leaving for Paris or returning from there, usually on her own. She was also observed in the company of various men, who included the good-looking Pierre Guille, the friend of Madame Morel, and the mysterious Marc Zuorro. Rouen thrived on gossip; it appeared to be the principal way of passing the time. In February 1934 Beauvoir was desperately trying to disentangle herself from some of it which linked her to Zuorro. In the end this situation was only truly disentangled when Sartre returned for the Easter holidays and with charm and humour explained that Beauvoir was *not* conducting a secret love affair with the bisexual and devious Zuorro. The rumour then spread that Mademoiselle de Beauvoir was 'kept' by a wealthy senator and had advised her students to adopt a similar arrangement. She had in fact made one or two concessions to respectability, she no longer lent 'shocking' texts or novels to the girls and when asked about moral topics she referred the questioners to a conventional source book. In fact this 'immoral' woman was planning her next journey, which would be not to Paris but to Berlin, and she arranged to take German lessons, in the hope that a better knowledge of the language would lead to a more interesting stay.

Sartre greeted her in Berlin with a temporary wedding ring, deemed advisable because he had been lent lodgings in a house which was comfortable but highly respectable. She had been so impatient to join Sartre that she had not waited for the end of the Easter term and had even arranged her trip under false pretences. While visiting a Paris psychiatrist on behalf of a friend she had persuaded him to state, on a medical certificate, that she herself was suffering from stress and needed a rest from work. In addition to her need for Sartre she wanted to escape from Rouen and she was curious to assess Marie Ville. In fact she found that the girl was no threat to her own relationship with Sartre, she was even likeable, if not very intelligent. Beauvoir realized that Marie and Sartre regarded their liaison as something temporary, like her own wedding ring: useful in the circumstances. Marie's husband was apparently unconcerned about the episode and Sartre *had* told Beauvoir from the start of their relationship that he would inevitably acquire 'contingent' loves. Beauvoir herself did not feel jealous. However, 'it was the first time since we had known each other that a woman mattered to Sartre and jealousy is not a feeling that I underestimate nor one of which I am incapable'. She had experienced it temporarily when Sartre was still intimate with Simone Jolivet. However, despite the 'contingent' nature of his affair with Marie, Sartre must have come very close to her, for he discovered her secret, possibly one reason for her strange behaviour: she had been raped by her father when she was very young.

Despite the presence of the Brownshirts in Berlin the French teachers made the best of the situation. Sartre showed Beauvoir something of the nightlife of the city in all its decadence, which Christopher Isherwood described unforgettably in *Mr Norris Changes Trains* and *Goodbye to Berlin*. Beauvoir was saddened when an anti-fascist rising in Austria was suppressed fiercely by

Dr Dollfuss.[1] She had understood how deeply serious the situation had become. However, 'we refused to touch the wheel of History, but we wanted it to turn in the right direction . . . Otherwise we would have had too many things to reconsider.'

However, Beauvoir was still more concerned with her personal affairs than with developments in the outside world. Colette Audry in Rouen had warned her not to stay away too long, and even Sartre advised her to return. At this Beauvoir flew into a rage. Was he afraid she might lose her job? Was he anxious to work without interruption on *The Transcendence of the Ego*, his current preoccupation? Or did he want to spend more time with the dreamy, distant and undemanding Marie Ville? History does not relate, but it has been noted that after Beauvoir's visit to Berlin Sartre gave up the idea of staying in Germany for another year.

Later that year, in summer, Beauvoir joined Sartre again in Germany, and this time the news from Austria was even worse. When Dr Dollfuss was assassinated the travellers decided not to go to Vienna as they had planned. When she recalled this incident Beauvoir thought that, instead, they should have gone there rapidly. 'But we were so imbued with the optimism of the period that, for us, the truth of the world was peace.' There was a disagreement between the partners: 'I hesitated, out of pure schizophrenia to change our plans, but Sartre refused categorically to undergo the boredom of a city disfigured by a ridiculous drama.' They visited Munich and enjoyed the Passion Play at Oberammergau but as their arrival in Nuremberg coincided with a fascist rally they were glad to leave Bavaria. In Dresden Beauvoir was told by a cloakroom attendant that it was 'not done' to use lipstick. They visited Czechoslovakia but they were glad to return to France. However they were soon disillusioned there because the right wing had made only too much progress. What was to be done? It was a British poet, Stephen Spender, writing in 1951 his vivid memories of Berlin and other cities, who underlined the failure of the European intellectuals during the mid-1930s.

[1] Engelbert Dollfuss (1892–1934): Austrian politician. Chancellor, 1932–34, he led the nationalist totalitarian movement which superseded democratic government in Austria. Opposition from Nazis within Austria led to tension with Germany and Dollfuss was murdered during an abortive Nazi revolt in 1934.

The so-called 'Pink Decade' had followed the American 'Lost Generation' of the 1920s. The writers had wanted to act but had not known where to start. 'We were divided,' wrote Spender in his autobiographical *World within World*, 'between our literary vocation and an urge to save the world from Fascism. We were the Divided Generation of Hamlets who found the world out of joint and failed to set it right.'

The same situation emerged in France the year after Beauvoir's visits to Germany, when the First International Congress of Writers for the Defence of Culture met in Paris in June 1935. Writers, many eminent, many to become eminent later, arrived from fourteen countries and talked for four days. They included Brecht, E. M. Forster, Waldo Frank, Pasternak. There was no voting, the speeches were never collected for publication and if many stimulating and radical ideas were put forward any conclusion remained a question no one could answer, without of course commitment to a political party: how would you choose between fascism, which was bourgeois and capitalist, and Soviet Communism, with all the loss of individualism it implied? You couldn't. Paul Valéry, the great poet, had concluded some time earlier that there could be no united front among writers. The writers who attended the congress achieved little more than the expression of their ideals.

In Rouen, as 1934 passed, life and work for Beauvoir began to gather momentum. Suddenly there was an end to boredom. Before Sartre's departure for Germany she had taken the trouble to help a student with the problems of her work at the lycée and gradually the student became a friend. Her name was Olga Kosakiewicz.

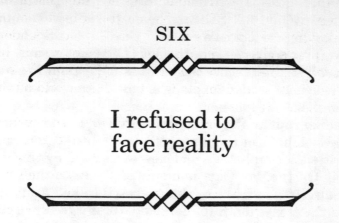

SIX

I refused to
face reality

'She talked to me about Baudelaire and God,' said Beauvoir later as she remembered her first encounters with Olga, the girl who seemed so different from all her previous students. Born in Moscow in 1917, Olga was the daughter of a Russian émigré engineer and his French wife – a former governess-teacher in Russia – who now lived at L'Aigle near Honfleur in Normandy. Colette Audry had been the first teacher at the Rouen lycée to mention the 'little Russian girl' to Beauvoir, and all the staff found that she had 'personality'. At first Beauvoir noted only her fair hair, her pale face and the extreme brevity of her essays. Many years later both teacher and student described their early encounters, explaining why their relationship was memorable from the start.

Olga had come to the Lycée Jeanne d'Arc when she was fifteen, shortly before Beauvoir took up her post. In 1978, in a filmed interview, the former student, an elegant, fair-haired, chain-smoking lady of sixty-one, remembered her arrival clearly. There had been rumours about the new teacher of philosophy. 'We were threatened,' said Olga Kosakiewicz, 'by an enormous lady whom you didn't know . . . an enormous lady who had been a teacher of philosophy for centuries in Rouen. No doubt she came from Rouen and would die there.' Olga and the other students thought they knew about this teacher, Beauvoir did not. 'We thought we were going to have her,' Olga remembered. But the rumour had been no more than gossip. 'So when we saw le Castor, *c'était formidable*, it was wonderful. She was beautiful, she was young, she wore make-up, she looked alive.'

Beauvoir remembered the schoolgirl Olga: her essays were not bad, but when the teacher asked questions, Olga never said a word. The former student explained why. 'Because I was shy,' she said, 'and then,' she told her former teacher, 'you asked questions in a rather abrupt and not very amiable way.' This criticism made Beauvoir look back at the image of herself in the classroom, and she admitted her faults as a teacher: 'I was rather fierce with my students.' On the day Olga unexpectedly rose to the top of the class Beauvoir had been unable to restrain her irony. As she returned the essays (on Kant) she said, 'To my great surprise the best composition I have received was the one by Mademoiselle Olga Kosakiewicz.'

If Beauvoir, as a former teacher, was honest about her style, Olga, as a former student, was honest about the teacher also: 'She didn't like us and we knew it.'

Beauvoir did not entirely accept this criticism. 'That's not altogether true,' she replied, 'but I have had more amusing classes.'

Olga insisted: 'Yes, we knew it! It wasn't very pleasant.'

The former teacher made another confession about her attitude during this early part of her career: 'I was fairly interested in the best students, but I really paid no attention to those at the bottom of the class.'

When asked if she made any effort to come closer to these less intelligent or less industrious girls she gave a straightforward reply: 'No, I was rather élitist, I spoke for the best students.'

Olga herself was an emotional student, a creature of extremes: she broke down completely when she took the 'mock' test before the *baccalauréat* and then finally passed the examination with brilliance. Beauvoir took some interest in this unusual student, but still regarded her as a student and no more. She came to understand how the girl's background had made her so different from the essentially bourgeois schoolgirls of Rouen. Her father had talked to her about life in the aristocratic circles of Moscow and recounted old Russian legends, while her mother had encouraged Olga and her younger sister Tania to read and listen to stories that were well in advance of their ages. The girls had learnt about classical mythology, the Bible and Buddhist legends, but there was no encouragement to believe in God or any other deities they heard about. As a result Olga was precocious in some ways; she pleased the literature teachers at the lycée but irritated the others because she lived in a world of fantasy.

Her personal development was thus eccentric and her academic results unpredictable. As a little girl Olga had thought of becoming a dancer, then an architect. After her *baccalauréat* however her parents decided that she must desert fantasy for reality and study for a career: they decreed it must be medicine, which she could study in Rouen. It was a subject Olga hated. She soon gave up serious work and preferred to lead a bohemian life spent mainly with a group of young 'Romanian and Polish Jews, driven out of their own countries by antisemitism, studying in Rouen because life was cheaper there than in Paris'. Olga asked Beauvoir to explain to her what it meant to be a Jew. Beauvoir replied firmly that Jews did not exist: 'There are only people.' The relationship between the teacher and her former student continued, Beauvoir liked 'her ways of feeling and thinking', but she did not regard her as a friend: 'To me, she was only a child and I did not see her often.'

In the meantime Beauvoir had been preoccupied with her two visits to Germany and with her attempts to fill the time during Sartre's absence. She gave lessons in philosophy to Lionel de Roulet, one of Sartre's students, whom she introduced to her sister. Hélène de Beauvoir was still living in her parents' apartment in the rue de Rennes, but she had rented a small studio and worked hard at her painting. 'Her life was difficult from a material point of view', Simone remembered, 'and very austere; she tolerated it with a good humour that I admired.' In fact Beauvoir came to Paris as often as she could and the two sisters went to theatres and cinemas together. When Beauvoir saw Katherine Hepburn in the film of Louisa Alcott's *Little Women* she felt ten years younger, remembering her 'adolescent reveries'. She also visited 'Camille' and Dullin both in their Paris apartment and in the Normandy farmhouse which they had restored as a holiday home. 'Camille' remained 'theatrical' even in the country and liked to dress up in peasant-type clothes. She had

Simone de Beauvoir

previously announced that she intended to 'seduce' Beauvoir but then gave up the idea, treating her friend in a condescending manner. Beauvoir had grown tired of her 'narcissism' and her 'coquetry', she was no longer impressed and more convinced than ever that she had no need to feel jealous of her.

She tried to make the best of the Normandy countryside, although she never actively enjoyed it. Occasionally she would escape into the past and once, near Lyon-la-Forêt, she discovered a cottage with irises growing in its thatched roof. She stayed there alone for a few days, relishing every detail from the red tiled floor to the apple-blossom and the cocks crowing at five o'clock in the morning. She set up a table under one of the trees and 'became once again the little girl doing her holiday tasks beneath the catalpa tree at Meyrignac. I gave her the thing she had dreamt about so often, in many forms: a little house of her own.'

It was easy enough to look back, but what of the present, and even more important, what of the future? The present offered no comfort, no stimulus. During the academic year 1934–35 all developments in the outside world increased the menace that had already darkened the political sky in Italy, in Germany and in France. Mussolini was preparing the invasion of Ethiopia. Pierre Laval, who had been French Prime Minister from early 1931 to early 1932, was appointed Minister for Foreign Affairs in autumn 1934. He was ready to negotiate with Mussolini and also with Hitler, who officially became Führer in August 1935. The coal-rich Saar district to the north-west of the Moselle area in the north, transferred to France after 1918 as part of the compensation settlement, voted overwhelmingly in 1935 to return to Germany. In France various right-wing parties had now become so powerful that they launched several new periodicals, including the unashamedly fascist *Gringoire*. Sadly, it became the favourite reading of Georges de Beauvoir. Along with *Candide*, *Je suis partout* and various other weeklies the principal purpose was to attack, as viciously as possible, politicians of any left or centre party. The left wing still aimed to support moves for peace while the Communists were forced into contradictory attitudes towards any possible increase in French military strength. In one sense this confusion helped Beauvoir: 'I took advantage of this indecision to safeguard my own serenity: since nobody understood precisely what was happening why not admit that nothing serious was taking place?' The situation was useful in the preservation of her escapism: 'I calmly took up again the thread of my private life.'

That private life, despite Sartre's return to Le Havre, remained disappointingly neutral. Beauvoir was dejected by the failure of her last attempted novel and was afraid of making the same mistakes again. She decided that while waiting until she was in a better frame of mind she would spend some time in the study of history, which she regarded as one of her 'weak points'. She soon began to feel better. At the same time she caught some of Sartre's enthusiasm for Husserl and they discussed him whenever they met. As she became fascinated by the 'novelty and richness' of phenomenology she appeared to have lost nothing of the early excitement she had felt while still a schoolgirl: philosophy, she had thought, 'went straight to essentials', and now she believed that she had never come so close to the truth.

After two years at the Lycée Jeanne d'Arc Beauvoir had given up any attempt to make new friends in Rouen. She saw 'only Colette Audry and Olga'. Her former student had failed her preliminary medical exams and 'she had lost all enthusiasm for study, which bored her; the certainty of a second failure and her parents' displeasure saddened her.' Olga was growing up fast, and she was also drifting. There seemed only one solution for her, the presence of her former philosophy teacher: 'She only regained a little confidence in herself and any zest for life when she was with me.' It was a new experience for Beauvoir and she began to feel differently about Olga: 'I was touched by this and went out with her quite often.'

At least Beauvoir had a good deal of free time. She enjoyed her visits to Le Havre to see Sartre and found the town infinitely more entertaining than Rouen, more international, while even the bourgeoisie seemed better-tempered and active: 'big business was carried on by modern methods; people lived in the present, instead of burying themselves in the past'. Beauvoir found endless ways of spending her time there. She could gaze with fascination at the old docks and the red light district, she could eat plums in brandy while looking out across the 'green rough sea', with Sartre she could take the boat to Honfleur, a picturesque little port thirty miles or so across the estuary of the Seine. The two friends found in Le Havre a café-restaurant, Chez Alexandre, which possessed a strange glamour, especially for Sartre, who later transposed it, renamed Chez Camille, into his first novel, *La Nausée*. As Beauvoir recalled it, nothing could sound less appealing, for throughout the year the strange artificial lighting made the place with its half-dozen tables look like an aquarium. 'The proprietor, who was bald and melancholy, served the meals himself; the menu consisted almost exclusively of eggs and canned cassoulet.' Predictably there were not many habitués, apart from 'three young kept women' who talked only about clothes, but the two future novelists were fascinated by the atmosphere of the place and began to invent additional and colourful details: 'As we were *romanesque*, we suspected Alexandre of drug-trafficking.'

But there were no new friends to be found, even in Le Havre. Beauvoir and Sartre were limited to seeing their old friends in Paris and sometimes visitors from the outside world came to Normandy – Paul Nizan, for instance, who had just spent a year in the U.S.S.R. When it was time for the Christmas holidays Beauvoir, the leader in any journeys with Sartre at this stage of their lives, persuaded him to go skiing near Chamonix. Winter sports, she recalled, had recently become accessible to the less privileged. She relished the cold, white world, the clean air. But the couple did not desert the intellectual life – they took with them 'a big book about physiology; we were particularly interested in the nervous system and recent research into chronaxy', a term which has vanished from medical and general dictionaries. It was concerned with 'The time required for the excitation of a nervous element by a definite stimulus; the minimum time at which a current just double the rheobase will excite contraction.'

Despite all these diversions the *romanesque* that Beauvoir and Sartre found or invented in Le Havre was no substitute for the life they wanted for themselves, the creative life, the writers' life. The view of their own present and future was grey. In the grey month of November 1934 they sat under the veranda of the Café des Mouettes in Le Havre and 'spent a long time regretting the monotony of our future'. During those heady days after the *agrégation* results and after their pact together they had not seen themselves as teachers in the provinces, unpopular with most of their colleagues and forced to live in their own recent past, close only to old friends who tended to be more successful than they were. 'Our lives were pledged to each other, our friendships fixed for ever, our careers were set and the world pursued its course.' This was Beauvoir at her most pessimistic. 'We were not thirty years old and nothing new would ever happen to us!' When life seemed particularly bleak Beauvoir's extremism made her forget the optimism of which she had been so proud and she would succumb once again to the fear of death which had often haunted her adolescence. She revealed her emotional self, especially when her defences were broken down by alcohol: 'If one evening I drank one glass too many I would shed floods of tears; my old nostalgia for the absolute would re-awaken: once more I would rediscover the vanity of human aims and the imminence of death.' There was one easy escape: 'I reproached Sartre for allowing himself to be taken in by that hateful mystification: life.' Both partners attempted to analyse in different ways her low state: 'Sartre denied that truth could be found in wine and tears; according to him, alcohol depressed me and I was wrong in advancing metaphysical reasons for my state.' Later, Beauvoir reflected further on the two essential truths 'between which there is nothing to choose and which must be faced together: the gaiety of existing and the horror of finishing. But at that time I alternated between one and the other. The second would carry me away in brief flashes only but I suspected that it was the more valid.' She was no longer the optimist she had been a few years earlier.

At a more mundane level Beauvoir, who was now twenty-six, felt that she was growing older. She did not worry about superficial evidence and there was no sign that her health or her appearance were affected. She was more concerned about her reactions to the outside world, or rather the lack of them: 'From time to time I complained that everything round me was losing its colour.' She was afraid that she could no longer feel anything. 'My curiosity still found something to feed upon: it no longer encountered impressive novelties.' She may have disliked Normandy but she did not blame the countryside or the weather or the lycée or the bourgeois of Rouen; she knew very well, with hindsight, the true cause of her depressed state. 'Reality seethed around me, but I made the mistake of not trying to enter into it; I contained it in schemes and myths which were more or less worn out: the picturesque, for example.' She felt she had slipped gradually into a dull and uncreative way of life. 'It seemed to me that things were repeating themselves because I was repeating myself.' She maintained that these negative feelings were only intermittent and towards the end of her life she denied that she had felt depressed in her late twenties.

She also denied that Sartre was depressed but he, writing in December 1939, three months after his call-up into the army, did not even pretend he had been anything else. 'At twenty-eight I was unknown, I'd written nothing good and I would have to work very hard if I ever wanted to write anything worth reading.' He then described his discussion with Beauvoir at the Café des Mouettes, using a few sentences almost parallel with her own memories, a situation which occurred more than once in their work. In these *Carnets de la drôle de guerre*, which were not published until 1983, he was more outspoken than she had been: 'We were tired of our precise, intellectual examinations of conscience, tired of this virtuous and dutiful life we were leading, tired of what we used to call our "constructions". For we had "constructed" our relationship on the basis of total sincerity and complete mutual devotion and we sacrificed our moods, and all possible disagreement there could be within us, to this permanent and *organized* [his word was *dirigé*] love that we had constructed.' He was writing some five years after the discussion at Les Mouettes and he added his diagnosis of their shared state of mind: 'In fact we were suffering from nostalgia for a life of disorder, a life of confused, imperious, instant abandon, a sort of darkness contrasting with our translucent rationalism, it was a way of drowning within ourselves and feeling without knowing that we were feeling.'

He wanted to be a student again, free to do exactly as he liked when he liked. He did not question the relationship with Beauvoir but he was beginning to wonder perhaps if its basis had been too intellectual. Was literature really more important than life? What was life? Sartre, who had seen himself as an anarchist, was feeling old. Beauvoir had known, during their early time together in Paris, that he did not want to enter the adult world, and if she did not always want to face reality, he, at this stage of life, could not bear the idea. In 1935 he would be thirty, and the idea terrified him. On his return from Germany his colleagues had laughed at his pot belly. During a recent summer holiday Beauvoir had noticed something else: 'I was beginning to lose my hair . . . When I noticed it – or rather when *le Castor* . . . noticed it with a cry – it was a symbolic disaster for me.' He was not much concerned with the idea of death, he said, but he could not tolerate the 'irremediable and tragic' problem of growing old. 'And for a long time I would massage my scalp in front of the mirror, baldness was becoming for me the tangible sign of ageing.' Fortunately for him the progress of his balding slowed down, probably through good luck rather than massage.

Did Sartre unconsciously search for 'a life of disorder'? Perhaps not, but it came about, as disorder usually does, in an unexpected way. At first Sartre seemed to seek the 'consolation of philosophy'. He put aside the still unfinished *Melancholia*, which eventually became *La Nausée*. He had failed to find a publisher for *La Transcendance de l'égo*, written after his study of Husserl, but one of his former professors now asked him to contribute to a series of books on philosophical themes. Entitled *L'Imaginaire, psychologie phénoménologique de l'imagination* (1940), Sartre chose to write about aspects of the imagination and the problem of the image, which interested him deeply. He planned a major work in two parts, the first critical, the second more original. The first part was published in 1936, but the second, creative part, though ready for publication, did not appear until 1940. He found this work absorbing but tiring and he began to prolong his working hours by taking pep pills, meaning inevitably that he needed sleeping pills as well. At this juncture the possibility of a new kind of experience came his way.

He had always been interested in 'dreams, hypnogenic images, the anomalies of perception', and would ask his friends to recount their dreams to him. Early in 1935 a former student colleague, by now well known for his work at the psychiatric hospital of Sainte-Anne in Paris, asked Sartre if he would accept an experimental injection of the drug mescalin, the same drug used later by Aldous Huxley in an attempt to open the 'doors of perception'. Sartre was told that the experience would not be pleasant, but he would probably have some interesting visions and if he were to behave oddly afterwards any side-effects would last only for a few hours. In fact Sartre seems to have lived through nightmares, perhaps the result of his depressed condition or his consumption of pills. His visions included a threatening orang-outang outside the railway carriage window as he returned to Le Havre, and he imagined the acorns at the tips of Beauvoir's shoelaces were about to turn into gigantic scarabs. Later he was convinced that houses had grinning faces, clocks had the heads of owls and he was being followed by a lobster.

Unlike the poet Gérard de Nerval, who had walked about Paris in the mid-nineteenth century accompanied by a lobster on a lead, Sartre had no control over the crustaceans which sometimes pursued him. They tended to appear when he was either on his own, or feeling depressed. Nerval, after all, had been mentally unbalanced and eventually committed suicide. One day, when Sartre and Beauvoir were walking through dreary country near the railway line outside Rouen, the unhappy teacher announced that he was suffering from a 'chronic hallucinatory psychosis' and was on his way to madness. Beauvoir protested angrily, 'not, for once, from optimistic prejudice but from common sense'. She knew, she added, how easily Sartre's imagination could lead him towards catastrophe, and she gave him her instant diagnosis: ' "Your only madness is that you believe yourself to be mad." He replied in sombre tones: "You'll see." ' Doctors confirmed that his condition could not have been caused by the mescalin and they did not even advise him to take a rest. He must work hard and not spend time on his own, for solitude brought the lobsters on stage. Beauvoir could not be with him all the time, obviously, but she solved the problem: she would entrust him to someone who was virtually free all day because she had no intention of doing any work, and that was Olga. She was convinced he had been overworking though at the same time she admitted that she was angry with him: 'He had no right to assume moods which threatened the things we had constructed together.' Was she afraid she could no longer say 'We make one together?' Beauvoir, who knew very well that psychology was not her 'strong point', felt she could not do too much to help Sartre. On balance, however, she was sure she had been right: 'I would certainly not have helped him by sharing his fears.'

By now Olga, once 'the little Russian girl', had come much closer to Beauvoir. Their friendship had grown quickly and deepened in intensity. There was a magnetism about Beauvoir that drew admiration and love from women, and was to do so for the rest of her life. 'At first,' Beauvoir remembered, 'it was Olga who wanted the friendship, Olga who created it.' Beauvoir's analysis of this friendship was surely correct: 'An attachment can only be strong if it asserts itself against something.' Olga, she saw, 'was more or less against everything', while she herself was free of all restraints: 'nothing oppressed me, while everything crushed her'. Like Zaza in the past, the girl found herself caught in the trap of bourgeois convention, symbolized in this case by her parents' decision that she must conform and train for a profession. This may have seemed an enlightened attitude in some ways, but these parents had brought up their elder daughter on memories of a vanished aristocratic past which she could never inherit; and it was too late now for her to leave the fantasy world she had entered as a child. Olga, like Zaza, loved her parents, but she could not accept their programme for her.

Olga failed her examinations a second time simply by not taking them, and her parents threatened to send her as a boarder to an educational establishment in Caen. She was desperate, and Beauvoir was the only person who could help her. Olga's former teacher was nine years older than she was and Olga was the first of many young women who looked up to her as a rôle model. She was different from all other women in Rouen, both at the lycée and outside it, and she lived in the unconventional way she had chosen for herself. Olga believed that Beauvoir had attained everything she wanted, especially freedom. Beauvoir responded to the girl's appeal, she gave her confidence in herself, and instead of remaining at a distance, as she always did when encountering new acquaintances, she allowed Olga to come very close to her. The girl 'reached me through the single vulnerable point in my heart: through the need she had of me'.

Olga in her turn had much to offer Beauvoir. In the first place the older woman appreciated the girl's attractions, 'the charm of her face, her gestures, her voice, the words she used, the stories she told'. But there was much more: the girl's intelligence, her sensitivity, her straightforward 'authentic' quality, her total lack of hypocrisy; she always said what she felt. Beauvoir saw in Olga some reflections of herself. Olga too was an extremist; she was capable of dancing until she collapsed. She was also a person of paradox. Her apparent passivity on certain occasions 'was not indolence but a challenge to all kinds of tyranny'. Theirs was far from a one-sided friendship, the two women shared their memories, their attitudes, and Beauvoir could talk to Olga 'more intimately than to any woman of my own age'. Her pleasure in talking was increased because Olga would listen to her 'passionately'. Soon they knew each other's background in almost every detail: 'She told me about her past and I described to her a good deal of my own.' Beauvoir did not tell everything – that 'transparency' was reserved for Sartre.

This friendship saved Olga from misery, but what was to be done about her career, about her life? What practical steps could Beauvoir take? It was Sartre who came to the rescue. If Olga hated medicine, then she must give it up. Since she had been good at philosophy she could take her *licence* with a small group of students he was teaching in Le Havre. He and Beauvoir would collaborate in the preliminary coaching she would need. Beauvoir persuaded Olga's parents that the plan was a good one, Olga would live in Rouen and all would be well.

The appearance of Olga had given a new dimension to Beauvoir's life but she herself was not to be deflected from her own personal programme. She was approaching thirty and she was as determined as ever to achieve her true personal independence through her writing. She had studied Husserl with Sartre, but she had no wish to join her partner in writing on philosophical themes. She knew that she assimilated new ideas quickly and more precisely than he did. She maintained, not modestly but truthfully, that since she could produce no original ideas of her own she offered no resistance to a philosophical text, she could understand it and received it passively, analysing any weakness. Philosophy had always meant, and would continue to mean a great deal to her: 'If a theory convinced me, it did not remain exterior to me; it changed my relationship to the world, it coloured my experience ... philosophy for me was a living reality. It afforded me satisfactions of which I never tired.' Yet it was Sartre, not Beauvoir, who wrote on philosophy. She wanted 'to communicate what was original in [her] own experience'.

Although that experience was limited in some ways, she now wanted to develop an adequate technique that would transform it into fiction and make it meaningful for her readers. She decided now that she would write a series of linked stories with some characters appearing in several of them. There would be no more attempts to solve the problems of the world by constructing a huge edifice of plot and modelling herself on Stendhal. There was to be one more important aspect to this new book. Under the title of *Quand prime le spirituel* it was to be her first publishable writing, but, significantly, publication did not take place until 1979, when she was seventy-one and all her major work had been published.

Her material was predictable enough, made up of her own experiences and those of her friends. She used a fine phrase to describe her principal target, the profusion of crimes, petty and grave, caused by what she called *mystification spiritualiste*, 'spiritual dishonesty'. This expressed her horror of bourgeois society, which she mentioned at every possible opportunity. How could she press home the attack on the misdeeds committed in the name of religion? She decided to give the book a title based on a well-known work by Jacques Maritain, the Catholic philosopher, teacher and writer, a convert in fact from Protestantism. His book (published in 1927) was called *La Primauté du spirituel*, and Beauvoir made an ironic adaptation of the title. Her novel is known in English as *When Things of the Spirit Come First*. Its five prose pieces succeed, with a struggle, in earning the title of stories, and when they were eventually published the French publishers, Gallimard, added the word *roman* (novel) on the outside cover, although not on the title page. In her preface to this 1979 publication Beauvoir explained that in writing these stories she was rebelling against the 'bad faith' which had oppressed her for a long time. The people who had suffered through this bad faith had been the young women she had known personally and she criticized them indirectly for being 'more or less consenting victims'. She was preoccupied with the destructive hypocrisy of their parents, particularly their mothers. The 'lives of girls and women', formed her subject matter, as it had done in the early failed novels and was to do in several future ones.

Some of the girls and women in these stories are memorable: Chantal, the lycée teacher, who includes something of Beauvoir and something of a teacher colleague in Rouen, and 'Marguerite', who embodies another aspect of Beauvoir herself. Zaza, inevitably is there, known as Anne, but she is not half as real as she was to become in the memories of her which Beauvoir recalled some thirty years after her death. Anne's mother is a cruel and highly exaggerated portrait of Madame Lacoin and all similar bourgeois mothers. A long section in the story entitled 'Anne' shows through a monologue how this 'devout' mother prays for the strength she needs to handle her daughter more firmly, and justifies her repressive attitude towards the daughter whom she thinks she loves. It is the most bitter attack on *mystification spiritualiste* that Beauvoir ever wrote, but if it has the strength of exaggeration it does not compensate for the failure to convey a moving, fictionalized portrait of Anne herself. The author admitted this failure. The drama of Zaza's death had affected her so deeply during her youth that she never succeeded in translating the experience into fiction.

Beauvoir, the learner-novelist, struggled to make the best of her limited experience. There is a good description of what it was like to work in the Bibliothèque Nationale and there is one amusing scene which the author probably did not invent, for in all her writing life she invented very little. It proves how well Beauvoir could handle irony, even at this stage, and there is also a glimmer of feminism, which otherwise, on her own admission, meant nothing to Beauvoir in the mid-1930s. The heroine of the story, Lisa, goes to the dentist, who, when she is not capable of replying, talks to her about theosophy. He appears to be a caricature of any old-fashioned 1930s man, for he tells Lisa that if she goes on working too hard she will lose all her teeth. He adds, significantly, 'Pretty women should not be allowed to study.'

In this book Beauvoir used elements of her own experience and aspects of her own character, fitting them together like pieces of a jig-saw puzzle, grafting characteristics of one person on to those of another. Chantal-Beauvoir, the lycée teacher, befriends her students but refuses to help one of them who has become pregnant: she is not so much recommending moral austerity as indicating that the girl must assume responsibility for her own behaviour and its consequences. Outside her academic life Chantal is also regarded as a bad influence on Anne, just as Beauvoir had been seen as a bad influence on Zaza.

Some episodes seem to reflect a kind of wish-fulfilment. For instance when Chantal visits Anne she takes beautiful clothes, whereas Beauvoir, visiting Zaza, had to be lent clothes because her own were so dowdy. There are unconvincing men, unsuccessful marriages and moments of masturbation; if the episodes are not all well narrated, Beauvoir was at last on her way to becoming a novelist and her dialogue was acquiring speed and conviction. The writing took her two years, and in 1937 her book was rejected by two publishers, Gallimard and Grasset. The public was not ready for a book which attempted to describe, indirectly, some of the problems of women.

Sartre, who had not yet published a novel, gave Beauvoir valuable advice: why did she not put more of herself into her writing? He was not interested in all these vague women, but he knew that *she* had something more to say. *Mettez-vous dedans*. He was telling her to express herself at a much deeper level, to go beyond incidents she had personally seen or experienced. She must interpret, without being didactic: that was surely what Sartre meant. She was struck by his remarks 'and even intimidated', she said in 1978, during a filmed conversation with Sartre. At the time Sartre gave her this advice he may still have believed, or thought he believed, that literature was more important than life. Beauvoir considered the implications of Sartre's advice: 'I thought that if anyone dedicated themselves to writing in this deeply committed manner, it became something very serious, like love, life, death . . .' She added that she hesitated a long time before approaching her work in this way, but in the end this is what she did.

Beauvoir had no readers beyond Sartre and a few friends, until 1943, when World War II was nearly over in France. After the two years' work on *Quand prime le spirituel* she may have been more disappointed by its rejection than she cared to admit. Significantly, two of her future heroines, Denise in *Le Sang des autres* (*The Blood of Others*) and the narrator in the story 'L'Age de discrétion' in *La Femme rompue* (*The Woman Destroyed*) were deeply upset by reactions to their books. Denise becomes hysterical when two men give her direct, even brutal critiques of her novel, while the other heroine fails to see what all her friends have seen, namely that her latest book of literary criticism has nothing new to say. She begins to wonder if she is ageing. However, Beauvoir stated calmly that she 'buried the novel with a smile'. She could allow herself the smile because the Grasset reader had included at least one encouraging sentence in his report, mentioning 'gifts' which 'allow the hope that one day you will write a successful novel'.

What would she write about next? Women, no doubt, but only as individuals, not in a social context. She noticed relevant stories in the newspapers. The swindler Stavisky, who died at the beginning of 1934, had left a beautiful widow, Arlette, a former fashion model, and her situation interested Beauvoir: 'Are there limits,' she asked, 'and what kind of limits, to the loyalty which a man and a woman who love each other owe mutually to each other?' She was not indifferent to some of the women she saw in Rouen, and remembered that she, Sartre and Olga 'were usually more curious about women than about men'. They liked to watch and listen to the women's orchestra which played at one of the big cafés, and paid great attention to the *entraîneuses* at the Océanie Bar. Beauvoir had been equally interested in the prostitutes she had encountered in Montparnasse when she was a schoolgirl. In her favourite Cintra Bar Beauvoir noticed a very different kind of woman: 'The director of a major fashion house often came to hold discussions with suppliers and customers round one of the barrels which served as a table; we observed her *avec sympathie*; intelligent women, business women, were not common at that period; we appreciated her elegance, her lack of self-consciousness, her scathing and authoritarian attitude.'

In the meantime, what had happened to the plan for rescuing Olga? The girl had been allowed to enter that *huis clos*, the Beauvoir–Sartre partnership, and Beauvoir called the new arrangement *le trio*, the triangle. It was a kind of family, a 'chosen' family, the only kind that Beauvoir admitted. The conventional family horrified her, she felt that she had suffered from its constraints during her early life and since then she had been convinced that human relationships should be 'continually re-invented'. In practice she and Sartre had adopted Olga. Strangely, a similar idea had occurred to them many years earlier, a kind of fantasy, at the time when they were occasionally Monsieur and Madame M. Organatique. Talking to a pretty salesgirl who had been drinking too much in a Paris bar they had thought 'Why don't we adopt her?' There was no question of taking the idea seriously but it may have lain dormant in their joint unconscious. Beauvoir referred to the trio as the 'work of Sartre', and it was soon obvious that as a means of educating Olga it was a waste of time, despite the careful syllabus and timetable drawn up by the two teachers. Olga preferred eating sweets to summarizing a chapter of Bergson and Beauvoir realized, late in the day, that she was not interested in 'abstract speculations'. Beauvoir's lycée colleagues and few friends were sceptical about this triangular arrangement and could not understand why the two intellectuals were so overwhelmed by this irresponsible, deceptively fragile young woman who seemed to exercise a kind of magic power.

The relationships between the three members of the trio were of unimaginable complexity, especially since the two teachers tended to discuss them in terms of phenomenology. In simpler terms the situation was a mixture of the sophisticated and the primitive: Olga loved Beauvoir and liked Sartre. Sartre and Beauvoir maintained the terms of their contract, and Sartre fell in love with Olga. In his *Carnets de la drôle de guerre* he described two of the most dramatic years of his life. It was one of the most revealing descriptions Sartre ever wrote about his own emotional state, recalling it in the autumn of 1939: 'I was at my lowest ebb at the moment of my madness and my passion for O.: two years. From March 1935 to March 1937. The madness pushed back the limits of the plausible: from that moment I abandoned my bourgeois optimism and I understood that everything could happen to me as well as to other people. I entered a world that was darker but less insipid.' Sartre had never imagined that such things would change his life, his feelings for Beauvoir were part of their 'constructions' together and feelings for any other woman belonged to the 'contingency' arrangement. 'As for Olga my passion for her burnt away my humdrum impurities like the flame of a Bunsen burner.' He suffered: 'I became as thin as a cuckoo and distraught; farewell my comforts.' He also described how he and Beauvoir had reacted together when they encountered someone so unimaginably different from themselves. 'And then, le Castor and I underwent the breathtaking experience of that naked and instantaneous conscience, which seemed only to feel, with violence and purity.' He had believed that thinking was infinitely more important than feeling, a belief that underlined his own faith that literature was more important than life. 'I rated her so highly that for the first time in my life I felt humble and disarmed in front of someone and I wanted to learn. All this was useful to me.'

If Olga's presence had scared away the lobsters which haunted Sartre's worst moments of depression it almost destroyed Sartre's belief in his future as a writer: 'I began to doubt the possibility of salvation through art.' Without this 'salvation', without his writing, there would be nothing left of Sartre.

How did a girl of eighteen or so, as Olga had been in 1935, come to threaten both the separate and shared lives of two older intellectuals? In the first place she was young and shared their anarchism, which before the arrival of Olga in their lives they had felt in danger of losing: 'Together we hated crowds on Sundays, ladies and gentlemen who were *comme il faut*, the provinces, families, children and all forms of humanism.' The relationship reached a level of mystical exaggeration, for Beauvoir admitted that she and Sartre practised 'the cult of youth, its chaos, its revolts, its liberty, its intransigence'. The partners invested Olga with values and symbolism. She became 'Rimbaud, Antigone, *les enfants terribles*, a black angel who passed sentence on us from the height of a diamond sky'. Olga herself was not pleased by this elevation, she would rather have remained herself. Beauvoir, like Sartre, was fascinated by someone who could only respond through her emotions and, unlike herself, could only live in the present.

What did Olga look like? It was possibly Sartre who wrote the best description of her when he introduced her as 'Ivich' into his novel *L'Age de raison (The Age of Reason)*: 'Her face was largely hidden by her fair curls, which she had brought right forward to her nose, and her fringe reached down to her eyes. In winter the wind blew her hair about, and exposed her large pallid cheeks, and the low forehead that she called "my Kalmuck forehead" – revealing a broad face, pale, girlish and sensual, like a moon between clouds.' Sartre believed that Olga had 'class', he seemed to find a kind of poetry in her. She was 'fey', she was intelligent but non-intellectual, gifted in some ways, but untrainable, incapable of application and discipline, the opposite of all that was Latin and cerebral and hard-working in Beauvoir.

Hélène de Beauvoir visited her sister in Rouen and painted a portrait of Olga with the cascade of fair hair that poured over her face. She observed the triangle. Olga was 'very capricious', she remembered, *'très fantasque*, she had a Slav charm which fascinated Sartre'. He was also intrigued, Hélène remembered, by an encounter with someone who possessed the 'power of inaction'. If Simone found Olga astonishingly 'authentic', incapable of any dishonesty, reacting only through her emotions, Hélène saw her somewhat differently: 'she considered us as patient workers, and in a way, she despised us'. If she had no gift for work, she had such a talent for idleness that she could spend hours on end doing nothing. At the same time she despised anything 'too natural: she didn't want to sleep at night, she drank tea to keep awake'. She didn't eat so that she would not put on weight, she would not make any plans, she would merely condescend to read, for that did not curtail her liberty.

However, Beauvoir needed Olga. Through her, she said, she had discovered the pleasure of giving. It became usual, after the publication of *The Second Sex*, to say that Beauvoir knew nothing or understood nothing about motherhood, but through her relationship with Olga she experienced something very much like it: she admitted that she had known previously how moving it was to feel useful, how 'disturbing' it was to believe that she was 'necessary'. Olga's affectionate response, she said, gave her so much pleasure that if she had been deprived of it she would have been sad.

But no 'mother' has an easy life. She was made not only sad, but angry, by Sartre's behaviour. He had fallen in love, she convinced herself, partly out of jealousy. He could not bear to see Olga showing an interest in Marc Zuorro, for instance, while Beauvoir did not enjoy seeing Olga and Sartre go off happily on some outing together. On one occasion when this happened she was so upset, as she sat in a café with Zuorro, that she could not eat her scrambled eggs.

Yet Beauvoir had to admit that Olga's presence had revolutionized Rouen, for in her company the town became 'iridescent'.

The two women both had rooms at Le Petit Mouton, a so-called hotel, now vanished, half respectable, half *maison de passe*, or house of assignation. The place was so 'picturesque' that mice would run over Beauvoir's face as she lay in bed at night. There were love-affairs of all kinds among her friends, homo- and heterosexual, and melodramatic behaviour, including wife-beating, among the tenants. The place allowed teachers 'exiled' from Paris, and their students, to entertain each other as best they could. Beauvoir and Olga would drink far too much cherry brandy and once Olga fell asleep on the stairs. Beauvoir taught her young friend to play chess, but when they played at a local café they were driven out by other players because they were not up to standard. Simone Jolivet came to Rouen and decided that Olga, like her, carried a 'demonic sign' and she declared her to be her 'god-daughter before Lucifer'.

Beauvoir admitted later that she felt 'uneasy' during the years of the trio. She did her best to cope with every minor shift in the emotional reactions between them, but one thing stands out: she herself must have behaved with incredible patience and fair-mindedness, for even though she understood and loved both Sartre and Olga she cannot have anticipated every aspect of the girl's wayward and potentially destructive behaviour, nor all the childish attitudes of Sartre. She had assumed a difficult if not impossible role: she was not Olga's mother, and no longer her teacher, she was a friend of a very special kind, she had shown courage in agreeing to experiment with a new kind of quasi-family, the 'reinvented' family. It was her responsible attitude which helped her to be so tolerant, especially as she felt that she and her own happiness were sometimes in danger. Sartre's behaviour was not impressive. With hindsight Beauvoir referred to his 'imperialism' and, understanding though she was, always the first to hear details of his personal life as well as his ideas and theories, she did not disguise her impatience when he described at length Olga's every mood and his reactions to them. She never said outright 'I was jealous', but she was shaken by some of her arguments with Sartre, even if they were not bitter. 'I was led all the same to revise certain postulates which I had previously taken as agreed; I admitted that it was a mistake to blend together another person and myself in that dubious and over-useful word "we".' She also had to admit that individuals, as individuals, underwent experiences in different ways on their own. 'I had always maintained that words fail to express the actual presence of reality: I had to accept the consequences.' She had learnt, through the trio-triangle, one of the most important lessons of her life: 'When I said "we make one together", I was avoiding the issue.' Not even the unique partnership with Sartre was safe from emotional dangers and, like marriage, it needed concentration, work. 'Harmony, between two individuals, is never "given", it must be continually fought for.' Most people make similar discoveries during their lives, but for Beauvoir they came as a shock. She had not realized that a woman and a man see things differently and Sartre, who sought out 'live' stories in the newspapers and argued about them, now argued about a crucial stage in their own lives, separate lives. Beauvoir also learnt to see Olga as Sartre saw her and she, who had experienced such difficulty in relating to others, now saw that such relationships were possible, inevitable. It was part of adult life, and a useful part of a novelist's training.

In the meantime she had to deal with Sartre more as a headmistress or a dean of women than as a mother. She was beginning to take control of all that truly mattered in their joint personal life. They had always criticized each other's manuscripts – that was easy enough – yet only Beauvoir could have 'managed' the trio. She had never felt disadvantaged by her femininity, now it enabled her to understand those two complex characters, Sartre and Olga, and their equally complex relationship. No man, and Sartre least of all, could have resolved the situation, in which a basic friendship continued to exist. Beauvoir possessed the instinctive strength to deal with circumstances in which intellectual analysis and 'transparency' were useless. Just as she had told Sartre in a common sense way that he was not mad, Beauvoir now told him not to be ridiculous. He had begun to think that 'art seemed very useless when faced by this cruel, violent and naked purity'. Such was his image of Olga. But Beauvoir had to talk him out of these exaggerated, romantic notions. 'A conversation with le Castor revealed to me again my rotten attitude [he used the word *saloperie*] and turned me away from this morality.' There could be 'salvation through art', but the artist has to suffer the plus and minus of life first. He suffered: Olga did not accept him as a lover, she preferred independence.

When, in 1974, nearly forty years later, Beauvoir questioned Sartre at length about his relationships with women she asked him:

'Have you sometimes been rebuffed by women? Are there women with whom you would have liked certain relationships and you didn't have them?'

Sartre defended himself: 'Yes, like everyone else.'

Beauvoir perhaps enjoyed a moment of revenge: 'There was Olga.'

Sartre: 'Yes.'

Beauvoir: 'But it was such a confused situation!'

Sartre: 'Yes.'

It was rare for him to remain monosyllabic. She asked him nothing more about Olga on that occasion.

During the years 1935 and 1936 Beauvoir was preoccupied with the hothouse life of the trio and with her attempts to write a good novel, but she realized that on the French political scene, which she had found 'confusing', much was happening. During May 1935 Pierre Laval, the Foreign Minister, negotiated a pact with the U.S.S.R., to be ratified the following year. The Communists scored much success in the local elections and the various parties of the left wing began to move more closely together. By the early summer the establishment of a 'Popular Front', a coalition of all these parties, with Communist support, already seemed a possibility. As a result the celebrations on July 14th, Bastille Day, were particularly festive. Beauvoir and Sartre went to the Bastille to watch, for 'We shared this enthusiasm to a certain point, but it did not occur to us to march, sing and shout with the others.' Beauvoir was at pains to define the limits of their commitment: 'Events could rouse within us strong feelings of anger, fear and joy: but we did not participate; we remained spectators.' In January 1936 the right-wing Pierre Laval fell from power and the manifesto of the Popular Front was published. By June the Front was a reality and Léon Blum, an experienced politician, a lawyer and an author became Prime Minister. Beauvoir and Sartre welcomed the Popular Front – cautiously.

That same summer brought a change for Beauvoir more important to her than any developments in the outside world. At last she was to leave Rouen. In the autumn she was to take up a post at the Lycée Molière in Passy, a smart district of Paris, while Sartre was to take up a new teaching post in Laon. During her four years in Rouen Beauvoir, like Sartre in Le Havre, had been bored and depressed, written her failed 'Stendhalian' novel and her set of linked stories, which had been shelved for the time being. However, these years were far from wasted, for Beauvoir had found her true strength and begun to feel confident about her future. She had seen Sartre through his depression, his post-mescalin madness and his destructive infatuation with Olga. Both partners had learnt from Olga: she was to become the starting-point for Beauvoir's first published novel, *L'Invitée* (*She Came to Stay*), completed in 1941, and also to become 'Ivich' in Sartre's series of novels *Les Chemins de la liberté*.

Beauvoir was also becoming socially aware: she had told her girls that there was more to life than marriage, she had refused to support the government's campaign for a higher birthrate. She had questioned the right of the Rouen bourgeoisie to bring up their daughters in the old-fashioned, conventional, sex-conscious way. She had made one valuable adult friend, Colette Audry. In 1978 Audry asked Beauvoir if she remembered a conversation they had had together, years earlier, in Rouen. She herself felt uneasy about the way women were treated, even in political circles. She remembered what Beauvoir had told her: 'When a woman is intelligent, when she knows what she wants, she can manage.' Audry took the conversation further: 'Listen, I would like to write a book about women, there must be a book about women.'

'Write it then!' Beauvoir replied. Audry remembered her brusque manner; she had spoken 'just like that', as though scolding her. The two women met again after the war and Beauvoir mentioned their previous discussions: ' "That book about women, I think I'm going to write it." And it was *The Second Sex*.' Audry, the activist, had thought about the book, and talked about it, but it was Beauvoir, the theorist, who wrote it. Perhaps she owed more than she knew to the 'provincial boredom' of Rouen.

The summer holidays arrived. Travel was almost as important to Beauvoir as writing. The previous summer she had spent some three weeks alone walking in central France, joined later by Sartre, who had accompanied his mother and stepfather to Scandinavia. This summer of 1936 was to be more adventurous. The partners left for Italy, going to Naples and Sicily by way of Grenoble, Marseille and Rome. They did not take Olga with them.

SEVEN

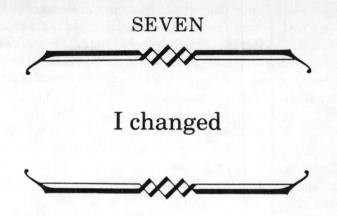

I changed

1936 was a bad year. In March Hitler occupied the Rhineland, and despite this violation of the Versailles treaty he encountered only non-effective protests from France and Britain. In May the Italian leader Mussolini captured the capital of Addis Ababa in Abyssinia after a seven-month campaign of territorial expansion for his fascist, impoverished country. The Emperor Haile Selassie had gone into exile, first to Palestine and later to Britain, while King Victor Emmanuel III of Italy was declared Emperor of Abyssinia in his place. The first disruption in Spain came in mid-July, after six months of a Popular Front government which possessed only a narrow majority. The army was powerful, as it had been for more than a century, and a military coup d'état was more likely in Spain than in most other European countries. General Franco, backed by anti-socialist, pro-clerical factions was considered so dangerous politically by the government that he had been sent to the Canary Islands as governor, where he was thought to be out of the way. However, from there he flew to Spanish Morocco where he masterminded a military uprising, captured Melilla on the Mediterranean coast and, back in the Canaries, seized the capital, Las Palmas.

The Spanish Civil War broke out officially on July 18th, just as most people in France and other neighbouring countries were preparing their summer holidays. Beauvoir was 'disturbed' by this news, but not seriously, for she was apparently unaware that the Spanish left wing had lost most of its support since the elections of 1931, when the republic was established. For the time being she clung to her old optimism and packed her bag for Italy 'in a carefree mood'. Her first visit there in 1933 had been cut short through lack of money, now she looked forward to seeing, with Sartre, more of the country she had found so attractive and continued to do so for the rest of her life.

After first spending ten days in Rome the tourists were overwhelmed, fascinated by the poverty-stricken squalor of the poor districts in Naples. Houses unfit for habitation and dirty streets teemed with people, 'naked, scabby children', some people with running sores on their bodies and 'faces as livid as abscesses', others fighting over remnants of food in the gutters. Beauvoir was horrified by everything she saw, all watched over by the statues of the Virgin Mary. She admitted however that she and Sartre did not truly understand how and why these people lived as they did. She realized that since the two of them 'failed to understand the depth of this poverty, we were capable of finding some of its effects attractive'. They found the mothers de-lousing their children, the craft-workers in the street, the fruit-sellers cutting up water-melons, 'picturesque', but they tried to look at another aspect. They liked to think this poverty 'destroyed all the barriers which isolate men and diminish them'. Life was communal and public: 'all these people lived in the warmth of a single womb: the words inside, outside, had lost their meaning'. Beauvoir noticed too that there was a good atmosphere among the people: 'up and down the streets there ran smiles, looks, voices, friendship', and this *gentillesse* impressed the French tourists. Sartre too seemed to appreciate the 'transparency' of the situation: everything was out in the open, nothing was hidden or secret, except prostitution, for the fascists had cleaned up the brothels. Later Beauvoir remembered her main impression of Naples: 'Human life is exhibited in its organic nudity, in its visceral warmth; it is under this aspect that it astonished, saddened and fascinated us.'

The partners took it in turns to organize the tourist expeditions this year. Sartre noted, in a letter to Olga, that Beauvoir was 'thrilled' by the sordid scenes she saw between the central station and the docks. Beauvoir searched for an explanation of her own reaction: why was she so excited by this display of social horror? In the past she had often mentioned her delight in the sordid picturesque but had linked it with her interest in alienation or her cult of the solitary life. In looking at Naples she worked out one interpretation of her attitude, which was shared by Sartre: unknown to themselves, she thought, 'We must have been dedicated humanists, for the conscientious bourgeoisie, the believers in social hygiene, the Communists, all the rationalists and all the progressives, condemn, for good reason, this filth and the obscurantism which preserves it.' Her interest was theoretical, not practical, but she believed it proved her acceptance of reality: 'In making an emotional compromise,' she maintained, 'one proves that one loves men not as they ought to be, but as they are.'

Even while on holiday, Sartre did not lose the image of Olga. He wrote to her regularly and she replied. He needed to communicate to her his reactions to Naples, reactions so intense that sharing them with Beauvoir was not enough. From Naples he wrote to Olga one immensely long letter which brought his reaction to life so close to literature that it later formed the basis of his story *Dépaysement*. The printed version of the letter (published by Beauvoir in 1983) runs to some thirty pages, with two breaks: 'A passage is missing.' Were these missing pages or paragraphs personal, even intimate in tone? Or were they merely lost? This is the only letter from Sartre to Olga published to date.

Both Beauvoir and Sartre took their tourism seriously and she in particular was determined to miss nothing. They reached the summit of Vesuvius partly on foot, since they could not afford the rack-railway. In any case Beauvoir believed in 'conquering landscapes by leg-power' and Sartre had no choice but to follow her. They preferred Pozzuoli and Pompeii to Paestum, where their first sight of a Greek temple left them cold. Beauvoir made a short trip on her own to see Salerno and Amalfi, after which they went to Sicily together. Following their 'initiation' in Naples, the poverty of Palermo seemed bearable. 'It teemed with the picturesque and local colour and I was delighted by it.' One day they were the only adults in a marionette theatre, where they ate sticky grapes and felt very happy. As they returned by sea from Syracuse and Messina to Naples, the thought of her inevitable return to France began to encroach and Beauvoir became

171

irritated by Sartre's reaction. 'While we were sailing under clear skies [he] read the newspapers, he talked to me about Spain and Germany and the future, where the skies were far from clear.' By the time they reached Rome on their way back to France, his mood had changed completely. The trip was ending, his old worries began to haunt him again: the political situation and his relationship with Olga. Beauvoir could not bear the idea of returning to Paris. 'I was frightened. Were the lobsters going to come back?'

In Rome, they succeeded where, on their earlier visit, they had failed: they stayed out in the streets all night until dawn, then went to a hotel to sleep. However, Sartre later made an admission which confirmed Beauvoir's worst fears: 'All that night a lobster had followed him.' Beauvoir remembered what had happened in Normandy: when Olga was with Sartre, during his post-mescalin convalescence, the lobsters had disappeared. Did he become depressed at the thought of returning to the unresolved situation of the triangle and the awareness that Olga did not respond to him sexually? Or did he want to show Beauvoir that he was still just a little 'mad' from time to time and in need of sympathy?

The political problems that darkened the end of the partners' holiday intensified. By the end of 1936 the internal situation in France had already deteriorated, despite the promises held out by the Popular Front in July, while the progress of the war in Spain did not cheer the French left wing. While remaining a 'spectator' when the Popular Front introduced the forty-hour week, along with paid holidays for workers, Beauvoir was much more concerned about the French government's reaction to the war in Spain. If she had been only moderately disturbed about the rise of fascism in Italy and Germany she was deeply moved by the plight of the Spanish republicans and the refugees who now came into France. Her immediate reaction was personal: her first holiday abroad had been spent in Spain, during the first summer of the Spanish republic, while during her second visit in 1932 she had seen the devastating gulf between rich and poor. The war quickly involved her younger friends: Stépha's Spanish husband Fernando felt impelled to return to his country on active service. Jacques-Laurent Bost, one of Sartre's favourite pupils, wanted to volunteer but the veteran André Malraux reminded him that he did not know how to handle a gun. Malraux himself, with his wife

Clara, had originally gone to Spain a few days after the outbreak of war and later commanded an air squadron. He had taken part in a good deal of action and wrote much of his experience into his reportage-novel *L'Espoir*, published in 1937.

Beauvoir and Sartre had no intention of joining the intellectuals from France and many other countries whose idealism took them to Spain. 'There was no question of our going to Spain: nothing in our lives disposed us to such a *coup de tête*.' When Beauvoir saw that neither the French nor the British government was going to intervene in the war she felt angry, indignant, but what could she do? 'Our political impotence, far from providing us with an alibi, broke our hearts . . . We were isolated, we were nobody: nothing we could say or write in favour of intervention would have the slightest effect.' It was too late now for any persuasive, theoretical contribution; international diplomacy was governed by appeasement and non-intervention although it was clear to everyone that Franco's supporters, the Italian and German fascists, were not only intervening, they were virtually conducting the war, while the Soviets backed the Republicans.

Beauvoir's emotional response to the war and the sinister implications behind it was strengthened by a simple message which rang out all over Europe and has since become a legend. The message came from a woman member of the Spanish Cortes, Señora Dolores Ibarruri, known as 'La Pasionaria'. ¡*No pasarán*! (They shall not pass!) These defiant words surely helped to stimulate the Republican cause. The response from individuals was strong, but from governments it was non-existent. The French intellectuals soon understood, with immense sadness, what was happening. 'Spain,' Beauvoir remembered, 'was no longer the land of hope, but the scene of a battle the outcome of which was now in doubt.' That battle was not confined to Spain, it became worldwide, even if the fighting was in one place only. Creative people, seeing the implications of the conflict, felt personally involved.

As for Beauvoir, she was quick to emphasize that intellectuals might not be very useful in a battle zone, they might get in the way. Her former student colleague, Simone Weil, teacher of philosophy and an unfailing supporter of the underprivileged, rushed off to the front in her usual Quixotic style. 'She demanded a rifle,' Beauvoir remembered, 'she was posted to the kitchen and upset a bowl of boiling oil over her feet.' She became a useless casualty. Colette Audry, another former colleague and the only politically active woman Beauvoir knew, went off to Barcelona where she met some Trotskyite leaders and made speeches to groups of sympathizers. 'She came back euphoric and happy, but we doubted if her speeches did any good.' Though the war upset her, Beauvoir still preferred theory to action.

If she was disturbed by the tragic events in Spain she was at the same time deeply preoccupied with her own personal situation. Her return to Paris meant that she had to reassess her lifestyle, in which there were three elements: her teaching work, which gave her financial independence, her relationship with Sartre and her own dominating urge to become a writer. Her students at the Lycée Molière reacted to her as the girls in Rouen had done in 1932. She presented herself to them as a kind of actress playing the part of a philosophy teacher, at the same time enhancing her appearance and presence as though to prove that she was no machine for the production of knowledge, no abstraction. She was first of all a woman, and not 'just' a woman, she was a person in her own right. One of her former students, Sarah Hirschman, was so impressed by her new teacher that she remembered precise details about her twenty years later: she wore a lilac silk blouse, a black pleated skirt, high-heeled shoes. No more of those dull, sensible clothes that supplied the uniform of women teachers for so long. As in Rouen, make-up was still important to Beauvoir; her lipstick was cherry-coloured, she used blue eyeshadow, black mascara and an eyebrow pencil.

She obviously enjoyed wearing eye-catching clothes as a kind of anti-establishment gesture, and she was still compensating for the time when she had been a badly-dressed teenager whose mother did not consider such things important. In later life she seemed anxious to prove that she had never aspired to expensive 'bourgeois' tastes by saying, 'I have never been elegant,' and, Sartre, towards the end of his life, once referred to clothes as part of 'purely feminine values', 'minor values which do not correspond to an eternal feminine reality'. Sarah Hirschman remembered too that her teacher would buy the well-known women's magazine *Marie-Claire* and put it down on the desk beside her handbag.

Beauvoir herself, again late in life, denied that she ever bought magazines of this sort. She did not *want* to remember. As a teacher she was not easy to follow in the classroom, for she spoke very fast, a habit she never lost, and she did not always proceed logically with her explanations. Although never very interested in the students at the bottom of the class, as in Rouen, she would explain difficulties when asked. The girls admired her, and part of the admiration consisted of curiosity and gossip. This gossip was more accurate than the stories that had circulated in Rouen. If Mademoiselle de Beauvoir dressed unconventionally for a teacher, her man friend, said to be her lover, was rumoured to appear in the classroom wearing a roll-necked sweater instead of the conventional shirt and tie. Other pieces of gossip were absolutely true: Mademoiselle de Beauvoir hated cooking, never did any and always ate in restaurants. She was also a writer, apparently, although nothing was known about what she wrote.

Passy, where the Lycée Molière was situated, is a respectable area of the city and Beauvoir had no wish to live there. When one of her former colleagues from Rouen, also now teaching in Paris, had taken a three-room apartment, Beauvoir had contemplated doing the same thing, but she had no money with which to buy furniture. At the same time she was 'terrified' at the thought of going round the offices of estate agents and actually moving in. Was it the idea of some sort of solitude that frightened her, or was it the boredom and drudgery of domestic chores? She decided, along with many writers of her generation and later, that it was better to take a room in a hotel, which would 'free [her] from all worries'. She chose the Royal-Bretagne in the rue de la Gaîté in Montparnasse. She still felt as she had on arriving in Marseille: her immediate surroundings were of no importance to her. The concept of 'home' meant little or nothing to her at this stage of her life. She preferred the busy atmosphere of the city and its people round her: 'I didn't mind having one room only, I didn't mind if it was not attractive: I had Paris, its streets, its squares, its cafés.'

In particular she had Montparnasse, the left bank quarter where she had been born, the quarter which, as she said many years later, gave continuity to her life and work. In the mid-thirties Montparnasse, although slightly past its peak, was world-famous, still the most lively place in Paris, especially popular with foreign residents and tourists from every country in the world. On her return to Paris Beauvoir had considered which of the various cafés to adopt as her centre, her *quartier général*, and chose Le Dôme, which was very popular among writers. Twice a week she went to the Gare du Nord to meet Sartre as he arrived from Laon. After a drink in an ugly, gloomy café – such places appealed to them – they would go down to Montparnasse, and from the *terrasse* of Le Dôme they could indulge in that age-old Parisian pastime: 'I enjoyed watching the people come and go.' No district anywhere in the world was more international than Montparnasse and people were on show, almost as though in a theatre. 'There is no place,' to quote Sisley Huddleston, a former Paris correspondent of *The Times*, who had lived there happily, 'which puts itself in such full view as Montparnasse. On a fine summer evening there are thousands of chairs and tables, thick-set, covered only by the sky, and lit up by a million-candlepower electric lights.' Beauvoir and Sartre, with their friends, could often be found at one of those tables. 'Montparnasse does not intend to be overlooked; and it is not overlooked.'

Beauvoir examined carefully the people who surrounded her. 'On the whole, in Paris, as in Rouen, the women seemed to us more amusing than the men.' She would have seen and heard the famous Kiki de Montparnasse, artists' model and painter herself, who was still croaking out songs in 1950, hoping to earn herself a meal. There were women of every possible kind: 'At night, tall American women would get drunk in majestic fashion. Women artists, artists' wives, models, little actresses from the Théâtre Montparnasse, girls who were pretty or less pretty, more or less completely kept by men, we liked to look at them dreaming over their café crèmes, gossiping with their young friends, showing off in front of their men . . .' More and more Beauvoir liked to look at women. 'They dressed cheaply, but not without care; some of them wore old-fashioned clothes bought at the flea-market.' Montparnasse was famous for the strange garments worn by the habitués: Cocteau once said they were left-overs from seaside holidays, and they looked odd in the city. Beauvoir noticed the anonymous women, the occasional eccentrics; she was not searching out the famous or fashionable.

She had chosen Le Dôme not merely for its entertaining view of the human landscape, she also liked to work there, and the café supplied her with a kind of study. She liked to shut herself into *un boxe*, a kind of pew-like cubicle well away from the *terrasse* and the street. There she could feel, as she had felt in Marseille, that writing was not such a lonely pursuit after all: 'German refugees would be reading the papers and playing chess round about me; foreigners of all nationalities would hold passionate discussions, but in a low key: their murmuring did not disturb me; solitude in front of a blank sheet of paper is austere; I would look up, I could be certain that people existed: that encouraged me to write words which perhaps, one day, would reach someone else.'

'Someone else' – she had no need to look for friends now. She found again her old friends, including Stépha, and her newer friends from Rouen, who were also in Paris now. Zuorro was teaching, living also in Montparnasse, in the rue Delambre, just off the central boulevard. Jacques-Laurent Bost was studying for a *licence* degree at the Sorbonne and living not far away in the Place Saint-Germain-des-Prés. Perhaps Beauvoir had not anticipated that one more friend would arrive in Paris so quickly: Olga. How could a girl of nineteen, who had been fortunate enough to attract the wondering friendship of Beauvoir and Sartre, be expected to remain in the small Normandy town of L'Aigle with parents who were displeased with her? She was not studying, she was doing nothing. Since her parents would not give her permission to come to Paris she came without it and took a room in the Royal-Bretagne in order to be close to her mentor, Beauvoir.

Beauvoir was genuinely fond of Olga and had not contemplated abandoning her. Would the trio come into being again? It looked as though the trip to Italy had in fact been merely a temporary escape from the emotional hothouse. Beauvoir had always believed that its creation had been due to the dreariness of life in Rouen, but the complex situation that had developed was now part of life. In the first place, how was Olga to support herself? Beauvoir and Sartre were both generous, but they were far from rich and they believed, she in particular, that everyone, including every woman, should achieve a reasonable degree of financial independence. As a temporary move Olga took the only kind of job available to her – she worked as a waitress serving tea 'in a kind of cafeteria in the boulevard Saint-Michel which was also a library and a discothèque'. Beauvoir, however, saw that this was 'no solution'. Sartre seemed to be hoping for another kind of development: Olga enjoyed his company and the two of them would often 'wander through Paris until dawn, delighted to be together'. Beauvoir was not delighted when Sartre took up his old habit of trying to discuss with her everything that Olga said and did. She could see no solution to the whole tedious situation.

However, early in 1937 there was a solution, one that nobody had anticipated. Two events occurred almost simultaneously in the lives of Beauvoir and Sartre, causing another change for her and revealing the complexities and in particular the closeness of their relationship. In the first place Beauvoir became ill, overtaken in the late winter with a congestion of the lungs. Her circle of friends could not believe that such a thing could happen: Beauvoir was *never* ill, she was tough, she could walk for miles, she could work for hours, nothing daunted her. She could not believe it either. When in the end she had to be taken by ambulance to a clinic in Saint-Cloud the experience shook her. She had believed that such things happened only to other people, and now they were happening to her. 'So anything could happen to me, as to anyone else: what a revolution!' Although her remark was at least half-ironic, it proved that she had been living in a strangely isolated position, trying to discover her own true personality and come to terms with it. She constructed a drama out of her illness, which had made her realize how far, during the last few years, she had drifted into an unnatural situation. As she recovered she admitted to herself that she had unconsciously been living under strain, with her 'hands tightly clenched', and now it was a relief to shed her responsibilities for a time, to depend on others. She confessed that the trio in the end had been too much for her: 'The trio, with its anxieties and obsessions, had put me under such pressure that exile was restful to me.' Everyone close to her helped her through the crisis: her mother, her sister, Madame Morel, Olga, Bost and Sartre.

Whenever Sartre could leave Laon for Paris he went out to Saint-Cloud to visit her, and on one occasion, a few years later, while writing his *Carnets de la drôle de guerre*, he remembered these journeys, for they coincided with another important event of the year. Sartre was dutifully attentive to Beauvoir but he admitted he was not thinking only of her: 'It was the end of my passion for O. I was nervous, anxious,' still hoping, it appears, 'for some impossible rapprochement.' The partnership had obviously come near to disaster. Past and future seemed to be mingled in his thoughts, along with images of the love that was an axiom in his life and the contingent love that had affected him so deeply. Somehow he reconciled his feelings for both women, so different from each other, so complementary in their importance to him. The qualities within Beauvoir that he appreciated most were the very ones that had kept the trio together, and the reason he was thinking of some 'impossible rapprochement' was due to a new situation.

The trio-triangle, 'the work of Sartre', as Beauvoir had described it, was exhausting for everyone concerned in different ways. It was Olga's confused state which led her to carry out one supremely 'authentic', i.e. totally honest, genuine act. During a visit to Simone Jolivet and Charles Dullin in Paris she had taken a lighted cigarette and pressed it into her hand with 'maniacal patience'. Beauvoir saw the gesture as Olga's 'way of defending herself against the disarray into which this complex adventure had thrown her'. Suddenly, Olga herself made a more straight-forward gesture to end the 'disarray'. She had become closer to Jacques-Laurent Bost, whom she had met in Rouen and now saw regularly because Beauvoir and Sartre enjoyed his company. This pleasant, intelligent young man had also attracted the attention of the bisexual Marc Zuorro, who had in fact fallen in love with him. One evening Zuorro left Olga and Bost in his room listening to his records. Returning earlier than he had expected, he looked through the keyhole. He saw the couple in each other's arms, kissing. He was heartbroken. Olga and Bost were happy and Sartre realized that he had lost Olga. Beauvoir was relieved that the trio was over, and she saw its ending as a triumph of friendship. The triangle had resolved itself into a group of three friends, the three separate individuals who had originally formed it. Later, Bost and Olga married.

Beauvoir soon recovered and started her convalescence in Paris. Sartre had found her a better room, still in Montparnasse, in the rue Delambre, and in the same hotel where Zuorro lived. Since she could not yet go out, Sartre would bring her lunch. He would go to the Restaurant La Coupole, which was close by, and bring her 'a portion of the *plat du jour* . . . walking carefully in order not to spill anything'.

La Coupole was never a centre of gastronomy, but the meals helped Beauvoir to recover. Her doctor helped her further by recommending convalescence in Provence, and the thought delighted her. She went first to Bormes-les-Mimosas on the Mediterranean coast to the east of Toulon. Between going for short walks and eating crême de marrons, for she had been told to put on weight, she read such contrasting authors as Faulkner, Mazo de La Roche, Moravia and George Orwell. She was soon well enough to walk a good distance and her greatest delight was to go into village post offices and find, poste restante, 'letters from Sartre, each time like an unexpected gift'. For two months or so these letters were the only events in her life.

Sartre spent a great deal of time writing to Beauvoir, and he was always impatient for her replies, 'for things are still idyllic between us despite the distance'. No separated lover ever remained so close to his partner. She was 'totally present, in flesh and blood', he visualized her wearing her 'little white raincoat and [her] blue hat'. He read her letters carefully, even the descriptions of the Provençal landscape which did not interest him directly, 'but I feel so tenderly towards you that I want to feel as much as possible the things that happen to you and the objects which surround you'. His hotel room in Paris was haunted by her presence, especially since she had left there a little 'postilion-style cap'. He described also at immense length all that was happening among their friends in Paris, for if she had been there this is what they would have seen or talked about.

There had been another development in Sartre's 'contingent' emotional life, which Beauvoir knew about, for she was always told everything. No sooner was he forced to relinquish Olga – and he may even have tired of the struggle – than he at once found a replacement for her. This was none other than Olga's younger sister, Wanda, whom he always called Tania. She had followed Olga to Paris. Sartre still responded to the Slav charm he had first encountered in Rouen, but there was no question so far of another triangle situation. The girls were alike in many ways: photographs reveal the same fair hair, the same high cheekbones and hollow cheeks below them. In character too they were similar in some ways – they seemed to be gifted for something, but since they were incapable of concentration it was not clear if they would ever achieve anything. Wanda thought she was interested in painting and Sartre thought she had *un joli coup de crayon*, she drew very 'prettily'. He enlisted the help of Hélène de Beauvoir, asking if she would give Wanda some lessons and allow her to work in her studio. 'He even made me write to her parents,' Hélène remembered, for Wanda was only eighteen at the time. Some responsible person must be available close to her in Paris, otherwise she would never be allowed to leave home. Sartre even drafted the letter which Hélène was to send. She thought it contained some silly phrases and wondered what the Kosakiewicz parents would think of her. However, Wanda duly arrived, Hélène found her a pleasant enough girl but she was as lazy as her elder sister. She would come into the studio and lie down. 'Oh, Poupette,' she would say, 'I feel tired just seeing you at work.' There were in fact few more industrious people than the de Beauvoir sisters and Sartre. The sisters did not share Sartre's admiration of the Kosakiewicz idleness, their belief in independence would not allow them to do so, and Beauvoir had been known to laugh at Sartre's attitude to Wanda. She was genuinely fond of Olga but there is no evidence that she did more than tolerate the existence of Wanda.

During the separation occasioned by Beauvoir's convalescence Sartre told her in his letters all about the letters he himself did or did not receive from Wanda, and about the letters he wrote to her. Beauvoir read all this patiently. Her patience during the years of his 'passion' for Olga had paid off, the three of them were still friends and Sartre could write about Olga now as though she were a fictional character, which she indeed became, later.

While Beauvoir was still convalescing Sartre had some further news to recount. His novel *Melancholia*, which had preoccupied him for so long, had at last been accepted by the publishing firm of Gallimard, after some earlier confusion when it had been rejected for the firm's literary review *La Nouvelle Revue Française*. *Melancholia*, re-titled *La Nausée* by Gaston Gallimard, was not likely to gain a wide audience, for it had only a minimal plot, and apart from this one publishable book, compared to Kafka by one publisher's reader, Sartre had so far written only a few short stories. However, his letters made good 'fiction', even if he was recounting true events. Beauvoir received amusing descriptions of how Olga and Sartre now felt about each other. During a dinner at La Coupole she was *étrange et douce*. 'She didn't hate me and even looked at me with a kind of tenderness and even regret, but it was the way you look at an old garter . . . belonging to a woman you had once loved very much.' Olga, reported Sartre, now saw herself, 'with a comfortable sadness, as a crushed flower'. Most reassuring of all to Beauvoir was Sartre's new reaction: he found it all 'rather comical'. He was aware of how deeply he had changed, even though he had some regrets: 'Alas, poor Castor, a month and a half ago I would have found it all simply devastating.' 'Transparency', the freedom to express everything he felt, suited Sartre, and in Beauvoir he had the perfect confidante. Not everyone had her gift for listening, and Sartre knew that she would prefer 'stories rather than protestations of love'.

Despite his preoccupations in Paris Sartre's concern for his convalescent friend had not faded. He was now afraid she was walking too far. When she told him about some new minor ailment he gave firm instructions: 'If it lasts I beg you to go to *Marseille* and see a good doctor – an *expensive* one. I think nothing of that twenty-franc doctor.' He told Beauvoir he loved her very anxiously and very deeply. 'Send me a telegram with your news; if you're not well and if you need me, say so, I'll leave next Friday if you want me to.' He meant what he said; he often told her that he was going to see someone, usually a woman, because he had *promised* to do so. He was also aware sometimes of his own virtue. On one occasion he said he had written so many letters that the skin was peeling off his fingers, on another he was so busy that he had no time for '*les états d'âme*' – no time to be soulful.

Sartre, however, had plenty of time for sexual adventures and plenty of time to recount them. His recent and long-awaited literary success, the acceptance of *La Nausée*, and Beauvoir's absence, plunged him into a state of sexual and confessional energy that became nothing less than hectic and euphoric over the next few years. Some time in May 1937 he explained what happened when he went up to his hotel room with a friend of Beauvoir, the painter Germaine Pardo, who was known as 'Gégé'.

He had merely intended to retrieve a suit to be taken to the cleaners –

> (hypocritical little man, the good Castor will say. Good Castor, my intentions were pure, I swear it) and then I was faithful to thee, Cynara, after my fashion. Like that, because it happened, it had to. I kissed her on the cheek, she kissed me on the mouth. I took off her jacket, she took off her dress and her knickers. I went to bed with her. She told me that she loved me and I didn't believe it. I told her I liked her a lot and she believed it. She said: 'I almost enjoyed it.' Then I gave her a copy of *Erostrate* [a short story he had just written] to thank her.
>
> We went downstairs again, she was attentive to me, the way women are when they're happy. I took her back to her husband, I went to Le Sélect for a drink, I caught my train.

It sounds like an embryo short story by Sartre.

He ended this particular letter to Beauvoir with a touching message. In her recent letters, he said, 'you sound so happy that I was moved to tears. I love your little solitary activities, walking around, reading and sometimes drinking your little quarter bottle of wine. I love you. I'm very impatient to see you again – but I've not forgotten your dear face in any way. Will you be very plump?'

Beauvoir's convalescent letters meant a great deal to Sartre, even though he was teaching, writing short stories, seeing many of his Paris friends and conducting his current contingent love-affair with Wanda. There was near telepathy between Beauvoir and Sartre: 'I was very moved when I received your Tuesday letter and tears came to my eyes at the thought that there were tears in yours. Even at a distance, you see, it's catching.' He *had* to write to her, and even if his mother gave him money to go to the barber's, he could not get there because he preferred to spend the time writing to her, as he sat in La Coupole. He was broke, so broke that he actually stole thrillers from outside a bookshop; he could not afford to buy them. He told Beauvoir: 'Yes, *bon Castor*, I stole them', as though purging his guilt. She, in the meantime, was very happy as she walked over the slopes of Sainte-Baume, the mountain range lying across the two départements of the Var and the Bouches-du-Rhône. Her happiness was obvious to Sartre 'just through the way you're writing, the lines go up towards the top corner of the page'. He was quite honest about the contents of her letters, they were 'a little too full of nature for my taste, but since it's you who are looking at this nature everything interests me . . .' He even went to sleep thinking of umbrella pines and a brilliant blue sky.

Beauvoir was essential to his life. She had realized this ever since 1929 and if, during the most complex moments of the triangle situation, she had felt anxious, her confidence had grown during her convalescence, partly perhaps through the incessant exchange of letters. She understood very well that the Kosakiewicz sisters could supply Sartre with aspects of 'traditional' femininity, but though the girls enjoyed the company of intellectuals they were not intellectuals themselves. Sartre clung to Wanda, but he admitted to Beauvoir that she had 'the brains of a dragonfly', and he found that very difficult. Both sisters were probably more interested in themselves than in Sartre, while Beauvoir was profoundly interested in Sartre. In some ways she saw him as another aspect of herself. They complemented each other. If he dominated her in some ways he still wanted her to be independent of him. He appeared to behave independently of her but he needed her. How could he have coped with his hyperactive life without her? If he could not talk to her he had to write to her. He could not function without a listening, under-standing partner.

By the early summer of 1937 Beauvoir's convalescence was over but she still longed for country air, for real walking and climbing, no more gentle strolls. She and Sartre planned to go to Greece during August but she needed to fill in a few weeks before their departure. She set off therefore for the Col d'Allos region in the Alpes de Haute Provence and spent a cheerful active time there climbing and even sleeping rough.

It was late July or early August 1937 that Beauvoir and Sartre left Marseille for Greece, and Bost went with them. Much of the trip seems to have been highly uncomfortable, but that did not worry Beauvoir. She loved travel and always wrote detailed descriptions of her visits to any country. Her accounts of these journeys mark stages in her own development, and if she was changing in some ways she still visited the *bas-fonds* of Greece with an eye directed mainly at the picturesque. To her surprise

Athens was 'disorganized, dreary, and extraordinarily poor'. It was also deceptive: 'At first sight, I found great pleasure in the working-class streets round the Acropolis – little pink or blue houses, low-set, with flat roofs and outside staircases.' Then came an unpleasant surprise: 'One day, as we were walking by, children threw stones at us: "Oh, they don't care for foreigners," we thought calmly.' She admitted that poverty did not yet upset her deeply, but she seemed to notice it more than ever. 'During the 30s, although we were indignant about the injustice of the world,' she remembered, 'it could happen, especially when we were travelling, that we were side-tracked by the picturesque and took it for granted, as something natural.' She excused herself and her friends by deciding that the stones had not been aimed at them personally. They deceived themselves, she admitted: 'We defended ourselves against the realities which might have ruined our holiday.' In the Greece of Metaxas,[1] Beauvoir discovered, there was a kind of wretched poverty different from that of Naples: the Neapolitans had at least been happy, the Greeks were miserable.

The small party saw a good deal of Greece, although Bost could not stay there as long as the others. On his return to France he was supposed to send them money at Salonika but it took so long to arrive that they could only just afford to eat. Sartre, impervious to 'curiosities of nature', refused to travel north to see the extraordinary Meteora, an isolated outcrop of precipitous rock crowned with medieval monastic buildings. He was ready to board the steamer for Marseille. Beauvoir realized that he had often agreed to her plans in order to please her, but now she was deeply upset, for she hated changes to her *Guide Bleu* travel schedules. She sat in her cabin and again wept 'tears of rage'.

However, the holidays were not over for her, since she had agreed to go on a walking tour of Alsace with Olga, who had spent some time there in Strasbourg as a child. Sartre returned to Paris to find that Olga was unwell and he was worried: he thought she

[1] General Yanni Metaxas (1870–1941): Greek soldier and politician. Chief of the General Staff, 1913–16, he resigned and went into exile. He later returned, entered the government and assisted in the restoration of King George in 1935. A year later he assumed autocratic powers and led the government until his death in 1941.

was now pregnant by Bost and, in her usual dramatic style, had decided to kill herself. He was relieved when this suspicion proved unfounded because, as he told Beauvoir, 'That would have cost us 1500 francs,' a good deal of money. 'That' would have been an abortion. Her trouble was an early sign of tuberculosis, from which in fact she was to suffer later. Sartre seems to have behaved like a typical failed lover, turned devoted father-figure. Olga now said she was jealous of Beauvoir because *she* had been to Greece with Sartre and she, Olga, had not. However, Sartre reminded her that she really *did* want to join Beauvoir in Alsace, and put her on the train. The two women enjoyed the countryside, but they were soon so short of money and so cold that they were 'not sorry' to be back in Paris.

Life in Paris, in the autumn of 1937, was now very different, because Sartre had been appointed to a post at the Lycée Pasteur in Neuilly. To solve the problems of the unmarried marriage, the couple took rooms in the Hôtel Mistral in the rue Cels, still in Montparnasse, but the rooms were on different floors. 'In this way,' Beauvoir said, 'we had all the advantages of a life in common, and none of its drawbacks.' She now deserted Le Dôme when she wanted to write, preferring her hotel room because it had bookshelves and a desk, and she no longer needed the reassurance of other people around her.

She had been comforted in a small way when the publisher's reader at Grasset had seemed hopeful of her literary future, although her linked stories had been rejected, and she had listened carefully to Sartre's advice when he had told her to put herself into her writing. Slowly she began to think harder about the novel which was to take her some three or four years to write, the novel which in the end had to wait until 1943 for publication, *L'Invitée (She Came to Stay)*. That autumn even Olga began to work, taking up at last Beauvoir's idea, supported by ex-actress Simone Jolivet, that she should train for the theatre. At first she was so terrorized by Charles Dullin, director of L'Atelier, who had agreed to give her an audition, that she went into hiding for a time and was even unfriendly to Beauvoir.

Beauvoir herself regarded the autumn of 1937 as one of the most disturbed and unsatisfactory periods of her life. If Sartre was close to her and Olga at least thinking about some sort of career, the state of the outside world was less than reassuring. In France the Popular Front collapsed, Camille Chautemps followed Blum as Prime Minister but was no more effective. The right wing continued to make progress and cause trouble. The international scene was even more frightening: fighting between the Chinese and Japanese, and an ever-closer alliance between Germany and Italy, who were supporting General Franco in Spain. Beauvoir was so dismayed by all she heard that she tried to ignore it, but failed: 'I did not want to admit that war was imminent, not merely possible. But it was no good playing the ostrich, burying my head in the sand, the threats that were growing round about me were crushing me.' Somehow she had to learn to face the world and made the admission: 'I changed.'

She was not the only one in her circle to change, even if the reasons were different. She was more dismayed than ever when Stépha's husband Fernando Gerassi came back from Spain on leave again. 'He was much changed, he was no longer cheerful.' Like everyone fighting in Spain he could not forgive the French and the British for their bland refusal either to intervene or to help the Republicans. His vituperation became personal: ' "*Salauds de Français!*" he said. He seemed to include Sartre and me,' Beauvoir remembered, 'in his rancour.' She attempted to excuse the two of them: 'That seemed unfair, since we hoped with all our heart that France could come to the help of his country, but his anger was little concerned with nuances of this sort.' Hope was indeed not enough, but Beauvoir was still not ready for action of any sort, even if restricted to polemics. A little later she and Sartre read Malraux's novel *L'Espoir* (*Days of Hope*) based on his recent active participation in the Civil War. Beauvoir admired the way in which he treated 'themes new to literature: the relationship between individualist morality and practical politics; the possibility of maintaining humanist values in the midst of war'. Although sharing with Malraux a preoccupation with such problems in the abstract, Beauvoir was not yet ready to contemplate such themes in a more practical manner.

She was to admit later that 1937 had left her only 'vague memories'. She went to concerts and enjoyed listening to Marianne Oswald, the German-born music-hall singer who fascinated the French intellectuals. In particular Beauvoir relished the anarchist songs specially written for her by Jacques Prévert, but on the whole she confessed to a feeling of stalemate, she even found less entertainment in 'observing the people whom I met'.

The year ended with a skiing holiday at Megève: a family party, for Sartre, her sister and a friend, plus Bost, went too. They took lessons and in the evening read new translations of Pepys' *Diary* and Swift's *Journal to Stella*. Beauvoir barely glanced at the newspapers. Despite the self-awareness of change, her transformation into a social being was still far from complete.

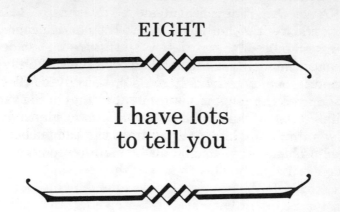

EIGHT

I have lots
to tell you

1938 was so crowded in more ways than one that both Beauvoir and Sartre had indeed 'lots to tell' each other, to quote a phrase she used in a letter written to him at the end of July. One early event of the year was the publication of Sartre's novel *La Nausée*, to a good critical reception. Its dedication was significant: *Au Castor*. If his Castor had been going through phases of change, Sartre was also changing, more rapidly in some ways, and taking a stronger interest in politics. If war should break out, as seemed possible, he would be called up into the army, and therefore he was personally concerned. His old friend Pierre Guille now regarded him as 'politically extreme', and the friendship cooled. Other friends, such as Marc Zuorro, also became more distant, and it is possible that they saw the Beauvoir–Sartre relationship as so exclusive, so mysteriously close, that they felt themselves to be on the periphery.

During this same year Sartre had also published one story, *Le Mur*, and was writing others. His burgeoning literary success, combined with Beauvoir's various absences from Paris, seemed to drive him into a series of further sexual adventures, all of which he felt compelled to describe to her in detail.

In the meantime there were early holidays which they spent together, starting with a short Easter holiday in the Basque country. They also visited La Rochelle on the west coast, where Sartre had spent a good part of his childhood. There they had discussed the story he was currently writing, the memorable *Enfance d'un chef*. They also made a 'pilgrimage' to Rouen, finding no trace of the 'hothouse' where they had formerly lived. Beauvoir remembered the trip later: 'The future . . . had detached itself from the moments of which it had been the very flesh: in the streets and in our memory only skeletons survived.' Since they had not enjoyed the town it is strange that they went back, but presumably they wished to carry out an exorcism, to convince themselves that they had escaped from the provinces and the emotional problems they had made for themselves there.

For their principal holiday that year they had planned a trip of six weeks in North Africa, but that was not due until August. At Whitsuntide Beauvoir left Paris on her own for an expedition on foot and by coach through the Auvergne and the Limousin. She wrote a few letters to Sartre during the trip but they would hardly have entertained him because they were rather tedious descriptions of the countryside. Beauvoir was often reminded of the many holidays she had spent as a child in her grandfather's house and one day, while walking through rocky gorges near the picturesque town of Saint-Flour in the Auvergne, she remembered something that had happened when she was very young: 'I was thinking about my childhood again and one of my oldest memories came into my mind: the flower that I had been accused of picking in Aunt Alice's garden; I told myself that one day I would like to revive, in a book, that distant little girl; but I doubted if I would ever have the possibility of doing so.' Fortunately, as part of her quest for self-discovery, which was for her, as she later realized, the start of independence, she made that opportunity for herself. Meanwhile she remained faithful to her early principle, life before literature.

In July 1938 she and Sartre separated for a time but kept in close touch by letter. Many years later Beauvoir carefully censored her description of the separation and of how they both spent the time: 'Since Sartre was detained in Paris,' she remembered, 'I went walking in the Alps . . .' giving the impression that she had gone alone. Sartre was 'detained in Paris' mainly because he was pursuing various 'contingent' love-affairs. He wrote to Beauvoir that he missed her, he was sorry that she had left him for this walking trip: 'absurd little globe-trotter, you would still be with me now, all smiles, if you did not have this strange mania for devouring kilometres.' In the meantime he indulged what others might call his 'strange mania': he called it *'les vicissitudes de la galanterie'*. He saw Olga often but was hoping for much more personal success with her sister Wanda.

While waiting for her to arrive in Paris the time passed pleasantly enough for him. First there was 'Lucile', one of Charles Dullin's drama students, who made advances to him and led him to tell Beauvoir that she was full of 'mysteries, eternal feminine and all that sort of thing', which held no charm for him, at least in this case. Beauvoir knew that he found nearly all women interesting and attractive, but she must have been reassured when he admitted he had learnt something: 'Ever since the Olga business, anything that has the slightest resemblance to *le passionné*, even if it's just a little excitement, I knock it on the head at once, through a kind of deeply embedded fear.' He added that this reaction applied not only to Olga but to 'everyone', meaning presumably every woman who impressed him.

When Sartre was thinking out a series of novels which he hoped to write, entitled provisionally *La Révolte*, the intended epigraph for this work was: *Le malheur, c'est que nous sommes libres*, 'unfortunately we are free'. That was part of his trouble: he had decided he was totally free, in sexual life as in everything else, and now his freedom had led him into a kind of sexual anarchy, a state of potential polygamy which he could no longer control. Perhaps he was too free? In any case, he described every detail of his emotional and sexual life in his letters to Beauvoir, and he assumed that she would read them without any personal or moral criticism. She had accepted that Sartre's sexual needs, like the man himself, were far from average. Total sex still did not interest him greatly or he would not have described himself as *plutôt un masturbateur des femmes qu'un coïteur*. Beauvoir knew that he 'liked touching', he even liked touching and holding her letters.

When she read these almost daily letters, which were always lively and amusing, was she jealous and angry, as many women might have been? Did she want to know what happened in bed between Sartre and a student from the Atelier theatre drama school, whom he had in fact 'stolen' from his former colleague Maurice Merleau-Ponty? The girl, Colette Gibert, had been warned by her aunt: Sartre lived *maritalement* with Simone de Beauvoir and 'no woman can resist him'. No details of the entire story and its background were omitted in letters to Beauvoir and Sartre assumed that she would react unemotionally as though she were reading a piece of fiction. 'Let's move on to the [Gibert] affair', he wrote on July 14th. 'It's going too well: yesterday I kissed this girl and she sucked my tongue with the power of a vacuum cleaner, so much so that it still hurts . . . She seems very pleased with the way things are proceeding. But don't worry, no vows have been exchanged.' Did she worry? Not in the least.

She had been delighted to receive his letters, she read and re-read them: 'They entertained me greatly,' she replied on July 22nd, 'and I'm waiting impatiently for the next instalment – I find Gibert *très sympathique* and this story elegant.' Gibert apparently envied Beauvoir's position as *maîtresse en titre*; it seemed unassailable. Beauvoir herself, however, was shocked to hear that Merleau-Ponty had abandoned 'his role as an impartial and peaceable monk. My love, you are very kind to have told me all this so well in detail.'

There was indeed no shortage of detail, especially since Colette Gibert offered Sartre the delights of novelty: it was 'the first time I've been to bed with a girl who's brown, or rather black, totally Provençal, *pleine d'odeurs* and curiously hairy', while her body itself was whiter than his. Beauvoir received many cheerful pages in this vein, and found the hothouse of sexual encounters in Montparnasse hotel rooms infinitely less dangerous and stressful than the emotional hothouse of Rouen with its long-drawn-out, unresolved problems. In the meantime Sartre had learnt that Merleau-Ponty was indeed in love with the girl and he, Sartre, was afraid that *she* might fall in love with him. 'I told her . . . that certainly I was in love with her but there was no place in my life for her . . . I talked to her not only about you but also about Tania [i.e. Wanda]', and she replied that she knew all that, 'there's no need to make a point of it'. However, it was Colette who made the point, after one of those nights of 'love', that she was not jealous of Wanda, who occupied second place in the hierarchy of Sartre's women at the time. 'I would never accept what you offer her, I'm jealous of Simone de Beauvoir.' Wanda was just another contingent love, she thought, of temporary importance only. Beauvoir received a deep if indirect compliment from this girl: 'I've always wanted to be with a man the way you are with Simone de Beauvoir. I think it's marvellous.' How many young women, since 1938, have said the same thing – and they are still saying it. In his letter of July 14th he added one sentence of further reassurance to Beauvoir: 'You must realize, *mon charmant Castor*, that in the midst of all these storms, I manage to be entirely united with you.' Even he seems to have realized that his words might not sound very convincing. 'It's not obvious in this letter, I've got too much to say. I kiss you tenderly, *mon charmant Castor,* and I'll write to you at length tomorrow.' A few days later he was writing to her from the Petit Mouton hotel in Rouen, where Beauvoir had once lived. He was staying there now with Wanda.

Sartre continued to tell Beauvoir everything and she accepted his 'transparency'; it was an essential part of their relationship. If she had not been told everything, what might she not have imagined? The total frankness of their exchanges can be wondered at, laughed at, envied, but any criticism of their attitudes is a pointless exercise. At this period of their lives Sartre had more to tell than Beauvoir, for his acknowledged 'polygamy' was not matched by any nymphomania on her part. In one way she was continuing, in a different dimension, the role she had begun when she first advised him about his early writing: she had read everything he wrote, and continued to do so, she was always his first editor. She did not at this point edit his love-affairs, but she listened. She was not ironic when she told Sartre how much she enjoyed his letters and the Colette Gibert story. These details amused her and she was confident of her own place in Sartre's life. His letters were more entertaining than the average novel and Beauvoir, a hopeful novelist herself, relished the opportunity of seeing how he handled this material. Did he still believe that literature was more important than life? Admittedly he had mastered the art of writing rather more successfully than the art of living, because apart from his relationship with Beauvoir he was still behaving like an adolescent boy and could not always find his way out of the entanglements he had so cheerfully created. But that was his style, and few men ever enjoyed life more than he enjoyed the life he had chosen for himself.

Beauvoir had written to Sartre on July 22nd addressing him as

'*Mon doux petit mari*'. She wrote as often as she could from the Alpine heights, describing all the details of her adventurous trips. She had left Paris on her own and near Geneva had been joined by Bost, one of the very few people in her entourage who could walk and climb as well as she could and also enjoyed camping. They left together for a short, sometimes hazardous holiday, coping with shortage of money, shortage of accommodation and a scarcity of places to eat. Beauvoir cut her hand on a rock, felt her heart beating fast as the two of them climbed higher, suffered from changeable weather, sunstroke and indigestion. But she enjoyed it even more than she had hoped. Hardly a day passed without letters between the Alps and Paris and at the end of one letter she remarked tersely that she had received 'passionate letters from Védrine', thanked Sartre again for his long entertaining letters and felt impatient to see him, adding, 'I love you passionately . . . I kiss you tenderly.' Of 'Louise Védrine', one of her former students, much was to be heard over the next two years.

Writing from Albertville in Savoie five days later Beauvoir told Sartre she loved him very much and that 'something very pleasant has happened, something I had not expected at all when we left – I went to bed with little Bost three days ago – naturally it was I who suggested it to him . . .' After all, she was older, and the young man knew she was 'bespoke' to his former teacher. She sounded immensely happy: 'We spend idyllic days and passionate nights.' She added that she found it *drôle* that she was now going to spend two days with Védrine, who had fallen in love with her. Beauvoir's emotional and sexual life was no less hectic than that of Sartre at this point and it did not affect her feelings for him in any way.

Over several future decades Beauvoir the writer used much of her own experience twice over in her work. By far the best account of what may have been her first 'contingent' heterosexual love can be found in *L'Invitée*, which so far had not made much progress. In it she describes how Françoise, a Beauvoir-figure, living with Pierre, a Sartre-like figure, has an enjoyable affair during a holiday in the mountains with Gerbert, younger than herself and vaguely involved with Xavière, the girl who preoccupies Pierre just as Olga had preoccupied Sartre. In 1984 Beauvoir told her first biographers, Claude Francis and Fernande Gontier, that the incident, the start of a fairly long relationship, happened 'just like that', just as she eventually wrote it down in the novel.

During a peasant-style dinner in a remote country inn Gerbert outlines his views about women, the views of a young man who saw the other sex as possessing more limitations than charm.

' "I don't think I'll ever love any woman," ' said Gerbert.

When Françoise asks why, he tries to explain.

' "I don't know . . ." he hesitated. "You can't do anything with a woman: you can't go for walks, or get drunk, you can't do anything, you can't make jokes and then you have to make a whole lot of fuss over them, you always feel you're in the wrong . . ." ' He explained further, 'with conviction': ' "When I'm with people I like to be just the way I am." '

Françoise hastily makes it clear that she is not this kind of 'traditional' woman, and tells Gerbert not to stand on ceremony with her. He is apparently not aware that she feels sexually attracted to him. He laughs.

' "Oh, you! You're like a man!" he said gently.'

An ambiguous remark, perhaps. Françoise/Beauvoir could be a good friend, and she did not wish to be treated as a fragile being. At the same time Gerbert/Bost was aware of this friend's bisexual nature, he knew how deeply Olga had been attracted to her and how later students had developed 'crushes' on her.

Beauvoir's two characters spend the night in a barn and it is Françoise who eventually finds the courage to invite Gerbert into love-making. It was *tendresse*, affection, not just sensuality, she tells him later, that made her want to be in his arms. He maintains that he also had been trying to make advances to her. It is a moving, unsentimental scene, ironic in its way, but expressing, perhaps truthfully, how Beauvoir entered the world of contingent love. She did not do so casually, as Sartre usually seems to have done, for sex without affection meant nothing to her. Later in life she said that this attitude was typical of her generation; it was due to the way she had been brought up. It was in any case part of her own nature.

Another part of her nature was less orthodox, but an essential element in her relationship with Sartre: her acceptance of 'transparency', their agreement that they should always tell each other everything. Again, she translated her own experience into the story of Françoise. When her heroine returns to Paris early one morning, she finds her regular partner, Pierre, still in bed. She asks him at once if he had received her letter. With a smile he says he was not very surprised by the news of her love-affair. Françoise replies that *she* was surprised by the affection Gerbert felt for her. She felt the same way, and one thing in particular delighted her: ' "Our relationship has become so deep but it's remained light-hearted." ' Pierre decides that both Françoise and Gerbert were lucky, and then she has one final question for him: ' "Do you see anything wrong in it?" '

' "Certainly not," said Pierre.'

If this is 'exactly', or even approximately, as it happened in real life, and if it was normal for Sartre/Pierre to be told about this happy contingent love, transparency was not extended to Olga/Xavière. She was told nothing. Although this incident was not mentioned in the letters from Sartre that Beauvoir published, with some censorship, in 1983, one of his July missives includes what may have been an indirect and reassuring reference to it: 'My love I have your long letter and I love you. Don't worry, there will be as many little *Erlebnis* [emotional experiences] on my side as on yours and they will cling together and we will love each other very much and very passionately.'

After this July filled with *les vicissitudes de la galanterie*, for Beauvoir in the Alps and Sartre in Paris, they met in Marseille and sailed to Morocco for their main summer holiday. In view of the summer heat these weeks cannot have been very comfortable, but the partners preferred their own cheap, independent way of travelling. Beauvoir enjoyed the more obviously touristic aspects of Morocco and remembered for instance the naked tattooed woman who smoked a cigarette skilfully held in her vagina. Years later she was to be deeply upset by the way women were treated in most of Africa, but she was not yet thinking along these lines. On this occasion she was much more distressed by a problem which affected society as a whole. She went in search of the urban 'picturesque', as she usually did, but not for long: 'In Casablanca the European quarter bored us; we sought out the shanty towns which we found only too easily; life there was even more ghastly than in the worst districts of Athens.' What upset her most was the direct cause of the misery: 'It was the work of the French; we passed through these places in haste; we were ashamed.' When she had first broken away from her family in 1929 Beauvoir had looked at the world with Panglossian optimism and had felt certain that the scourge of 'colonialism' would soon disappear. She realized now how wrong she had been, and later the bloodshed of the long, if undeclared, Algerian war, which broke out in 1954, was for her the ultimate tragedy.

1938 was not a year for cheerful summer holidays. In March Hitler had annexed Austria. Sartre was usually an optimist about politics, but even he was worried now. In September Beauvoir set out on another walking tour, again accompanied by Olga, and this time they decided to go to the Basses-Alpes. Beauvoir soon began to wonder if she should have left Paris, mainly because she did not like being separated from Sartre. She reacted like a young girl deprived of her father-figure. 'When I'm with you,' she wrote, 'nothing seems terrible, even leaving you – but when you're far away the slightest fear is unbearable. I love you passionately – I'm empty and miserable without you.' Although at first she had been pleased to see Olga again she soon found her irritating. She wanted Sartre.

He had told her earlier not to change her plans, but in late September, as the two women were on their way to Gap, a letter from him ordered them back to Paris at once. Sartre believed now that Hitler should be resisted. Many French reservists had already been called up. Czechoslovakia was now seriously threatened. Back in Paris, Beauvoir at last began to read the newspapers, a sign of the change within her. She felt *radicalement désemparée*, completely at a loss. A remark by Sartre's stepfather, Joseph Mancy, summed up the way many disillusioned French people felt at the time. He thought they should resign themselves 'to becoming a second-rate nation and to living for several years behind the Maginot line'. The French military chiefs had in fact put most of their faith in this line of fortifications built in the early 1930s along the eastern frontier of France. It was to prove ineffective, mainly because the Belgian government refused to allow its extension northwards along their border with France. However, when the Munich agreement was signed on September 29th between Hitler on one side and the French,

British and Italian leaders on the other, the threat of war seemed to fade. Beauvoir, like most apolitical people in France, 'rejoiced without scruples. I felt I had escaped from death, and for ever.'

Although aware of the change in her attitude towards the outside world she was still ready to postpone her acceptance of all that was happening in Europe. Disaster could not, must not overwhelm her, she thought, it must not interfere with the life she had planned for herself. Was she selfish, self-centred? She was like nine-tenths of her French intellectual contemporaries, convinced that she could do nothing. Later she would feel guilty, but for the time being, she was glad that life seemed to be going to plan, life to be experienced and enjoyed, providing her with 'lots to tell', in personal letters and later in literature.

NINE

I committed myself to literature

During the autumn and winter of 1938–39 Beauvoir felt confident at all levels, despite her suppressed fears about the political situation. She enjoyed her small classes at the lycée, which were more like tutorials, and several students became friends. She was so optimistic about the novel on which she was embarking that she felt she was entering the 'splendour of new worlds'. She no longer felt old, as she had done in Le Havre, expressing her mood by choosing a new set of clothes with particular care. She ordered a fine woollen suit, 'a pleated skirt, black and yellow blouses with which I wore black and yellow cravats. I changed my hair style; I followed fashion and piled my hair up on top of my head.' She went further: she even chose a hat: 'In the spring I bought myself a black boater which I wore with a little veil.' Her memories form a picture far removed from the turbaned and trousered Beauvoir of the 1960s and 70s, who denied angrily that she ever looked smart. But in 1938–39 she felt differently: 'I thought I looked elegant and I was proud of the fact.'

Conscious of herself as a woman, she began to be hopefully conscious of herself also as a working novelist. Unfortunately, like everyone else in France, she could not escape the uneasy atmosphere of the months that followed Munich and she had to admit to herself, with the utmost reluctance, that war was now inevitable. Her fear was almost outstripped by her guilt, for she had recognized at last just how consistently she had played the 'ostrich' – her word – and she was ashamed of herself. The change within her deepened and marked a watershed in her life. 'War could no longer be avoided. But why had we reached this point? I had no right to complain about it, I had not lifted a finger to prevent it. I felt guilty.' She remembered something that Paul Nizan had said: 'Political commitment could not be avoided in any way.' She now agreed with him that 'abstention is in itself an attitude', and accepted the indirect criticism: 'I felt stabs of remorse.' What could she have done? As a potential writer she could presumably have expressed opinions or made emotional appeals, and helped, like Colette Audry, in what is now called the raising of consciousness, which she was to do with unfailing conscientious persistence later in life. But not yet: 'Decidedly,' she felt, 'I was born lucky; misfortune would never overtaken me.'

However, she was moving away from her old attitudes. Earlier the outside world had seemed irrelevant, subsidiary to her own problems. By now she had accepted the existence of other people, she was aware of a different dimension to life, she was on the way to becoming a social being. There had already been a vast change within her when she had deserted her bourgeois background in 1929 but now she needed to escape for a second time, for if she had created a new kind of life for herself she saw that it was not the ideal life. She could say 'I changed', but at the same time she was reluctant about the very change she experienced: 'I obstinately banked on happiness.'

There were two aspects to this longed-for happiness, related to each other in a paradoxical way: there was the personal link with Sartre, which she regarded as indissoluble, and the simultaneous establishment of her own individuality. Without this independence the unique relationship with Sartre could not exist, but how were these two apparent opposites to be reconciled? She convinced herself now that any intellectual and emotional dependence on Sartre was 'immoral', and she must destroy it. But how? The only way she could do so was to take responsibility for some action, one that would affect her alone. She did not see any obvious action she could take in real life. She decided therefore to identify herself closely with the heroine of the novel she was now writing, *L'Invitée*, as it was finally called. She would project herself into the story, invent the necessary action, and as her heroine carried it out she hoped she herself would indirectly solve the personal problem that obsessed her, the problem of her separate, self-controlled existence. It was an ambitious plan: could she succeed? Could literature elucidate life?

So far all her attempts at fiction had failed, especially when she had written about events and attitudes outside her own experience. She seemed to be developing so slowly that her father, who had encouraged her early reading and writing, began to wonder if she would ever become a novelist. 'If she's got something inside her, she must get it out!' he said. She realized she would have to be patient. After all her failures of the last few years she knew that her present concentration on writing was no easy option, it was a challenge. Earlier, life had seemed more important than literature, but now the two were inseparable. She had learnt what most writers learn, if they had not already known it by instinct: 'Literature appears when something in life goes wrong.' The stress of the trio had almost upset the life she had established with Sartre. She had survived this crisis and was forewarned to some extent about the future of their relationship. So it was time to write, seriously; the tension in the outside world changed her, matured her and settled her future; 'History took hold of me, never to let me go; at the same time I committed myself totally to literature.'

Beauvoir was keen to work on her novel but she had no intention of giving up 'life'; 'my enterprise was my life itself, I thought I held it in my own hands. It had to satisfy two demands that in my optimism I did not separate: I wanted to be happy and to own the world.' She wanted everything: why not? She was glad to escape from her lycée work whenever she could and spent the time on active exploration-style holidays. 1938 had ended with further skiing at Megève and during the first quarter of 1939 Beauvoir made three trips into the French provinces, visiting Provence, the Basses-Alpes, Burgundy and the Jura. From there she went to Geneva in order to see the paintings brought there for safety from the Prado in Madrid. She had understood that the Civil War in Spain, now nearly three years old, was in reality a war at one remove between fascism and democracy. By now events in the sphere of politics were no longer distant and other people were no longer members of an alien species, figures in a 'picturesque' landscape. By late spring in 1939 she concluded that she had 'renounced my individualism, my antihumanism. I learnt solidarity'.

But 1939 brought other, less abstract problems, for she had to work out some vital details in the structure of her novel. In essence the story was so close to her own recent life that it was near-autobiography. As she thought about her characters, Beauvoir, despite her wish to achieve independence from Sartre, was ready to consult him professionally. She thought she might oppose to the heroine, i.e. herself, a figure based on the personality of Simone Weil, whom she regarded from a distance with increasing admiration.

This admiration of Weil, who believed in direct, practical action, reflected the change within herself. Weil, who was a year younger than Beauvoir, acting virtually alone, gave her entire self to the support of the poor and underpaid, wherever she encountered them; she even worked alongside them on assembly lines in an attempt to understand their life. She was an activist, Beauvoir was a theorist. Weil possessed political insight: as far back as 1933 she had written a forthright analysis of the origins of Hitlerism and later she attacked the evils of bureaucracy, especially as they had become evident in the U.S.S.R. Beauvoir's intention of opposing two different types of women in her novel might have been valid. Sartre, however, thought nothing of it. He explained to Beauvoir that a Simone Weil figure was unsuitable for this intended protagonist. She was a communicator, she could not present 'a conscience closed in upon itself', which he saw as necessary in the circumstances. What about using Olga instead, so different from Beauvoir herself and her projected heroine? The novelist, ready as ever to be influenced by Sartre, recalled that she was 'convinced on the spot'. However, she took care to explain at this point that she had not originally intended to write a novel which included a version of Olga, she had planned the central theme of her book before the trio was set up. In other words, she had begun to think about the problem of establishing independence long before she wrote *Quand prime le spirituel*.

While working on those stories in Rouen Beauvoir had had to contend with Sartre's difficult behaviour when his 'passion' for Olga led him into a state of confused depression. Now, despite his advice to her about the new book, he did not make the writing of it any easier for her. His behaviour had assumed a recurrent pattern, for he proceeded to complicate their joint loves by falling in love again, despite his continued pursuit of Wanda.

His new love, the third person joining his relationship with le Castor, was the red-haired Jewish girl of Polish origin, 'Louise Védrine', who was already in love with Beauvoir and had been writing her passionate letters. She had become an admiring, adoring friend of both partners. Forty-four years later, in 1983, Beauvoir published thirteen letters written to the girl by Sartre in 1939. She added a brief editorial note to the effect that Louise was 'a friend of mine with whom Sartre began a liaison, quickly ended by the war'. She said nothing about her own relationship with the girl, which had become sexual. Sartre knew these details, for he received the confidences of both his Castor and Louise Védrine, while the three of them often exchanged and passed on each other's letters. Sartre wrote to Louise Védrine as though dedicating his entire life to her, he tried to comfort her because she was convalescent and lonely. He hoped that Beauvoir was going to see her every day, he wished he could be with her.

Beauvoir did in fact go to see her in the nursing home where she was recovering from an operation, but was annoyed on at least one occasion when Louise's mother, who clearly distrusted her daughter's attractive teacher friend, would not leave the two of them alone together. Louise sometimes wrote a note to Sartre and gave it to Beauvoir to forward. Sartre himself was having a tedious time because he had agreed to spend a short holiday with his mother and stepfather in Saint-Sauveur-en-Puisaye, the Burgundy village where the writer Colette had been born. He was so bored, he wrote to Louise, that he thought about her all the time.

As for Beauvoir, she may have thought about Sartre, but she also thought about Bost, so much so that she went to see him in secret. Only Sartre knew that she had gone to Amiens, where their young friend was doing his military service. Olga must not know, Louise must not know. Beauvoir had to establish an alibi, and broadcast the story that she had gone to stay with Madame Morel, hoping desperately that she would not be found out. In the train on the way north to Amiens Beauvoir wrote to Sartre, explaining how she had seen Olga shortly before leaving Paris. Olga 'talked to me at length about Bost but I've no remorse as far as she is concerned, but an impression of underhand futility which will fade when I see Bost but it destroys my pleasure in leaving . . .' Sartre was still the only person she cared for: 'At the moment I would like to see you and only you; everything is so complete, so necessary and so happy with you, *vous autre ma vraie vie* . . .' But she still went to see Bost. She enclosed a letter which Louise had written to Sartre.

He had the task of explaining to Louise why Beauvoir seemed suddenly to have deserted her. '*Mon amour,*' he wrote, 'I really don't know what to say to you about Castor's departure.' Fortunately he was able to produce a plausible excuse on her behalf and he sounded highly convincing: 'I can imagine how empty Paris must seem to her and how impatient she is to see something of the countryside. You know that about the month of June she has a terrible and imperious urge to see something green.' This urge was something that Sartre could not share. 'Personally I don't really understand that but I know it exists. She needs it as much as she needs to eat when she's hungry.' He worked hard to comfort the girl: 'Don't take her behaviour as showing a lack of affection. I know, better than you can know, how much le Castor loves you.' He seemed to envisage the formation of a second triangle: '. . . in any case, our future is your future; there's no difference and le Castor lives in a world where you are everywhere present at the same time.'

He told Louise to be confident and patient, he tried to make up for Beauvoir's absence. Despite his efforts, it looks as though Louise, like Olga before her, still preferred Beauvoir to Sartre. 'And if you're a little sad in your love for Simone, remember,' he wrote hopefully, 'that I love you passionately in the meantime.' In the meantime also he wrote to Beauvoir, saying that he was *tout en idylle* with her.

In Amiens Beauvoir did not see as much of Bost as she had hoped, for the time they had planned to spend together was interrupted by his military duties. However, she made the best of it, as she told Sartre: the long wait for the young man to appear 'has provided excellent circumstances for reading Heidegger[1] whom I've almost finished and understood at least from a superficial point of view.' There was another aspect to this

---

[1] Martin Heidegger (1889–1976) German philosopher, a student of Husserl. He

situation: 'It could be very useful in a novel and even in many ways depending on whether it is developed towards *le passionnel* or left as contingent, just as it was.' She may not have progressed very far with her novel but she was certainly gathering material fast and thinking about technique. She took her manuscript everywhere with her and went on writing whenever she had the chance.

Beauvoir and Sartre were to meet in August for their summer holiday together, but there was one problem: they had no money, they could not afford to go abroad. Sartre had promised Wanda he would take her on holiday but now he hoped to persuade her to stay in Paris, which would be much more economical. 'Only, if she refuses, I'll have to make the trip.' Beauvoir was also told that if the two of them stayed with Madame Morel at Juan-les-Pins that would be economical too. Sartre was trying to carry out his promises to everyone and seemed to feel a little guilty about his Castor. 'As I don't want you to suffer, this is what I suggest: on leaving *cette dame* [Madame Morel], a walking tour for two weeks which will allow us to see again the Causses, l'Aigoual, Cordes, Albi' (in south-western France). After that, taking coaches, they would follow the Pyrenees from Foix to Pau. He seemed anxious to please her: 'Don't be sad, *mon cher petit*, I'll walk as much as you want me to, I'll be easy-going and attentive.'

Beauvoir patiently accepted Sartre's proposed holiday compromise. She expected Sartre to behave like this, it was his nature. She had accepted him 'for better or for worse', and she was presumably satisfied with his 'better' side, which was dedicated to her. She saw nothing 'wrong' in his attitudes or behaviour and in any case she herself was not living a conventional emotional life. She had accepted the young Bost as her lover, although he was the official partner of her close friend Olga, whom she herself had

was concerned all his life with the 'question of being' from the time he published the unfinished *Being and Time* in 1927. Later he applied himself to the study of being as a whole, going beyond the limited question of human 'being'.

He used Husserl's phenomenological method for 'the investigation of the extreme states of mind in which, according to Existentialism, the situation of man in the world is revealed' (Anthony Quinton, *Fontana Dictionary of Modern Thought*, 1977). He denied however that he was an existentialist.

Despite his important contribution to 20th-century thought Heidegger's reputation has been clouded by his apparent adherence for a time to the principles of National Socialism and his failure after World War II to condemn the atrocities of the Hitler regime.

loved sexually in the past. She also accepted sexual advances from Louise Védrine. Should admirers of Beauvoir and Sartre accept their tolerance of each other? Yes, they have no choice. No wonder both partners used the phrase *on ne fait qu'un*: we are one together. No two people ever achieved such unity despite the paradox of what might sound like promiscuous behaviour. 'Contingent' is a much better word, its philosophical context deeply reassuring.

Beauvoir was in her early thirties now, deepening her intellectual background by reading Heidegger, working on her novel when she could, but most of her effort was spent in dedicating herself to the relationship with Sartre, listening to the problems he created for himself and pursuing her own friendships which varied from the *tendresse* of contingent love for Bost to an *amitié particulière* with Louise Védrine. If the Munich agreement had made Beauvoir feel she had 'escaped from death' Sartre's behaviour during 1939 made it an almost impossible year for her. He had given in to Wanda, as he almost always did, and by the end of July he took her to Aigues-Mortes in Provence.

He also took her virginity, and Beauvoir was told the details. He added that he considered the man's role in a 'devirginization' to be ridiculous, and declared that 'I must love her the way I do in order to carry out this sordid task'. He honestly told Beauvoir all the primitive vindictive plans that Wanda had worked out in her 'dragonfly' mind: she tried to make Sartre promise that he would not tell Beauvoir all *she* would tell him about Olga. 'You know I'd told her in the past that I would repeat everything to you,' he said. Sartre was naive about women in some ways but he had noticed something else: 'I have the impression that she had made up her mind gradually to demolish the "friendship" that I have for you.' He added one comment on all this that might have enraged Beauvoir but perhaps reassured her at the same time: 'It's rather amusing.' He also said he was so short of money that he and Wanda lived on fruit and sandwiches and even economized by sharing a bedroom.

Beauvoir was confident enough to accept and even enjoy Sartre's descriptions of his amorous antics, sometimes reminiscent of a bedroom farce. She had been jealous of Simone Jolivet in the early days, curious about Marie Ville, while Olga and

Louise were friends of hers. Wanda seemed to offer more of a threat, but at least Beauvoir believed she could rely on Sartre's earlier statement that he was 'through' with *le passionné*. In any case, while he was with Wanda, she set out again on a walking and climbing expedition, not this time in the Grandes-Alpes, but in the less demanding hills of the Basses-Alpes and the Alpes-Maritimes. She was joined for a time by her friend Stépha's husband, Fernando Gerassi, but unfortunately he proved to be no good at climbing and no better as an aspiring holiday lover: 'He made a few advances to me the first two nights,' Beauvoir informed Sartre, 'but they were very discreet. I hope to be alone again tomorrow . . .'

As the weeks of summer continued to pass the partners remained in close touch by letter. Sartre was looking forward to meeting Beauvoir in Marseille, and he hoped they might even reach Portugal together. He was so anxious to have news of her that he would 'even read avidly descriptions of walks in the beautiful countryside'. While telling her of his intimate moments and quarrels with Wanda he added that he missed her but knew how she would respond: 'Whose fault is that, you'll say? Mine, no doubt, but you're like Paradise Lost. I love you.' He wanted to end with more loving remarks but couldn't: 'Goodbye, delightful Castor, she has just come in and I'm finishing this letter in front of her. You know my feelings but I daren't write them because they could be read upside down.' Sartre was even reduced to going to the post office in secret to collect letters from Beauvoir. Wanda was a tyrant.

He parted from her to join Louise Védrine at La Clusaz in Savoie. Only Beauvoir knew of this last and secret 'vicissitude' of the summer. In later life, when Sartre was asked to talk about his relationships with women he would explain that the beauty of women helped, he thought, to compensate for his own ugliness. He maintained that men were 'comical', he soon ran out of conversation with them. As his letters prove, he could 'love' several women simultaneously and it has been said that his attitude, including the 'transparency' pact with Beauvoir, was not 'normal'. But what was normal about Sartre? He did not relish total sexuality, he thought 'parents are like knives plunged into the heads of children and they cut their thoughts in two'. He hated fresh food; he thought it should be cooked, processed into an artefact. His capacity for work was nothing short of phenomenal, as his future output was to show. He ignored any illness in himself and later lived on stimulating drugs in a way which would have killed any 'normal' person.

And how 'normal' was Beauvoir? She was a unique, individual woman, otherwise she would not have made the original contract with Sartre and remained faithful to it, after her fashion, in the same way as he did. She was no feminist yet, but she was proving herself something of a superwoman, working on her novel through endless interruptions, Sartre's polygamous life, her own bisexual adventures and the depressing atmosphere of the post-Munich year. When younger, both she and Sartre had been fascinated by extremes of human behaviour, they had studied abnormal people because they believed this was one way of understanding human nature and all its potential. Perhaps they found these extremes, even this 'abnormality', in each other.

They went on writing to each other and to Louise. It has been said that both he and Beauvoir were consciously writing letters, even at this stage of their lives, with an eye to future publication. Despite their dislike of 'traditional', 'bourgeois' writing, they had inherited the French tradition, aristocratic as well as bourgeois, which included the production of intimate journals and private letters as a kind of literary genre. To write was to live and letter-writing was like breathing. On August 4th Sartre wrote to Louise ('Ma chère petite flamme'), told her he loved her passionately and described how he had met Beauvoir in Marseille. She was punctual, as usual, wearing 'her little pink and blue dress', and so sunburnt that she was 'a delightful little monster'. He wrote on as though composing another short story, and Louise was included in it. They had talked a lot about Louise: 'At whatever moment of the day you were thinking about us, we were thinking about you, we were talking about you.'

The reunited partners took a room near the old port in Marseille with a splendid view of the sea and there they had 'a vast philosophical conversation in which you [Louise] were very much involved'. He had agreed with her in an earlier letter that they would always tell each other everything, as he and Beauvoir did, and he carried out his own directive. He also described happiness *à deux* the way he and Beauvoir enjoyed it. They went to a café in the evening. 'It was dark, there were no street lamps, a gentle darkness fell from the trees, you could hear people . . . but you couldn't see them. It was cool, it was very poetic and we talked about philosophical truth . . . Then we went to bed, blissfully happy, our heads full of words.'

The next morning they went to a café where Sartre could write this letter and read the newspapers. Beauvoir, he said, only understood fashion magazines, the type of periodical she later denied ever looking at. By chance their friend Paul Nizan and his family, who were on their way to Corsica, arrived at the same café. They all had lunch together and Beauvoir remembered later that Nizan was optimistic about the international situation, maintaining that Germany would soon be subdued. Since he was an active political journalist his audience believed him. Their old friend from student days had published several books by now, fiction and non-fiction, and in 1938 he had won the Prix Interallié. As he disappeared after the lunch party, carrying a rubber boat in the shape of a swan that he had just bought for his children, Beauvoir and Sartre did not know that they would never see their student comrade again.

They had to wait in Marseille for news from Madame Morel for they could not go to her house in Juan-les-Pins until she arrived from a stay in Portugal. Fortunately for them the young Bost appeared on leave from military service. Bost did not enjoy the bullfight they watched at the Marseille bullring, and the French visitors found it a second-rate affair after the corridas they had seen in Spain. Bost's dislike of bullfighting was attributed to his Protestant background.

August brought the last few weeks of holiday. At the Morel villa, 'Sull'Onda', which had a garden and private beach, there were several guests, both family members and friends. Good times alternated with family rows and silences. Sartre remarked to Louise that Beauvoir was surprised and shocked by this example of *la vie de château*, this life of leisure, for it was something she did not really care for. Perhaps she remembered her aversion as a girl to the horrors of bourgeois life; but she herself admitted that she had not yet learned to combine work and holiday. She had however given Sartre some more valuable editorial advice; one chapter of the novel that would eventually be *The Age of Reason* had been found 'boring' but now, after he had worked on it, embodying her suggestions, she found it very good.

For her part, Beauvoir was learning to swim, instructed by Sartre. He thought she was 'terrifying', she took it all so seriously and concentrated so hard. Sartre told Louise all about it and added that Beauvoir's swimsuit was 'very humble compared to the complicated two-piece costumes' worn by other women.

The *vie de château*, which included lunch parties for ten people lasting all afternoon, was clouded not only by the various personal problems of everyone in the house, and the arguments between them, but by the darkening international scene. Beauvoir transferred her feelings of foreboding to the sea: she felt that something was lurking beneath the surface of the water – not an octopus (Sartre had a phobia about them), but some kind of poison. 'This calm, this sunshine were deceptive: suddenly everything would be torn asunder.'

It was the Germano-Soviet non-aggression pact of August 23rd, 1939 which 'tore everything asunder'. Beauvoir had hoped against hope that the peace would hold, guaranteeing her happiness. Now she realized that 'Darkness was falling over the earth, and entering into our bones.' She reacted by admitting that her friend Colette Audry and the Trotskyists had been right: 'Stalin didn't care a damn about the proletariat of Europe.'

It was time to leave 'Sull'Onda' and everyone wondered 'in what circumstances we would meet again'. Beauvoir and Sartre, determined to spend a few days together on their own, went to Carcassonne by train and saw at least some of the places they had planned to visit, although they did not reach Portugal.

It was hard to escape signs of imminent war, reinforced by memories of old conflicts. The train to Carcassonne was crowded with regular soldiers who had been recalled from leave, and though Beauvoir hated the restored medieval fortified *cité*, with its impressive ramparts and fifty-three towers, she was able to escape for a time and drink white wine 'under the arbour at a deserted *guingette*'. Here the tourists talked about 'the war and the post-war', they were at least 'happy to be together as [they] faced up to the disaster'.

Sartre at least was not yet convinced there would be a disaster, and wrote to Louise that he 'really didn't think there would be war'. However, he also talked about the 'post-war', because he had plans: 'Even if there is a war there will be an afterwards, for the three of us.' No wonder he and Beauvoir had talked so much about Louise in Marseille; they definitely seemed to be creating a 'family' trio again. In later life Beauvoir remembered the Rouen trio as 'the work of Sartre', and perhaps he at least hoped that history would repeat itself in a more satisfactory form. The earlier trio had given Beauvoir many problems but she was not against a 'family', provided it was a 'chosen' family, one she had helped to choose from among friends – 'Friends,' as the British writer Hugh Kingsmill once described them, 'God's apology for relations.' The group that seemed to be in formation was not only a chosen family, it was an extended family, and even, in its way, an incestuous one. There would presumably be several sets of partners: Beauvoir and Sartre, Beauvoir and Bost, whom Sartre liked, Beauvoir and Louise, Louise and Sartre. In Rouen, Olga had preferred Beauvoir to Sartre. Louise seemed to feel the same way, unaware perhaps that in Paris yet another girl student, Nathalie Sorokine, was also becoming attached to Beauvoir. Sartre, in his usual optimistic way, tended to simplify the whole situation. For the time being however she accepted what he said, as she usually did.

As the summer of 1939 ended everyone's future hung in the balance, and the two friends saw the war coming literally closer every hour. They reached the picturesque town of Mont-Louis in the Pyrenees, near the Spanish frontier, crowned with a château, haunted by memories of early religious wars and fortified by the famous Vauban in the seventeenth century. Here they were jerked away from history, for the mobilization posters, calling up reservists, began to appear on the walls. Sartre's class was not yet listed, and surely there was no more optimistic man in France than he was. He told Louise in a letter of late August that 'mobilization is not war', and since he had been trained for a metereologist unit he would never be sent to the front line. Nevertheless, prudence prevailed, the friends decided they would return to Paris in a day or two.

First they reached Foix, even more picturesque and historic than Mont-Louis. They rewarded themselves for their decision to return with a large, expensive lunch at the best establishment in the town, the Hostellerie de la Barbacane. During the lunch they discussed the series of novels Sartre was writing and he talked about the fourth and last of them, which never appeared. But what of *her* novel, which would express her independence from this man who seemed perpetually to dominate her? There is no evidence that they discussed *her* work, and in fact it was far from ready for publication or even submission to a publisher. During that year two unusual and very different first works were published, *Au Château d'Argol*, by Julien Gracq, a latter-day surrealist preoccupied with the unconscious, the mysterious and the magical, while the *Tropismes* of Nathalie Sarraute was one of the first hints of the *anti-roman*, even the *nouveau roman*. Beauvoir was not yet in a position to compete, for the complications of 1939 had given her little chance to continue with serious work. She had not made the task any easier for herself, she had set herself a seemingly insuperable problem: 'When one embarks on a large-scale work, written in a rigorous fashion, long before you finish it, you cease to coincide with it.' What professional writer would not agree with her? The change within herself, the threat to life in Europe, and most of all the end of the triangle situation with Olga and Sartre, had each brought difficulties. 'The novel had been conceived and constructed in order to express a past that I was in process of outgrowing.' At this period the woman and the author were two people, not one, and she admitted that she spent 'weeks and months . . . incapable of working'. When she was able to concentrate later she had to resurrect 'the world of the past'. Fortunately, in the end, she succeeded, but in the circumstances she needed every week of the several years she spent on the novel.

By the summer of 1939 the world in which she had begun the book was indeed slipping into the past. The world of the present was gloomy, unreal, uncertain. When, at the end of August, she and Sartre reached the station in Toulouse, the trains were so crowded that they had to let one go and then fight for seats on the next. In Paris everything was closed and all their friends were away. What could they do? They read every edition of the newspapers and went to the cinema. Sartre still felt that if there was a war it would not last longer than a few months, and at the

Café de Flore in Saint-Germain-des-Prés, where Beauvoir had first been taken by Olga, she heard various hopeful discussions about what might happen: 'If the Soviets allow Germany to start a war, it's because they're banking on world revolution.' There was one more possibility: 'If the fascists were liquidated, then maybe socialism could make progress in France and the whole of Europe.' This was the reason why Sartre, who had hated his military service, accepted the fact of his call-up, which even he now saw as inevitable. He continued to reassure Beauvoir that there was no need to worry about him, for he would never be near the front line, but she *did* worry for she did not really believe him. She tried to remain calm, but failed. 'I was frightened. I wasn't frightened for myself, not for a moment did I think of running away from Paris, I was afraid for Sartre.' Her attempts at maintaining fortitude by some intellectual self-control proved useless, her reaction was purely emotional, and no woman who lived through those days anywhere in Europe could fail to identify with her.

On Friday, September 1st, she went to Le Dôme and ordered coffee. The early morning paper had set out Hitler's demands, but did not comment on them. A waiter told her what was happening: ' "They've declared war on Poland." ' This latest and much feared news was in the midday editions. She felt numb. Sartre was mobilized, he had to leave for Nancy and the east the next day. Beauvoir went with him next to the Café de Flore where the clients had not yet come to terms with the drama round about them. Beauvoir decided that she must put all this into writing at once, the novel would have to wait. She began a journal. She noted that in Le Flore at least most 'people remained cheerful. I'm still thinking of nothing but my head aches.' In three lines she evoked the atmosphere of that evening: 'There's a beautiful moon over Saint-Germain-des-Prés, it looks like a country church. And in everything, everywhere, a horror: impossible to foresee, imagine or grasp anything.' Early next morning Beauvoir went with Sartre to the Gare de l'Est, he left for Nancy on the 07.50 train and she walked back to Montparnasse alone.

Sartre had just had time to visit his mother and to write to Louise, whom he had not been able to see as she was away from Paris. 'I'm not too sorry for *le bon* Castor who's totally brave and totally perfect, as ever.' He was heartbroken because *she* was alone at Annecy (near the Swiss border). No doubt he believed temporarily everything he wrote: 'I'll come back to you. I shan't be in any danger, I'm faithful, you know, and you'll find me again . . . Nothing can change us, my love, not you, nor le Castor, nor me. It's a bad moment in our story, but it's not the end of our life. There'll be a peace and an *afterwards*.' He would write to her every day if he could. 'But I wanted you to know that I love you passionately and forever.'

Later that day, in the train, he began to write to Beauvoir, telling her he loved her and needed her, he was thinking of her all day, following her through *her* day. He added that he was going to write to his parents and to Wanda. Beauvoir herself, also thinking of Sartre all day, could not write to him until September 7th, when she at last received his first letter and an address.

TEN

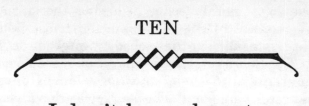

I don't know how to
deal with this war

When Beauvoir wrote the words 'I don't know how to deal with this war' she found it hard to believe that the war was really happening and felt she could not face the reality alone. On that evening of September 2nd she fled her hotel room and spent the night in the Gerassi apartment. Superficially the world had already changed: the streets were dark, the cafés were putting up blackout curtains and the local crêperie had already run out of flour. The next day, Sunday, September 3rd, Beauvoir lunched at Le Dôme with her friend Gégé and her future husband, Pardo. They joined Gerassi, who as a Spanish citizen, was not called up. The two men were betting that there would not be a war, Beauvoir was pessimistic and feared the worst. She was proved right. All peace negotiations had failed. The friends learnt the news at three thirty from the newspaper *Paris-Soir*: Britain had declared war at eleven a.m. that morning when a good part of its population were in church, praying for peace. France, the newspaper announced, would make its declaration at five p.m. that day.

The atmosphere was very different from that of August 3rd, 1914, when many men had volunteered cheerfully to join up, and their wives had optimistically supported them. The words of 'La Marseillaise', *Aux armes, citoyens! Formez vos bataillons!* had little relevance in 1939. Beauvoir saw no optimism whatever; people were in a state of depression and shock. A succession of feeble governments, outbreaks of social unrest, continued economic problems, the growth of fascist-minded parties in France, the long moral decline following the unsatisfactory Treaty of Versailles in 1919, all these factors had led the country downhill into a state of war that nobody wanted except Hitler. In *Le Sursis* (*The Reprieve*), Sartre's novel published in 1945, the second in his series *Les Chemins de la liberté*, one of the characters was to make a relevant point: 'The bourgeoisie don't want war . . . They're frightened of victory, because it will be the victory of the proletariat . . .'

After learning that the war, the unthinkable war, had actually begun, Beauvoir went back to her room in tears and began to tidy up in an obsessive way, finding one of Sartre's pipes and some of his clothes as she did so. Her mood was black: she knew that if Sartre was killed she would not go on living: 'That makes me feel almost calm but in the case of B. [Bost] it's intolerable and mingled with a kind of remorse if I survive him.' Although she became calmer and went to the Café de Flore to write to the young man, she could not stop thinking of him and the danger he might soon be in. That night she slept in the Pardo apartment in the rue d'Assas and next day went to the lycée in Passy to collect her gasmask. In France, as in Britain, everyone was terrified that the Germans might use poison gas in attacks on the civilian population, as the Italians had done in Ethiopia.

Beauvoir's *Journal de Guerre*, most of it published for the first time in 1990, shows her uninterested in the wider problems of the war or in any action connected with it. Her attitude was not new. In 1936, despite her deep sympathy with the Spanish republicans, she had seen no point in going to Spain. She could not now volunteer for any relief work, she could not drive a lorry or nurse the sick even if she had wanted to because it was important for her to earn as much money as she could. She had to support herself and help Sartre support those two idle sisters Olga and Wanda. The odd life-style of the group had run them into debt and Beauvoir had even borrowed money from Louise Védrine's father, who was a dealer in pearls. In any case experienced lycée teachers, including teachers of philosophy, were very much needed now that the men were called up, even if the immediate academic future was obscure. Also, despite everything, she still wanted, more than anything else, to continue and finish her novel, she even thought she might start work at once, 'but not in my room, in a café', for there she would not be alone. Understandably, Beauvoir found it difficult to settle down; she would concentrate on her journal instead, she decided, for in this way she could keep on writing, she could preserve the immediacy of the situation and at the same time occupy part of her day, blunting the edge of her anxiety.

She decided to read another journal, the early diaries of André Gide, which had been published that summer. The entries he had made on the outbreak of war in 1914 expressed a strange contrast with the declaration of September 3rd, 1939. In 1914 he had been confident: 'The wonderful behaviour of the government, of everyone and of all France, as well as of all the neighbouring nations, leaves room for every hope.' Gide's later journals, published in 1945, show that in September 1939 he was no longer hopeful. He was deeply disturbed by the threat to the European cultural heritage: 'Yes, all that might well disappear, that cultural effort which seemed to be so wonderful . . .' A little later, on October 30th, he wrote a sentence that could have applied to Beauvoir and the literary ambitions of her group: 'It is by insisting upon the value of the particular, it is by its force of individualization, that France can best and must oppose the forced unification of Hitlerism.' Gide was seventy when he wrote this, and a prophet in his way. Beauvoir, in choosing to read him at this juncture, was unconsciously living out his principles.

However, if she did not know how to deal with the war, she spent the early years of it trying to deal with her personal life, groping her way, with varied success, through a labyrinth of sexual and emotional relationships which could hardly have been contained within half a dozen novels. The complexities of her situation were not suddenly brought about by the war, they were already in place; the people were already there: Sartre, Bost, Olga, Wanda, Louise Védrine and Nathalie Sorokine occupied her entire life, she would have to direct them like actors on a stage, or, to adapt her earlier phrase about herself, like characters in a novel. She still felt desperately lonely: 'I go to the hairdresser, he styles my hair beautifully, I feel sad as I come out because I've no one I love to show myself to.' Fortunately her most desperate worry was allayed fairly quickly – a letter from Sartre, his first

217

from the war zone, arrived on September 7th and she replied at once: 'What a delight to have your address at last, to feel in touch with you . . . I'm not thinking about the day when I'll find you again, and I never think about the past . . . But I don't need to find you again, I'm not separated from you, I'm always in the same world as you.' She told him she felt calm, but 'without regrets, without desire, without hope . . .' She also told him what she had told her journal: if he died, she would not survive him.

But Sartre was not the only man in her life: 'The only painful thing from time to time is panic about Bost, anxiety for him so violent that I feel almost crazy.' She would go for long walks thinking about him and skip any passages in her current reading that referred to war: 'Atrocious state of mind . . . almost every evening . . . Bost is dead, in the morning he is sometimes alive.' This love may have been contingent, but it obviously meant a great deal to her, for Bost was young and their sexual life together was more straightforward and satisfactory than the complex intellectualized ménage with Sartre. By September 9th she at last had a letter from Bost, who was temporarily in a safe area. She felt that shackles had fallen away, she experienced 'physical liberation, I'm going to live through a whole day without feeling afraid'. She then continued in the same vein that Sartre had followed in his letters to Louise in August: 'All at once I find again if not memories then at least a future: we shall all find each other again, we'll love each other, we'll work, life will have a meaning.'

The next day, September 10th, Sartre received his first letter from her and their daily exchange was established, they were 'talking to each other', she felt cheerful, a new kind of existence had begun. The time passed with Olga in parcelling up books for the two soldiers, painting the windows with dark blue paint in compliance with blackout regulations, and listening to records with friends. 'It's a strange life of leisure that I'm leading,' wrote Beauvoir, 'futile, without much meaning but – it's scandalous – full of charm. I haven't yet realized that it will go on for a long time, I'm not thinking about the future.'

Beauvoir settled down to some extent but she was soon involved in a small-time life compounded of affection, deception and a curious disregard for the war, as though she had returned to that earlier state of mind she thought she had outgrown: she could hardly bear to accept this war because it was an attack on her personal happiness. The war did not bring out in her any kindheartedness towards her family, for when she called on her grandmother in the rue Denfert-Rochereau she remarked only that she was 'really senile'. She was equally offhand about her own mother, who was temporarily in the Limousin, and spoke of a possible visit from her sister as a kind of threat. When she went to see Sartre's mother she noted that the visit was 'tedious'. Perhaps she was irritated by Madame Mancy's comment about Sartre's conscription: 'It will be good for him, it will show him that one can't live the way one wants to.'

When she wrote to Sartre she was already telling him not to mention in his letters to Olga and Wanda anything she had said. She re-read old letters from him, she looked at old photographs, shed a few tears and told Sartre more about her feelings for Bost, especially after she had had a discussion with Olga about the young man. 'I asked [Olga] what she would do if he died; she said that she had immediately wondered about this, it would be a great misfortune but not a disaster because their relationship was very pleasant but there was nothing essential in it for her.' Beauvoir's reaction to this made her sound like a scheming, predatory woman: 'That pleased me; moreover I've no remorse as far as she's concerned and I'm more and more determined, if he comes back, not to sacrifice him to her.' It looks as though the earlier resolution of the trio situation had been more apparent than real, it had done little more than end Sartre's 'passion' for Olga and then created a new variation on the same theme: a trio consisting of Beauvoir, Olga and Bost. Beauvoir passed on to Sartre her disapproval of Olga's attitude: she did not seem to care for Bost; even in tragic and touching matters, she thought, 'there's a deep frivolity within her'. But she still enjoyed Olga's cooking; macaroni one evening, rice the next. It did not occur to Beauvoir at this stage of the war to cook for other people or even for herself.

Nobody, nothing in Paris could give her the happiness brought by Sartre's letters, expressing all that she meant to him: 'For me,' he wrote, 'you are more solid than Paris, which can be destroyed, more solid than anything, you are the whole of my life that I shall find again on my return. I love you passionately.' Presumably, despite the correspondence he was conducting with Wanda and

Louise, he meant it, after his fashion. Sartre could write endless letters to an infinite number of women, because he had little to do at his army post, he could work on the novel he was writing and now began a journal, following Beauvoir's example. She had no chance to be idle. She was kept busy by Sartre's constant requests: could she try to see Marie Ville, who was in Paris, could she somehow bring Wanda to the capital, her letters from L'Aigle sounded so depressed. He wanted detailed accounts of everything Beauvoir did, everything she heard, could she send paper, ink, envelopes, books. She had all the responsibilities, he had few. When he asked about her work he seemed to enquire only *en passant*: 'I'm sorry the Café de Flore is closed . . . Are you going to write your novel?' She was not writing her novel, she was far too restless. Her lycée work was more or less arranged, but since the term did not start until mid-October she decided to visit friends while she still had the chance. She stayed with Simone Jolivet and Charles Dullin at their house near Crécy to the south-east of the city, then she accepted a pressing invitation from Louise Védrine to visit her in Quimper, Brittany, where she was staying with her mother.

The girl was waiting for her at the station, 'slim, graceful and *farouche*'. She was also tearful. Beauvoir had to stay in a small hotel, for Madame Védrine was still hostile towards her and was given to creating hysterical scenes. She maintained that her daughter had received from Beauvoir a love-letter which she intended to show to the Ministry of Education to cause trouble. Beauvoir told Sartre that her letters had been 'passionate' but not 'compromising'. The fact that she owed money to Védrine's father did not make the situation any easier, for she couldn't pay it back. She felt sorry for Védrine, but could not offer her any love. 'We go upstairs to my room. Embraces. But I no longer have any feelings of sensuality. Nor dreams, nor desires, it's also a kind of inhibition.' In fact she had a dream in which she and Védrine quarrelled violently over how they would 'share' Sartre when he came on leave. The dream was a warning, for the next day Védrine actually suggested that they should each see him for three days out of the six he would be allowed. Beauvoir told this much-desired man that she had 'trembled . . . with anger'. She had been disappointed in Védrine – she had hoped to find something more 'solid'. Instead she had found 'a very little girl, slightly distraught, too pathetic and disorganized . . .' She found that she herself was not in a mood for 'sentimentality', and only Sartre gave her any real satisfaction. Without him she felt 'hollow' and 'hungry'. At the same time she reassured him that Védrine still loved him and was hoping that the war would end his romance with Wanda.

If her entanglements with young women do not reveal Beauvoir the feminist they show her in formation, for during this brief stay she realized how far her young friend suffered from her dominating mother. Madame Védrine exhausted Louise so much she would cry and that in turn depressed Beauvoir. However, she realized how fortunate she was herself: 'I'm wonderfully lucky to have money and depend on no one; it can cause tragedy and horror, but I never feel depressed like Védrine or Kos. [Olga] because I feel free, I can dispose of my life and if necessary my death and I need not account to anyone except myself . . .' She hoped that Louise's father would arrange for her to live in Rennes on her own for if she stayed any longer with her mother she would go crazy. She realized too that she would have to have her in Paris occasionally, but felt 'detached' from her.

After these few days of drama Beauvoir spent a little time touring in Brittany on her own and despite her earlier promises to herself she sank into nostalgia whenever a place reminded her of Sartre: they had visited Brittany together in 1932. At Douarnenez she began to cry, remembering how they had discussed 'evolutionism and mechanism and animals' and how they had woken up cheerfully every morning in their twin beds. She needed Sartre and his tenderness very badly on September 25th, and she was full of remorse: 'I never told you enough how much I loved you, I've never been nice enough to you . . .' She spent a few happy days with Madame Morel at La Pouèze where she could rest, read and enjoy good food and wine. She was pleased to accept all this because she now had no money left at all. She then came back to Paris, accepted extra work at two other lycées and began to think out how she could defeat wartime regulations and arrange to visit Sartre at his military post. For the first time she realized that her independent life-style brought some disadvantages, for her migrant existence in and out of the

Montparnasse hotels made it difficult for her to obtain a certificate of residence, without which she could not be given a travel permit allowing her to go anywhere near the war front. Also, if she had been married to Soldat Sartre it might have been easier to invent some excuse for visiting him. She desperately needed to see him, for even if she dismissed his contingent loves as irrelevant to the relationship, daily letters could not replace physical *presence* and the all-important live discussion of each other's thinking, reading and writing. In the end, after bribing a concierge and going to two police stations, Beauvoir succeeded in complying with the regulations. She invented 'a sister with a bone complaint whom I was going to visit in Marmoutiers', not too far from Sartre's army post. It looked as though she would be able to travel east after all and the partners invented a coded language in order to discuss their plans and defeat the postal censorship.

October 1939 was a busy month. The lycée term began, ensuring Beauvoir's income for the time being. She left the Hôtel Mistral in the rue Cels for the Hôtel du Danemark in the rue Vavin, not far from the Luxembourg Gardens. According to Sartre October 10th was their tenth 'wedding' anniversary – their sexual relationship dated from 1929 – and he sent his partner a 'symbolic' flower petal, since he could not send a bouquet. She said the date was the 14th, but they did not argue about it. He overwhelmed her with heartfelt expressions of love, regretting especially that this was the first time they had not been together for a celebration: 'My dear love, you've given me ten years of happiness . . . I renew the contract at once for ten years . . . you are the most perfect, the most intelligent, the best and the most passionate.' She, writing on the 10th, was for once brief: 'You have made me such a beautiful life, my love, I owe you everything I have, everything I am.' Unfortunately, owing to postal delays, he had to wait for her letter. On the vital day – the 10th, as he saw it – he had no message from her and he wrote that it was a 'sad anniversary'.

In the meantime Beauvoir's entanglements with women friends continued. The Russian girl Nathalie Sorokine returned from the Pyrenees where she had been looking after children and was determined to get closer still to the teacher on whom she had developed a 'crush'. Beauvoir said later that 'My heart was empty and solitude weighed heavily upon me.' If her letters and her journal show that she was not solitary for more than an hour or so at a time in the hectic, unbroken round of Montparnasse life, she needed, apart from Sartre, some friendship which included a deeply emotional element, the kind of relationship she had experienced with Zaza at the Cours Désir and later, on a sexual level, with the young Olga in Rouen. The intense and unhappy Louise Védrine could not satisfy this need, although she would have liked nothing better. As a result, Beauvoir said later, 'I offered only feeble resistance to the efforts that [Nathalie] ['Lise' in the later memoirs] made to infiltrate my life.' This girl, an unwilling student of chemistry, lived in Paris with her parents who had come from the U.S.S.R. and were stateless persons. If Beauvoir had sensed violence in the past beneath Olga's quiet exterior she had no need to search for it in Nathalie; it was obvious in everything she said and did. At the age of fourteen she and a friend had already become experienced shoplifters, concentrating on the Uniprix section of the well known Printemps store for their 'work'. Nathalie stole knitting wool and sold it to her mother at half price, she also stole handfuls of pens and sold them to her classmates at school. One day she was arrested and her parents had been accused of complicity in the thefts. Eventually however the girl was released.

She was something of a mythomaniac, telling Beauvoir that her parents were very poor, persistently quarrelsome and given to beating her. Later she confessed that they did not ill-treat her. She worked hard to win Beauvoir's interest, waiting for her as she left her hotel in the morning for the lycée, waiting for her when her lessons were over, refusing to leave her room at night, sleeping on the doormat. She asked for lessons in philosophy, which she received, and regularly gave Beauvoir little gifts: chocolate, or a photograph album. She was jealous of Beauvoir's women friends and particularly jealous of Sartre. She had not yet met him but hated his image and hoped he would be killed, for she was convinced that Beauvoir only noticed her because *he* was not there. Later in life Nathalie wrote and had some short stories published but for the time being she was even jealous and dismissive of her older friend's work on her novel. ' "And that's why you refuse to see me," she told me with indignation, "to tell stories which haven't yet happened!" ' If Beauvoir grew angry with her the girl would begin to cry and then the teacher would give in to that near-motherly instinct which formed such a strong part of her character: 'The need she had of me touched me.'

Nathalie's need did not stop at schoolgirl admiration; she wanted something more. She had made sexual advances to Beauvoir the previous summer, and now continued in September and October: 'She drew me on to the bed, then with sobs, into her arms and against her mouth and after an hour she even directed my hand towards precise parts of her body . . .' She uttered endearments in Russian, and, wrote Beauvoir to Sartre, 'there's no escape, here I am, involved *dans une histoire*, and as she's very demanding and authoritarian I'm rather upset about it'. Beauvoir had not chosen to reject these advances, and she also began to make comparisons: 'She loves me at least as much as Védrine has ever loved me.' However, Nathalie did not receive much encouragement for the time being: 'As for me, naturally, I remained like a block of wood, by the end of the war I shall be a sexless being.' Which was far from the case.

Beauvoir admitted to Sartre that 'if Védrine did not exist I would certainly give [Nathalie] her place. In any case I shall see her a little this year and we'll see, but I'm a little anxious.' She could foresee more and deeper entanglements but if she wanted to escape she apparently did not know how to go about it. Nathalie hated Louise, which did not make life any easier for anyone, and was particularly jealous of Olga, to whom Beauvoir gave a good deal of her time. All these young women needed her dramatic individuality, her blend of aloofness, stability and controlling intelligence, for this was the figure she presented to her admirers. Sartre was probably the only person ever allowed to see any sign of anxiety or uncertainty within her. If she felt protective towards the small group she called her *charmante vermine*, she could also be highly critical of them at the same time, but, again, only when writing to Sartre: 'When I see all these failures, and all these likeable, weak little people like Védrine, Kos., etc., I find it pleasant to think how strong we are, you and I.' This complacent attitude reflects one of the many paradoxes in her character. She was proud of the way she and Sartre conducted themselves: 'I find that so far it's a success for our morality and our way of living.'

She was also ready to make Sartre responsible for everything: 'My love, you have succeeded not only in our relationship but truly in your life, your morality, and indirectly my life also . . .'

As soon as he heard more details about Nathalie, in early December, Sartre was pleased that someone new had entered Beauvoir's life: 'I'm glad you're becoming fond of Sorokine, she's a little companion for you and from your letters she seems quite delightful.' This impression of her was proved later to be optimistic. However, Nathalie was soon a member of the Beauvoir 'family' and met Wanda, of whom she was not jealous. The two girls shared at least part of a Russian background. Wanda found Nathalie good fun in some ways, but exhausting, for she asked so many questions. The girl's abrupt, violent manner upset Wanda: 'All these questions pierced me like so many dagger-thrusts,' she told Sartre. Everything Nathalie did showed her extremism, another element within her likely to appeal to Beauvoir.

When the girl began to occupy a more important place in her friend's life Sartre, who was told everything, never missed an opportunity to tease Beauvoir about her: 'So you're rather in love with your little Sorokine, *mon amour*?' He seemed to think he must offer some advice: 'But you mustn't drop her, at least? What's going on? What a lot of stories and love-affairs you have, *petit tout-charme*!'

In fact Beauvoir quickly forgot her depression of early September, and by mid-October she had learnt how to make the best of things. 'Le Dôme is still lively and amusing,' she told her journal, 'with something black and heavy which is caused by relations between France and overseas countries.' Was she thinking about the war, the non-war? There were few signs that she ever did. 'This morning there were lots of familiar faces. I'm remarkably glad to be in Paris. If it were only a question of a short-term separation between you and me,' she told Sartre, 'I should be leading a most satisfactory life.' As it was, she enjoyed herself. With Marie Ville, *la femme lunaire*, she went to a bottle party held by Youki, ex-wife of the Japanese painter Foujita and a painter herself, now married to the poet Robert Desnos. The two women entered 'a smoke-laden room, full of people and glasses of red wine and paintings by Foujita'. Beauvoir was fascinated by this group of cynical guests, their sexual games and their obscene language, but most of all by the confidences passed on to her by Marie Ville. These she hastened in turn to pass on to Sartre.

La lunaire had liked her, she confided, ever since the early days in Berlin, 'in one sense *against* someone,' Beauvoir added, 'this someone being you. She holds a big grudge against you . . .' Sartre had caused her a lot of trouble, she said, and she had never felt any passion for him. She was critical of Sartre, he overestimated people, the young woman thought, and that led them, Wanda, for example, to overestimate themselves. He even overestimated *her*, said Marie Ville. Then came a telling remark: 'I am the only one,' wrote Beauvoir, 'whom you don't overestimate and on the contrary you admit my perfection too coldly; she will have a word with you about it.' Beauvoir must have relished every word of this conversation, to which she added no comment of her own. Wanda, thought *la lunaire*, was a naive girl who believed everything Sartre told her. At four a.m. Marie, plus an unnamed blond male admirer, went back to Beauvoir's hotel room and sat on the bed drinking and talking about Sartre, Wanda and *la lunaire* herself. The self-invited guests left at seven and Beauvoir slept until noon. The war had not made much difference to the life of Montparnasse.

Beauvoir had been allocated extra teaching work and did not see how she would have time to work on her novel. But there was always time to write to Sartre. She re-read what she called his 'philosophical letter' which he had written on October 11th about consciousness. 'You're a fine philosopher, *mon bon petit*, you must begin to construct a system since you've got the time.' She could have been envious, she could have been ironic.

By late October Beauvoir at last obtained her permit to travel east to see Sartre and then proceeded with the rest of her plan. On October 30th she borrowed a pair of blue pyjamas from Olga, got into bed, feeling perfectly well, and called a doctor. He thought she might be suffering from muscular strain, opined that her cold feet were caused by indigestion, feared possible appendicitis but decided against it. Finally he gave her a certificate releasing her from school work for a week. She then sent Sartre a coded telegram saying that she was on her way and set out on a slow and complex journey. However, the experienced Beauvoir was never deterred by uncomfortable travel. She reached Brumath after midnight on October 31st and with the help of an army patrol found an icy cold room in an *auberge* called La Ville de Paris. She set out next morning to find Sartre and she met him by accident, walking down the street. He had not received her telegram. He had grown a 'horrible stubbly beard' which she hated. Despite the problems of accommodation the couple were able to spend a little time together. Sartre had accidentally referred to her as his wife, although all the local people knew he was not married. Beauvoir became his 'fiancée', ostensibly trying to locate a cousin whom he was supposed to be finding for her: probably no one believed the story. Sartre had shaved his beard at once.

Their time together during these precious few days was mainly spent discussing each other's writing and in particular the complexities of Beauvoir's emotional life. If Sartre had any such problems, they were presumably less urgent, and in any case there was nothing to be done about them for the time being. While he was on duty she read a hundred pages of his novel, eventually *L'Age de raison*. 'It was the first time I had read such a long passage and I found it excellent.' Her reaction was not merely personal, it was professional, as it had always been from the time when she had seen his first imitative stories ten years earlier. 'I noted a few criticisms, especially concerning the nature of Marcelle,' the heroine of the novel thought by some biographers and critics to be modelled in part on Beauvoir herself. She also read the *Carnets* or war notebooks that Sartre had begun to write. They were much more than a day-to-day account of his so-called military life and the novelty, for him, of living with a group of men. He was setting down in detail, his ideas, his theories, his earlier life and his reactions to other people. That entailed writing about Olga, whom he called 'O'., and also about Beauvoir herself. Naturally she was intrigued, especially when she learnt that he was writing the notebooks 'for her', and that he did not intend them to be published during his lifetime: they were for posterity.

She was also shown other intriguing documents, although they were not for posterity. These were the letters he had received from Wanda and from Louise Védrine. Wanda's letters, Beauvoir found, had 'much charm'. The partners talked about the two girls and were both 'rather surprised to find how much Védrine has lost in our esteem and affection'. The girl's future life with her two older friends was probably doomed. Then came a reassurance from Sartre about one of Beauvoir's own problems: 'I tell him that I often see in her a caricature of myself and he assures me this is not the case at all.'

Everything that Sartre said reassured her – as she had hoped – but the results were surprising: 'The serenity that Sartre gives me has only strengthened my desire to see Bost, but without any *passionnel*, placing it all much more on the level of friendship than of love.' Presumably she saw the three of them as a family, part of *her* 'chosen' family. However, Sartre had to help Beauvoir further with her problems vis-à-vis Bost. 'Sartre explained to me again how in a way I want my relationship with him to be as it is, how Kos. [Olga] is necessary for its equilibrium; Bost is not *mine* because I am not *his*.' Beauvoir tried to pretend she was not jealous of Olga: she did not tell Sartre in Brumath how she found one thing 'very disagreeable': 'He writes longer letters to Kos. than he does to me.' Perhaps he did not write every day. Also, Bost, she assumed, would be spending his leave with the same Kos. and not with her. She went to great lengths to avoid sounding like any jealous woman – she thought of former colleagues in a similar situation: 'Those passionate intellectual women who pretend they are choosing the sufferings they undergo, who think themselves superior only when they have reached the end of their tether.' She reckoned she had changed emotionally as in other ways: 'The fact is that it's new for me, this inner psychological life; earlier I had above all a moral attitude, I tried to believe that I was as I wanted to be.' She felt she was now more realistic about herself.

The developments this year in her feelings for Bost had led her into a new attitude: 'It amuses me like a new area; it would not amuse me to write about it because it's too facile', but she was ready now to discover and understand something which she considered to be new: 'It's a step towards a knowledge of myself which is beginning to interest me. I feel that I am becoming something well defined: in this I'm aware of my age, I shall soon be thirty-two, I feel I'm a complete woman, I'd like to know what sort of a woman.' There was one crucial aspect of herself that she wanted to discuss with the person who knew her better than anyone else did. 'Yesterday evening I talked with Sartre for a long time about a point within myself which interests me in fact, it's my "femininity", the way in which I am of my sex and not of it.' Her bisexual nature was confusing to her. When she adapted this passage for publication in her 1960 memoirs she wrote: 'In what way am I a woman and to what extent am I not one?' The original and edited versions of the journal do not differ greatly, but the edited version appeared well after *The Second Sex* was published. It seems evident that this major study grew from her personal sexual problems, for she had to come to terms with her own elusive nature. 'This should be defined and also in general what I ask of my life and my thought, and how I situate myself in the world.' She showed Sartre what she had written in her journal so far and he gave her the same advice as he had given several years earlier when he had read her first short stories: 'He tells me that I should develop further what I say about myself.' But she could not do so for the time being, and she envied Sartre, the soldier who was living a part-time war: 'Great intellectual emulation: I too should like to have the time to think more about myself . . .'

Why did Sartre repeat his earlier advice: write about yourself, look at yourself more closely? He too, like most writers, wrote about himself, but indirectly, and not exclusively. He may well have sensed from Beauvoir's earliest writing that her strength and her future lay in the analysis of her own feelings and experiences; he was proved right, for she wrote so intensely and so intimately about herself that readers could identify with her, even if they came from vastly different milieux and cultures. So far, he could see, she had not been much interested in the world about her and the political life that was beginning to preoccupy him. She had had difficulty in making contact with other people, but no difficulty whatever in writing about herself. Sartre may also have seen other reasons for encouraging this dissection of a woman's inner life: he himself wanted to know as much as possible about his partner, and since the 'race' of women fascinated both the macho and the intellectual elements in himself, he was perhaps constantly hoping for more illumination. He at least thought he found the 'eternal feminine' boring, but all his life women intrigued him. His advice to Beauvoir in 1939, in conjunction with her own complex emotional and sexual life, was crucial, even if it was not implemented at once. She told him that before she started on any such self-examination she was determined to finish her novel first.

Beauvoir's stay in Brumath lasted from November 1st to the 5th. Writing in his *Carnets* the following month Sartre compared her arrival there to 'a time-bomb, dislocating my calm a few days after her departure'. She travelled back overnight, took a taxi from the station to the lycée, where she arrived at 8.30, taught for two hours and slept through a meeting called by the headmistress about providing help for evacuees. In a sense she was glad to be back at the Hôtel du Danemark, for she felt as happy as she had felt in peace time. She was delighted to feel she was 'home', in the kind of environment which spelt home to her: 'I'm glad I shall be seeing Kos. again, it amuses me to think that the two Kos. [Olga and Wanda] are there, at the hotel, that makes me as it were *un petit foyer.*' She came back also to all her 'family' responsibilities, for she was in charge of expenses. She had taken money to Brumath to give to Sartre, but, he wrote, 'we loved each other so much that I forgot to take it'. So she had to send it, and Sartre called her his *'petit chef du budget'*, his little treasurer. Her work was made more complicated by the fact that neither she nor Sartre had a bank account at the time and they were always in debt, especially since they had generously assumed responsibility for *le petit foyer*, and Beauvoir did her best to help the troublesome but appealing Nathalie.

This poor girl was now in serious difficulties because her parents had begun to treat her badly and regarded her as a parasite. Beauvoir could not give her as much time and attention as she wanted – she always wanted too much of everything – because Louise Védrine was coming to stay for a few days. When Louise arrived from Brittany Beauvoir came out of the lycée to see both girls waiting for her, Nathalie hiding by a pillar. Beauvoir told Louise she had an appointment, they would meet later. She took Nathalie to lunch and later felt tense, knowing that she would soon have to abandon herself 'to the frenzied hands of Védrine'. This girl was jealous because Beauvoir announced that she would be seeing Olga for an hour or so every day. Later in the evening they dressed with care – Beauvoir wore a mauve blouse and a mauve turban – and spent the evening at Agnès Capri's cabaret. Louise was then smuggled into Beauvoir's hotel room and there followed a 'passionate night; the strength of passion in this girl is amazing. From a sensual point of view', Beauvoir told Sartre, 'I was more involved than usual with the vague and crude idea. I think that I had to "take advantage" at least of this body – there was a hint of perversity, which I don't much like, and I think it was simply the absence of affection: it was the awareness of finding sensual pleasure without affection, which in fact has never happened to me.' In her journal she added that it *had* happened once in a vague drunken way with Gerassi.

In a sense Louise existed on the fringe of the Beauvoir family. She had escaped her own family and was living in Rennes, although her life was boring and lonely. Beauvoir told her that 'she must live out our absence in its authenticity, that is to say live in a world orientated towards us and the places where we are, and not achieve false presences'. Writing short letters was no good: 'Instead of passing more time in creating real contact through letters, she prefers to meditate in the void and tremble and cry.' Beauvoir was convinced that her daily letters, with their incessant detail, kept her in touch with Sartre and all her correspondents; it was the only way to create a real presence. Beauvoir tried to make her friend see herself as the centre of her world, she must be a person, she must not live as though attached to Sartre and herself. Whenever Louise promised that she would try to improve, Beauvoir was touched, and had moments of admiration for the attractive girl who dressed so well. Olga, in fact, had dismissed her as '*une élégante*', and of no importance. Olga was never far away from Beauvoir, and one evening during Louise's stay in Paris Beauvoir remembered past happiness and contrasted it with the present situation: Olga assumed 'the attraction of forbidden fruit and it's Védrine who seems to be the old mistress, with her demands, her rights and her implacable presence'. She recorded this reaction after a night when the air-raid sirens had woken everyone in the hotel: but since Louise's presence there had to remain secret, they had decided they would stay in bed, and fortunately no one knocked on the door.

Olga did not possess Beauvoir's talent for keeping in touch with her friends through long, regular, detailed letters, and as a result she had lost contact with Bost, not for the first time: 'He complains,' wrote Beauvoir in her journal, 'that her letters are cold (that amuses me, for I think part of his complaint is due to the comparison with my letters).' Olga did not think about Bost all the time and wondered who could keep up a relationship with someone who could only be seen ten days every four months. Beauvoir knew that the young man's reproaches had upset Olga 'but that pleases me'. Not content with Sartre in her life, Beauvoir wanted Bost too; she was emotionally grasping. Although fond of the girl, she dismissed Olga's affection for him: 'I think he is safer with me than with her, I know how to love him better than she does . . .'

Beauvoir went on thinking about the situation and explained to her journal (and to her later readers) why she never stopped writing, even if her letters were often so repetitive, so flat. They kept her close to Sartre every minute of the day: 'I feel particularly happy because I feel truly I'm in the same life, the same world as Sartre; it's not a question of memory nor of waiting. I'm in the same world in the present and distance is not a separation.'

Somewhere, behind all the letters from *Votre charmant Castor* to her *Cher petit être*, the preoccupation with writing a novel and the endless café talk, with reading those amusing macho missives from Soldat Sartre, was the war. But where was that war? The British suffered naval losses, but little else happened. The French were short of armour and their air defences were weak. Sartre, who was grateful that the war gave him time to think and write, composed a literary, intellectual forecast, recorded by Beauvoir in her journal. He believed that this conflict would be 'a modern war, without any massacre, just as modern painting has no subject, music no melody and physics no matter'. His aphoristic pronouncement was neat, but was soon proved wrong. Late in November a subsidiary war broke out, and it was to last nearly four months: the U.S.S.R., in search of military bases and territory, invaded Finland and eventually acquired 16,000 square miles of land. (As a result, in 1941, the Finns joined the German attack on the U.S.S.R., hoping to win back what they had lost.) To the gossiping habitués of Montparnasse cafés that war was even further away than the Maginot Line. Beauvoir still showed little interest in the war, regarding it only as something that took Sartre and Bost away from her.

The war had given her more than enough to do, from earning as much money as she could to help support the 'family' to acting as wife and mother to Soldat Sartre. The lycée term would not end until mid-December. Beauvoir had escaped a possible move to Bordeaux with her students but had to renounce a possible second visit to Sartre, who had been transferred temporarily to Morsbronn-les-Bains, not too far from his previous post. The trip to Brumath had left her in a happy and constructive state of mind, she worked on her novel whenever she could escape from the young women she cared for but didn't care for enough. She felt she had endless responsibilities towards them: *Que de femmes sur mes pauvres bras!* exclaimed Beauvoir. She had obviously made difficulties for herself in accepting Louise Védrine's 'passionate' love and Nathalie's naive but determined advances. She was fascinated by her own attractiveness to girls and young women, all of which she reported to Sartre: one girl had said a few years earlier that she 'loved her as passionately as if she were a man', and she often received admiring letters. She remarked to Sartre, with cynical irony, that if this sort of thing went on, then by the time she was sixty girls would be committing suicide in the classroom.

At this period of her life Beauvoir was an immensely feminine woman, taking great delight in her clothes, her turquoise shantung blouse, her purple silk umbrella, her coral and gold ear-rings given to her by her sister, her turbans, her new coat — the list is endless and a reminder that Frenchwomen had not yet suffered any restrictions in what they could wear. She noted also anything new or attractive worn by her friends, Louise Védrine's fur muff or Nathalie's tartan hair-ribbon.

Her wish to know more about herself made her almost narcissistic. She became curious about the effect she had on other people: 'I've started an enquiry about how men see my physique: for usually only women find me pretty.' Jean Kanapa and another young man, previously students of Sartre, were asked for their opinions. One found her *'bien, mais pas dans le joli,'* while another found her *'jolie et même assez belle'*. The young actor Mouloudji was also asked his opinion and gave it in some detail: at first he had found her 'hard and abrupt, a woman who wasted no time, while Poupette seemed to resemble a housewife, which he found more reassuring, and then the other day at La Rotonde he saw that I was interested in the wine I was drinking and that I tell stories well – according to him I looked interesting rather than pretty.' She noted all this carefully. Mouloudji remained on the fringes of the Beauvoir family and several years later, when he had become well known as a writer, he included her in one of his novels.

In the meantime Beauvoir was also ready for any kind of distraction and entertainment. There was no shortage of entertainment either. Prices of seats at the opera had been reduced and evening dress was no longer obligatory, so Beauvoir and her friends, dressed in their informal best, were able to hear Gluck's *Alceste*, and Berlioz's *La Damnation de Faust*. They also went to the cinema where they enjoyed second-rate American movies, with the exception of one starring Shirley Temple, whom Beauvoir described scathingly as *une authentique petite ordure*.

Apart from teaching philosophy and writing fiction, Beauvoir could also have conducted the *courrier du coeur* in a woman's magazine or become the equivalent of a marriage guidance counsellor. Affairs of the heart preoccupied her deeply. She told Sartre she loved him more than ever, 'you are my daily bread, my little sunshine', and she consoled herself by wearing one of his white shirts. In her intensely feminine mood of late 1939 she was also prepared to use those old-fashioned feminine wiles whenever she thought it necessary. She was so preoccupied with Sartre's fascination for Wanda that she carried out a 'charm offensive' in the hope of coming a little closer to her. She found the girl attractive, with her fair hair combed flat, with 'a black pullover which revealed her neck, a light complexion, a young, heavy, slightly pathetic look'. She was interested 'in particular to discover what could please you in her. . . I've told you already, I'm not jealous of your feelings for people; but it's not only the subject of a novel, I'm jealous of their feelings for you. Wanda doesn't worry me because in her little consciousness you're such a strange being, so different from the one I love . . .' Louise Védrine on the other hand annoyed her because she thought about her love for Sartre as something too significant. Since Beauvoir knew that Sartre, like herself, was considering how he could end his relationship with this girl, she gave him advice, he must reduce 'slowly the passion' in his letters. It would all be difficult, but not tragic. Louise would live through 'many pathetic and horrible crises', but Sartre would have to take the final decision himself: 'It's your choice.'

So much for Beauvoir's preoccupations at the end of 1939. She maintained a love-hate relationship with Louise and reported to Sartre all her observations and complaints. When Louise wore 'her cossack hat, a blouse with a tie, she would look like a charming little boy if she didn't wear so much make-up'. Beauvoir still accepted her love-making and if she did not enjoy sex without tenderness she must have concealed her feelings well because Louise became 'ecstatic' about her affection. Unfortunately this passionate girl was clumsy, which led Beauvoir to speculate about women as lovers: 'Beneath her destructive hand I'm astonished at the awkwardness of women in acts where men are expert.' She tried to explain this: 'Is it because like the man in Gide's *Journal* they put themselves in your place, but it's their own self they put there, whereas a man is incapable of this substitution of the person and tries to give you pleasure as you are?' And in any case Louise snored.

It was obvious that this girl could not expect much future with Beauvoir and Sartre. Nathalie Sorokine on the other hand had shown herself to be much more understanding, even if Beauvoir found their sessions of 'ardent kisses and philosophy' exhausting. She was warming to Nathalie, who was generous, always bringing small presents, and showed an unexpected talent for caricature. Perhaps her very naiveté appealed to Beauvoir: 'She has brought *Le Mur* [Sartre's collection of stories] for me to explain the obscenities and I begin a whole course of obscene physiology but a man nearby has his eye on us and we go to my room. Kisses, but chaste – I would rather like *une passion avec elle* . . . *une histoire avec elle* because she charms me utterly.'

If all these confidences reveal the feminine Beauvoir, where was the feminist? On the whole hard to find, although she was all the time observing and appraising women, ready to teach them as well as to love them. She had noted with regret that some of her former students were doing poorly paid menial jobs and on visiting her old friend Colette Audry, now married, she found that she had become much more *une femme d'intérieur*. The only feminist in her immediate entourage was her sister Hélène, who has always maintained she was the first in the family to assume the role. If Simone for instance had avoided domesticity with ease Hélène had to make a more difficult decision, for her partner Lionel de Roulet suffered from ill-health. He had spent September with Hélène in the Limousin and 'she looked after him with devotion . . . and Lionel began to expose a theory to her, he believed there are two women within her: an affectionate, devoted woman made for marriage and maternity – and a strong artificially constructed woman, the woman painter whom he does not like.' On this evidence Lionel de Roulet would be classified today as a male chauvinist: 'He loved her more than ever this September he said because she looked after him and he adores being looked after.' Simone thought that he wanted 'to transform Poupette into a slave-wife – but he must have been disappointed . . . the first thing she greeted him with when he arrived in the Limousin was to say "you mustn't prevent me from working" '. He also wanted to change the nature of their friendship, seeking 'male–female relationships which would free him from having affairs: she protested, saying "I prefer you to have affairs, that lets me out." ' Nothing would stop the strong-minded Hélène from painting.

Her sister called her 'an odd little person'. 'She explained to me,' Beauvoir told Sartre further, 'that [Lionel] was perfect in friendship but that in love she is not pleased with his feelings because he shows so little affection and is dominating.' Though recording what Hélène had said, Beauvoir made no comment on her sister's clear-cut approach to what has since been accepted as a central problem for women. At the time she told Hélène to go away for she felt sleepy.

Beauvoir and Sartre continued all autumn and winter to write to each other every day. Sartre was still deeply attached to Wanda, and he was easily worried if for some reason or other she did not write to him regularly. After telling Beauvoir in mid-December that she 'made one with his life' he added, in brackets, 'I'm now going to write to Tania [Wanda] and tell her I love her passionately, it sickens me slightly.' After that faint show of guilt he continued to hope that he would soon be able to come on leave.

Beauvoir wanted to go skiing during the Christmas holidays, as she had done for the last five years. Sartre had told her it was dangerous to go alone, but fortunately his former student Jean Kanapa – who had earlier given an opinion about Beauvoir's looks – needed a companion and they left to spend ten days or so at Megève. Beauvoir remembered later that they got on well together 'in a curiously negative way'. They failed to find any shared topics of conversation and 'even at table, sitting opposite each other', they spent the time reading. In their way they were quite happy.

In the four months of the non-war Beauvoir had at first not known what to make of, she had felt confused and depressed, but after the reassurance brought about by a few days of Sartre's presence she spent as much time as she could working on her novel. She could have spent more, but she obviously did not try very hard to disentangle herself from the adoring women who took up as much of her days and nights as she would allow. They needed her, and in a sense she needed them, she needed talk and a show of affection. She consciously made and kept her life complex, and all this experience was to be reflected in *The Second Sex*.

The late 1930s had brought great changes in Beauvoir's approach to social and political life, she established her individual self but she remained a bourgeois intellectual living among the bohemian fringe of Montparnasse. So far the phoney war had not shown her how the working-class lived, and she had not sought them out, even as a sight-seer. Sartre, her women friends and her writing filled her fragmented existence, but this further awareness would come in time.

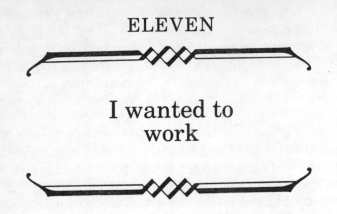

ELEVEN

I wanted to work

1940 began, and though Beauvoir frequently said that she wanted to work, or tried to work, her novel had not progressed very far. Her intermittent writing so far had coincided with two years of anxiety, uncertainty and fear caused by the political crisis in Europe. Four months of invisible war had so far made nothing easier. But time was her problem; she worked slowly and she was not prepared to give up much of her social life for the austerity of blank pages on the desk in front of her. One day in early January she was in a state of jubilation because she had revised twenty-five pages, after seven hours of work. She still had only a hundred pages ready and wanted to add another hundred in order to show them to Sartre when he came on leave.

As for her day-to-day emotional life, she returned from the skiing slopes to the Paris gynaeceum and on January 4th she entered into the *petite passion* with Nathalie Sorokine that she had hoped for. 'We began to kiss. I ask her, I have to, following our recent conversations: "Do you want us to have a really full relationship or stay this way?" – "Just as you wish." ' The girl was hesitant, wanted to go further but did not know what to say or do. 'I explained myself: "You said, Just as you wish, but if I asked the question, it's because I wanted it." ' Nathalie did not want them to be hypocrites. 'I say I'm not one.' The girl decided that it was not a good thing to stop half way. 'Then I begin to undress her a little and she says "Put the light out."' A further display of shyness. 'I take my blouse off . . . then she says firmly . . . "let's go through with it" . . .' and they got into bed. 'It's strange and pleasing to have her in my arms all inhibited by her nakedness and curious about the experience. I caress her a little, but in a limited way. No sensuality. Not for her either I think because she's rather frozen with shyness, but she's pleased because "we aren't hypocrites" and "It's intimate."'

Sartre was given the same account in the letter Beauvoir wrote the next day: 'She asked if I went to bed like this with you, if it didn't embarass me, if you walked about the room in the nude (I said you didn't).' And did he have hair on his chest? In her journal Beauvoir noted that Nathalie had 'the virgin's horror of the male', and she was 'amazingly virgin'. The evening ended happily at midnight, Beauvoir gave Nathalie the money for a taxi and slept well. She noted that she was 'relieved. I knew I had to go to bed with her and feared passionate outbursts, but she was pleasant and lightweight and unpredictable as she usually is.' The relationship was affectionate and, of course, contingent.

A few days later Beauvoir was again feeling cheerful. 'Do you know what's happening to me today?' she asked Sartre on January 9th. 'I am thirty-two. But I don't feel too much of an old woman; I'm in cheerful good health and I look fine.' She was going to celebrate with Olga and Wanda by seeing a Pirandello play at the Comédie-Française. 'I've dressed in my best this evening, with my earrings and a turquoise blue turban matching my blouse.'

Of the two sisters Beauvoir found Olga 'more interesting than Wanda but W. is more pleasant to look at', and if her charm was 'limited' it was 'less insipid, slightly rougher and harder'. Beauvoir was taking a good deal of interest in Wanda these days, she liked to talk to her, to describe her clothes and listen to what she said about her painting. She echoed Sartre's belief that these two sisters had 'class' and in order to show her own total lack of jealousy she told her *tout cher petit être* that she understood 'very well that you feel affection for this little person', i.e. Wanda.

It was Louise Védrine, for whom Beauvoir had few good words at this time, who understood what her friend was about. Louise saw no reason for being jealous of Nathalie, and saw herself as the centre of Beauvoir's emotional world – the world outside Sartre, that is – for on hearing about the *petite passion* she said, ' "That

239

provides you with material for a novel." ' Beauvoir seems to have felt genuine affection for Nathalie and she needed some physical response; at the same time, however, she was very ready to write down all these experiences – twice over, in her journal and her letters – as a kind of literary exercise, material to be kept in store for future fiction.

Fortunately there was at least one other diversion: Dullin's production of Shakespeare's *Richard III* at the Atelier. Since Olga was now making good progress as a student actress Beauvoir was taken backstage and enjoyed the play from the wings. The women, she thought, acted better than the men, but one thing in particular pleased her: in her novel she had already described backstage atmosphere when her hero, Pierre, was producing *Julius Caesar*, and now she was proud of herself, she decided she had got it 'right'.

Sartre, she hoped, would soon come to Paris, but his leave was deferred more than once, for there was no wife and family to give him any priority. In the meantime there was the problem of Louise Védrine, a problem the partners shared. Sartre had sent Beauvoir an extract from one of her letters, in which the girl had presumably told him she loved him exclusively. Beauvoir at once explained to Sartre that he had entirely misconstrued the situation: 'She is far from living only for you; she lives *formidablement* for me, and also for her work and endless little things she wants to do; there is an abstract tension in her relationship with you, she's been calculating: I've known him for six months and I haven't seen him for seven, and it is this idea of your useless love which is painfully in her mind. Moreover she is extremely happy at the moment.' There was no need for Sartre to feel guilty: 'There is no remorse to be felt about not seeing her.' As well as being his treasurer and acting as his first editor, Beauvoir was now organizing some aspects of Sartre's emotional life. At the same time she was as usual preoccupied with her own. She was rather amused to find both Védrine and Sorokine explaining to her separately how they felt about her: she must not imagine, they each said, that she had any duties towards either of them. They obviously wanted her love and were anxious not to antagonize her by making claims. Beauvoir valued some aspects of both relationships; she needed the *amitié amoureuse* supplied in different ways by both girls, and on days when she felt warm towards Louise she realized that she made sound and intelligent comments on her manuscript novel. She obviously felt more affection for Nathalie and provided the girl was not making any scenes Beauvoir would enjoy the evenings in which lessons on Descartes and Leibniz alternated with kisses and embraces. She also had to educate this innocent 'angelic' girl on such crucial topics as birth control and abortion, 'which interested her very much'.

Louise may have been 'extremely happy' in some ways but she was doomed. She was intelligent, but tried to dominate everyone, had little true understanding of philosophical concepts, would enter a room 'posing like a star', and, worst of all, on her own admission, she decided, 'correctly and sadly, I am not authentic'. If she was not 'authentic', not 'genuine', it is not clear why Beauvoir had accepted a sexual relationship with her during 1939, especially since she did not enjoy much of their time in bed together: 'in addition to the usual body smell of a redhead she had a strong and horrible smell which made things rather unpleasant . . .' She was acceptable as a friend, but no more. The problem now was how to end it all, especially since Beauvoir seemed incapable of making up her mind. On January 20th, after a discussion about love and morality, Védrine seemed to be making a comeback: 'I'm rather taken with her again, I'm drawn to her.' Beauvoir enjoyed dinner with her at Chez Lipp, the old-established brasserie near Saint-Germain-des-Prés, and they talked philosophy: 'The trouble is I can hardly discuss things with her because she contributes nothing personal, I can just explain things to her – or else we have to talk about her, it's the only topic on which she produces something new. We talked about Einstein and the non-Euclidean forms of geometry.' Yet only four days later Beauvoir found Védrine less intelligent than before and rather boring. She seemed incapable of a clear-cut decision.

At last, early in February, Beauvoir received a telegram from Sartre that he was on his way to Paris. She cancelled a meeting with Louise, saying that Bost was coming, for Sartre's arrival had to be kept secret from her. He did not want to see her. Beauvoir took his suitcase to the Hôtel Mistral and went to meet him in an old-fashioned, dark-panelled brasserie near the Gare de L'Est.

Suddenly he was there, 'surely the dirtiest soldier in France with his ragged cape, his enormous shoes, size 44 (five sizes too big) and his filthy uniform'. They 'found each other again' without any difficulty. Even when Sartre was with her or near her Beauvoir still had to write everything down in her journal. The leave was not merely an emotional reunion, it was intensely literary. No sooner had they reached the Hôtel Mistral than all was as before: 'We went to bed at midnight and talked until after 1. Sartre told me about his journey, showed me his notebooks and began to explain his theories to me.' She was happy. 'This seemed very precious but totally familiar to me, I don't feel I've been separated from him, there's absolutely nothing to be rebuilt between us.'

They spent the next few mornings in a café reading each other's manuscript novels and Sartre congratulated her on what she had written. Their time together was fragmented by her teaching work, and when Sartre went to other rendezvous she had occasional meetings with Védrine. With Sartre Beauvoir went to the cinema, walked and talked 'about simultaneity, time, the consciousness of others, and the discussion became heated'. Later Beauvoir remembered more about this first leave, especially Sartre's new programme for himself: he would no longer evade politics, but he would act on his own; he did not expect that those close to him would automatically agree with him. Beauvoir herself was interested in the philosophical basis of his changed outlook, but she only wrote about this later when she herself had caught up with his new concern about politics. 'His new morality, based on the notion of authenticity, and one that he tried to put into practice, demanded that man should "assume his situation".' In the Sartre–Beauvoir vocabulary an 'authentic' individual is spontaneous and self-creating, his thought stems from his own discoveries, not from outside factors or influences, and it remains consistent. Sartre at this period was especially concerned with the future of young people, the students, like Bost, whom he had recently taught: they must not be allowed to emerge from the war with feelings of guilt.

On the fifth day of his leave, when Sartre went to spend some time with Wanda, as had been agreed, Beauvoir dined with Védrine and went back to the Hôtel du Danemark. Nathalie came to see her and fell 'passionately' into her arms. In bed she read to her teacher what she had written about 'Proust, art and life; we have a discussion, I explain things to her, I am full of tenderness for her: I would have been captivated by this girl if only I had given a little of myself – but I've no wish to give myself . . .' They got up. Nathalie had almost finished combing her hair when Sartre arrived and she was disconcerted.

Beauvoir then went to a bar with Sartre and heard how he had spent his day. She herself was not precisely disconcerted but somewhat confused and depressed. Other women perhaps would have felt old-fashioned jealousy but Beauvoir's relationship with Sartre was unique and all feelings, however primitive, had to be analysed and rationalized. She admitted to her journal that the existence of the Kosakiewicz sisters was painful for her mainly because 'through the affection of Sartre or Bost they assume value and life again . . .' She did not entirely trust the sisters, they were accomplices in small ways, she felt, and she was upset by the possible image they had of her, 'this austere relationship with Sartre, this numb generosity, this slightly hateful presence that I represent in their lives'. Sartre also felt he was in a dilemma: but who, apart from Beauvoir, could possibly have tolerated the situation and worked her way through it? She could not do otherwise, for the situation itself could not be separated from Sartre, and life without Sartre could not be contemplated.

She was however intermittently without him during this leave and noted that she was not depressed simply because he was spending time with Wanda, 'it would be just the same if he were with his family'. She wondered how she could live through the next few months, but she heard from Olga that Bost was definitely arriving soon. That was going to cause complications – *quelle vie en casse-tête* – but she saw a comic film and felt better. The next day she spent a painful evening with Védrine: 'she sighed and dug her nails into my shoulder and we have to get into bed and embrace'. The embraces were punctuated by 'sentimental *bavardage* and passionate questions: do you love me? Are you happy?' She wasn't, but they dined Chez Lipp and discussed Kant, 'about whom Védrine said stupid things'. Beauvoir then warned her adoring friend that she would not be available for a few days because her sister Poupette was coming. She had already told her that Bost was there, in order to conceal Sartre, now Bost had to be concealed because otherwise Védrine would have been jealous.

The next day Beauvoir met Sartre at Le Dôme. 'He explained to me that he had been "morally uncomfortable" with Wanda, precisely because she was so nice to him, and wondered if it wouldn't be better to be faithful all one's life to one person'. That sounded dangerously like the unthinkable situation, marriage, and Beauvoir was not altogether pleased: 'I find it somewhat disagreeable to think about the attitudes of superiority that Wanda is taking towards me.' Olga, she thought, probably saw her as someone rather odd, but she did not worry about that. On the other hand she and Sartre were both rather depressed 'at feeling our lives to be so complicated and so encumbered'. But they had only themselves to blame and Sartre at least was contemplating one move towards simplification. 'We discussed whether or not he can break with Védrine and he's almost decided to do so, saying that the war has dried up all his feelings and they must wait for the end of the war before seeing each other again.' Later in the day they talked about Védrine again for a long time and continued talking – did they ever stop? – during most of their last night together at the Hôtel Mistral.

The emotional problems caused by Sartre's presence in Paris remained private, for most of Beauvoir's *Journal de guerre* was not published until 1990. Some parts of it, the more consciously 'literary' sections, were however included in the second volume of the memoirs, *La Force de l'âge*, which appeared in 1960. When, on February 15th, she accompanied Sartre to the Gare de l'Est at the end of his leave, she transformed her own emotional reaction into a short set piece of sociological literature.

'I am calm, but on seeing this departure as a collective event, I feel moved. The sight of all these men and women clumsily shaking hands on the platform brings a catch to my throat. There's a procession of women: mothers, but principally wives and girlfriends, moving away, their eyes red, their gaze fixed; some of them are sobbing. Barely ten or so old fathers among them; it looks primitive, this separation of the sexes, the men who are being carried away, the women going back towards the city.' Some of these were crying as they clung to their menfolk: 'You can feel a warm night behind them, and the lack of sleep, and the nervous fatigue of the morning.' The soldier nearest to the door stood back so that every couple could share a last goodbye kiss.

'The women stand in line and each one climbs up on to the step, I climb up too, then Sartre disappears inside. Collective and violent tension: this train about to leave, it's like being torn apart physically. And now it leaves. I'm the first to move away, very quickly.'

The departing soldier also wrote up this scene in his *Carnets*, the two pieces so close to each other in imagery that they lend credence to later rumours that Beauvoir and Sartre often composed together – no wonder he so often said *on ne fait qu'un*. He described this scene as a 'strange social event in dirty grey and muddy khaki, this totally primitive selection between men who were all being taken away and badly made-up women who looked ugly after a sleepless night . . . they were going to stay where they were.' Sartre felt no compassion; as he looked at the women of all ages, shapes and sizes, all red-eyed, nearly all crying, he found it 'almost comical'. He noticed one 'tall elegant blonde' who was not crying, and thought she was the most upset of all of them. He also remembered 'a young girl who looked exactly as women look when they return to their places after Communion'. Though Beauvoir and Sartre both used the word 'primitive', there was a fundamental difference in their reactions: Sartre saw the scene as an observer, while Beauvoir, as a woman, could feel as the other women felt.

Sartre began to write letters at once, as he always did, for both partners did everything they could to maintain contact hour by hour. He remembered that Beauvoir had been the first to leave the platform, and he hoped that the lycée had soon dried her tears. Though he had found the scene at the station 'almost comical' he remembered Beauvoir's tearful face at their parting quite differently: 'How beautiful it was, this face, *mon charmant Castor*, I know nothing more beautiful in the whole world and it's made me feel very strong and totally humble to think that it was for me that it was so beautiful.' Whenever he thought of her face tears came into his eyes.

Beauvoir did not need the lycée to dry her tears, there were not many of them and they were over as soon as she stopped a taxi outside the station. She then had a cheerful lunch with Nathalie and passed on to her all the gossip about Sartre and Louise. The day continued in its usual complex fashion, for in the early evening she met Louise, who was looking beautiful. Beauvoir felt 'slightly uncomfortable as I thought about what was in store for her', namely the break with Sartre, but in her letter to Sartre – began almost as soon as he left – she could at least tell him that the girl would possibly not be too upset. Louise complained that she had no 'shared life' with Beauvoir, and was 'haunted' by the Beauvoir–Sartre relationship: 'She wants to copy it exactly.' But what could have been more impossible? Beauvoir made her own attitude perfectly clear: 'I repeated to her firmly that she will never have more of my life, that I did not promise more, that I cling to my solitude and my liberty.'

The complexity of the day ended with one final stage of *la vie sentimentale*. Later in the evening Olga, she found, was being particularly charming and affectionate towards her, and she began to speculate on the possible reasons for it. 'I wonder,' she wrote in her journal, 'if this is not in some way against Wanda, in order to form a couple with me against Wanda–Sartre.' She repeated her suspicions to Sartre. No wonder he had once told her she was 'too much loved'. Everyone wanted her. Sartre had much more of her than anyone else but at thirty-two, during the standstill of the phoney war, with her 'real book' barely half written, she belonged surely to her fragmented self, even if she had not yet decided the true nature of that self, that woman, that femininity.

That night she slept for ten hours, sleep that she needed because she knew that *la vie en casse-tête* was imminent. Just after four in the afternoon, when she was giving a sociology lesson, one of the lycée servants told her that Monsieur Bost was in the *parloir* downstairs. Her hands began to shake, the blood rose to her cheeks and her voice gave way. However, she had to finish her lesson somehow. Then the two of them went for a long, long walk in snow-covered, sunny, blue-skied Paris. They stopped temporarily in the dark, old-fashioned brasserie at the Gare de l'Est where Beauvoir had met Sartre a fortnight earlier. She telephoned Olga to say they could not meet because her sister Poupette had just arrived in Paris. Olga did not sound too friendly; perhaps she did not believe the story. Beauvoir was so disconcerted by all this that she lost the letter she had immediately begun to write to Sartre about Bost's arrival and had to start all over again.

1. Simone aged 7 months, August 1908.

2. The Beauvoir family in 1915. Simone, aged 7, to the right. Her father in Zouave uniform. Photo taken near Paris.

3. Simone (right) and Hélène de Beauvoir with their mother.

4. Beauvoir at the Café de Flore in 1945
with the owner, Boubal, and her friend Gégé Pardo.

5. Jacques-Laurent
Bost on his
mobilisation,
November 1939.

6. Bost and Olga,
Paris, 1950.

7. Nelson Algren.

8. Violette Leduc, 1965.

9. Sylvie Le Bon de Beauvoir, at Elounda, Crete, August 1975.

10. Beauvoir and Sartre distributing
La Cause du Peuple, 1970.

11. Sartre's 69th birthday, 21 June 1974.
Luncheon in Sylvie Le Bon's apartment, Paris.

12. Sartre and Beauvoir on their way to a radio broadcast.

13. At home, May 1983.

In her journal she noted that in addition to her happiness with Bost she was very much aware of their life as a group: 'This war is truly lived by us together, and together we await our future, it is not a question of each person awaiting their own.' Bost was more than a Sartrian clone, but he was not an outsider; Sartre had been his teacher and that link kept everyone close. The young man was very upset that he had missed Sartre by one day.

If Beauvoir thought of herself as living in a group and used semi-technical philosophical jargon to describe the situation, life for the time being was *à deux*. She and Bost went to a hotel in the Place Denfert-Rochereau, L'Oriental, which was 'luxurious and warm', decked out in velvet with a pink counterpane on the bed. The night was 'tender and passionate' but Beauvoir slept badly because the room was too hot and she was over-excited. However, she happily read Bost's notebooks about his military life, while he read Sartre's *Carnets* and the manuscript of his novel. They were able to spend most of four days together, Beauvoir read affectionate and confessional letters from Sartre as they sat together in cafés. She was immensely cheerful for she had realized that Bost cared for her and for Olga in totally different ways. Was she vindictive or just helpfully honest as she explained to him that the girl was probably superficial and never thought about anything except *des histoires de bonne femme*? In any case Bost cared for Beauvoir enough to hope that she would come to stay near his camp in the Seine et Oise.

Beauvoir had not had Sartre entirely to herself during those ten days of leave and his letters reminded her of the fact. 'I loved Wanda very much,' he wrote, 'and she seemed to love me.' Beauvoir had to listen to admissions of guilt concerning herself; he thought he hadn't been nice enough to her and he was sorry about something else: 'I've given your little knife to Tania . . . I was fond of it while I was here [i.e. at the front]. Only it didn't cut any more and then . . . I wasn't at the war, I was in Paris . . . But I was wrong and I'm beginning to regret it.' Beauvoir was spared no proof of his 'transparency'. On reaching his unit (temporarily at Bouxwiller) he smoked his pipe close to the stove 'thinking of you happily. From time to time I also remembered Tania clasping me in her arms and saying: *Mon tout chéri, mon tout chéri*, and that moved me too. But it's strange: today memories of Tania have faded, now there's only you.' Beauvoir, conditioned though she was, probably did not find it strange at all. Wanda, on her side, found it strange to learn from the *Carnets* that Sartre had *une vie intime*, for she had assumed he hadn't. Her reactions to the *Carnets* were inevitably different from those of Beauvoir; she was 'deeply shocked' by some entries. Several of those fourteen notebooks were lost and only five have been published to date, therefore it is impossible to guess what facts or thoughts had upset this surprisingly prim girl.

During those ten days so important to her emotionally, Beauvoir noted all the details in her journal. Sartre wrote down his memories and interpretations in his notebooks: 'Only excellent things. No hours were wasted. I don't think it could have been better. I've seen le Castor and T. [Wanda], I was not alone for one moment . . . People did not disappoint me, on the contrary. There was even one happy surprise – which belongs to my private life.' At which point he became reticent, remembering perhaps that Wanda would soon be reading these *Carnets*. He may even have been censored later by his editor, his adopted daughter, Arlette Elkaim-Sartre. A month later, in a letter to Beauvoir, he reminded her of what had happened during his leave: 'During my leave you noticed, in Paris, that in our physical relationships, I had changed.' At the start of their sexual life together she had apparently found him 'slightly obscene', but things were different now, better in some ways: 'Perhaps physical relationships lose something of their strength this way, but they gain in *propreté*' – they were presumably more straightforward.

As he looked carefully at Paris, he saw the city where Beauvoir, like everyone else, had been living a life of strange charm against a backdrop of superficial near-normality. 'I wasn't much aware of the war there,' Sartre confirmed. 'In the streets perhaps, in the evening. But in the carefully chosen places where we went with le Castor, the war had barely upset anything . . . About half way through my leave I began to notice the high proportion of old, infirm people and I felt Paris to be a bloodless city, drained by the haemorrhage of all its men.' There was no good jazz. It was Beauvoir who made him aware of 'something more subtle': 'It was a city of men without features.' She equated this situation, depressingly enough, with *'une vie de famille'*. He went further, noticing that most people 'don't talk about the war and sometimes even amuse themselves. Yet I know that their destiny is fixed, like that of dead people.' They were just waiting for the end of the war, 'which does not depend on them'. They accepted the war, they let it wash over them. 'Yes, Paris seemed to be like a family vault . . .' One thought cheered him: 'I was alive in that proud, dead town and I was alive precisely because I didn't belong to it.' In war conditions soldiers have often felt this distance from their old life, while women in many ways took over responsibility from them, as Beauvoir did on Sartre's behalf. Sartre was reminded now of experiences that Beauvoir and he had shared during holidays abroad, looking at splendid Greek or Moroccan cities inhabited by 'dead people'. He was not referring to the truly dead, but to the living.

Once Bost had left, Beauvoir summoned her sister to Paris from the Limousin. This time she did not have to lie to anyone. Poupette wanted to go to the Bobino music-hall where there were some good clowns and 'Edith Piaf, who looks hunchbacked and hydrocephalous and made me cry'. Not surprisingly, perhaps, for Beauvoir realized that she was 'in a state of edgy sentimentality and terribly sensitive to songs'. That same afternoon she had had a difficult session with Nathalie, who cried during a lesson on Descartes, and Beauvoir decided that 'this mixture of *philo* and sentiment is absolutely intolerable'. She could have put a stop to it, but obviously she preferred their relationship the way it was, the way she had chosen. Nathalie, like Olga before her, was a 'chosen' daughter, after all.

Beauvoir had no 'chosen' sons, but now, shortly after the end of his leave in Paris, she had to deal with the boy Sartre. He appealed to Beauvoir, his 'morganatic wife', as he called her, for help vis-à-vis Wanda. There was nobody else from whom he could ask advice, this was a problem for the agony aunt, the *courrier du coeur*. He had to simplify life, he had duly broken with Louise, but Beauvoir had told him his letter to her had been too brutal, for she was more sensitive and intelligent than Colette Gibert, the girl with whom Sartre had enjoyed *les vicissitudes de la galanterie* in 1938.

It was Colette who had indirectly caused him trouble now. He had written letters to her during their liaison which the girl had kept and had recently shown to the actor Marcel Mouloudji. He in turn showed the letters to his friend Wanda and she, studying the dates, now accused Sartre of having embarked on his love-affair with her before ending his relationship with Colette. Sartre was desperate to keep Wanda's affection and at once asked Beauvoir for her opinion on a cruel letter he proposed sending, via Wanda, to the unfortunate Colette. He told her he had never loved her: 'I found you physically attractive although coarse, but there's a certain sadism in me that was drawn to this coarseness.' He alleged that his letters to her had been 'exercises in passionate literature' over which he and le Castor had laughed heartily. Beauvoir knew that Sartre had never truly cared for Colette, and by now she realized the lengths to which he was prepared to go in order to keep Wanda. She had agreed with him that Wanda was fussing about something she had already known about, but her reaction, combined with Sartre's own memories, now turned him into a guilty adolescent, confessing all his weaknesses to the one person who would listen to him patiently. 'Why did I need that girl? Wasn't I just playing the village Don Juan?' He realized Beauvoir would excuse his sensuality but 'In this case I accuse not so much my behaviour with her as my sexual personage in general . . . It seems to me that until now I've behaved like a vicious child in my physical relationships with people . . . this shows that something's very damaged within me . . . It's the atmosphere of *canaillerie sadique* that disgusts me.'

But he knew who was to blame. Though Wanda had been in the wrong in some ways *he* was the one to pay for all his past sexual life. 'It must change.' Beauvoir was asked three times in one letter what she thought of all this. He did not know what to think and longed for her advice. At the same time he returned to something Colette Gibert had said: she had been jealous of Beauvoir but resigned to the special status enjoyed by her immovable rival. She had accused Sartre of 'mysticism' in his attitude to her and now he exploited that crucial word, not irrelevant perhaps to his unique and near-unfathomable relationship with Beauvoir. His mother confessor received the full impact of his self-criticism but in writing it he did not seem to notice that he was hurting her at the same time: she had to listen to a quotation from his latest letter to

Wanda: 'You know very well,' he had written to her, 'that I'd trample on everyone (even le Castor despite my "mysticism") to be on good terms with you.' Transparency could go no further. This letter to Beauvoir, of February 24th, 1940, continued with more self-condemnation and reached a conclusion: 'I've never known how to conduct either my sexual or my emotional life; I feel deeply and sincerely that I'm *un salaud*, a bastard. And a small-scale bastard on top of that, a kind of university sadist and a sick-making civil service Don Juan. It must change.' He was full of good intentions. He added a list of books for Beauvoir to buy for him when she had some money and since he had no letter from her that day he was '*tout seul dans la merde*', all alone in the shit.

There was never any need to feel sorry for Sartre, who surely did not realize how lucky he was. Beauvoir not only uttered no complaints about his behaviour, but told him in loving, slightly maternal tones, how deeply she cared for him, how much she wanted to be near him: 'Oh my love,' she wrote on March 2nd, 'I love you so much, I would like to hold you tightly against me, to see your little face and talk to you; when I think that you were worried the day before yesterday because of me and my feelings or rather my judgments on you, when I imagine the strange state in which you were, I'm so impatient to see you that it makes me cry;' she felt he was near but far: 'it's as though I were seeing you through a transparent and deceptive pane of glass, I'm carried towards you, you're so close, I feel I'm going to touch you and then no, that's in the way, I have to write, letters take two days, and it takes two days for the reply to arrive, and letters are too short . . .' She excelled herself in outpourings of affection: 'How can you imagine, *doux petit être*, that I don't believe you're being honest and straightforward with me?' She approved of his break with Védrine, although both partners were to return to this problem later and 'It's true that the phrase you wrote to Wanda, "I'd trample on everyone" was unpleasant for me . . . but I got over it, and you must have been crazy, *mon petit*, to think that it would prevent me from writing to you.' She was upset to think that this was Sunday and she would have to wait until the following day for his next letter.

She learnt from it that he had been 'shaken' by her loving reply to his apparently heartless remarks about 'trampling' on her. He now felt that he was changing – but in fact he never did. He at least thought he was struggling with himself, he was half-convinced that he might overcome his sexual anarchy, his innate *machismo*, his self-confessed incapacity for human relationships. There was only one relationship that counted, the partnership with Beauvoir which was stabilized by its intellectual base, allowing them both to conduct subsidiary love-affairs, as they both wanted to, without any damage to their regard for each other. He was expert in professing love; she had greater warmth and emotional depth. His expressions of love *sounded* heartfelt enough, hers were less literary, more spontaneous, they were 'feminine' in the best sense of that much-abused word. Beauvoir, in Paris, beset with practical problems and jealous girls, had been able to sense precisely how, and at what point, she must 'forgive' Sartre, or even punish him, although she rarely did so. Sartre told her that he clung to her judgment 'more than I cling to anything in the world; scold me if I deserve it, I beg you'. During their early life together she had edited his manuscripts; now, after first refusing to do so, she was apparently 'editing' his private life. From now on, he decided, his personal relationships were going to be 'pure', straightforward. He thought she might distrust him and wonder if he would start telling her 'total lies and especially half-truths'. That would destroy him: 'My love, you are not only my life but the only honesty in my life.' And he made it clear that he knew why: 'It's because you are what you are.'

Paradoxically, perhaps, the partners were never so close as when they were apart, for it was their nature to write out their feelings in the greatest detail; they were obsessed by writing and went on with it in one form or another under all circumstances, sometimes even when they were together. 'You must blame me when I deserve it,' wrote Sartre, 'just as you must be severe about my novel when it's not good.' Beauvoir was reminded that she was his 'little moral conscience'. Which was more important to each of them, the writer or the writing? The two aspects of life were inseparable, their relationship, thanks to Beauvoir, had survived the crisis provoked by Wanda's unfounded complaints and Sartre's desperate bid to keep her. He felt now that 'contingent' arrangements must not be allowed to get out of hand, relationships must be 'complete'. 'There is no pain,' wrote 'Palinurus' in

The Unquiet Grave in 1944, 'equal to that which two lovers can inflict on each other.' Even the insensitive Sartre had realized how hurtful he had been, but there is no sign that Beauvoir set out to inflict pain, even if, in a display of delicate sado-masochism, he had practically invited her to do so.

In early 1940 Beauvoir was thirty-two, while Sartre would be thirty-five in June. The war coincided with the end of their youth and the beginning of their writing careers, even if nothing could be published for the time being. Both partners felt the years 1939–40 were crucial to them, but they were not thinking directly about the war. This spring season was to change the history of Europe, even of the world, but the separated partners were thinking principally of themselves, the war was a mere backdrop, inconvenient to Beauvoir even if Sartre still found it 'interesting'. Their separation forced them to think even more deeply about themselves, about their relationship, about their work, all intermingled. It had been a testing time – neither partner knew that worse was to come – but Sartre concluded that 'the only thing which it hasn't been necessary to change in any way, the thing which is utterly true and satisfying, is the love between the two of us'. As the two partners 'grew up' those letters grew into a novel more absorbing than anything else either of them wrote; the story they told was immediate, compelling. They kept each other's letters, until they finally reached the Bibliothèque Nationale in 1989.

If Sartre had to deal with the Wanda situation at a distance, Beauvoir lived in the day-to-day world of wartime Paris, coping with another of Sartre's emotional problems, one which in fact she shared. She continued to see Védrine and realized that the girl had accepted the break with Sartre with more stoicism than she might have hoped for, especially since the former admirer had written her a heartless letter. However, the break caused other problems. It had changed her own relationship with Védrine, they were now less close, and Beauvoir saw this as a hopeful sign: 'It brings the possibility of freedom, for she will soon be in need of a man.' The girl was talking about getting drunk. 'Soon she'll be on the look-out for an affair, then another love and I shall be liberated.' Beauvoir decided that she no longer found Védrine *sympathique* but she was concerned about a wider issue: 'I have

253

reproached the two of us,' she told Sartre, 'myself along with you moreover, in the past, in the future, in the absolute, about the way we treat people.' She had found it unacceptable – late in the day – to cause Védrine suffering, and how could it have been avoided – neither partner had treated her well. However, she was relieved that the girl was not too upset, and at least she was showing some guilt about the third party in their 'trio'. Sartre's excuse, echoed by Beauvoir, was that Védrine had no solid centre, she was not 'authentic'. As this vital word came into her head Beauvoir began to worry about her own situation: *'Hélas*! if you were to abandon me through authenticity or any other whim, no I wouldn't bear the blow with the same dignity as Védrine, I can't imagine what I would become, the world would collapse beneath me.'

However, despite her display of love for Sartre and her fear of sharing Védrine's fate – surely a fear that was not very real? – she could not resist one touch of irony as she ended her letter of March 4th: 'I'm ashamed of letters so much shorter than yours, but at the same time I'm not living through such moral and emotional tornadoes; my life is even and calm and well imbued with the satisfaction of good work completed and all these delights on the horizon that I'm hoping for.'

She had high hopes for the future, thinking of the Easter holidays, for she was fairly sure she would be going north to see Bost and would come back to Paris for Sartre's next leave. However, when Beauvoir told Sartre that her life, unlike his, was calm and tranquil, she had spoken too soon. As soon as she left Paris to visit Bost at Charmont in the Marne it became temporarily complex, frustrating, and alarmingly dramatic. She made a bad start by taking the wrong train from the Gare de l'Est, remembering so vividly Sartre's departure on September 2nd by the 07.50 to Nancy that she climbed into it herself. She was horrified by the discovery of her mistake and only reached her destination, after various train changes, in the late evening. All was darkness and confusion, no Bost, no taxis, no rooms to let. Eventually she found somewhere to sleep and next morning came to the house where Bost had booked a room for the two of them. He was there, asleep.

But the drama was not over. A nearby garage-owner had noticed her arrival, knew she was a stranger and reported her mysterious presence to the police and the military authorities. Surely she was a spy? Her visa was not complete, she had failed to show it on arrival for the necessary stamp of approval. Unfortunately for her there had been intelligence reports that a woman of similar appearance was being sought in the area. She had to admit that she had come to see Bost. She could show identity papers proving that she was a respectable and respected lycée teacher but even that was not enough. The investigating officers went through all her papers, her journal and the manuscript of her novel. Worse still, they read Sartre's *Carnets*, which she had brought to show Bost, and decided that he was a Communist. Therefore his lady friend must be dangerous too. Unexpectedly one of the army officers recognized her: he had encountered Mademoiselle de Beauvoir while she was teaching in Marseille and a little later she had examined him in philosophy when he took his *baccalauréat* in Caen. Unfortunately she had given him a bad mark: zero. Beauvoir, who wanted to be well known as a writer, did not relish being so well known as a teacher. She was very nearly sent back to Paris, but after she had pleaded her innocence with tears and feminine wiles, she was eventually allowed to stay. She left Charmont for Nettancourt, slightly further to the east, between Châlons-sur-Marne and Bar-le-Duc in the Meuse.

In Nettancourt she and Bost were at last lucky, she found a room in a house where there was a kitchen with a large table and a stove on which they – Bost, that is – could cook. Shopping was difficult and Beauvoir ventured out as little as possible. They succeeded in preparing meals, although Beauvoir's menus when on her own consisted of canned herrings and apple purée. She was delighted by the table not so much for eating on as for writing on, and whenever Bost was away on duty she worked hard at her novel. The atmosphere of this quiet house was more conducive to work than the cafés of Montparnasse. She missed Sartre's daily letters, for some of them had gone to the Charmont poste restante and had to be recovered. Although she was fond of Bost and delighted by the time they managed to spend together she told Sartre – for she wrote every day – that *he* was her 'only comfort'.

Sartre needed comfort too, for Wanda had not written to him, he could not understand her silence and was afraid she might be pregnant. Beauvoir replied that this was very unlikely. He was due to come back to Paris for his second leave at the end of March, and since she was with Bost it was arranged that Sartre should see Wanda first. Emotional life at least was once again calm and tranquil, after its fashion, even if Sartre's days were to be divided up like a school timetable.

In the outside world, which preoccupied Sartre a little but Beauvoir, apparently, not at all, tranquillity seemed to be fading, for during March and April 1940 there were signs that the *drôle de guerre* was becoming somewhat less *drôle*. During the previous autumn France had promised to help Finland resist the invading Russians but in the end, like Britain, had done nothing. When, in March, the Finns eventually gave way to the Soviets, public opinion forced the resignation of the Prime Minister, Edouard Daladier. His place was taken by Paul Reynaud, regarded as more energetic, but when he decided to retain Daladier as Minister of Defence, any activation of the war was unlikely. There was soon another disaster, although this time French forces were less involved than the British: Hitler's armies occupied Denmark without meeting any resistance and soon controlled all the ports in Norway, although Narvik in the north was temporarily recovered by the Allies. The inefficiency of the French and British intelligence services was such that the French Prime Minister had had no warning of the German attack – he heard of it first through a dispatch from Reuters. This unexpected campaign in the north affected Beauvoir at once because she was instructed by Sartre, who had heard the news on the radio, that she *must* read the newspapers, something she still tended to avoid unless some crisis was likely to affect her personally. Sartre now pointed out to her that 'this could well decide not the outcome of the war but its duration'.

In the meantime Beauvoir had seen Sartre for his second period of leave at the very end of March. The partners had recovered from the stormy discussions of the previous month. They both remembered something more important to them than Sartre's sexual anarchy. Writing after his departure he mentioned their 'serious and weighty conversations' and to Beauvoir these formed the highlight of the leave. They had been reading and discussing by letter Saint-Exupéry's recent book *Terre des hommes* (translated in 1947 as *Wind, Sand and Stars*). She saw the work as reflecting the qualities that had been emphasized by Heidegger. She was impressed: 'In describing the world of the aviator Saint-Exupéry also transcended the opposition of subjectivism and objectivity; he showed how diverse truths are revealed through diverse techniques, each one expressing however the whole of reality, none of them possessing any privilege in relation to the others.' Beauvoir felt that the author had made the reader 'present in detail at the metamorphosis of earth and sky experienced by a pilot at the controls of his plane'. It was the emphasis on individual experience, freedom of choice and personal responsibility which to Beauvoir and many of her generation made Saint-Exupéry's writing 'the best possible, the most concrete, the most convincing illustration of the theories of Heidegger'.

Beauvoir was ready to learn of Sartre's progress with his new theories, later to be expressed in his key book *L'Etre et le néant* (*Being and Nothingness*), but she was not always ready to accept everything he said. As they walked round the damp, dark streets near the Gare du Nord in Paris there was a disagreement between them which she did not forget. They were discussing the problems of *dépassement* or transcendence and the connection between 'situation and liberty' when Beauvoir raised an interesting question: 'What transcendence is possible for a woman in a harem?' She was beginning to think about women in a situation of subjection, but Sartre, preoccupied with theory, was convinced that her point was irrelevant. He believed that 'even this enclosed existence could be lived through in different ways'. Beauvoir obviously saw the problem from a more practical angle and it was one to which she would eventually return. She did not agree with Sartre. 'I resisted for a long time and I only gave way superficially.' She remained convinced that 'in principle, I was right'. She gave one reason for her attitude: 'In order to defend my position I would have had to abandon the position of individualistic, namely realistic, morality, which we had assumed.'

Was there a more personal reason? She admitted all her life that she did not consider herself an original thinker, she believed she had nothing to add to the theories and ideas put forward by Sartre. At the same time was she perhaps unconsciously behaving

257

in an old-fashioned 'feminine' way, allowing Sartre to believe he had won the argument simply because he was a man? She obviously did not want any ideological rift between them, she had succeeded in preventing an emotional break, and since the possibility for live discussion was so restricted at the time, she was prepared to make the concession, temporarily at least, and equally prepared later to explain that she nad done so unwillingly.

Serious topics were not regularly mentioned in the daily letters or the *Journal de guerre*; the separated partners wanted personal details, and they preferred to keep any discussion of abstract concepts for the times when they could talk *tête-à-tête* and argue over a café table. The day-to-day, hour-by-hour life of late 1939 and most of 1940 described in the letters, is concerned, especially for Beauvoir, with the minutiae of their own relationship, their complex friendships and love-affairs with other people, and the extent to which they depended upon each other. When Beauvoir published Sartre's letters in 1983 she added a careful preface, for they dealt with the 'recent past'. She explained her presentation: 'I did not feel I had the right to publish them in entirety. I have not modified one iota of what concerns my relationship with Sartre. But to avoid embarrassing third parties – or those close to them – I have suppressed passages, changed names.' She added that she had decided herself on 'nearly all these alterations. Some were required by Madame Elkaim-Sartre.' Behind that brief sentence there may well have been some argument, to put it mildly, and Madame Elkaim-Sartre, Arlette, the daughter whom Sartre later adopted was far from pleased by the appearance of the letters. However, the absent Sartre was no doubt on Castor's side. He had told her in 1974, during the recorded *Entretiens* published along with *La Cérémonie des adieux*, what he felt about his letters: 'They were the transcription of day-to-day life . . . They were spontaneous . . . I thought . . . that these letters could have been published . . . I had a very slight ulterior motive that they would be published after my death . . . In fact my letters have been the equivalent of an account of my life.' The extent to which his letters had been censored did not become clear until Beauvoir's own letters appeared in 1990, her adopted daughter Sylvie Le Bon de Beauvoir having published them *en intégralité*.

258

To those who read the Beauvoir story only as it appears, neatly tailored in the later memoirs, the letters are surprising, for they are not in any way 'literary'; the writer, who was very often tired and harassed, was chatting spontaneously and telling Sartre everything. Even the journal was intended for him, he was its first reader. She tells him all the details of her emotional life with Louise Védrine and Nathalie Sorokine, along with her swings of mood and her uncertainties. One day, or rather night, she would 'hate' Védrine, a few days later she would be drawn to her, then she would find her 'inauthentic'. She felt affection for Olga and yet she would go in secret to see Bost, the girl's official partner, and even indicate to him that Olga was not very intelligent. She would read, in secret, a letter from Bost to Olga and feel disappointed because it was so affectionate.

Yet all through this confused and confusing life she somehow persevered with her novel and responded to Sartre's pioneering thought, which was later to condition the whole post-war generation. Unconsciously, through her chaotic experiences and close observation, she laid the foundations for her own later work, her support for the women so badly in need of education and help. Women, she began to see only too well, had no freedom, and because of their orthodox conditioning and their destructive mothers – both Védrine and Nathalie suffered in this way – they had not even developed the *will* to be free. They could only complain to anyone prepared to listen and ask for affection, usually in a hopeless, demanding way. Beauvoir earned their admiration and love because she had understood or somehow learnt how to find freedom. Could she have done so if she had not had the good luck to encounter Sartre? Probably not, and therefore in some ways it was a limited freedom, but she knew this very well, she knew, or thought she knew, how to manage it and she knew the price: she needed Sartre and as a result she accepted his needs, which did not always make life comfortable for her. With Sartre in the background she overcame her uncertainties and as a writer she learnt how to use both her problems and her solutions to advantage. Despite Sartre's constant presence the essential conquest of freedom within her own mind was achieved by Beauvoir on her own. If she had been truly independent of Sartre and everyone else she would have been an inaccessible heroine, almost a saint, a martyr, an equivalent of Simone Weil. Fortunately she was a woman, an emotional woman, intelligent, capable of extremes, but a woman with as many failings as any other, and that is why every detail of her life, especially her early life, will continue to fascinate future generations. It fascinated her, she was watching herself grow up, which is why she wrote down and preserved so many documentary details. She also had a readymade, immediate audience, Soldat Sartre, who wanted to be entertained with news of all that was going on in Beauvoir's mind and in Montparnasse.

As 1940 progressed the partners needed each other's letters as desperately as ever, but for the months of April, May and June only a one-sided correspondence has been published, for Beauvoir's letters are missing. Sylvie Le Bon de Beauvoir has explained that they may have been lost in view of the 'events', namely the collapse of the French army and all that followed. Beauvoir left Paris for a few weeks, then she had no address for Sartre, because he became a prisoner of war. Beauvoir wrote, or at least preserved nothing of her journal during March, April and May. Sartre continued to write letters virtually every day and Beauvoir replied. Did she exercise any further censorship? It is not clear. It is however totally clear that Sartre experienced another of his recurring emotional crises over Wanda, the girl who continued to mean so much to him, and as usual, when he recovered, Beauvoir was still there. She always was there.

TWELVE

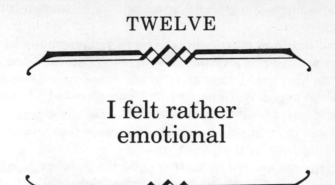

I felt rather emotional

During the late spring and early summer of 1940 France, within the space of a few weeks, was overcome by the worst military disaster in its history, which had known many. The Prime Minister, over-optimistic about developments in Norway, made a hopeful speech telling the public that Hitler's route to Norway and its valuable mining resources had been cut; however, he was quickly proved wrong, for Narvik was abandoned. Sartre was even more optimistic than Paul Reynaud. He wrote to Beauvoir on April 11th: 'Have you seen? The war news is good, the Germans have been damn stupid and now they're paying for it.' He misinterpreted most of the situation: 'I imagine there's going to be trouble somewhere (but probably not in France) and I'm beginning to hope that the war won't be as long as I'd feared.' Although he was on so-called active service he was dependent for news on rumours and on the radio bulletins he could hear in the local *auberge* if he was lucky, but he could not see many newspapers. He compared the war to reading a thriller, as he began to see hard news emerging from a fog of rumour. He again instructed Beauvoir to read the papers. She was unwilling, as usual in Paris, and she was much busier than her distant partner: in addition to her teaching work she still had all the problems of day-to-day life. She had to scrape together enough money to subsidize the insatiable Sartre, find the time to buy and send him books and writing materials, help the vague and incompetent

Olga and Wanda fill in official forms and manage the allowances they received from Sartre, administered by her, and often wasted by them.

She had another role, infinitely more responsible and important; she was Sartre's critical muse. She had found the draft prologue to his novel so bad that he had developed a complex, he said, and scrapped it. In spirit she was always at his side: 'I'm totally and perpetually in contact with you, *doux petit*. All the time I'm working on my novel you're present as a severe little critic and its *for you* that I'm correcting, much more even than when I'm inventing . . . I'm putting right the imperfections you've pointed out.' She felt she had not seen enough of him during his second leave but he in fact felt that they had been particularly close: 'I don't think we've ever been closer together,' he found, [you] had 'entered into my ideas so well and made them yours and sometimes followed me and sometimes gone far beyond me . . .' He didn't think he could manage without her, and if she died, 'I wouldn't kill myself but I'd go completely mad. So let's stay very much alive, my love.' In mid-April she seemed to him just as young as she had been ten years earlier and he clung to her 'a thousand times more'.

Both partners maintained their intense efforts to bridge the gap between Paris and Sartre's military base in the east. They both felt they were not succeeding, for various reasons. Beauvoir was humble, finding her letters were '*pas assez gentilles*', while Sartre was faintly guilty as he ate an omelette with her 'poor little sous'. However, there was literature to keep them going. At the end of April he learnt that his stories, *Le Mur*, had won him the Prix Populiste. He had asked Beauvoir's earlier advice: *she* must decide about his entry, whether he should agree to be a candidate. In the meantime she had made definite progress with *her* novel, Sartre had found it 'excellent', she must now show four hundred pages of the manuscript to Brice Parain, the Gallimard reader. At the time he was in the army, allocated to messenger work as a cyclist, and could only be seen, it was thought, on Sundays between five and nine p.m.

Sartre spent a good deal of his time, when not writing or reading, in teaching himself to type, playing chess and ping-pong. Beauvoir occasionally visited her parents; she did not enjoy her mother's cooking very much, but it saved her a little money. She still had to cope with the feminine entourage she called '*ma charmante vermine*', and especially the problematic Nathalie, who was still jealous of Sartre and hoped he would stay away for three years. She called him '*crevette*', shrimp, and he was particularly annoyed when she tried to spread a rumour that he was impotent. However, he still wanted to hear all the news about her. Sometimes he praised Beauvoir's severity, sometimes he warned her not to overdo it. He even gave her advice about how to conduct the relationship. 'As for Sorokine, I find her instability rather irritating, as you do, but you must consider that there are many affectionate gestures which even a well brought up man can allow himself when dancing with a woman, gestures which a woman dancing with another woman should not allow herself. It must be rather irritating for her.' It was the sort of situation which fascinated Sartre. 'Even if she loves you in a rough sort of way this story makes me laugh, *mon petit*. How nice and delightful you are in the midst of all that, *petite trop aimée*. Not more than you deserve, surely, but more than you want to be.'

In mid-May 1940, Beauvoir may well have felt that she was not loved enough. The unique and polygamous Sartre, having decided a few months earlier that he must reform his personal and sexual life, was now swept away on a tide of love and compassion. Wanda had written to him, she was ill, she had to be X-rayed and she had said, 'How much I want you to come, to come at any price.' Sartre told Beauvoir at once, on May 12th, saying that 'It's odd, she's becoming more and more "my child", as Z [Olga] was for you at one time.' His next remark was even odder: 'I've just written to her that if she wants it and the wait is not too long, I'm ready to marry her in order to have three days' leave. I think this will not be pleasant for you; although it's purely symbolic it commits me up to my neck.' Sartre himself was not altogether happy about his Quixotic idea: 'I myself find it very displeasing, not so much because of that but because of my family from whom I'll have to conceal it and they'll certainly find out one day.' He sounded like a conventional bourgeois or a guilty adolescent. Did the man who wrote to Beauvoir every day with outpourings of infinite love merely assume that she would accept his latest plan in her usual understanding way? Was she still prepared to believe, as the

263

medieval Eloïse had believed, that 'the only bond between lovers should be love'? Sartre wanted to do everything he could to help Wanda. 'In compensation,' he told Beauvoir, 'I'll still take a day to see you.' That was less than kind, considering the depth of love he professed. And did he really care for Wanda, was she a helpless child? If she was found to be not too ill 'I'll excuse myself on the grounds that no marriage leave has been granted since the Holland business or that the waiting time is too long and then there's no point in it'. He was anxious, as ever, for Beauvoir's reaction and advice: 'What do you think? Do you reprimand me?' He ended his letter by saying, 'I love you with all my strength, *mon charmant Castor, mon amour.*'

The casual announcement of his marriage proposal to Wanda was one of the greatest cruelties towards his *charmant Castor*. Did he think she would laugh it off? Did she complain? Was she angry, his 'little judge'? How quickly did she recover from this latest emotional shock? There may have been good reasons for her current letters to have been 'lost' but it is more likely that she reacted as she had done two months earlier, she forgave the insensitive man and suspected no doubt that he would soon forget his headstrong plan. She may have censored his replies to any reaction of hers, but she had allowed him to have a trial run: he was to repeat this performance in the future.

The Holland business: on May 10th Hitler's forces had attacked Holland, Luxembourg and Belgium. Four days later Holland acknowledged defeat. The Germans moved swiftly through the Belgian Ardennes and quickly reached northern France. The war had not only begun, it seemed to be nearly over. Sartre reported that there was a curious feeling among his soldier companions, 'almost relief'. He wondered how Beauvoir felt about it: was she in a state of 'agitation, gloom or in that happy indifference that you sometimes feel?'

In Paris nobody could feel indifference, least of all Beauvoir. On May 10th, unfolding her newspaper as she walked down the boulevard Raspail, she had read the headlines. 'I sat down on one of the benches and began to cry.' What could have happened? 'Had there been treason? I could not think of any other explanation.' Military inefficiency, political ineptitude, public complacency, moral decline: these various factors were not fully appreciated by many French people until long after the war was over. Beauvoir herself had hardly registered them, she was even more unrealistic than most French intellectuals. Early in May Paul Nizan had been shot at the front, before the end of the month Bost was seriously wounded. Sartre continued to write garrulous 'reassuring letters' and the French Prime Minister said in a radio speech that he believed in miracles, because he believed in France. Beauvoir was not taken in, but jumped to conclusions: 'That meant, obviously, that it was all over.' What could she do? The inhabitants of Paris had not yet taken fright and begun to leave the city, but they all began to wonder when, rather than if, they should do so. There was a semblance of normal life, and Beauvoir could still go to Le Dôme. 'I imagined with anguish the arrival of the Germans, their presence. No, I did not want to be confined until the end of the war in this city which would be transformed into a fortress; I did not want to live for months, maybe longer, as a prisoner.' But she realized that she could no longer control her own situation, for 'materially, morally, I was obliged to remain there: life had definitely ceased to obey my wishes'. She could not leave Paris for she had to conduct the *baccalauréat* examinations at her lycée in mid-June. She could not continue with her novel, she could barely read. She spent her evenings at the cinema or the opera – the entertainment world had not yet closed down.

Ironically, Sartre described himself as 'little more than *un travailleur de roman*. That's all I do and I'll soon have finished.' He found the war 'interesting' and did not think that civilians would be bombed. Wanda was not too ill and there was no more talk of marriage because all leave was cancelled in any case. More importantly, Beauvoir's own place in his affections was no longer threatened: 'At the moment the war has aggravated the sense of hierarchy to the point where you are the only person in the world who counts for me; I no longer think of anyone but you.'

Fortunately she could still live on letters from Sartre, who had more time than ever to write since the German advance had so far by-passed his unit. He continued to send requests for books, ink and paper but was soon more concerned with re-orientating Beauvoir's management of the group of young women close to one or both partners. She was told to put the Kosakiewicz sisters on a train to Normandy at once. They were unwilling, she was firm, and they went. Beauvoir was also instructed that if Paris was evacuated, '*You must absolutely*, if it is practically possible, take Sorokine with you. Too bad if her mother curses you.' She would save the girl from the chaos of enforced evacuation, lack of money and isolation. 'Take her with you and if it costs us a little money, too bad ... And then, most important of all, we are privileged people and that will be the only concrete help that I understand and permit: total help to one individual.' Beauvoir herself was not forgotten. When Sartre speculated on 'the possibility of a life in which I couldn't write or publish what I write, and one in which we would have many material deprivations, if I think I'd be leading this life with you, I think I could still find happiness in it'. He thought about her all the time, he said, except when he was playing chess.

By Sunday, June 9th, 1940, the news from the war front sounded irrevocably bad, for French forces in the north-east were falling back. Beauvoir had spent the previous evening at the Opéra with Védrine, listening to Dukas' *Ariane et Barbe-Bleue*. The girl wore 'her pretty red dress over which she had slipped a red scarf; we had bought some cakes in a nearby pâtisserie and settled down in a box'. Afterwards, walking down the avenue de l'Opéra, they had argued fiercely about the music – Védrine disliked it, Beauvoir defended it. Only afterwards did they talk about 'the war, about a possible defeat'. Suicide was a possibility, thought Védrine; no, said Beauvoir. She felt it was interesting to go on living, there was 'just that tragic interest' that she had now felt for a month, 'despite everything'. Sartre's optimism had probably been contagious in the end, and Beauvoir, the hopeful novelist, could not restrain her curiosity, although she admitted her characteristic emotional reaction: 'I felt the German advance as a personal threat, I had only one idea in my head, not to be cut off from Sartre and Bost, not to be caught like a rat in occupied Paris ...' Anti-aircraft fire could be heard, there were clouds of white smoke in the sky, but Beauvoir spent her Sunday reading and listening to music. In the evening she heard from Védrine that the *baccalauréat* examinations had been cancelled, teachers were free, and the girl offered her an escape: why should Beauvoir not leave Paris with her and her father, who planned to drive to the west? In this way she could stay with her friend Madame Morel near Angers.

She agreed to go, feeling that she would never see the city again. She packed a few possessions, leaving 'all my books, papers and old clothes. I took manuscripts, notebooks and clothes that I liked.' She spent the night in Védrine's hotel but got up early next morning to rescue the letters from Sartre and Bost which she had been keeping in the Lycée Camille Sée, mainly to prevent them being lost or read by other people in her hotel room. She hoped to take Nathalie Sorokine with her to Angers, but as a foreigner the girl would have to wait a week for a permit. Beauvoir worried desperately about Sartre: 'I realized that he would be a prisoner of war for an indefinite length of time, that he would have a horrible life, that I would have no news of him' – and 'For the first time in my life I had a kind of *crise de nerfs*; for me this was the worst moment of the entire war.'

Fortunately she had repaid her debt to Monsieur Védrine, fortunately his hostile wife was not there. After some reluctance he agreed to make room for his daughter's friend alongside his account books, his valuable stock of pearls and the woman employee whom he was taking as a passenger. Before they left Paris Beauvoir just had time to go to a café and write to Sartre and Bost, sobbing as she did so at the anguish of separation. After an overnight stop at Illiers (Proust's 'Combray') the refugees continued westward through Le Mans in the Sarthe, and at Laval, further west still, Beauvoir left the others, having found she could take a coach to Angers. She had to stand most of the way but by eight in the evening she reached the town, which was crowded with people who had fled from Paris, the north and the east. A few years later Beauvoir re-lived this journey in what was to be her second novel *Le Sang des autres*. Understandably she added dramatic highlights. In 1940, on June 11th, Madame Morel's daughter met her by car and she was soon safe at La Pouèze. The house was full of refugees, and Beauvoir shared a bedroom with a poodle, who was 'rather too friendly, especially towards the morning, but he didn't disturb me too much'.

Thanks to Louise Védrine, who would have done anything to help the young woman she adored, and to Védrine's father, Beauvoir had been lucky, and her escape from Paris had not brought her any suffering. Thanks to her generous friend Madame Morel she could now rest and was given breakfast in bed every day. There was only one disappointment: there were no letters for her. She had assumed that letters from Sartre and Bost would have been forwarded from Paris; it had not occurred to her that the owner of the Hôtel du Danemark might have had other things to worry about.

As the news spread that the Germans had reached Le Mans, about fifty-five miles away, some of the village people fled from La Pouèze, leaving it deserted and silent. From the Morel home 'we could hear cannon and the sound of explosions: the petrol storage tanks in Angers had been blown up ... Lorries full of French soldiers, all singing, passed through.' Four 'elegant' French officers stopped their car to ask the way: they wanted to find out if the Germans had reached Angers. A column of tanks went past, moving west, as the soldiers had done. Beauvoir remembered vividly the extraordinary scene, dramatizing it with herself as the central and only character. All the house shutters had been closed. 'I remained alone, by a window, looking through the slits in the shutters at the empty street. There was bright sunshine. I felt I was living through a science-fiction novel; it was still the familiar village but time had turned upside down. I had been projected into a moment outside my life. This was no longer France, it was not yet Germany: it was no man's land.' A large detachment of German soldiers moved into the village and to everyone's surprise they were not barbarians: they 'did not cut off children's heads, they paid for their drinks and for the eggs they bought from the farms, they spoke politely'. But they were Nazis nonetheless: they told Beauvoir, when they found her reading in a field, that they liked French people; 'it was the British and the Jews who had led us into all this trouble'.

Operation Dynamo, the official name for the Dunkirk rescue of British and French troops, was over. The Prime Minister, Paul Reynaud, urgently needing to replace incompetent military leaders and ministers, recalled Marshal Pétain, who was eighty-four and had been French ambassador in Spain since the end of the Civil War. The government, or more precisely the Council of Ministers, moved from Paris to Tours, and later to Bordeaux. Political machinations led right-wing, pro-German cliques to the forefront, and Reynaud resigned on June 16th. Britain was determined to continue fighting, France wanted an armistice, and it was the right-wing Pétain's voice, 'military and paternalistic', that Beauvoir heard on the radio on June 17th. Four days later the terms of the armistice were made clear. Only one thing mattered to her: what was happening to the French army, what was happening to Sartre? 'Had he managed to return to Paris? How could I find out? There was no telephone, no post, there was no way to learn what was happening there: the only solution was to go back.'

She felt she had already been away long enough. 'And I wanted to see Paris under the Occupation, and I was bored.' She left the relative safety and comfort of the Morel household on June 28th and accepted a lift back to Paris with a Dutch couple. But there was not enough petrol, hardly any food, and finally, in La Ferté-Bernard, not yet half way to the capital, Beauvoir accepted a lift in a German lorry. It left her in Mantes where she found a further lift with a Red Cross car, which took her the remaining twenty-five miles to a deserted Paris. The owner of the Hôtel du Danemark was surprised to see her for she had not expected her to return and had thrown away all her belongings. Fortunately she had not thrown away a letter from Sartre, but it belonged to history, for it was dated June 9th and contained no real news.

Passing the Café Dumesnil, in Montparnasse, Beauvoir caught sight of someone she had not seen for some time: her father. Although they had a drink and a sandwich together he had only depressing rumours to pass on to her, for he thought prisoners-of-war would not be released and were probably starving to death. A visit to her mother was no more cheering: 'I don't think I could ever have felt so low as I did during this return through the empty streets, beneath a stormy sky, my head on fire, my eyes burning as I thought that Sartre was literally dying of hunger.' She looked around her: 'The houses, the shops, the trees in the Luxembourg Gardens all remained; but there were no more people, there never would be any, and I didn't know why I survived in this absurd way.'

Habit took her back to Le Dôme, where there were few clients. She could not stop thinking about the one man she wanted to see. 'I almost hoped I would find Sartre, all smiles, sitting on the terrasse.' There was no Sartre, but her old optimism quickly returned: 'All at once, suddenly, I believe in an *afterwards*: the proof is that I've bought this notebook, some ink and I've written down the events of these last days.' Writing saved her. She found a part-time teaching post at the Lycée Victor Duruy and she also found again Nathalie Sorokine. The girl had attempted to leave Paris by bicycle but the Germans had sent her back. Nathalie had at once 'found', i.e. stolen, a bicycle for her friend and taught her to ride it. Beauvoir began to reorganize a life for herself, although it was a lonely one. Since her grandmother had gone to stay with Beauvoir's parents she could again take over her apartment at 91, rue Denfert-Rochereau, which she had occupied in 1929 after leaving home. She discovered a way of spending her afternoons: she would go to the Bibliothèque Nationale and read Hegel.[1] She found him difficult but calming. Though she could not concentrate on her novel for the time being it was never far from her mind and in Hegel one day 'I found a passage which I copied out, it would form a wonderful epigraph for my novel': 'Each conscience seeks the death of the other.' She did not forget it.

France was coming to terms with its defeat. The interim government was now established at Vichy in the Auvergne, some 180 miles south of the capital, and outside the occupied zone. On July 10th Marshal Pétain, by a large majority, was granted full powers as Prime Minister and on the same day he declared himself 'Head of the French State'. Conditions for ordinary people varied widely across the country, and in Paris Beauvoir found food, but no films worth seeing. There were not many German soldiers in Montparnasse and none at Le Dôme, for a notice appeared forbidding them to enter, although she did not know why. On July 11th life in one sense began again for her, for she received a note from Sartre, written on July 2nd. He was in a prison camp near Baccarat, the town famous for its crystal glass works, not far from Strasbourg. He had been taken there on June 21st, his thirty-fifth birthday. 'I'm a prisoner and very well

---

[1] Georg Wilhelm Friedrich Hegel (1770–1831): German philosopher whose influence on the theories of Marxism and existentialism was important. His *Phenomenology of Mind* was published in 1807. He hoped that philosophy could assume the status of a science and he sought some form of rational religion which could serve as a model in the development of personality and morality. He was also concerned with the philosophy of history, of art and of religion and with the history of philosophy itself. Sartre's key work *L'Etre et le néant* (1943) owes much to Hegel.

treated, I can work a little and I'm not too bored and I think I'll soon be able to see you again.' He hoped she would write to him and tell him everything. 'Send me a quick parcel of something to eat, for we're getting rather thinner here. I've a good figure but I don't want to become concave.' Beauvoir noted her reaction: 'This letter matters hugely, and it's nothing at all. All the same, I can breathe a little more easily.' Her letters began to reach Sartre by the end of July and he could say 'my life has changed'. His optimism had hardly been damaged, 'and I've always told you, as long as there are the two of us, I'll know how to be very happy again'. But love was not all. 'With the food send me *in particular pain d'épice* and chocolate.'

Sartre, surrounded with 7000 other prisoners, and busy with *L'Etre et le néant*, was happier than Beauvoir, who felt lonely, seeing only Olga, on a brief trip to Paris, and the unpredictable Nathalie. Though her presence helped her former teacher in some ways, this girl was still difficult and exhausting. She would refuse to leave her friend's apartment before the curfew, although it was now as late as 11 p.m. and once, when Beauvoir threw her out, she spent the night asleep on the doormat.

Beauvoir had hoped Sartre might be released during the summer, or early autumn, for optimism and rumour had led him to believe so. 'If I find you again, I find my happiness again, and I find *myself* again.' He advised patience and discouraged her from coming to Baccarat, for the journey meant thirty-two hours of travel for a kind of prison-style visit lasting twenty minutes. One day, he wrote, she would certainly see him appear from 'behind the statue of Balzac', at the Carrefour Vavin in Montparnasse. His hopes of early release were dashed for in mid-September he was transferred to a camp near Trier in Germany, close to the border with Luxemburg, where he settled down to a privileged and busy life. He was allowed to sleep in a bed, worked as an interpreter, a hospital aide, a teacher. He also wrote a successful play, *Bariona*, which was to be performed in the camp at Christmas time. Everything entertained him but he was disappointed by the lice: 'They don't bite, they brush against you, and the remarkable thing about them is their extraordinary prolificity.' He read Heidegger, continued to write and said he had 'never felt so free'. How lucky he was! He had published

La Nausée just before the war; *L'Imaginaire*, the revised second part of a book he had been asked to write while in Le Havre, and published in 1936 as *L'Imagination*, had appeared in March 1940, despite the initial reluctance of his publisher and had been a great success with students at least. *Le Mur* (1939) had just won the Prix Populiste, but it was the work in progress now, the philosophical work and the first volume of *Les Chemins de la Liberté* that were to transform Sartre into a leader of his generation. Captivity was shaping his career.

Beauvoir, 200 miles away in Paris, was 'free' in a different kind of way, for the war had brought the summer term to an early close. In some ways life in Montparnasse seemed to continue for her as though very little had happened; cafés and restaurants were still open. When her young friend Bost had recovered from his war injury she spent ten days with him in Montpellier, where he was convalescing, and she also took a short holiday with Louise Védrine, cycling round Brittany for a week. News of Sartre was so intermittent that she felt discouraged from writing every day, and then, when letters came more regularly, she wished she had written more often. She had heard that letters to prisoners should not be too long and craftily discouraged other people, including Sartre's mother, from writing too often, lest the prisoner might be forbidden to receive so much correspondence. Although she missed Sartre desperately she had consolations: Bost returned to Paris and when the autumn term began he took a post as *surveillant-professeur* at a school in the Denfert-Rochereau district. He was sorry that he had to teach philosophy, but he was quite well paid. Beauvoir saw a good deal of him, mostly, it appears, in secret, but when she saw him 'officially', about once a fortnight, Olga was jealous, 'a pure tyrant'. The 'family' situation was changing, or rather shifting: Nathalie found a young man she could sleep with and quarrel with, while Védrine, as Beauvoir had foreseen, began to contemplate marriage with a fellow student, which took place in the spring of 1941.

During her brief escape from Paris and in the absence of news from Sartre and Bost Beauvoir had not had the heart to write. When she could at last exchange news and ideas with Sartre once again she recovered something of her underlying ambition. She continued studying Heidegger for she wanted to stay close to the course of Sartre's thinking. She had written rather wistfully in mid-July that she had had 'a brief moment of intellectual warmth, I wanted to do some philosophy . . .' The intellectual life of the capital was suspended, and Beauvoir had no contact with writers. Many of the older ones – André Gide, Blaise Cendrars, Colette – were in the south, living in the relative comfort of the unoccupied zone. Aragon was in Nice while André Malraux, released from a detention camp, was at Cap Saint-Martin. The Americans Gertrude Stein and Alice B. Toklas were having a not unpleasant time near the Swiss border. In Paris Adrienne Monnier succeeded in keeping her famous library and bookshop open, helping among others the Hungarian writer Arthur Koestler who had gone into hiding even before the *drôle de guerre* ended, because the French regarded him as an enemy alien with dangerously left-wing views.

Publishing did not come to an end but obviously it changed. The publishers Bernard Grasset and Robert Denoël sided with the Vichy government and the German occupants. The astute Gaston Gallimard had removed his business first to Normandy, then to Carcassone in the south, but with his staff soon returned to Paris. The novelist Brice Parain, editor and reader for Gallimard, had already shown interest in Beauvoir's novel, and she decided she would go and see him. He explained to her how far publishing had been affected by the Occupation, how the German Ambassador, Otto Abetz, although reputedly a Francophile, had drawn up a list of forbidden works. These included anything by a Jewish author, from Heinrich Heine to Freud, and anything too 'patriotic', such as the writings of General de Gaulle, whose activities as an overseas resistance leader were obviously a threat to the occupiers' regime. As time went on the effects of the censorship were found to be patchy and unpredictable, but for the moment any author had to take care, he or she might be forced to write about the past or about an idealized future with no obvious location. If the writing concerned the present time, then the subject and the interpretation must be handled with care and have no relevance to the current situation of France or to any way of thinking that might draw disapproval or anger from the authorities. Predictably, the early war years did not see the publication of many outstanding books, but in the abnormal climate works on philosophical themes were 'safe' provided they dealt with abstractions only. An established author could be published in France, if he obeyed the rules, and for this reason François Mauriac's *La Pharisienne*, one of the last of his better novels, was to appear in 1941. That same year also saw the publication of a small masterpiece, Aragon's poems *Le Crève-coeur*. These lyrics kept imaginative writing alive and seemed to contain a message of hope.

By the end of 1940 Beauvoir had worked her way through alternating moods of misery and elation. At one point she could not even make notes for her journal, for she was haunted by a 'map of Germany, with a black frontier of barbed wire, and then somewhere is the word Silesia, and then phrases overheard such as: "They're dying of hunger." I hadn't got the heart to continue; the *tête-à-tête* with the paper was unbearable for me.' At least she was able to write to Sartre, who hoped she would write every day, for now there was no limit to the letters he could receive, although he could not send as many as he wanted, despite the regular smuggling of correspondence by civilian staff, visitors and escapees. She was still agitated by imaginary worries: she thought Sartre's head would have been shaved and at the mention of the 'hospital' where he worked for a time, she was panic-stricken: was he dying of typhus? She was disappointed that her efforts to arrange his release through various contacts were not successful, but in the end she felt calmer.

Eventually she was able to settle down to creative writing again. She began to see now that writing in itself was a form of indirect resistance to the Occupation, to the cultural darkness that was threatening to engulf Europe. 'There was no encouragement to think that Germany might be defeated . . . But I made a kind of bet: what value would there be in hours spent vainly writing if tomorrow everything collapsed?' There was another side to the question: 'If ever the world, my life, and literature were to find a meaning again, I would reproach myself for the months and years wasted in doing nothing.' She made herself work. 'So I installed myself at Le Dôme in the mornings and late afternoons in order to compose the last chapters of my novel; I revised the entire book.' It was hard work and any writer, amateur or professional, can feel sympathy for her. 'It did not excite me; this book expressed a period of my life that was over; but in fact I was impatient to leave it behind and I attacked the work with vigour.'

During the winter of 1940–41, even colder than the first winter of the war, she left the Denfert-Rochereau apartment and moved back to the Hôtel du Danemark. 'Coal was short, my room was not heated, the sheets were icy cold, I went to bed wearing ski trousers and a pullover.' Beauvoir now spent as much time as she could in her two favourite cafés, Le Dôme and Le Flore, the two stable points in her life. The cafés were able to produce at least some heat, even if a glowing stove usually entailed dealings on the black market. The atmosphere was very different now. Instead of the refugees of the pre-war years she saw Germans, who were now allowed to enter, and she also saw them eating 'butter and jam, entrusting packets of real tea to the waiters'. Life was truly hard for most of the French, and especially hard for Beauvoir as she tried to come to terms with her isolation and her confused response to the defeat of France. No one could escape the situation and the 'ambiguous solidarity' it produced. 'In this occupied France the mere act of breathing implied consent to oppression; even suicide would not have freed me from it, it would have consecrated my defeat; my salvation was linked to that of the entire country.' The most depressing aspect of it all was the realization of her own guilt: 'This situation had been imposed upon me, but my remorse had revealed to me that I had contributed to its creation.' She knew that during the 1930s she had closed her eyes to the entire world of politics, national and international. She had barely read the newspapers, she had on her own admission behaved like the ostrich, she had buried her head in the sand. She felt guilty that her generation had let down young people, young men like Bost. Preoccupied with her own individual destiny, her conviction that nothing could obstruct her happiness and her ambitious belief in literature, she had been one of the many French intellectuals who had chosen to ignore the inevitable decline and defeat of the country. She had looked with curiosity at poverty and deprivation, but only from a distance, finding it 'picturesque'. The German Occupation of France was not 'picturesque'.

But what could she do now to remedy the situation? Nothing. 'I blamed my old inertia, I found nothing more to do than go on

living, surviving, waiting for something better to happen.'
Beauvoir could go to the theatre but she could not listen to any
uncensored radio broadcasts and naturally she refused to read
German-controlled newspapers and magazines. She was not
totally alone now for Olga, and Wanda too, had both returned to
Paris. Nathalie Sorokine was still close to her and would not go
away, despite her unromantic love-affair with the young man
who she had hoped could help her escape from home. She had
hoped earlier that Beauvoir might come to her rescue by giving
her an allowance, but this was something Beauvoir could and
would not do. She was always ready to help but refused to do
anything that might encourage the girl to be even more irresponsible than she was by nature. Nathalie responded to her with a
fierce remark which has often been quoted: Beauvoir was cold, she
said, she was 'a clock in a refrigerator'. She was of course far
from cold; all her reactions to the events of 1939 and 1940 showed
her to be a deeply emotional woman, just as she had been an
imaginative, romantic, even violent adolescent. She had responded to the suppressed violence within Nathalie to such an extent
that Sartre had occasionally told her not to quarrel too much with
the girl. No doubt the two women argued partly out of frustration,
for Beauvoir in particular suffered at least three different kinds of
deprivation: she missed the presence of Sartre, even if their sex-
life had always been low-key, she was denied the intense
intellectual discussions which she found essential and stimulating, while wartime conditions made it exceptionally difficult to
finish her novel, especially since publication seemed a remote
possibility. Nathalie's deprivation was simpler but intense: she
suffered from lack of love.

When she was depressed Beauvoir may well have seemed
unresponsive or obstinate on occasions, for she could see no end to
the current gloom. She wrote pessimistic letters to Sartre but
fortunately she received optimistic ones in return. On October
26th, 1940, he took care to remember an important event which
had taken place, according to him, on October 10th, 1929: 'My
love,' he wrote, 'it's our eleventh anniversary. I feel very close to
you, I love you.' She assured him constantly that she loved him
but at the same time, though she rarely admitted to straightforward jealousy, she kept a close eye on the Sartre–Wanda

situation. In January 1941, when Wanda was in Normandy with her parents, Beauvoir tried to find out a little more about it: 'This afternoon with Bost I went into Wanda's room.' There she read the girl's diary: 'I saw in her *journal intime* that along with excellent feelings for you she was deeply annoyed because on two occasions she had received news of you through me.' She herself was irritated by Wanda's idleness and was no longer operating a charm offensive towards her. She had had enough of her, a feeling that was reciprocated. 'Moreover, she hates me, and that's why I've given up taking any interest in her.'

Fortunately these petty problems did not occupy the whole of her life, for she rediscovered the 'consolation of philosophy'. She still found Hegel interesting when she talked to her students about him, but he only reinforced her feelings of intellectual deprivation: she desperately needed 'solid conversations'. 'At this moment I'm aware of my metaphysical situation as intensely as in my youth, no doubt from solitude, and it's the one true richness in my life.' It contrasted with her day-to-day life: 'all our little world is really rather little', she admitted to Sartre, and she longed for his return.

Two months later, in March 1941, Sartre's optimism was justified: he reappeared in Paris. He had obtained 'unofficial' release from prison on health grounds, having drawn attention to his near-sightless eye in a pathetic way: 'Problems with balance', he had told the doctors. He was then given civilian status and with the help of German civilians outside the prison camp he escaped. He made his way to Paris as quickly as possible and moved into the Hôtel Mistral. Beauvoir followed, taking a room of her own.

Despite her relief and delight, Beauvoir admitted she had problems of readjustment. The intense correspondence of the last eighteen months had kept the partners close in most ways. She had worked for him in Paris like any willing wife while maintaining an independent existence of her own with Bost and her young women friends. What she found hard to understand now was his changed attitude towards politics, public morality and action in general. He immediately criticized her for buying tea on the black market and for signir.g a statement, as all lycée teachers had to do, that she was neither a freemason nor a Jewess. He wasted no time. 'That first evening he surprised me in another way; if he had returned to Paris it was not to enjoy the delights of liberty, but to act. In what way? I asked him in astonishment: we were so isolated, so powerless!' He was not prepared to accept that. 'Precisely,' he told me, 'we must shatter that isolation, we must unite, we must organize resistance.' Beauvoir confessed that she 'remained sceptical', the kind of response that has led many people to criticize her as unwilling to take any action. She understood the romantic side of Sartre's nature: 'I had already seen Sartre evoke unexpected possibilities in a few words, but I was afraid this time he was nourishing illusions.' She was more realistic than he was, but so far her vision, unlike his, was limited to the personal situation.

Undeterred, he approached many old friends, and sought out new ones, forming a group called 'Socialisme et Liberté', whose first meeting was in Beauvoir's room in the Hôtel Mistral. Some of the members were in favour of carrying out individual attacks. 'But none of us,' Beauvoir remembered, felt qualified 'either to manufacture bombs or to throw hand grenades'. If she had been less preoccupied with her many personal problems she might have discovered earlier, as she and Sartre did now, that there were already many other concealed resistance groups among the intellectuals and teachers. They had remained so deeply hidden because they were working in great danger and were not able to achieve very much. Nothing daunted, Sartre asserted that if Germany won the war it must at any price be made to lose the peace, and that was a job for the intellectuals; it would involve the kind of educational work they were well equipped to do. Unfortunately this 'privileged' group had not yet discovered how to make contact with ordinary people, ordinary readers, unlike 'Vercors' (Jean Bruller), a professional illustrator wounded on active service, his book, *Le Silence de la mer*, describing how one Frenchman and one young girl 'resisted' in silence, was printed and distributed cautiously the following year in a dangerous operation in which everyone involved, from the printers to the women sewing the pages together, were virtually risking their lives through this kind of resistance commitment.

Sartre soon came to terms with the strange life of occupied France and realized something of Beauvoir's experience so far. He came to understand what Gide had once written about the captive bird: it was better to remain in the middle of the cage. Later, Sartre wrote in *La France libre*, a periodical published in London, a memorable, possibly optimistic account, of what life had been like: 'No, the Germans did not walk through the streets with weapons in their hands; no, they did not force civilians to give way to them . . . in the Metro they gave up their seats to old ladies, they easily became emotional over children.' Some Germans would even display 'a naive goodwill', but received no response from the French, who kept their distance. Then Sartre made his most important point: 'But it must not be forgotten that the Occupation was part of everyday life. When a man was once asked what he had done during the Terror [of 1793] he replied: "I went on living." We could all make the same reply today. For four years [three in Sartre's case] we went on living and so did the Germans, in the midst of us, submerged and drowned in the unanimous life of the big city.'

Sartre was soon integrated into his old life again, he returned to teaching at the Lycée Pasteur and continued to write. Beauvoir herself went through a further period of deep change. She was infinitely happier after her partner's return, but a combination of his new attitudes and her own experiences reversed some of her earlier reactions to the outside world: 'Events had changed me; what Sartre had previously called my "schizophrenia" had given way to the counter-arguments inflicted upon me by reality.' She had reached an important stage of intellectual maturity, for the adolescent illusions she had preserved for so long had finally faded: 'I admitted at last that my life was not a story I was recounting to myself, but a compromise between the world and me.' This acceptance of reality led her into a mood of optimism and creativity, it changed the whole course of her life and writing, and the fact that the process had taken so long meant that the change was profound and lasting. Beauvoir no longer felt that 'setbacks and adversities were unjust: there was no way of rebelling against them, you had to find a method for circumventing them or accepting them'. Everyone in France, as they 'went on living', was following the same course. 'I knew that I would probably have dark hours to traverse, that maybe I would be swallowed up in the darkness for ever: this idea did not horrify me.' How different she was now from the Beauvoir of the 1930s! As she faced the reality she had rejected for so long she now found she had entered a new and constructive phase: 'Through this renunciation I gained a kind of insouciance that I had never known before.' The weight of her anxieties, real and imaginary, was suddenly lifted, and she felt she could begin to enjoy life in the active way she wanted: 'I took advantage of the spring and the summer; I finished my novel; I made notes for another book.'

1941 was hardly a year for optimism at national level. Admiral Darlan, who had become the virtual second-in-command to Pétain, committed the Vichy government to providing naval assistance to Germany, although the Germans did not entirely trust him. Though Sartre had been restored to Beauvoir, her sister Hélène had been trapped in Spain since the débâcle of 1940 and could only now communicate with her family through the Red Cross. In July Beauvoir's immediate family was further depleted, for her father died at the age of sixty-three, after suffering a relapse, hastened by malnutrition, following a prostate operation. He had been deeply depressed by the war and the occupation, for they meant that his former idle, enjoyable, nineteenth-century life-style was over for good. His daughter was surprised by his 'indifference' to the idea of death, for she herself had always been terrified by it. 'I admired the way in which he returned so peacefully into the void' and she admired another aspect of his attitude: 'He asked me if, without upsetting my mother, I could prevent any priest from coming to his bedside: she complied with his wish.' Beauvoir failed to understand the passage from life to death: 'I was present when he died . . . trying vainly to understand the mystery of this departure into nothingness.' She registered curiosity, but could find little to say about the man who had taught her to love books and encouraged her to write. 'I remained a long time alone with him after the final spasm; at first, he was dead but present: it was he. And then I saw him move rapidly away from me: I found I was bending over a corpse.' Her memories of his death are so laconic that they might well lend support to Nathalie Sorokine's accusation that she was cold. Was she unconsciously taking a form of revenge, aware of the way he had wanted her to be a freakishly brilliant student, remembering the years when he had grown distant from her mother and even treated her badly? Had Sartre replaced Georges de Beauvoir in some ways as her father-figure? Possibly. In any case she chose not to recall any affectionate feeling for the amateur actor who had preferred costume and make-up to a disappointing everyday life.

Nathalie herself now emerged from adolescence to become a tall, handsome, fair-haired young woman, despite *une lourdeur de moujik*; she was plump and always hungry. She had accepted Sartre in the end, although she had first pursued him along a street between Passy and Montparnasse, intending to attack him with a large safety-pin. By the summer she had stolen an extra bicycle for Sartre, who now planned, with Beauvoir, to visit the unoccupied zone in the south. This was to be more than a summer holiday. They hoped to gain supporters for 'Socialisme et Liberté', for it had soon become clear that very little could be achieved in Paris; it was too dangerous, especially so for a group of intellectuals with no experience of subversive action and no talent, it must be said, for practicalities. Beauvoir remembered clearly all the details of their journey. Crossing into the 'free' zone was not too difficult, but their visits to André Gide in Grasse and André Malraux in Saint-Jean-Cap-Ferrat were unsuccessful. Neither of the two eminent writers could give them any encouragement or advice, beyond caution. Malraux thought it would be better to postpone any action until the U.S.S.R. changed sides and until the U.S. came into the war, for he was convinced that all this would happen. Beauvoir and Sartre decided that they could not persevere with this approach and returned reluctantly to Paris.

On the way to Grenoble, where they were going to see Colette Audry, Beauvoir, while riding down a steep hill, crashed into a pair of cyclists coming towards her, fell off her bicycle dangerously close to a precipice, suffered bad bruising and losing a tooth, which became embedded in her lower cheek. She was lucky, for she could easily have been killed. The very next day she was brave enough to continue the journey by bicycle and finished her holiday and her convalescence at Madame Morel's house once again.

On their return to Paris they found the atmosphere had changed for the worse. The German occupiers 'no longer spoke of friendship, they uttered threats'. Would-be resisters were punished or shot. Beauvoir and Sartre saw that it would be far too dangerous to continue their secret resistance with 'Socialisme et Liberté'. Too many of their friends and former students disappeared – sometimes their fate was known, sometimes not. Reluctantly Sartre realized his project was at an end; there were no more secret meetings in hotel rooms. He concluded, as Beauvoir herself had decided earlier, that 'writing was the only form of resistance accessible to him'. Both partners have been criticized, usually by people who did not live under the German occupation, for giving up too easily. However, they were both better at writing than fighting, as their future was to prove.

The shortage of food forced Beauvoir into a completely different way of life from the one she had led virtually ever since 1929. She had always had a hearty appetite, and having lost a good deal of weight she at last discovered what all housewives had always known: she would have to shop and cook herself in order to survive. She had always thought that eating in restaurants was preferable to eating in her hotel room; it saved time, it was more sociable. She disliked cooking and preferred to be poor through eating out rather than better off and housewifely. 'I had little taste for domestic tasks and in order to deal with them I had recourse to a familiar procedure: I made an obsession out of my food problems and persevered with it for three years.' She learnt to cater as she had learnt to swim, by taking it very seriously, carefully collecting food coupons from Sartre, Bost, Olga, Wanda and Nathalie, spending as much time as she could searching for any food available on the free market. 'This kind of treasure hunt amused me; what a windfall if I found a beetroot or a cabbage! The first lunch we had in my room consisted of a "turnip choucroute" that I tried to improve by adding a bouillon cube.' Patiently she would sort dried beans, removing those infested with weevils. This was work she had always avoided, but now, characteristically, she made the best of it. She filled her store cupboard with pasta or oat flakes, gloated over her hoard and refused to allow the slightest waste: 'I understood avarice and its delights' and since she so much enjoyed eating she could say

> the alchemy of cookery pleased me. I remember, in early
> December, one early evening when the curfew – fixed at six
> o'clock, following an assassination attempt – imprisoned me
> in my room. I was writing; outside all was silent as the desert;

a vegetable soup was simmering on the stove and smelt good; this appetizing smell and the hissing of the gas were companionable; I did not live the life of a housewife but I had a glimpse of her delights.

Who could describe this near-motherly Beauvoir as 'a clock in a refrigerator'? She truly cared for her little 'chosen family'. In her kitchen she seemed so different from the Montparnasse intellectual all her friends knew that one of them, Marcel Mouloudji, found her good material for caricature. This talented, penniless, malicious young man who acted, sang and wrote a little, was a friend of Wanda's and it was he who had shown her Sartre's letters to Colette Gibert, in 1940. Later, in 1945, he won the Prix de la Pléiade for his novella *Enrico* and went on to a double career as writer and singer. Much later he published two comic autobiographical novels about his wartime adventures, and one of them was *Un garçon sans importance* of 1972. It contains a farcical description of a dinner he ate with 'Eugénie Leguen' (Beauvoir) and 'Sarbakane' (Sorokine). They had intended to make soup out of ersatz babyfood but by mistake they had used a flour-based glue. The women at least pretended to enjoy it, while the narrator of the novel, Mouloudji, suffered, and pondered about the implications of their behaviour. He imagined them belonging to a secret resistance group and felt he could not join them, for if they could not handle small problems of cookery, how could they be trusted with important matters of any kind?

Beauvoir had recovered most of her old optimism, partly perhaps because Sartre never lost his. 'We had decided,' she remembered, 'to live as though we had been assured of final victory in the end', and in fact during 1941 she was to see Hitler invade the U.S.S.R., to his cost, while in December, after the Japanese bombing of Pearl Harbour, the United States entered the war as Malraux had hoped. Beauvoir in fact maintained a day-to-day cheerfulness in inverse proportion to the worsening conditions of life in Paris. Food and clothing were hard to find. She wore wooden-soled shoes, as British women did, and ski pants whenever she could in order to keep warm. She admitted to neglecting her appearance and did not even seek to replace her lost tooth, mainly because she had no social life and now saw so few people. The shortage of electric power made professional hairdressing difficult and therefore 'turbans were fashionable: they replaced both hat and hairstyle'. Beauvoir had worn a turban since the early days of the war, causing Sartre in October 1940 to call her a 'little Hindu'. She had found these twisted scarves to be practical and they suited her; now she 'adopted them completely'. Little did she realize at the time that years later Simone de Beauvoir's turbans were to become world-famous and that journalists were to ponder on the psychological reasons for concealing her hair.

In the meantime the revised manuscript that she had been so anxious to complete found its way into the Gallimard office. Significantly it was not Beauvoir who took it there but Sartre. Either she thought he could exert more influence over the reader and editor than she could, or the book had already receded into her personal past. It was the summer of 1942 before she received a firm decision about its fate. She went, not alone, but accompanied by Sartre, to see Jean Paulhan, whose opinion was crucial, in his apartment on the Ile de la Cité.

'It was a beautiful day and I felt rather emotional,' she remembered. Beauvoir often denied that her novels could be called *romans à clé* but in this she deceived herself, as was demonstrated by Paulhan's first question which also proved there was an aspect to the book likely to excite gossip. Paulhan was intrigued to know 'whether Dullin really resembled the character of Pierre', 'hero' in one sense of the book. Apart from this he had one important criticism:

> He considered my style too colourless and asked in a kindhearted way:
> 'Would it be too much trouble for you to re-write the book, from start to finish?'
> 'Oh!' I said, 'that would be impossible for me: I've already spent four years on it!'
> 'Very well then!' Paulhan went on, 'in the circumstances we'll publish it just as it is. It's an excellent novel.'

Why then had he made such an alarming suggestion? 'I didn't work out whether he was paying me a compliment or whether he thought that my novel was the kind of book considered to be a good seller.' Paulhan was in fact repeating what Brice Parain had told Beauvoir in 1941, something she had passed on to Sartre. He had seen that the criticism was aimed at the new, non-literary tone he and Beauvoir had both developed. 'You and I,' he wrote to his Castor, 'believe that one should write as one speaks.' It was the only way to establish a direct, personal style.

'But the essential thing,' Beauvoir remembered, 'was that my book was accepted.' Understandably perhaps she felt 'not so much delight as relief'. It was nonetheless the start of her literary career, all she had to do now was to find a better title, and her suggestion of *L'Invitée*, instead of *Légitime défense*, was accepted. The stimulus to her ambitions had an immediate result: she had already begun a second novel and now went on with it enthusiastically. She knew she had to wait until the following year to see her first book published, but after four years' work it did not seem long until the summer of 1943, the date she had been promised.

The four years' work had taken the painful trio episode into the past, although none of its members ever forgot it, and while Louise Védrine was close to the 'family' circle there had even been a danger that a second one might have been formed. During the time she had taken to write the book Beauvoir had not only survived separation from Sartre and accepted his sexual anarchy, she had lived through two aspects of her own development which were to determine her personal future and her most important books. After many hesitations she had begun to control her own life as an independent individual and she was slowly becoming a member of society; she had 'learnt solidarity'. She did not yet see herself consciously as a *woman* member of society for she had not examined in detail how and why the life of a woman differed from that of a man: that realization, with the experience gained during the first few years of the war, was still to come.

THIRTEEN

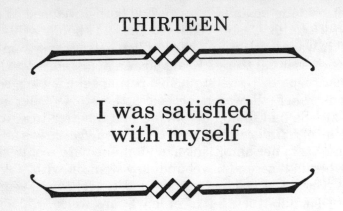

I was satisfied
with myself

There was nothing smug about the self-satisfaction Beauvoir now began to feel; she was honest about her achievements and proud of them, after such a long probationary period, yet conscious of the problems that lay ahead for her. After the acceptance of her novel she at once went on holiday with Sartre in the Basque country on the Spanish border and the south-east of France, later spending some time with Madame Morel. On returning to Paris for the autumn term she may well have wished she had not stayed away so long: 'I had an unpleasant surprise: the owner of the Hôtel Mistral had not kept my room.' It was virtually impossible in the autumn of 1942 to find a furnished room with a kitchen attached, for most people in Paris, even the intellectuals, had come to understand, reluctantly, that home cooking was the only means of survival. Eventually Beauvoir moved into the Hôtel d'Aubusson, virtually a slum building in the rue Dauphine which ran down from the Carrefour de Buci to the Pont Neuf in the 6th *arrondissement*: 'an iron bedstead, a wardrobe, two wooden chairs, peeling walls and a weak yellow light bulb in the ceiling; the kitchen also doubled as a *cabinet de toilette*'. The staircase was 'icy, damp, mouldy and evil-smelling', but she had no choice and stayed there nearly two years. She had to tolerate something else: Sartre had moved into the same hotel and in order to economize Wanda moved in with him, thus saving the rent of another room, which Sartre would otherwise have had to pay. She did not complain either when she had to move her belongings in a hand-cart; she was glad that 'a host of conventions' had been swept away. 'I also liked this semi-equality which was forced on to us; I had never had a taste for privileges.' She decided that she would prefer a socialist regime, provided its basis was sound, to 'bourgeois injustice'. She would even tolerate 'extreme asceticism' but confessed that she would miss the long holidays she enjoyed so much.

As autumn advanced, day-to-day life grew even more complex. The German occupiers were becoming more severe because the tide of war seemed to be turning against them. On November 4th Rommel lost the second battle of El Alamein in Egypt to the Eighth Army of British and Commonwealth troops. Gradually all Axis forces were driven out of Africa, and already on November 8th an Allied Expeditionary Force landed on the Algerian coast. The inhabitants of metropolitan France were heartened by this news, but equally dismayed by the immediate German reprisals: the so-called free zone in the south of the country was no longer free but occupied, for the Germans realized they must defend the Mediterranean coast. Two weeks later the French fleet destroyed itself at Toulon, carrying out a secret order made by Admiral Darlan in 1940: at all costs it must not fall into the hands of the Germans. Darlan had moved away from the Nazis and appeared to be ready to support the Allies, but he was assassinated in Algiers in late December 1942. In addition to this turmoil the Germans in France turned more fiercely against the Jews, who were ordered to wear an identifying yellow star on their clothing, although Beauvoir noticed that most of those who frequented Montparnasse and Saint-Germain-des-Prés seemed skilful enough to avoid this badge of discrimination.

She continued to look after the small 'family' who surrounded her and Sartre, none of them equipped to earn much of a living, even if the Kosakiewicz sisters hoped to make names for themselves. Mouloudji introduced them into his novel, calling them 'Volga' and 'Loubia'. Wanda had recently decided that she hated painting and now, with prompting from Sartre, wanted to become an actress like Olga. Beauvoir did everything she could to minimize the problems of cold and hunger for her group of young friends. She now found herself entirely responsible for Nathalie

Sorokine, because the girl had broken away definitively from home. After leaving her former lover, who was 'bourgeois' and unsatisfactory, she now found another, a young and attractive Jewish boy of Spanish origin, known as 'Bourla'. However, he was far from attractive to Nathalie's parents, for he could not offer the girl any security, although the couple were affectionately happy together. Nathalie's mother knew that Mademoiselle de Beauvoir, a popular teacher, had a strong influence over her headstrong daughter and she asked for support. Could she not persuade Nathalie to give up Bourla and return to her previous lover, who was usefully well off and would make an excellent husband? Beauvoir, predictably, refused. The mother was so angry that she complained to the education authorities, accusing Beauvoir of *détournement de mineur*, corruption of a minor. Unfortunately the authorities supported Madame Sorokine, and Beauvoir, despite her good record of twelve years' teaching, was deprived of her post and of any status within the field of higher education. The Sorokine family were immigrants to France, but they adopted the kind of behaviour that Beauvoir detested utterly: the conventional, money-based authoritarianism of the French bourgeoisie. She had attacked it in theory; now she had seen it in operation at first hand, which strengthened her resolve to oppose it fiercely for the rest of her life.

After her dismissal from lycée work Beauvoir no longer had the steady income of a civil servant but she relished one thing: she was totally free to concentrate on her own writing, and with some financial help from Sartre she could manage. She had helped him when he was an impoverished conscript; now, as he awaited the publication of *L'Etre et le néant* and the production of his first play, *Les Mouches* (*The Flies*) he was ready to help her. In fact he found for her a useful radio commission through a journalist named René Delange, director of the old-established, near-collaborationist but useful weekly *Comoedia*. The commission involved a series of twelve sketches, one to be broadcast every month during the following year, 1944: 'The idea,' Sartre told her, 'will be given to you, you'll do the dialogue – each one will last ten minutes.' He explained what she would be paid and added, 'I accepted on your behalf with enthusiasm.' Beauvoir said later that she had forgotten through what kind of 'trick' she had obtained this work but remembered that she had to write descriptions, or rather evocations, of old historic fêtes dating from the middle ages onwards. The idea was useful because it could not contravene the censorship regulations in any way. With help from Bost, Beauvoir carried out the commission, and the programmes were duly broadcast from Radio Vichy during the following year. If they have been preserved, nothing of them has been published to date. Beauvoir needed something to do, and she needed the money, even if it came indirectly from the collaborationist government. She did not assume the austere attitude of someone like Blaise Cendrars, who maintained a protest silence during the four Vichy years. Beauvoir's protest, during the war as before the war, remained one of apathy, despite her efforts to explain that for her at least writing was the only form of action she could take.

However, authors, like most of the French population, now began to see gleams of hope in the news from the war fronts, even though that hope had to remain muted for the time being. At the end of January in 1943 the Germans were defeated at Stalingrad in the U.S.S.R., and 90,000 soldiers of the Reich were taken prisoner. By September Allied troops had conquered Sicily and Italy. Even Beauvoir was watching military and political developments now. After Sartre had reluctantly brought his resistance group 'Socialisme et liberté' to an end he was invited by the Communist intellectuals to join the Comité National des Ecrivains and he agreed to attend their meetings. Beauvoir could not go with him because she was not yet a published author: 'I regretted it a little; I would have liked to meet new people.' She claimed that she had been a supporter of 'Socialisme et Liberté' because it had been a 'dangerous improvisation' – and it must have brought out her sense of adventure – but she did not care for the 'official and routine-style atmosphere' of the C.N.E. about which she now heard. Yet she understood that Sartre wanted to go and she was glad that the two of them still belonged to what was called the 'intellectual resistance', though she felt protective about Sartre: 'I was rather worried each time he went [to these meetings] and during all the time he was absent.' She had followed Sartre into a new phase of politically conscious life: 'I was all the same very pleased that we had emerged from our isolation, especially since I had often felt how much Sartre suffered from passivity.' She herself was content to protest against the German domination in theory only. Sartre had begun to contribute to underground newspapers and journals, but she herself had not yet thought of expressing herself through journalism.

Authors naturally hated the censorship of literature, but they could not complain that nothing was published during the German occupation. Albert Camus, who had come to the mainland from his native Algeria in 1940, was making a name for himself, and Sartre was impressed by *L'Etranger* (*The Outsider*). Raymond Queneau, admittedly no beginner, was able to bring out *Pierrot mon ami* in 1943, an amusing novel destined to have a long popularity in Britain as well as in France. During the same year Saint-Exupéry's *Pilote de guerre* appeared and found great success. Some of the leading French writers remained silent, or had left the country. Jules Romains was in North America, Georges Bernanos in Brazil, while some, like André Malraux, published only in Switzerland. Rather than watch German films in the cinema the curfew-bound population discovered that they could even enjoy evenings at home, provided they had something to read. Soon there were not enough books, either new or secondhand, to go round.

Beauvoir was too cold to write in her miserable room in the rue Dauphine. Since the street was not far from Saint-Germain-des-Prés she would spend as much time as she could in the Café de Flore, arriving about eight in the morning. She kept vivid memories of the special kind of life that went on there. If she arrived early she could sit 'in the best place, the one where it was warmest, next to the stove'. The owner of Le Flore, who has earned himself a place in the literary history of occupied Paris and its aftermath, was Paul Boubal, who had a slightly square, 'solid Auvergnat face', and a bad temper for at least an hour or so in the morning. Wearing his blue apron he would come down from his own apartment before eight o'clock and unlock the doors. He would nag his staff, deal firmly with his trade suppliers and complain about the customers, for they would even drink ersatz coffee without daring to object. 'If you gave them shit, they'd eat it!' he would say. Like other Auvergnats in the restaurant and café business he had been very successful and his café had already become a regular meeting place for theatre and film people before the war. Simone Signoret, for instance, had found her first film roles through meetings at Le Flore. The well-known personalities had not deserted it; Jacques Prévert and his friends still came, so did Picasso, as did younger writers, Dominique Aury and Arthur Adamov, or younger ones still, including Marcel Mouloudji, who, while there, occasionally found himself a small part in a film. He was beginning to write, and Beauvoir would correct his grammar and spelling for him. Boubal the businessman could not bear him as a client because he was always badly dressed and since he was constantly broke he would occupy a table for hours while paying for only one drink. Boubal himself, despite his high-handed attitude, was always popular, for somehow he succeeded in 'importing' food from his native Auvergne and would supply it to some of his regular customers, even if they did not always pay him for it: often, like Mouloudji, they had no money.

Sometimes Vichy supporters and anti-semites found their way into Le Flore, ignored by the right-minded regulars. If a stray German came in he soon sensed the hostility around him and left. Boubal was partial to Beauvoir and Sartre, who spent a vast amount of time there, so much so that the young Bourla used to say: 'When they die someone will have to dig graves for them under the floor.' At least they paid for their ersatz coffee. If the air-raid siren sounded Boubal 'would push the customers out at once and bolt all the doors; he would give favourable treatment to Sartre, myself and two or three others: we would go up to the first floor and stay there until the all-clear sounded.' Beauvoir soon learnt how to take the maximum advantage of the situation: 'In order to avoid this disturbance, and also to escape the noise on the ground floor I acquired the habit in the afternoons of going up to the first floor immediately.' The Café de Flore, once the scene of Apollinaire's 'Wednesdays', had become a literary centre again: 'A few other writers installed themselves there, also no doubt for the same reasons as I did; pens ran over the paper: we might have been in a well-disciplined classroom.'

Mouloudji, the young man of many gifts, never forgot the café, and in his novel *Un Garçon sans importance* he called it 'Sainte-Boubal', or even 'Sainte-Boubal la Désespérée'. After he had become a successful writer and singer he enjoyed making teasing references to the intellectuals he had seen working hard at the start of their careers. In his story he called them 'the abstracts' and gave an easily recognizable portrait of the obvious leader, 'Garap', namely Sartre, described as a 'dwarf'. Sartre has made several appearances in fiction, sometimes under his own name and usually portrayed in an unflattering, if comic, vein but most novelists, with the exception much later of Violette Leduc, have either been too polite or too timid to introduce Beauvoir in any guise. Mouloudji was neither. In his novel he described her at work, writing as usual in a café.

> At last Eugénie Leguen appeared in the glass-panelled doorway . . . She trotted along between the chairs up to her usual place, opened her exercise book and took out her inspiration. It was not the moment to disturb her. Impassive despite the continual to-ing and fro-ing of the customers she began to write, like a vertical sleeper linked to reality by the device of her moving pen. How impressive she was as she wrote, with her air of possessing second sight! . . . She emitted such a powerful atmosphere of concentration that you could no longer see her; there remained only a motionless form, while her mind, frolicking elsewhere in typographical meadows, gathered up sentences, images and ideas which she affixed to the blank pages.

1943 was a crucial year for both Beauvoir and Sartre. Despite the three years' difference in their ages their destinies had been parallel ever since the *agrégation* of 1929. Sartre's play *Les Mouches*, his first apart from *Bariona*, performed in the prison camp, was premièred in June. Jean-Louis Barrault had considered it but was deterred by the big cast of extras required and also by the play's message: in Beauvoir's words it 'exhorted the French to liberate themselves from their remorse and assert their right to freedom'. Sartre was making one of his first statements of the existential principle: each individual must be responsible for himself and his own liberty. Even though he was addressing his audience through the myth of Orestes and his defiance of the gods, the German occupiers were not likely to be taken in. However, Charles Dullin eventually produced the play in June 1943 at the Théâtre de la Cité in the Place du Châtelet. This was correctly the Théâtre Sarah Bernhardt, temporarily deprived of its name due to the stringent anti-semitism of the occupiers, for the great actress had been Jewish. Theatre-going was popular, despite curfews and powercuts. A surprising number of theatres were open, for Paris had succeeded in remaining something of an entertainment capital, though the German occupiers on the whole preferred to go to the opera, where they were less troubled by any language problem.

There had not yet been time or opportunity for wartime Paris to see plays in which a well-known story from classical times was combined with a subversive message. The play was not censored, either because the officials concerned did not grasp its potentially dangerous meaning, or because some German intellectuals admired the work Sartre had published so far and realized that he was an intelligent interpreter of various German thinkers. Heidegger, after all, who had influenced Sartre so strongly, supported the Nazi regime and never officially recanted. In adapting the Electra story from the *Oresteia* Sartre was in one sense following recent tradition in France, for Cocteau had used classical themes in the 1920s and Giraudoux had produced his *Electre* in 1937. The French dramatic critics took care not to discuss Sartre's barely coded statements about personal responsibility and liberty. They preferred to examine the literary aspects of the play, praised Olga, who, under her stage name of Olga Dominique, struggled with the part of Electra and despite her inexperience partially succeeded. The decor, costumes, masks and statues, designed by the sculptor Adam, also caused controversial comment. Critics writing in the German-language newspaper *Die Pariser Zeitung* spoke favourably of the play, but the public did not favour it with good attendances and after a few weeks theatres went dark for the summer. Dullin, however, brought the play back into a repertory season in the autumn.

The production of *Les Mouches* gave Sartre his start in theatrical work and had an immediate effect on Beauvoir: she now wanted to write for the theatre herself, especially since she had attended every rehearsal and reacted to the contagious excitement generated by a first play produced in difficult circumstances. All her life she had been a regular theatregoer, she had been delighted to see her young friend Olga making progress as an actress and she relished the immediacy of audience response.

Like most of her projects, her ambition to write for the theatre was realized in the end but she had to wait two years before the curtain went up on her first and, as it happened, her last play.

Temporarily at least the atmosphere of her personal life with Sartre was less intense than it had been during the long separation of the early war years. The partners had in one way settled down, always of course living in separate hotel rooms. Sartre had not become monogamous – that would have been a denial of his nature – he still spent much time with Wanda and did not dare allow her to see him writing a letter to Beauvoir. After encouraging Wanda to take up a career in the theatre, as her sister had done, Sartre took care that she did not miss rehearsals or performances, and later in fact he wrote plays which included roles designed for her. As for Beauvoir, sexual jealousy now seemed even less important than it had been in the past. She valued Sartre most of all as her intellectual partner and they both relied closely on each other for discussion and criticism of their work: writing had taken over her life. In some ways she had perhaps moved closer to Sartre's way of thinking: when young he had thought literature was more important than life, while she believed the opposite. The war, and their own experience, had changed both of them. They had achieved a balance between writing and life – for how could the first dispense with the second? They were both busy, happy, sensing that they were in their different ways on the verge of success. Their early need to write as a form of personal self-fulfilment was now being slowly trans-muted into social and political commitment. In that commitment, however, Beauvoir never lost sight of the personal, highly individual starting point which was to characterize her entire work. She was still closer to Sartre than to anyone else, and though she had known for a long time now that she would always have to share his emotional and sexual life with other women this made her cling more passionately than ever to the relationship of cerebral give-and-take that has given the couple a unique place in twentieth-century history. At the same time her contingent sexual partner, Bost, was still close.

Suddenly, thanks to Sartre, Beauvoir found herself writing fiction and non-fiction at the same time, and writing much faster than she had been able to do with *L'Invitée*. In the few months before *L'Etre et le néant* came out Sartre's name already carried a good deal of weight in publishing, and a new word was suddenly in use among writers on philosophical themes, editors and critics.

'Are you an existentialist, madame?' The question was put to Beauvoir one day in the Café de Flore by an acquaintance of Sartre, Jean Grenier, a publisher's reader who had been trained as a philosopher. She maintained that she did not know what the term meant. Out of context this may sound strange, but she went on to say that she understood very well the term 'existential' when it was used as an adjective, for she had studied Kierkegaard, Hegel and Heidegger, quite apart from her discussions with Sartre over the last few years. It was the use of the adjective as a noun, applied to a person, that temporarily confused her, especially since another philosopher who had recently begun to use it, Gabriel Marcel, was a Christian thinker and therefore occupied a position a long way from hers. She did not want to accept an over-simplified label and when Grenier invited her to contribute to a collection of essays on philosophical themes she told him she could add nothing to *L'Etre et le néant*.

She was then informed that she could choose her own subject, and when Sartre encouraged her she agreed to take part in the project, for she had wanted in any case to write something about 'the relationship between individual experience and universal reality'. She interrupted work on her second novel, *Le Sang des autres*, and launched into an essay which she entitled *Pyrrhus et Cinéas*. Within three months she had finished it, but either Grenier's project collapsed or Beauvoir's contribution outgrew it. It was to be published the following year by Gallimard. At this point Beauvoir confidently took stock of her own achievement so far: '*L'Invitée* would appear within one or two months. And I thought that with *Le Sang des autres* I had made progress. I was satisfied with myself.'

While waiting for *L'Invitée* to be published Beauvoir spent three weeks cycling alone in the centre of the country, starting from Roanne, some forty miles east of Vichy. She was able to enjoy meals which, compared to those available in Paris, seemed luxurious: 'radishes, a huge dish of spinach, excellent potato croquettes and two bad apricots.' Riding south-west she went through the Limousin on her way to meet Sartre at Uzerche and visited the house where she had been so happy during her childhood holidays. She did not go hopefully *à la recherche du temps perdu*, which was just as well: 'I spent a day at Meyrignac with my cousin Jeanne, surrounded with a swarm of fair-haired children. The house had been enlarged, the wood-store, the shed and the laundry had been made into living-rooms; there was no more wistaria on the walls, no more bignonias, statues of the Virgin stood under the trees and the landscaped garden was fenced with barbed wire. I did not find much of the past again.'

L'Invitée finally appeared in the early autumn of 1943, and Beauvoir had the strongest possible reason for self-satisfaction. The years of hard work seemed justified. When he read some of the early chapters Sartre had referred to it in his letters as 'your little book' but finally elevated it into 'an excellent novel'. Physically speaking it was, is, far from little, for in the French paperback Folio edition of 1986 *L'Invitée* is just over 600 pages long and amounts to some 170,000 words. In 1941 Brice Parain, the Gallimard editor, had decreed that the first two chapters must be omitted, which meant that the novel was long, but not too long. These chapters, which Beauvoir saved, were published in 1979 and prove that the editor was on balance right, for they tell the story that the author had, by then, told in her memoirs. Her family and friends are there, with new names. At school Françoise, the heroine, meets a Zaza-like figure, called Elisabeth, who asks her if she is a materialist or a deist. At the end of the deleted chapters Françoise shyly meets Elisabeth's brother Pierre, who seems set for a successful career in the theatre.

At the start of the novel in its published form Françoise and Pierre have been living together for some time, she is writing a novel, he is playing the name part in his own production of Shakespeare's *Julius Caesar*. Françoise has invited a young girl, Xavière, to stay with them in Paris, for she hates life in Rouen. Beauvoir, narrating much of Olga's earlier life, did not change the name of the town, as though taking her revenge on its dull, bourgeois citizens. The title given to the British and American editions of the book, *She Came to Stay*, misses the point: the girl was *invited* to Paris, she did not merely arrive or stay on in a casual fashion. The basic plot, which could be that of any romantic novel, re-tells the Beauvoir–Sartre–Olga story and develops the account of Beauvoir's liaison with Jacques-Laurent Bost, as already mentioned. Xavière is so tiresome that surely no reasonable people would tolerate her for half a day. But Françoise and Pierre are not reasonable people, they are in essence serious intellectuals living according to their own rules in a kind of *huis clos*. They are both fascinated by the 'authentic' quality they see in Xavière: to them she is spontaneous, honest, independent, conditioned only by herself and not by any inherited codes of rules imposed from outside.

Pierre falls 'contingently' in love with Xavière but his love does not last, for when she is committed to him he considers she is no longer 'authentic'. She had previously been so authentic, so free, that like Olga, she had deliberately burnt her own hand with a cigarette in confused self-punishment when she felt guilty about her behaviour. When Xavière seems to love the young Gerbert, Pierre is jealous, then Xavière is angry when she discovers that Françoise and Gerbert have had a brief if 'contingent' love-affair. By the last chapter the two men are on their way to the war, for this is 1939. All the suppressed emotionalism in the two women comes to the surface and Françoise has to decide between the girl and herself: she chooses herself and kills Xavière. The violence is indirect, conducted by remote control: she turns the gas taps on in the girl's bedroom and opens the valve in the kitchen. Beauvoir herself knew that the murder was unconvincing, and not even those 'lost' chapters about Françoise's youth could have laid foundations that would have developed her into a killer. The author, who maintained that she had thought about this plot before the triangle situation developed in her own life, justified her heroine's symbolic action by adding as epigraph the sentence from Hegel she had noticed in 1940: 'Each conscience seeks the death of the other.'

The philosophical aspects of this behaviour fascinate academic critics who have compared Beauvoir's treatment of the Otherness theme with that of Sartre in *L'Etre et le néant*. She is less pessimistic than he is and more concerned with the translation of concepts into action. She had a woman's instinct for relating abstractions to human behaviour, and without it she would never have become a novelist. In *L'Invitée* there is a graceful passage, salvaged fortunately from one of the excised chapters, which surely only a woman could have written, describing Françoise's recollection of an old jacket she had once seen on the back of a chair. She raises an age-old philosophical problem: if she were not there to see it, did the jacket 'exist'? It appears in the novel when Françoise is in a café by herself, thinking that she is 'exiled from the whole world', while Pierre and Xavière are together in another café. She remembers then an incident from her childhood:

> Her old jacket was hanging over the back of a chair . . . it was very old, it looked worn out. It was old and worn but it could not complain as Françoise complained when she had hurt herself: it had no soul; it could not say to itself 'I'm an old worn jacket'. It was strange; Françoise tried to imagine what it would be like if she could not say 'I'm Françoise, I'm six years old, I'm in grandmother's house'; if she couldn't say anything at all to herself; she closed her eyes. It's as though one did not exist; and yet other people would come there, they would see me and talk about me. She opened her eyes; she saw the jacket, it existed and it didn't realize it existed, there was something irritating about it, a little frightening. What's the point of existing, if it doesn't know it exists? She reflected: 'Perhaps there is a way. Since I can say "I", suppose I said it for the jacket?' It was rather disappointing: there was no point in her looking at the jacket, seeing nothing else and saying very quickly 'I'm old, I'm tired', nothing new happened; the jacket remained there, indifferent, totally extraneous, and she was still Françoise. Moreover, if she became the jacket for a moment then she, Françoise, would know nothing more about anything . . .

When this recollection appeared in the novel the phrase 'it had no soul' was removed.

Beauvoir the novelist 'existed' and was mentioned as the new '*romancière*', a convenient French term which fifty years later would be dismissed by many as sexist. An inescapable atmosphere of femininity does indeed permeate *L'Invitée* but never turns it into what is unkindly called 'a woman's book'. The men characters, Pierre and Gerbert, are little more than two-dimensional, even if Pierre is potentially interesting as an amalgam of Sartre and, as Paulhan had discovered, Charles Dullin, the theatrical producer. The analysis of Françoise by the author as intense, loving, possessive and finally destructive, is so *nuancé* that it almost justifies Beauvoir's preoccupation with herself. Françoise appears too good to be true, taking all responsibility for everyone and receiving little understanding in return. She might have reduced Xavière's undoubted power by laughing at her, but in this world peopled only by writers, artists, actors or singers there is much seeking of entertainment but no straightforward humour. Xavière herself almost laughs at her friends when she tells them ironically how orthodox they are, within their own set of rules. Why doesn't Françoise simply walk out on Xavière and Pierre? In the end she does so by committing the murder, but in doing that she is in one sense destroying herself. By stressing the fact that she had made a responsible choice, and 'chosen herself' she forgot perhaps that she was making a negative choice. As with all Beauvoir's future fiction, the autobiographical element is constantly fascinating.

Xavière and Françoise dominate the novel, and the older woman's love for the girl, which also embodies a degree of hate, brings both of them to life. Without the novelist's detailed observation Xavière might have been an unconvincing caricature of the ultra-feminine. When Sartre used Olga as a model for Ivich in *L'Age de raison* and its sequels, he obviously saw her as more eccentric. For Beauvoir Xavière is highly visible, with her beret, her flowered blouse or her new blue dress; her fair hair is mentioned too often: had no one ever had fair hair before? Françoise is sometimes aware in a confused way that she loves her physically, especially when they dance together. 'She felt Xavière's lovely warm breasts against her, she breathed in her delightful breath; was it desire? But what could she desire? Her lips against her own? This body abandoned in her arms? She could imagine nothing, it was only a confused need to keep this lover's face turned perpetually towards her and to say passionately: she belongs to me.' How much did Olga 'belong' to Beauvoir? Would there have been a novel without her? The author maintained that she had changed Olga's character when translating her into Xavière, but the book itself was dedicated to Olga. Pierre, even if permanent, seems less important to Françoise and hardly earns the reader's sympathy, for he is infinitely less interesting than Sartre. In a book so deeply concerned with sexual relationships there is no overt sex to be found, partly because it rated so little in the Beauvoir–Sartre partnership and partly because the characters are so deeply absorbed in their talk over the café tables or their observation of people's behaviour at parties or in the theatre.

Women are the stars of the book, both Beauvoir and Françoise look at them admiringly, assessing their talents, their movements, their clothes. Françoise envies their natural-seeming skills, while she, when dancing for example, is sometimes as intense as Beauvoir had been when Sartre was teaching her to swim. Elisabeth, the painter, is the most unhappy character in the book, in love with a married man who does not leave his wife. She is typical of a vast number of dissatisfied women caught in a triangular situation different from that of Françoise, Pierre and Xavière. There is violence within her too, she imagines weapons in her hand, but she is not sure whom she wants to kill, her lover, his wife or even herself. In one of the deleted early chapters Elisabeth makes a significant remark about her career. She wants to be a painter, not a 'woman painter'.

'I would hate to be a Marie Laurencin. I don't know how talented women can be slaves to their sex.'

'I've often complained about not being a boy,' said Françoise, 'they're free.'

'Oh, a woman can have exactly the same life as a man nowadays,' said Elisabeth, 'the trouble is, nine-tenths of them are wet.'

At the end of the twentieth century many women, feminists or not, would agree with her.

Beauvoir had always wanted to bring Zaza to life, and a part of Zaza went into Elisabeth, although the author denied it. Unconsciously perhaps she had rescued her from being a bourgeois wife but realized that creative women do not escape emotional problems: after all, she had known them herself. *L'Invitée* is far from a feminist book in the 'normal' sense, but it expresses the starting point of all Beauvoir's thought: you must be a person, you must choose your own existence, you alone are responsible for it, you must be 'authentic'.

When, in 1942, the Gallimard advisers vaguely hoped that the author might re-write the book, they obviously wanted it to be more orthodox in style, more 'literary', perhaps. Since it has not dated in essence, later readers do not realize how original, and therefore strange, it sounded when first read – sounded, because its life is in the dialogue, usually the beginner novelist's greatest problem. However, Beauvoir was no beginner, and Sartre had been advising her for years to put more of her real self into her writing. Brice Parain had told her as far back as 1941 that her characters spoke a kind of Montparnasse language but Sartre, when consulted, fiercely denied any such thing: there were as many 'languages' in Montparnasse as there were little groups, and he believed that the style of dialogue used by Beauvoir and himself was an amalgam of influences. The style owed something to their 'bourgeois origins', student slang, Olga's individual way of talking, and most importantly *'notre language, c'est nous'*, expressing directly, spontaneously, what their characters felt. He advised her strongly to change nothing, and she didn't. Later he took her to task for correcting her proofs badly and went through a hundred pages again for her.

After the publication of *L'Invitée* Beauvoir claimed that she was detached from the novel. Not perhaps as detached as she thought, for though she had finished explaining the novel she continued to explain how she felt about it: 'My optimism demanded that my life should reflect continual progress and authorized me to look with disdain and a light heart at this beginner's work which I now regarded only as a frivolous love story.' Since she had now lost her earlier apolitical attitude she had become ambitious for other attainments: 'I dreamt now of vast *romans engagés*: novels committed to ideas, especially those touching on politics.'

However detached she may have felt, the book was at last on the reviewers' desks and in the shop windows. Beauvoir remembered both the literary and the personal reactions. One of the first reviews she read was written by Marcel Arland, a novelist and former Goncourt prizewinner, a friend of Jean Paulhan and a director of the book review section in *Comoedia*. Beauvoir, like many other writers, but not Sartre, was prepared to forget the pro-Vichy attitude of the paper because Arland seemed to take her book seriously. However, he regretted that her 'characters were obsessed by *des histoires de lit*' – by sex – and many other reviewers 'denounced the immorality of the milieu I was

301

describing'. She remembered however that in Vichy France official propaganda emphasized all the old-fashioned conventional values while at the same time she forgot that most of her readers did not live *en vase clos*, in Montparnasse, as she did. Outside her immediate circle of intellectual friends her readers were mainly middle-class, as they were for almost all of her life, and they were obviously just as unprepared for 'contingent' love affairs as they were for the discussions of 'authenticity'. If they were looking for overt sex, they would not find any. Her own personal reactions, and those of other people towards her, were fascinating. She felt she was 'suddenly, a writer. I did not conceal my delight.' She remembered how she had felt when she was an adolescent: 'At last I had kept the promises I had made to myself at fifteen . . . I had crossed the first threshold: *L'Invitée* existed for other people and I had entered public life.'

She never forgot the reception of this first book: her friend Marc Zuorro dismissed it as fit for railway bookstalls; the Catholic thinker Gabriel Marcel saw Xavière as 'a perfect incarnation of the Other'; Cocteau wrote to her with praise. Various women, influenced by the book and the publicity, made advances to her; she avoided them and they were not pleased. Men were more ready to condemn the book but she was particularly moved by one good-looking, impoverished young man who offered her the most valuable gift that could be imagined in that autumn of 1943: English cigarettes.

There were not only critical and personal reactions to the novel, there were rumours of a much more important literary, near-'official' response. Beauvoir had been told by her publishers a few months earlier that she could possibly be a candidate for the prestigious Goncourt prize. She was naturally excited by this development. On the day of the time-honoured luncheon ceremony, when the prizewinner was chosen, 'I was working as usual,' Beauvoir remembered, 'upstairs at the Café de Flore; but I was awaiting with some impatience the telephone call which would give me the result.' She was behaving in what might be described as the old-fashioned feminine way: 'I had put on a new dress, made for me at La Pouèze under the direction of Madame Morel in a fabric that was ersatz but a beautiful electric blue; I had exchanged my turban for a swept-up hairstyle, which was more *recherché*.'

However, she was apparently not upset when she heard that 'the prize had been awarded to Marius Grout', a name unknown outside France today, for his novel entitled *Passage de l'homme*. A little later Beauvoir was again mentioned as 'well placed' for the Prix Renaudot. This time the prize went to André Soubiran, the well-known popular writer on medical themes. She accepted these disappointments 'without pride and without indifference'; she was happy that she had made new friends, and she had 'written a real book'.

Although she did not lose touch with her immediate young 'family', Olga, Bost and Nathalie, Beauvoir suddenly found herself, now that she was a published writer, received into a new circle of people, all well known in the literary and artistic world. They included the former surrealist Michel Leiris, best known for his work with the Musée de l'Homme and his book *L'Age d'homme*, later a brilliant translator, and his wife Zette. Beauvoir also met the novelist Raymond Queneau, and was charmed by Albert Camus, who was just beginning to be better known. In describing why she felt drawn to him Beauvoir summarized her own development so far: 'His youth and independence brought him close to us: we [i.e. Sartre and herself] had developed without any link with any school, we had been solitary; we had no domestic circle [Camus' wife had remained in Algeria], nor what is called "milieu".' Café life in Montparnasse or Saint-Germain-des-Prés apparently did not count as such. 'Like us, Camus had moved from individualism to commitment.' Beauvoir appreciated his ambition and his refusal to take himself seriously, and she also knew that he carried out important secret work for an underground resistance network. Another aspect of Camus also pleased Beauvoir: 'He knew how to smile in a detached way at things and people, while dedicating himself intensely to his enterprises, his enjoyments and his friendships.' He obviously shared much of her own attitudes, and he gave her immense pleasure when he read her second novel *Le Sang des autres* in typescript and told her that it was a 'fraternal book'.

This was the novel she had begun to write as soon as she had finished *L'Invitée*. Though the question of personal relationships still preoccupied her, she wanted to write about other, wider concepts, she wanted to discuss many moral issues which now dominated her thinking and she chose to set her story against the background of occupied France, in which she was still living. When she had finished *Le Sang des autres*, Camus asked Beauvoir to give her manuscript to Les Editions de Minuit – Jean Bruller's own firm which had brought out his short novel *Le Silence de la Mer* – for clandestine publication, but France was liberated before it was printed.

1943 was a year of intense activity for Beauvoir, now totally 'committed to literature'. After her slow start as a writer she completed the essay commissioned by Jean Grenier in three months, while Sartre wrote his play *Huis clos* in less than three weeks. Camus again took a hand in its history, for he was keen to play the role of Garcin in the play and also to produce it, for he was now fascinated by the theatre. It was in Beauvoir's hotel room that the rehearsals began, with Wanda cast as one of the two women. Significantly perhaps the play's first title was *Les Autres*, (*The Others*), indicating that Beauvoir and Sartre were still thinking along parallel lines, however different their actual writing at the time.

As soon as she had finished *Le Sang des autres* Beauvoir, who seemed in a great hurry to pour out all her ideas into books, continued to make up for lost time on early rejected work by thinking about a third novel. She had found a title in advance, *Tous les hommes sont mortels* (*All Men are Mortal*), emphasizing a fact that she did not like to acknowledge. The year seemed to be ending more cheerfully. The French Committee of National Liberation had been formed in Algiers in the summer, directed by the two generals, de Gaulle and Giraud. The latter was soon eliminated. In September–October came the first liberation of French territory: Free French troops drove the Italian occupiers out of Corsica, an important strategic gain.

Beauvoir herself might have participated more actively in intellectual resistance but, though she believed she had forsaken her earlier 'individualism', she was too much of an individual to contemplate joining a political party or tolerating any form of bureaucracy. As a published writer she could now have joined Sartre at the meetings of the Comité National des Ecrivains, to which he went three times a week. The objectives of the Comité were high-minded: they intended to save the honour of French literature and punish any traitors. They also intended to include among their members all types of believers, political and religious, supporters of General de Gaulle – naturally – also Communists, democrats, Catholics and Protestants. If idealism in itself is never boring, attempts to translate it into action, even intellectual action, can be difficult and frustrating. As every political activist knows, the machinery of democracy, in its struggle to be fair, can easily produce a dull evening, while if there is any drama and excitement the result can easily be anarchy. Beauvoir had achieved no political thinking of her own, in this field she remained in the shadow of Sartre, as she honestly admitted. 'My agreement with Sartre was so complete that my presence [at these meetings] would have repeated his own in useless fashion.' She wanted the excitement that these meetings could not produce: she might have gone if she could have joined when the Committee was formed, and if the sessions had been truly interesting: 'but Sartre found them rather tedious.' She said that she would have liked to 'do something'; but she was not attracted by 'symbolic participation and I stayed at home'. Beauvoir regarded herself as 'committed', but her commitment was limited by her deeply ingrained belief: in her case action remained intellectual action, she was a writer, and she would express her ideas in her books or not at all.

The year was ending. Beauvoir had now moved into the Hôtel de la Louisiane in the rue de Seine, so had Sartre, so had Nathalie Sorokine and her student lover Bourla. Sartre's room was small, bare and bookless, but Beauvoir lived in relatively grander if somewhat incongruous style: 'In my room there was a divan bed, bookshelves, a large solid table and on the wall a poster showing a British horseguard soldier.' On the day she moved in Sartre upset a bottle of ink on the carpet, which was at once removed by the owner: 'But I liked the wooden floor as much as a carpet. I had a kitchen. From my window I could see a large expanse of roofs. None of my resting-places had ever come so close to my dreams; I imagined I would stay there until the end of my days.' This was far from the case.

1943 was the year of *L'Invitée*, which was to take its place among other classic novels about the human triangle in its various forms, from *La Seconde*, which Colette had published in

1929, to *Jules et Jim*, which Henri-Pierre Roche wrote in 1953, supplying François Truffaut with one of his most lasting film successes. For Beauvoir, as she prepared to go skiing with Bost in the coming January, 1943 had been the year when her life as a writer began. Her life as a feminist had developed no further than her perceptive descriptions and analyses of women characters in her first novel. But it was a start.

FOURTEEN

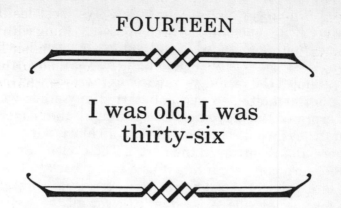

I was old, I was thirty-six

On January 9th, 1944, Beauvoir had indeed become thirty-six and now she was at last a writer. She had been hoping for this ever since her last years at school, she had wanted, through her writing, 'to burn like a flame in millions of hearts', and she had thought that if some adolescent, 'someone like me', were to weep over the novel she would write, it would be a 'novel in which I would tell my own story'. This was in fact a highly coloured evocation of her future writing, and if *L'Invitée* did not cause tear-stained faces at least the author had made direct contact with readers, and thus achieved her ambition. She had pursued a single track unswervingly, never losing her belief that life must come before literature, for if one wanted to write fiction, as she did, what was to go into that fiction, if not life? Life had to be seen, analysed, interpreted, criticized, praised, condemned, but most of all – first of all – life had to be lived. Even Sartre had tacitly accepted her order of priority in the end; his first writing had failed because it had been near-pastiche, unrelated to life. For Beauvoir however, this same belief in life as the start of writing had entailed the coming to terms with the reality outside, a major and long-postponed step for her. In the end she had come to see that reality entailed the understanding of other people's behaviour and then the forging of relationships with them.

The first half of 1944 in fact brought Beauvoir a social life so crowded and cheerful that the word 'relationship' is too abstract a term to be used in the same context. She was now invited to parties and dinners by many of the new friends she met. She and Sartre were lucky enough to join in a reading of Picasso's play, *Desire Caught by the Tail*, which he had written in 1941 in veiled protest against the Vichy regime and the Occupation. Picasso himself attended the reading, Braque was there, as was the actor Jean-Louis Barrault. The cast out-starred any other who may have interpreted the play later, except that all the readers were amateurs: they included Michel Leiris, Dora Marr, Sartre, Camus as compère and Beauvoir in the part of The Cousin. She did not praise Picasso's play, regarding it as a throw-back to the 1920s, even a late echo of Apollinaire. However, she congratulated herself, for she felt she 'existed' a little for all the well-known people present and realized that within a few months after the publication of her novel 'the world had grown wider and richer'. She had seen herself as something of an actress and had tried to enhance her appearance: 'Olga had lent me an angora pullover in a beautiful red; Wanda, a necklace of big blue beads,' and indeed she scored a success: 'Picasso delighted me by congratulating me on this colour combination.' Beauvoir blossomed: 'I smiled, others smiled at me, I was pleased with them and with myself,' she felt flattered, and friendship, she remembered, 'turned her head'. She explained later why she allowed herself to enjoy this type of bourgeois-style social life: there was a 'secret and violent after-taste' to it all, for virtually every guest at these evenings of entertainment could well have been in danger for some reason or other.

When Beauvoir remembered later the parties she and her friends had given and attended in 1944 she seemed to feel that she had personally invented the whole concept of party. She even mentioned an essay written about herself by the journalist and critic Geneviève Gennari who noted the number of *fêtes* that occur in her novels. Beauvoir decided that a *fête* was 'an ardent apotheosis of the present in the face of anxiety about the future'. She took good times seriously, it was her nature to do so, she felt impelled to analyse them. Later she realized that the somewhat febrile social life of this period and the excitement among the intellectuals formed perhaps an unconscious anticipation of German defeat and Allied victory. There was an echo, dimly realized, of all that was happening at a different level throughout France. The resistance movements had strengthened, their direction was at least partly co-ordinated, even if the British and U.S. Allies were still diffident about the leadership of de Gaulle whom some believed to be potentially a military dictator. There was no doubt that the *maquis* (the resistants used this Corsican term, evoking wild, impenetrable country, to describe themselves) now included an increasing number of Communists. Though the Germans were not yet defeated, there was a pervasive feeling that they would not win the war. If Beauvoir's memories of good times sound strangely insensitive against the background of the war and suffering that still extended over so much of the world they showed how much the people of Paris needed escape of some sort and described honestly how one section of the intellectuals spent their time in the last few months of the German occupation.

Beauvoir preferred parties to politics. She had spent all her twenties trying to escape politics, and Sartre had had to nag her into reading about them in the newspapers. Now, following the profound change within her during the crucial years of 1938–39, she could no longer claim the belief in anarchy which, she had once thought, justified her early inaction. During the first months of his life in the army Sartre had written to Beauvoir that the war 'interested' him. Now politics 'interested' him even more, but his intellectual independence never allowed him to join a party. In this aspect of life Beauvoir followed him. If she had been attracted by the spirit of adventure and potential violence that had surrounded 'Socialisme et Liberté' in the early days she could not tolerate the inevitable tedium and minutiae of political life, though later she was to take a more positive political stance and translate her thoughts into writing.

There was however a related area of life and thought which preoccupied her much more deeply and led her to assume a much more creative, if still theoretical, attitude. This was the whole area of morality. In early life Beauvoir had been the intensely emotional Catholic child of a conventional, practising Catholic mother, and though she soon lost her faith in God she never lost a belief in individual morality. How does an atheist see the structure of morality? Can such a system be established, and if so, on what principles? Sartre, while writing *L'Etre et le néant*, had indicated that he would write another book dealing with ethics based on the existentialist credo he had just set out, but he never did. The task, with some prompting from him, but mainly through her own choice, fell to Beauvoir.

Even before the publication of Sartre's book in mid-1943 the themes and vocabulary of the 'new' philosophy, which in many ways was far from new, passed into the day-to-day talk of the Paris intellectuals. Beauvoir's answer to Jean Grenier, when he asked her if she was an 'existentialist', was contained in her long essay *Pyrrhus et Cinéas*. It was a rich and stimulating piece, Beauvoir's first non-fiction, an ambitious attempt to project the main tenets of the existentialist creed into a moral dimension. That creed was based, in Sir Anthony Quinton's memorable phrase, on man as a 'self-creating being who is not initially endowed with a character and goals but must choose them by acts of pure decision'. Beauvoir, starting from this assumption, expressed indirectly the intellectual situation in which she found herself after five years of war and many years spent in the study of Hegel, all of this in close association with Sartre. She introduced her knowledge of history and literature to impressively good effect. The adventurous King Pyrrhus of Epirus is contrasted with the cautious Cineas, a Thessalonian who was his chief adviser, although the essay is not given any dramatic form. The author's mind was obviously teeming with ideas, which she links skilfully with references to past writers, such as Voltaire,[1] Benjamin Constant,[2] Kierkegaard, the inevitable Dostoevsky, dear to the existentialists, and, of course, references to Sartre himself. The problems of personal responsibility, the limits of human endeavour, the non-existence of God, relationships with other people, communication, action: these

[1] Voltaire (François Marie Arouet de) (1694–1778): the major part of his work expressed his philosophical views. While affirming the existence of God, he condemned all dogmatic religions, especially Catholicism and its priesthood, which he regarded as a source of intolerance and superstition. The dominant trait of his writings on political as well as religious subjects is lack of respect for existing institutions and contempt for authority. He was thus very much a dissident influence and paved the way for the French Revolution.

[2] Benjamin Constant (1767–1830): novelist, philosopher and politician, best known for his short novel, *Adolphe*, and for his passionate and intellectual friendships with Mme de Charrière and Mme de Staël among others.

are some of the problems that Beauvoir attempts to elucidate.

Existentialism in its serious aspects was much in the air; it had not yet been turned into a new and picturesque version of pseudo-intellectual bohemianism. The intelligent reading and thinking public wanted to understand more about it, they needed readable commentary: such work of Sartre that had been published so far was not easy reading, however much it fascinated professional thinkers. How would this new 'ism' affect moral attitudes; how were people to behave towards others if the rules laid down by Christianity were swept aside? Beauvoir attempted to supply the answers; she was the ideal intermediary between Sartre and the hopeful people who were anxious to re-orientate their thinking and living.

It cannot be said that *Pyrrhus et Cinéas*, despite the energetic clarity of the style, supplied a positive moral code built on a rational analysis. Sixteen years later, Beauvoir found it necessary to re-examine her essay. She was aware that her attitudes were subjective, and some of them had not changed a great deal, including her belief that in wartime there must be an acceptance of violence. She professed she was not pleased at her failure to escape all individualism and believed that the book reflected her own earlier mood at the age of twenty, when she had asked 'What is the use of it all?' Perhaps she remembered her early total devotion to a Christian God followed by an equally total rejection. She was particularly anxious to point out that she had trusted her own wishes and deliberately chosen the doctrines which encouraged her in that attitude. She considered that everything in her personal history destined her for existentialism and her own responsibility for every aspect of her personal life. However, the *Pyrrhus et Cinéas* piece, she said later, interested her only as a stage in her own development, for she decided the 'streak of idealism' she could not lose invalidated her theories. With her usual honesty she made no attempt to justify any aspects of her work which she considered unsatisfactory, but her decisions about precisely what was unsatisfactory were obviously in themselves subjective. By the time she recorded her later revised opinions of this early work she was less interested in the abstractions she had been trying to interpret, and had become absorbed by an in-depth examination of herself in her volumes of memoirs. She valued evidence of how she had felt and thought at any particular period of her life, for she was convinced that the chapters of her own history would help all her readers in the interpretation of their personal experiences.

When writing this early essay she had emphasized her belief in man and his capacity for giving a meaning to his life, something he could do without any outside intervention. However, recalling this work in 1960 she added something she would not have admitted earlier. She was 'never to lose sight of that dizzy void, that blind darkness from which came all the desires and impulses (*élans*) of mankind'. She had not lost all sense of mystery and all fear of death. Until the end of her life she remained a convinced atheist but she was always honest enough to admit that the harsh light of existentialist thought never reached into that one dark corner of her mind. The young Simone had thought of becoming a nun and then felt guilty because her feelings about God had grown lukewarm. That little girl never disappeared completely and it may have been partly the memory of her, plus the moral teachings of her mother, however different from her own beliefs, which caused Beauvoir for the rest of her life to remain preoccupied with the problems of ethics.

Despite the accelerating hopes of German defeat and Allied victory, or perhaps because they were so well founded, conditions in France, during the early months of 1944, worsened. The Germans had not bombed Paris severely for they had hoped to preserve it for themselves as ultimate conquerors of France. The British, however, determined to destroy enemy communications wherever possible, had no compunction about bombing French railway stations, including those in the capital. Accordingly the Gare de Montparnasse, not far from Beauvoir's hotel, was one of their targets. One night Sartre persuaded her to treat the air-raids as a theatrical display and, as the walls of the Hôtel de la Louisiane shook, they watched from the roof: 'The horizon was ablaze, and what a fantasia in the sky! I was fascinated and forgot to be afraid. This chaotic spectacle lasted for two hours.'

Daily life grew more complex and austere; there were more power cuts and Beauvoir went to almost any lengths to secure food. After all, she was still responsible for feeding Sartre and her young 'family'. She learned from Zette Leiris of a reliable source of food at Neuilly-sous-Clermont to the north of Paris. The concierge at the Saint-Gobain glass factory there apparently sold meat illegally. Beauvoir, accompanied by Bost and their bicycles, made the twenty-eight-mile train journey to Chantilly. They then cycled for a further twelve miles or so, and triumphantly bought fresh beef along with cultivated mushrooms that were being grown in a disused quarry.

There were only too many other reminders that the war was not over and that the Hitlerite regime had to be feared as much as ever until the very last moment. Beauvoir was made bitterly aware of this by a tragic event within her 'chosen' family. Her young friend Nathalie was still living happily with her Jewish lover Bourla, who one day visited his father, and decided to stay in his father's apartment overnight. By a cruel coincidence the Germans visited the house in the early morning; father and son were taken to Drancy prison and a little later executed.

Beauvoir was deeply upset by this tragedy because she had regarded Nathalie and Bourla – he was only nineteen – as *les petits*, the children. Beauvoir knew that the relationship between herself and Nathalie was complex, but she genuinely loved these youngsters. They had occupied a room not far from her own in the Hôtel de la Louisiane, and sometimes she would go to say goodnight to them. The girl demanded a kiss, so did Bourla. The shock of the boy's death made her painfully aware of 'the capricious horror of our mortal condition', she was overwhelmed by a despair so intense that it was 'truly infernal'. Eventually she recovered from her gloom because her old optimism, 'the splendours of the future', took hold of her again.

Early in 1944 Beauvoir's first radio programmes were broadcast, members of her 'family' participating in the production. The young Bost had helped her assemble the documentation and Olga took part in one of them, reading François Villon's famous poem, 'Ballade de la belle Heaulmière'. Life went on. The end of May brought an important theatrical event for Sartre: the première of his one-act play *Huis clos*, produced by Raymond Rouleau at the Théâtre du Vieux Colombier as the first part of a double bill. It was infinitely more successful than the feeble comedy which followed it (the order was later changed) and was destined to make history: when the time came to record the story of Saint-Germain-des-

Prés and the post-war social phenomenon that claimed to be inspired by 'existentialism' there had to be a starting-point. With hindsight it was not too difficult to establish it as the première of *Huis clos*.

The message of the play, 'Hell is other people', was easier for the audience to absorb than the half-concealed, politically orientated subversion of *Les Mouches*. Beauvoir, delighted by the success of Sartre's play, was now more keen than ever to write for the theatre herself. She had made a first attempt a year or so earlier, wishing to deal with the 'relationship of individual experience to universal reality'. She had imagined 'that a City state demanded one of its most eminent members to sacrifice a life: that of a person who was loved, no doubt'. She wanted to show the changing moods of the main protagonist: 'The hero began by refusing; then he was carried away by concern for the public good; he agreed, but then fell into a state of apathy which made him indifferent to each and all.' The author then proposed an interesting development: 'Someone, *probably a woman* [my italics] succeeded in reviving egotistical passions within him: only then did he find again the will to save his compatriots.' However, Beauvoir found her scenario 'too abstract', her play never received a more precise plot or a title and she introduced her ideas into *Pyrrhus et Cinéas* instead.

Now, in the early summer of 1944, she looked further for a dramatic subject and eventually found one while she was reading a vast historical work in search of yet another plot, the theme of her projected third novel. Her inspiration came from the Swiss historian Simonde de Sismondi, who early in the nineteenth century published *L'Histoire des républiques italiennes du moyen âge*. He himself was of Italian descent and this detailed, twelve-volume study exerted a strong influence later on the Italian liberal tradition. It contained many astonishing and true stories, and among them Beauvoir found a recurring theme that suited her present purpose: in the Middle Ages, when a city was besieged and short of food it was the practice to get rid of the 'useless mouths', namely women, children and old people – Beauvoir listed them in that order – so that food supplies for the men defending the city would last longer. She began to speculate 'on the feelings of the victims and of the fathers, brothers, lovers, husbands and sons who had condemned them'. Then she sought a more positive approach and imagined a situation in which 'a city which had just won a democratic regime found itself threatened by a despot'. She admitted that her current preoccupation with moral problems led her to consider 'the question of ends and means: does one possess the right to sacrifice individuals to the future of the community?' She wanted to involve her characters in a political, philosophical and moral dilemma.

The plot of her two-act play was simple: the besieged city of Vaucelles, in fourteenth-century Flanders, cannot hold out until promised help from France arrives, for there is no food. Jean-Pierre has refused all responsibility for municipal administration and the management of food supplies, but when he learns that women, children and old people are to be liquidated he realizes that he must take action. He urges everybody to disobey the order that will lead to their death. Louis, the leader of the council, eventually persuades his colleagues to change their minds. It is decided that the entire population will leave the town and confront the enemy. As the gates open on this brave adventure, the outcome of which remains unknown, Louis makes a short, melodramatic speech: 'We fight for liberty, liberty will triumph through our freely given sacrifice. Whether we live or die, we are the victors.'

Parallel to this grandiose theme a more intimate human drama develops. Jean-Pierre loves Clarice, Louis's daughter, while her own fascist-minded brother Georges makes incestuous advances to her and is furious when he hears she is expecting Jean-Pierre's child. Clarice tries to kill herself, is prevented and makes her existentialist point: *Chacun est seul*, 'each one of us is alone'. In her own later assessment of the play's merits the author said nothing about the role of women, but specialists in women's studies have built up *Les Bouches inutiles* (*Who Shall Die?*) into an important pre-feminist tract. Beauvoir, however, did not intend to limit the implications of her drama – she was concerned with the problems of humanity in which women and men are equally involved. While concerned with the sufferings of all French pople during the Occupation, she was at the same time unconsciously remembering the problems experienced by women, especially in wartime. The shortage of food was more than a material problem, it symbolized a deeper hunger for spiritual and moral values.

As with her first and second novels, Beauvoir had to wait patiently before her play could be produced. In the meantime living conditions became still worse. Parisians had very little to eat and in cold weather Beauvoir resorted to a rabbit-skin coat. Any women rich enough or clever enough could of course dress well even during the worst of the Occupation, for the *grands couturiers* managed by various means, some of them not too honourable, to continue profitably in business, and they could still export to neutral countries. Beauvoir now saw no point in paying any attention to her appearance and still had not consulted a dentist about the tooth she had lost in the cycling accident of 1941. After all, she realized, 'I was old, I was thirty-six.' The five years of war, which coincided for her with the writing of her first two novels, her first long essay and her play, combined with the emotional intensity of her bisexual life, had left her exhausted. Even if the cult of the young which followed the war had not surfaced, her remark reflects an attitude typical of European women, especially those in Latin countries. Among the French bourgeoisie an unmarried woman of thirty-six would certainly be regarded as 'old', an attitude which probably helps to promote an important French industry: the preserving and restoring of beauty. Later, especially in the documentary film based on *The Second Sex*, Beauvoir launched a particularly bitter attack on the beauty institutes, their directors and their clients. To her, nothing was more dishonest. Indirectly she taught women how to develop their own individual beauty along with their personality. In early middle age she herself was handsome, though she had never been pretty. She never made any secret about her age. Despite her response to Sartre, Bost and several women she always remained essentially herself, never losing that intellectual curiosity and mental energy which set her apart. She had not needed existentialism to discover herself, although it helped her to focus the direct look, the direct thought, which before 1938–39 had been turned too often inwards. Now her intense blue-eyed gaze encountered the outside world, not merely the individuals, but groups of all kinds.

At the beginning of the war Beauvoir, like most women in

Europe, had had to accustom herself to a social life without men. She had always experienced deeply affectionate relationships with women, ever since the days of Zaza, but she had given little thought to the group which made up half the world, women, ordinary women. As she joined the ordinary women who were trying to buy food for their families and send parcels to their menfolk in the services, Beauvoir began to look further than her companions in the lycée staff rooms or hotel bedrooms. 'I knew few women of my own age and none who led the existence of a traditional wife; the problems of Stépha, Camille [Simone Jolivet] Colette Audry . . . or my own problems seemed to me individual and not generic.' Beauvoir had met the Leirises and the playwright Armand Salacrou and his wife, but these ménages were indeed not 'traditional'. She had begun to look about her more closely. 'On many points I had realized how far, before the war, I had committed sins of omission: I knew now that there was a difference between Jew and Aryan; but I had not realized that there was a feminine condition.'

Strange, perhaps, in someone who had appreciated the obvious femininity of Olga and Wanda and the agonizing dependence of Védrine and Nathalie Sorokine. 'Suddenly I met a great number of women who were over forty and who, despite the diversity of their opportunities and their merits, had all had an identical experience: they had lived as "relative beings".' She described how she began to learn more about them: 'Because I was a writer, because my situation was different from theirs and also, I think, because I was a good listener, they told me many things; I began to realize the difficulties, the deceptive opportunities, the traps and obstacles that most women found in their path; I felt also to what extent they were at the same time diminished and enriched.' She herself had always been aware of the potential enrichment, for she had had the best of both worlds. Soon she was to pay attention to those who had been less fortunate. 'I did not yet allow much importance to a question which affected me only indirectly, but my attention was aroused.' How few women, at the end of the war in France, had the privilege of being 'married' yet free: Beauvoir did not realize to what extent she would set an example to future generations. Her life during the war proved a paradox: was it possible for women, in the words of the French proverb, to have *le*

317

beurre et l'argent du beurre, to have the butter and the money for the butter, to have their cake and eat it? Men, after all, had always had it. In some ways, during the war, Beauvoir had lived like a man, remaining independent financially, despite the give-and-take she operated with Sartre when they were both in debt, trying to support a group of young women who were obviously extremely lazy. At the same time Beauvoir had mothered all her young friends in practical matters and chosen to show her affection for them by accepting their desperate demands for sexual caresses.

In mid-July, 1944, a member of the important resistance group known as 'Combat' was suddenly arrested, and since Sartre was in touch with the group through Camus, his name was compromised. Camus advised both Sartre and Beauvoir to disappear from the Paris scene for a time and they took his advice. After spending a few days in the apartment of their friends, the Leirises, they went out to Neuilly-sous-Clermont (where Beauvoir had bought black market food not too long before) to the north-east of the city. They stayed there for three weeks or so in an *auberge* which was also the local grocery store. They did not hide, but continued with their writing on the ground floor bar. They felt this location to be useful because they could easily return to Paris 'when things started moving', that is when the hoped-for liberation became imminent. They were determined to witness the coming of freedom.

They did not have long to wait for the drama of the Liberation, for by the second week in August even the French newspapers and radio, not merely the B.B.C. in London, told the excited population of France that the American divisions had reached Chartres in north-west France, only fifty-five miles from Paris. As soon as they saw that the war was virtually won Sartre and Beauvoir cycled to Chantilly, from where they were able to take a train to the capital. Unfortunately the R.A.F. chose to attack the train, causing some casualties but leaving the locomotive undamaged. Beauvoir remembered later how she lay on the floor of the compartment listening to the machine-gun fire but felt nothing, for everything seemed unreal. She was afraid only when it was all over. Eventually the train reached Paris and Beauvoir's memoirs recall the never-to-be-forgotten events of the next few weeks. By mid-August, no food, no gas, only a makeshift stove heated by burning newspapers, invented by Bost. The last rumours, the last sniping and then, on August 25th, the arrival of the Allied armies in the city. In her 1960 memoirs Beauvoir gave a good and, as usual, a personal account of how her war ended, the war she had done nothing to prevent and nothing to conclude. 'It was over,' she wrote. 'Paris was liberated; the world and the future were restored to us, and we threw ourselves into it.' In saying 'we' she was presumably thinking not only of Sartre and their small 'family', she had learnt to think of society.

As Beauvoir thought over what she had learnt from those long years 1939 to 1944, when no one close to her was lost, with the exception of Sartre's brilliant friend Paul Nizan and the young Bourla, she returned to one of her deepest and most disturbing problems, her fear of death. Many writers have felt the same fear and many more have encouraged and helped their readers to come to terms with it. The English William Hazlitt was one of the most persuasive analysts of the problem, especially in his essay on the subject written in the early 1820s, in which he offers a kind of solution: 'A life of action and danger moderates the dread of death.'

Beauvoir had on the whole been lucky to escape danger during the war but there remained action, and for her action could only be writing; she knew no other. In the late summer of 1944 she was beginning to think about her next novel and in the meantime she was able to practise a skill she had barely had the chance or the wish to exercise so far – journalism. Camus had commissioned Sartre to write a long reportage for his newspaper *Combat* on the liberation of Paris, and Beauvoir did more than help him. Seven articles were published, *Un promeneur dans Paris libéré*, and Beauvoir probably wrote them all: she later said that she did. She certainly supplied information and acted in her usual role as Sartre's editor. He signed them. Her name was not added to his; he was already well known, she was not. Despite the novel and a few articles she had published she was not known as a journalist, and after all, she was a woman, she was still expected to know her place. Where Sartre was concerned, she did.

FIFTEEN

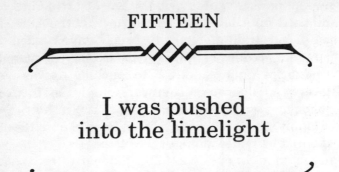

I was pushed
into the limelight

She wanted success but it was not her nature to seek the limelight. However it soon shone over her. In the autumn of 1944 Beauvoir could have returned to teaching, for her suspension following the complaint by Nathalie's mother had been lifted. But it was too late now, for the teacher, although remaining a teacher in various indirect ways, had been transformed into the writer. Sartre too had left the lycée classroom for ever, since the success of his play *Huis clos* in May 1944 had brought him more commissions of all kinds and the beginnings of fame. His reputation began to spread outside Paris and soon outside France. Sartre and Beauvoir, after their long slogging climb, the failed books and adverse circumstances, suddenly found they were nearing the top of the hill, they could even see the country which lay beyond. If the French had needed General de Gaulle as a leader in 1944, and continued to need him for a long time, the intellectuals needed a leader too. During the Occupation nothing had been straight forward, attitudes, behaviour and writing had been ambiguous, there had been compromise, hypocrisy, secrecy, censorship. The Liberation produced a kind of editorial euphoria and writers of very different convictions could be found contributing to the same periodicals. However, this literary and political coalition did not last long. The old-established reviews eventually resumed publication, their editors free at last to write and publish as they chose. But where was this intellectual leader? All the obvious creeds, right wing, left wing, Catholic or Communist, had failed. André Gide? François Mauriac? Louis Aragon? Even André Malraux, the man of action, did not seem to have anything to offer the emerging and restless younger generation.

The vacant place for the intellectual leader was filled – by Sartre. In 1944, he was thirty-nine, he was left-wing in a liberal but independent way, he belonged to no political party, he was an individualist, he wrote clearly and, most of all, his years as a teacher had kept him in touch with young people, he knew how to talk to them, he even knew how to listen to them. Despite the complexities of his personal behaviour everything about his thought and writing was coherent: he had spent several years writing *L'Etre and le néant* and a few weeks writing *Huis clos*, but in the end both works expressed the same themes: they reminded everyone that they must think for themselves, both about themselves and about their relationships with other people. And they must act. In 1926, when he was twenty-one, he had written to Simone Jolivet that fame tempted him, and most of all he was ambitious to create, he had to create something, it didn't matter what. Now he set to work. Before 1944 was over he had begun to create the most radical and influential periodical of the postwar years, one which has outlasted his death, and almost, it must be said in 1990, his reputation. The small committee which planned *Les Temps modernes* (named after the classic Chaplin film) was formed in the autumn of 1944 and included, in addition to Sartre as the prime mover, his former associate Raymond Aron, who had come back from Britain, another former colleague, Maurice Merleau-Ponty, Jean Paulhan, Michel Leiris, Albert Ollivier (one of Camus' colleagues on the newspaper *Combat*) and Simone de Beauvoir.

Her name was not added to those of the other members merely because she was Sartre's permanent companion, for her reputation was growing as fast as his. Her essay *Pyrrhus et Cinéas* came out just over a year after *L'Invitée*, in the first publishing season after the end of the Occupation (autumn 1944) and it was a great success. Everything about it was new, but not in any obscure way, for the new thinking was in the air, especially in the air of Saint-Germain-des-Prés; it only needed to be crystallized. At the same time the author was not an obscure academic, she could be seen, handsome and distinctive, with Sartre in the Café de Flore and other haunts in the area. The news had spread also that her second novel had been accepted by Gallimard, who were publishing *Les Temps modernes*. Her close friends also knew that she had started to write a third novel.

1945 was a hectic year for those countries which were still fighting a war, and in France, against the background of bitter recriminations, personal and judicial, that have not ended to this very day, the intellectuals mobilized themselves for another kind of action. Sartre and his associates had been thinking about their periodical ever since 1943, but it could not be published until they had received an allocation of paper, which was in short supply and sought by every editor and publisher in the country. In the end it was Beauvoir, accompanied by Michel Leiris, who went to see the Minister of Information, Jacques Soustelle, to ask for the paper supply. There was some delay, inevitably, but in the end the paper allocation was won, and the first issue of the magazine appeared in October 1945.

In the meantime Beauvoir experienced her first transformation into a celebrity. Quite apart from her own plans for work she was grateful for invitations and commissions, for by mid-January 1945 Sartre had flown to the U.S. to represent *Combat* and although she was pleased on his behalf she may have hoped to go with him. She was convinced that she herself would receive an invitation fairly soon but now found herself separated from Sartre for four months. There could be none of the daily letter-writing that had been so important during his time in the army, for so far there was no air-mail postal service for civilians. However, she was more than busy, working at her third novel *Tous les hommes sont mortels*, and awaiting the publication of her second, *Le Sang des autres*.

In January that year she met Cyril Connolly, editor of the celebrated and regretted London magazine *Horizon*. In the issue for May he referred to the 'three literatures' that had appeared in France since the war; the literature of collaboration, of which he said nothing beyond a few names, the literature of Occupation – 'those researchers into the human spirit, the meaning of words, myths and symbols, the fate of a man at a level sufficiently deep to evade the political censorship' – and the first two names he gave were those of Sartre and Camus. The third literature was that of resistance.

When Connolly went to Le Flore, Sartre was 'absent from his favourite table' – he was probably in the U.S. already – but Beauvoir was there to receive him. He referred to her novel *L'Invitée*, 'about the whole ambience of the Flore', and she showed him details of the planned first issue of *Les Temps modernes*. Connolly borrowed a piece for his own magazine: it was one of Sartre's important statements about commitment in literature. Sartre maintained that the Occupation had taught French writers their responsibilities: he held 'Flaubert and Goncourt responsible for the repressions which followed the Commune, because they wrote not a single line to prevent them'. Perhaps it was 'none of their business, but was the Calas case the business of Voltaire? the sentence on Dreyfus the business of Zola. . . ?'[1]

Soon after Sartre's departure for the U.S. Beauvoir gave a lecture to a group of students, mainly Catholics, at the home of Gabriel Marcel, the exponent of Christian existentialism. Her views, not surprisingly, were opposed to his. She had taken with her a Turkish-Jewish student named Robert Misrahi, whose studies had been partly financed by Sartre. She described him as 'an existentialist and a Zionist' and he took it upon himself to defend her so violently against the predictable arguments of Marcel that the audience took a dislike to him. After the lecture Robert Misrahi listened carefully to her as she explained that it *was* possible to build a system of morality on the concepts set out in *L'Etre et le néant*. He urged her to write it, and since *Pyrrhus et Cinéas* had been a success the previous year she began to think seriously about a second, more detailed book on the subject.

Soon afterwards she made her first journey outside France for six years. Her sister Hélène had married Lionel de Roulet in Portugal, not because she was interested in the respectability of

[1] Voltaire's hatred of intolerance and injustice led him to campaign vigorously for the rehabilitation of Jean Calas and other victims of religious and political persecution. Four years before the end of his life Emile Zola (1840–1902) successfully espoused the cause of Captain Dreyfus, entering the controversy with great vigour with his letter to *L'Aurore*, beginning with the words 'J'accuse'.

marriage but in order to stay with him in the event of a German invasion. When he joined the Institut Français in Lisbon he invited his sister-in-law to come to Portugal and give lectures on life in France during the Occupation. On the way Beauvoir stopped briefly in Madrid, and became aware of how deeply her outlook had changed since her first visit to Spain with Sartre in 1931. The picturesque no longer moved her, she realized only that Franco had supported Hitler and had done nothing whatever to relieve current poverty. In Portugal things were not much better, though she was able to eat well and buy some good clothes.

Reading the articles she later wrote for Camus' *Combat* newspaper in Paris one is inevitably reminded of her visit to Greece in 1937. She had wondered then why children were throwing stones at her party of three, now she was horrified by the Portuguese children begging in the streets while the well-fed bourgeoisie at the café tables urged her not to give them anything because they would only spend it on cigarettes or sweets. Beauvoir signed her articles with a male pseudonym, Daniel Secrétan, for she did not want any recriminations to worry her brother-in-law in Lisbon. The pieces she wrote contained nothing but gloom about the poor people of Portugal: no food, no clothes, no houses. She began to develop a method which she was to use for the rest of her life in her polemical non-fiction writing. She quoted statistics, often very telling ones: the amount of the bread ration, the rise in the cost of living, the birth rate compared to the death rate. Five hundred grammes of bread per day might have been tolerable but in the more remote places there was simply no bread at all. Many men could not work because they were so hungry, there was of course a shocking amount of illness and the population had recently declined by ten per cent. Only two of her articles were published in *Combat*. The Portuguese propaganda services complained about the critical portrayal of their country's unashamed capitalism, with the result that the acting editor of *Combat*, Pascal Pia, decided to stop the publication of further articles. Camus himself was unfortunately away in the U.S. at the time. Another publication, *Volontés*, took over the 'Daniel Secrétan' work.

She was no longer the tourist looking for the picturesque; she had learnt realism. Her first reactions may have sounded emotional but she added sufficient cold fact to counteract any claim that she was writing as a sentimental tourist. There was nothing 'feminine' about her reporting, unless her response could be considered too 'emotional' for a man.

Was it 'emotional' or 'rational' to refuse her support for a mercy plea when the fascist writer Robert Brasillach was due to be executed for writing pro-Nazi articles during the Occupation? She had 'wept with rage' while reading these articles and did not sign the mercy petition on his behalf; Camus took the same attitude. At the same time she went to the trial, for she felt that having committed herself she could not then escape responsibility. Brasillach accepted the death sentence bravely, but this in itself did not move her. However, she was aware of a disturbing problem: the trial had in a sense transformed Brasillach, the executioner, into a victim, and the verdict seemed inhuman. Friends – Communist friends – told Beauvoir that if the case upset her, then she should not have come to court. Later she heard that Camus had changed his mind in the end and signed the mercy plea. *She* did not change her mind. Quoting Simone Weil, who had said that 'anyone who used words to tell lies should be put on trial', Beauvoir added that some words were 'as lethal as gas chambers'.

After four months or so in the U.S., where he had been reporting for *Combat* and *Le Figaro*, Sartre returned. He had, as usual, been faithful to Beauvoir in his fashion, that is not faithful at all. He had met someone who had previously admired him from a distance in Paris, and now, said Beauvoir, they were 'very much attracted to each other'. This was Dolores Vanetti, an actress who had played at the Théâtre de Montparnasse before 1939 and was well known at Le Dôme. She had since married an American doctor, but was not too happy. Although she herself admitted later that she did not fall in love with Sartre until their second encounter, later that year, this was no idle 'contingent' affair. Sartre had explained to her his special relationship with Beauvoir and they had agreed to treat *their* special relationship as short-term; it would come to an end when Sartre returned to France. However, when Sartre came back he found he could not accept that it was all over, he was determined to see Dolores again and arranged, without much difficulty, to go back to the U.S. in December for a lecture tour, visiting various universities.

Beauvoir, experienced now in the complex world of Sartre's women, made the best of things, as she always did. During July, while Sartre went to see his mother, recently widowed for the second time, at her country house in the Yonne, Beauvoir went on a short cycling holiday with the actor and producer Michel Vitold, going through the Creuse area, then through the Auvergne to Vichy. Vitold was by origin Russian, a brilliant cyclist, a cheerful companion and welcome contingent lover. He was a great admirer of Sartre and had been the first Garcin in *Huis clos*. Beauvoir wrote to Sartre giving all the details of their holiday, and she was often reminded of him when seeing places where they had been together. Vitold was obviously a great extrovert, they went bathing together, they tried sleeping out in the open though it was rather cold, and he pushed her and her bicycle uphill. They had a good deal to talk about, for Vitold wanted to produce her play, *Les Bouches inutiles* (he eventually did so), and was glad of a confidante, to listen to details of his troubled private life.

Ordinary day-to-day life was not yet easy, even in the provinces, and if the couple had not brought American food with them they would have felt hungry, especially, worse luck, after meals. They slept rough, on café benches and in a charcoal-burner's hut, and once in the back of a baker's shop. After they had separated at Vichy, Beauvoir continued on her own as far as the hilly Vercors district, between the Drôme and the Isère rivers.

When Sartre received all the news about her holiday with Vitold he replied saying he was delighted that she was enjoying herself and had not lost her youth. He hastily added that he had not lost his either; he was with Wanda at the time. He told Beauvoir that he very much wanted to see *her* again and when he was in Paris he felt lonely without her. He was pleased to learn that she was cycling along 'with the violence of her stormy nature'. Sartre now had little of the free time that he had enjoyed while in the army, and his letters to Beauvoir no longer have the bubbling warmth and tender intimacy of the early days. He did not write as often because they were usually not separated for very long. They still spent holidays together and during August they stayed at Madame Morel's house. They were there when the second atomic bomb was dropped on Nagasaki and the war in the Far East ended.

For Beauvoir however, the big event of 1945 was the publication in September of her second novel, *Le Sang des autres*, so successful that it went through thirty-two impressions in two years and was translated into more than ten languages. She had started it about four years earlier, but despite the long wait for completion it had not become 'historical', at least from the public's point of view. Its background was the resistance, but Beauvoir had not intended it as a 'resistance novel', for it was about the human situation and human relationships, and the war was in a sense incidental.

The plot observed the unity of time so dear to the classical dramatists, for the external action takes place during one single night, which Jean Blomart, a resistance leader in the midst of setting up an operation, spends at the bedside of the dying Hélène. During that night, by a series of flashbacks interspersed with straightforward incidents, the reader learns the life stories of both characters. Jean Blomart, born into a bourgeois family of successful printers, deserts them at the age of twenty and becomes a worker, joining the Communist party. He lives through the political problems of the 1930s and feels guilty when the brother of a friend is killed in a demonstration. He meets Hélène, who prefers him to Paul, her fiancé. Hélène is demanding, much concerned with herself and uninterested in politics and trade unionism. When Jean rejects her she despairingly accepts sex with another man, finds herself pregnant and has an abortion. Jean allows her to stay briefly in his house until it is all over. On the outbreak of war Jean is conscripted, and she tries, through an influential friend, to arrange a safer posting for him. Although they had decided earlier to get married he now realizes he cannot tolerate her interference and they separate.

During the Occupation the two of them meet again. Hélène has now accepted the reality of political life, is unafraid of danger and anxious to join in resistance work. Jean reluctantly entrusts her with a mission, she is shot in the lung and brought back to Jean's resistance cell to die. He now realizes how much he loves her. She dies in the early morning and shortly afterwards he finds the strength to take the decision that he had deferred the night before.

While she was writing the book Beauvoir had felt that it was an

327

improvement on her first novel. It is carefully constructed in thirteen chapters, is half the length of *L'Invitée* and, despite the flashbacks and occasionally confusing chronology, the background of the characters and their changing interplay are handled with economy and clarity. But fifteen years later Beauvoir was hard on her book, too hard. She found her characters thin and unconvincing and the whole novel too didactic. Because she had consciously set out to write a novel about responsibility and took as her epigraph the well-known sentence of Dostoevsky, one she had already quoted in *Pyrrhus et Cinéas*: 'Each of us is responsible to every human being', it would have been difficult to avoid a fairly obvious message. By 1960, when she criticized her own book so heavily, the pressures of the resistance and its immediate aftermath had faded and some of the appropriate lessons had been learnt. She herself had learnt much more about life and fiction writing, even if her plots and characters were more remembered than invented. *Le Sang des autres* is a richer book than she allows it to be. The use of her own experiences, including her flight from Paris in 1940, is less interesting than the use she makes of earlier memories. For example, one incident from her childhood had impressed her deeply. Louise, the devoted maid in the Beauvoir household, had left to get married, and then her baby died. The young Simone was taken to see her in her slum-like home and was upset by the poverty and deprivation she found there. In the novel she transferred this reaction to Jean Blomart, showing incidentally that a boy can grieve at such an occurrence just as much as a girl. At the same time this incident, and also the death of Hélène, form two of her many attempts to come to terms with her lifelong obsession: death. As with *L'Invitée*, endless details in the novel come from Beauvoir's experience: an army lieutenant is called Bourlat, as though commemorating the lost Spanish Jewish boy, Bourla. When a girlfriend of Jean's, Madeleine, goes to the front in the Spanish Civil War, she injures her foot by spilling hot oil over it, a clear recollection of what had happened to Simone Weil. Marcel, like Sartre, is sent to a prison camp in Baccarat, while the irresponsible Hélène, like Nathalie Sorokine (to whom the book is dedicated), steals a bicycle. Nathalie, incidentally, found the novel very boring.

The author considered that the character of Hélène was better developed than that of Jean Blomart, and she admitted modelling her partly on herself. Women novelists have always been criticized for their failure to portray convincing male characters, and if Beauvoir had improved her handling of this problem – the figure of the painter and sculptor, Marcel (said to be based on Giacometti, whom she knew, and Marcel Duchamp) is certainly interesting – the women are still more successful.

Beauvoir resented the labels attached to her book, as she resented all labels in literature and politics. She did not want it to be described as a 'resistance novel' or an 'existentialist novel', but, published as it was late in 1945, how could it have been regarded as anything else? Sartre's two novels, *L'Age de raison* and *Le Sursis (The Reprieve)*, long awaited, were also published at that time. The reading public of 1945, half-educated now about the new 'ism' and keen to learn more, wanted supporting texts. *Le Sang des autres* was such a text and it was a readable novel with no shortage of action. More people could share something of it than could share in *L'Invitée*, despite the common situation of the eternal triangle. The atmosphere in the earlier book was too cerebral, the emotionalism too fitful and confined to Françoise. In *Le Sang des autres*, despite the didacticism, the sexual feeling is warmer and shared by more people. Jean is more convincing than Pierre in *L'Invitée*, Hélène is infinitely more credible and more likeable than Xavière. A vast number of novels about the resistance were published, some outstanding, some more successful than they deserved, but this novel is about many other things too. In it Beauvoir acknowledges the lessons she had herself learnt about political apathy and personal responsibility, and passes them on. This novel deserves to be better known. She did not help it by her own criticism and it was not helped by a later interpretation: in 1984 Claude Chabrol made a film, *Le Sang des autres*, based on the story; it was one of his failures.

Two years had passed since Beauvoir had been asked 'Are *you* an existentialist, madame?' and she had not been able to answer the question with a Yes or No. Now, however, there was no escape, for aspiring intellectuals and the fringe of small-time writers who hovered round the offices of publishers, newspapers and magazines insisted that existentialism was not only an intellectual movement, it was a way of life. They suffered from hunger of all kinds, the food supply was still bad and spam did very little to help the taste buds. There was also a need for something beyond *les nourritures terrestres*. After the victory celebrations the political scene was confused and confusing, while fear about a possible third and nuclear war soon began to spread, leading to a demand for escape into the consolation of philosophy. The new religion was to be non-religion and as though by magic a high priest, accompanied by a priestess, had appeared, and they were usually to be found seated at a table in the Café de Flore. This table soon had to be equipped with a special telephone line because Sartre was much sought after and received endless calls. Despite the interruptions both he and Beauvoir still preferred to live and work in public rather than at home, for a café could provide food and drink, plus heating when necessary, eliminating all the tedious minor problems of domestic life. The décor for the new talkative literary movement was perfect. This corner of the 6th *arrondissement* had received its name from the church named after Saint Germanus. The building itself, if hardly beautiful after its nineteenth-century restoration, still stands, an island of near-peace at a busy, ever-more-commercialized crossroads. To the saint's name is added 'des Prés', meaning literally 'in the meadows', because this area, like Montparnasse and other *quartiers* of Paris, had once been a village.

Beauvoir's later account of the existentialist 'offensive' in autumn 1945 was low-key and modest, even though she had acquired some prestige in her own right through her novel and her long essays. She was now very busy. She published nothing in the first number of *Les Temps modernes*, which appeared in October, but the two following issues contained important articles – *Idéalisme moral et réalisme politique*, and *L'Existentialisme et la sagesse des nations*. She made a further contribution to the November issue by reviewing at length her friend Merleau-Ponty's book *La Phénoménologie de la perception*, based on his doctorate thesis and since then accepted as a major work of international value. Beauvoir was also invited to lecture at the Club Maintenant, where Sartre had recently, and literally, drawn the crowds.

However much Sartre thought of Dolores at this time – he had even dedicated to her his 'presentation' of *Les Temps modernes* – Beauvoir was constantly at his side during this hectic autumn and had become used to the titles accorded to her by would-be witty journalists. There was no escaping the religious theme: she was 'la grande Sartreuse', or 'Notre Dame de Sartre', and the two of them were constantly interviewed and photographed. When she later wrote about the Saint-Germain scene Beauvoir insisted that Sartre was the true celebrity, while she remained in the background. For the time being at least she seemed content to remain there, although she admitted enjoying her share of the fame, for it had come to her comparatively late in life. She was now thirty-seven, and she had been writing ever since she could remember. However, she soon found that there was no point in living in the limelight if it prevented the completion of any serious work. Sartre intensified his habit of supporting himself with alcohol and stimulants, for his mental activity was so intense that his physique could hardly keep pace with it. Beauvoir continued her lifelong habit of keeping an eye on Sartre and trying to minimize his excesses.

But fame had to be paid for: as the autumn passed there was no longer any chance of working quietly at café tables, and Beauvoir was reduced to working, without an audience, in her hotel room. She and Sartre soon spent more time in the downstairs bar of the much grander but unpicturesque Pont-Royal, near the Gallimard offices. The bar lacked café tables: Beauvoir missed them, for the small barrels supplied instead were adequate for glasses but not much use for writing on.

Did Beauvoir now think about those younger people whom she called the 'family', '*le petit monde*', '*ma charmante vermine*', who had taken up so much of her life during the early war years? Developments were both good and bad. Olga and Wanda were making some progress in the theatre, although any roles they obtained were small and did not earn them much money. Nathalie Sorokine had met Ivan Moffatt, a Hollywood scriptwriter working in a film unit of the American army. She became pregnant, married Moffatt and was preparing to join her husband in California.

The news of Védrine was not so promising, and in mid-December 1945 Beauvoir wrote to Sartre: 'She disturbed me and filled me with remorse, because she is going through a terrible and profound crisis of neurasthenia – and . . . it's our fault, I think, it's the after-effect, very indirect but severe, of our *histoire* with her.' Beauvoir thought that she and Sartre were at least partly to blame: 'She's the only person to whom we've really done harm, but we've done it.' When Beauvoir's letters were finally published in 1990 she and Sartre were described by some critics as twentieth-century embodiments of those wicked if entertaining seducers in *Les Liaisons dangereuses*: unlike the Marquise de Merteuil, Beauvoir did at least regret her behaviour. She explained to Sartre that the unfortunate Védrine had discovered her own masochism, on reading *L'Etre et le néant*, and that despite her marriage she was living through a kind of retarded adolescence. Beauvoir was obviously distressed and hastened to tell Sartre that she did not like to think that 'things will disappear without being shared with you'. She appeared to realize that her relationship with Sartre was not as invulnerable as it might have seemed earlier, and she knew she must work to preserve it intact. If she had hoped that Sartre might share something of her guilt over the depressed Védrine, she was destined to disappointment. There was little chance of the girl returning to a happy life: she had loved Beauvoir and seemed disinclined to look for happiness in any other relationship.

At the very end of the year, when Sartre had returned to the U.S. and Dolores, Beauvoir may have felt deeply worried about her own personal future. Fortunately her professional life was now occupying a great deal of time, even if it did not always bring her success. In November Michel Vitold at last produced her play *Les Bouches inutiles* at the Théâtre des Carrefours, but it did not enhance her reputation. She was unlucky in one way: her neighbour at the first night was none other than Jean Genet, the ex-convict writer taken up by Cocteau and more significantly by Sartre. Genet, who had recently enjoyed his first successes with the publication of some poems and his novel, *Notre Dame des fleurs*, told her in a forthright manner that this was not the stuff of drama. Olga played the part of Clarice, but she was hardly experienced enough to cause a sensation, metro trains rumbled nearby, the theatre was cold and the scene changes were too slow. One reviewer was kind enough to write that aspects of the play reminded him of the classical dramatist Corneille, but that did not save Beauvoir. After fifty or so performances *Les Bouches inutiles* was taken off, the author decided she had no talent for the theatre and made no further attempt to write a play.

Fortunately, she was now invited by the Alliance Française to lecture in Tunis and Algeria, where she enjoyed herself thoroughly, after making her first trip by air. She had become so used to walking in lonely regions of France by herself that she did the same thing among the sand dunes near Tunis. She fell asleep and woke to find 'a very dirty old Arab' sitting on her stomach. She managed to escape, after giving him money, and later learned that the threatening knife which lay beside him in the sand was there for cutting asparagus, not for murdering women tourists.

No sooner was existentialism launched as an intellectual fashion than it was attacked on all sides, sometimes by traditionalists and sometimes by journalists who were merely looking for something and someone to attack. Beauvoir found that men would glance at her strangely. If a woman was an existentialist – there was no escaping what had become a meaningless label – she must be immoral and dissolute. Would things have been different if she had been married to Sartre? There was no marriage certificate and no wedding rings, but were these two different from many couples? They had been fond of quoting Dowson's poem: 'I have been faithful to thee, Cynara! in my fashion', and it expressed their life-style very well. Even if Beauvoir constantly stressed that Sartre was famous and she was hardly so, he was the first to acknowledge how much he depended on her. He had written *L'Etre et le néant* but she had gone through the whole vast book with him, and for those who wanted some practical application of the ideas it contained it was she who had written *Pyrrhus et Cinéas* and related articles in *Les Temps modernes*. Sartre could have remained king of his unexpected castle without a consort, but it was useful to have one. Without Beauvoir the early existentialist era would have been like Bloomsbury without Virginia Woolf. It would have been abstract and dull.

Who would have thought that the heirs of Kierkegaard, Hegel and Heidegger would be subjected to the first postwar 'hype', even if the word was not yet much known in Europe? The hype endangered the serious interest in existentialism, and Beauvoir was quick to see that degeneration would quickly set in. During a lecture tour in Switzerland she found that she and Sartre were 'enthroned' like a 'Catholic king and his queen'. She thought they looked ridiculous, but especially herself.

It was a strange situation indeed. Her ambition had been to become a serious writer, and she had maintained that she had no philosophical ideas to add to those of Sartre, but she had spent a good deal of time working out the morality that was latent within them. Despite the journeys, lectures and essay-writing of 1946 she had never stopped working on a third novel, a long one again, and it was published at the end of the same year.

This controversial work gives a better impression of what was happening in Beauvoir's unconscious mind during the years 1943–46 than what she chose to remember later in her memoirs. She described the external atmosphere in which she began the novel, after reading Sismondi's *Histoire des républiques italiennes*, where she had found the theme for her play *Les Bouches inutiles*. She added too that her idea for a new hero was linked in one way to the conception of the previous one, Jean Blomart in *Le Sang des autres*. Her next hero would be the reverse of Blomart, who took all responsibility upon himself; the new one would decide he could achieve nothing. Her new novel was certainly different, for, set against a background of six centuries of history, it told the story of one man, Count Fosca, who was immortal. She intended to prove two things she regarded as important, and one of them mattered deeply to her in a personal sense. She was so terrified by the idea of death that she wanted desperately to state that immortality did not bring happiness, the infinite is no improvement on the finite. At the same time she believed that there was no way of improving the lot of mankind: each man, each woman would have to deal with his/her own individual problems.

When she wrote *Tous les hommes sont mortels*, Beauvoir used the story-within-a-story method, incorporating what amounts to an historical novel set within the life-story of an actress named Régine. She is self-centred, unsatisfied, demanding, and the reader does not sympathize with her in any way. Régine becomes curious about Fosca and when she learns about his immortality she hopes that if they love each other she can bring him back to normal life. He tells her the story of his life so far and between each period of his existence there is dialogue between the two of them.

Fosca lives in the city state of Carmona in northern Italy in the late thirteenth century. He is so ambitious for the prestige of his town that he assassinates its hated ruler and assumes power. The incident of *Les Bouches inutiles*, including the phrase itself, is built into the story of the town when under siege. Fosca finds life too short for the success of his ambitions and accepts the offer of the elixir of life, which makes him immortal without ageing. There are two results: he and his town become powerful, but as a human being Fosca is doomed to unhappiness, for everyone close to him grows old and dies. He even tries to kill himself but the elixir is all-powerful, he has to go on living.

He also has to move on in time and space. He soon outgrows Italy and by the sixteenth century he becomes close to the Emperor Charles V in Vienna. A hundred years later Fosca travels through the whole of the little-known American continent from south to north, befriending an explorer who eventually turns against him and then shoots himself. The fourth section of the story takes place in eighteenth-century France, when Fosca marries Marianne de Sinclair, an intelligent and sophisticated woman. They are happy until she learns the truth about her husband. The last section takes Fosca through the revolution of 1830 in Paris at the side of his grandson Armand and when the 1848 revolution comes he feels he does not belong to the same world as the young people and leaves them. He sleeps for sixty years and then spends the next thirty in an asylum. It is after this stay that he meets Régine and at the end, having told her his story, he walks out of her life. She realizes that she cannot make any true contact with an immortal. She is left alone and loses her reason.

When Beauvoir described how she set about writing the book she referred to the 'abstract' construction of *Le Sang des autres* and said of this new venture *'je rêvai'* – she allowed herself to dream. The novel is something of a fantasy and everyone can find in it what they are looking for. The French critic and biographer, Françoise d'Eaubonne, who knew Beauvoir well, thought that the author had exploited a lyrical vein which she had neglected during a long preoccupation with abstract thought, analytical dialogue and reporter-like prose. There is no means of knowing if her earliest writing had included the touches of poetry that occur here, but there is nothing similar in her work until the first volume of memoirs describing her childhood. In the novel, flowers, trees, buildings and many outside scenes are evoked in brief sentences which convey both image and essence. One night Fosca sees his young son in the garden with his friend Béatrice: 'they had twined garlands of flowers over their nightgowns; Béatrice had placed convolvulus in her hair and a heavy magnolia flower at her breast . . .' There are no purple passages, only memorable glimpses of worlds far removed from the eternal café tables of *L'Invitée*.

The author's messages come through to the reader despite the wide variety of contexts. Fosca discusses religion with Charles V, education with Marianne, but the conclusions are always the same: the only thing worthwhile is to act in accordance with one's conscience. 'If that is true, any wish to dominate the world is vain; one can do nothing for men, their well-being depends only on themselves.' The Emperor intended, through the grace of God, to achieve not the salvation of others, but merely his own. The emotional undercurrent to the fourth section of the book, when Fosca meets and marries Marianne de Sinclair, is particularly strong, for he feels that, now he has rediscovered love, he has become attached to life again: 'Now I am in love and I can suffer; I've become a man once more.'

Beauvoir, always a more emotional writer than might appear on the surface, wrote with deeper feeling here than in any other of her early fiction. Her distress about mortality is all-pervasive, and is never counteracted by any rational approach. Through Fosca's love for Marianne she also attempted, perhaps unconsciously, to indicate that her own love for Sartre, and all that it implied, compensated for the terror she felt at the inevitability of death. Or was she expressing her fear that this love might not last, might be as 'mortal' as the partners themselves?

Perhaps Beauvoir succeeded in reducing some of her fears by writing this long novel, which is isolated from the rest of her fiction but integrated within her early writing by its persistent message about self-reliance. Fosca's belief that love attaches him to the world does not solve the problems of his immortality but mitigates them for a time. On the whole the book creates a feeling of pessimism, mainly because the reader finds it hard to come to terms with the author's non-acceptance of death and her failure to overcome it.

Beauvoir seemed incapable of seeing the book dispassionately, no doubt because it embodied some of her deepest feelings, especially her atheism, perhaps even unconscious memories of her early emotional Christianity. Its publishing history has been intriguing, for the publisher, Nagel, who was a Communist, received conflicting reports on it. His wife liked it but many people didn't, thinking it was inferior to her others, 'as you know', he told the author. But the author did not know. She had heard a rumour that the novelist Raymond Queneau liked it so much that he had suggested a first printing of 75,000 copies. Her friend Michel Leiris, a surrealist himself, believed that she had 'used the fantastic too rationally', an astute comment which helps to explain the failure of the book with the reading public. The critic André Rousseaux – whom Beauvoir quoted with obvious malicious pleasure – wrote that he had misjudged her in the past and she would never write anything of value in the future. *Tous les hommes sont mortels* seems to have been a favourite with women readers. Hélène de Beauvoir and Françoise d'Eaubonne thought highly of it and by 1974 it had been translated into eleven languages. Readers in such different countries as the United States, Argentina, Japan and Czechoslovakia have been able to read this novel in their own language, but no publisher in Britain has felt moved to offer the book to the British. In 1981 the Queen of Denmark and her French consort, using a pseudonym, translated it into Danish. The Queen had first read the book soon after her marriage in 1967, having found a copy in her husband's library.

> Some time later [the Queen wrote in 1987], I read it once more and was captivated by the extraordinary tale itself and by the fascinating picture of European history which the author conveyed through the strange and troubled character of 'Fosca' . . . It was the book itself rather than the author which was of interest to me. It is deeply moving at times and it contains a warmth and compassion which somehow seem to

be lacking in Simone de Beauvoir's later work – though I freely admit that I have only read a small part of her oeuvre.

The critics reacted favourably to the Danish version, some, wrote the Lord Chamberlain, wondering why Her Majesty and His Royal Highness had chosen a 'juvenile work [sic] and not one of Simone de Beauvoir's later novels. Others emphasized on the other hand the importance of knowing the writer's line of thought when she was young.' In 1946, when the book was first published, Beauvoir was in fact thirty-eight, but she was young in two important ways: she had not yet written either *Le Deuxième Sexe* or *Les Mandarins*.

SIXTEEN

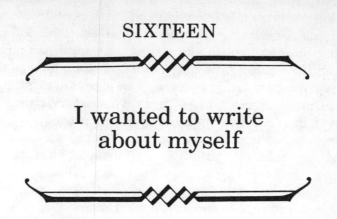

I wanted to write about myself

In some ways Beauvoir had never done anything else, she had constantly written about herself ever since adolescence, and although many writers behave in the same way they rarely concentrate on their own story with such intensity and with so little disguise as did Beauvoir. The starting-point always lay in her own subjective view, and however far this seemed to fade and become objective, in fiction and non-fiction, it never disappeared. *Tous les hommes sont mortels* had been about her own fear of death, her belief in the individual and his responsibility for him or herself. The novel had taken a long time to write, was not successful in 1946 and has received little critical attention, let alone approval. As though to compensate for this failure – it cannot be called anything else – the next few years, between 1947 and 1954, saw her two most important books and an unexpected development in her emotional life. This latter was to bring out all the femininity in her nature, leave her with unresolved problems for a long time and complicate the Beauvoir legend for ever.

In the meantime she returned to the ethical questions of which she never tired. After the prompting she had received from the young Robert Misrahi in 1945 she had made another attempt to prove that a moral system could be built up on a base of atheistic existentialism. Her long essay *Pour une morale de l'ambiguité* was first published in two parts in the January and February issues of *Les Temps modernes*, appearing in book form later in the same year, 1947. She began with an opening quotation from an existentialist *avant la lettre*, the sixteenth-century Montaigne: 'Life in itself is neither good or evil, it can contain good and evil depending on what you make of it . . .' Despite her passionate interest in the subject, and her conviction that she was the only thinker-writer attempting to clarify this aspect of existentialism, she was the strongest critic of her own work. Writing sixteen years later, in 1963, she emphasized how important it was in 1947 to correct misconceptions about existentialism, which was regarded as 'nihilist, miserabilist, frivolous, licentious, and despairing'. She considered that the polemical side of her book was valid, and she still approved what she had written about aestheticism and artistic commitment. However, she found that her proposed solutions were no better than 'the maxims of Kant'. In the second part of the three-part essay she attempted to give a series of 'portraits', illustrating for example the nihilist, the adventurer, the aesthete and others. These attempts, she found, were influenced by Hegel and were 'more arbitrary' and 'even more abstract' than his. Although this long essay has remained in print, followed by the shorter and earlier *Pyrrhus et Cinéas*,it has never found enthusiastic supporters. The important thing for Beauvoir was that she had carried out her plan and seen the results published, even if she later decided that, of all her works so far, this was the one which 'irritated' her the most.

However, by the end of January, before the second instalment had appeared in *Les Temps modernes*, she was no longer in Paris but in the U.S. Her ambition to go there, as Sartre had done, and to enjoy herself as a tourist, had been realized through a chance meeting at the Café de Flore with the former surrealist Philippe Soupault. He said he could probably arrange a lecture tour for her through the government department responsible for cultural relations and the Alliance Française. He kept his promise, and as a result she left for New York at the end of January 1947, travelling in the U.S. until the beginning of May, giving some twenty-four lectures all over the country at university and other locations, from New York to Los Angeles, Berkeley, Harvard, Yale, Princeton, Philadelphia and back to New York again. At the same time she was commissioned to write several important articles in large-circulation periodicals, including *Vogue*.

She had some friends in the U.S. and in New York was delighted to find again the Gerassi family. Stépha, her husband and son had left France in 1940, crossed Spain illegally and reached North America from there. Later Beauvoir planned to go to California to see her young friend Nathalie Sorokine, now Mrs Ivan Moffat, who had a little daughter. Most of all she was happy to meet again Richard Wright, whom she had encountered in Paris earlier. He had become internationally successful with the publication of *Native Son* in 1940, the first contemporary novel about a rebellious young black American. Five years later the appearance of his autobiography *Black Boy* maintained his reputation.

After the years of deprivation in France Beauvoir obviously relished all the comforts of American hotels and the usefulness of the drugstores, which she described as 'poetic'. She walked round New York and saw all the sights, especially those recommended by Sartre, or by Bost, who had been to the U.S. on an assignment for *Combat*. She enjoyed herself immensely but one deprivation remained: the absence of Sartre. Despite the end of the war and his intermittent but relatively close presence in Paris her feelings had not changed from the period of their separation and their intense daily letter-writing. Just as he had always begun to write to her in the train as he left Paris she now began to write to him as soon as her plane touched down in Canada on the way to New York. 'Do you remember,' she asked, 'this room where I'm writing to you, with its pale walls? You are so present to me here.' As she had drunk her quarter-bottle of champagne during the flight she had felt 'utterly happy. You were as close to me as if you had touched me; I feel that I shan't be separated from you for one minute, nothing can separate us.'

In 1948 Beauvoir telescoped together an account of this first trip to the U.S. and a second one she was to make seven months later into *L'Amérique au jour le jour* (*America Day by Day*). However, like her later memoirs, the book narrates only the surface happenings of her journeys and refers to many people by initials only, preferable no doubt at the time but unsatisfactory for the next generation of readers. Her letters to Sartre, published in 1990, supply a continuous and fascinating subtext to the more official account she wrote after the trip, giving her immediate reactions and proving the extent of her later memory lapses, both conscious and unconscious, when she was questioned by interviewers about the details of her earlier life.

In New York she found that her trip had not yet been officially financed, and Claude Lévi-Strauss, the social anthropologist, who was working at the time in the cultural relations department of the French Embassy, dealt with this on her behalf. He also filled in some background to her trip that was not too pleasing. The French officials in New York did not care for the Paris existentialists, whom they regarded as subversive left-wingers, and to receive a woman existentialist was almost more than they could tolerate. However, Beauvoir was there, and was soon much in demand by groups interested in France, in addition to the marathon lecture tour which had been at least partly arranged in advance. It probably did not occur to Beauvoir that her audiences were particularly curious about her simply because she was a woman, and a Frenchwoman. Her arrival had been backed up with a *New Yorker* article written by Janet Flanner at least partly after an earlier interview in Paris. The correspondent was delighted by 'the female intellectual counterpart of Jean-Paul Sartre', after having expected 'a grim half hour'. 'Mlle. de B. is the prettiest Existentialist you ever saw; also eager, gentle, modest . . .' After describing a typical Beauvoir day in Paris the correspondent quoted her talking about Sartre and Michel Leiris, who was described as an 'Existentialist poet'. ' "We have intellectual conversations," she said to us, with a sweet smile in which we detected no trace of pity.'

Other journalists referred to Beauvoir as 'elegant', a description that was quoted in a French biography published in 1985. She was still furious about it a year later and said that it was nonsense, she had *never* been elegant. She had forgotten perhaps that her American friends were determined to see her as elegant – a Frenchwoman arriving from Paris? How could she be anything else? She admitted that she had had one dress made, in a knitted fabric, 'deep blue with large green pattern motifs', but she had regarded it as a wretched concession to bourgeois orthodoxy. She had even wept from disapproval of herself but had to admit later that during the social whirl of New York the dress was essential. She was not a naturally good speaker, as the schoolgirls she had taught earlier had always known, and when writing to Sartre she made no secret of her attitude towards her audiences. Lévi-Strauss told her that she spoke too fast and was difficult to follow, but she brushed such criticism aside in the deprecatory style that was to be increasingly typical of her: 'But that isn't important because in any case these old hags don't understand French.' She was pleased nonetheless that most people she met understood her English, even if she could not always follow their American.

The literary agent Marion Saunders gave Beauvoir some stopgap money but this did not prevent her from being described as 'an old horror'. Another woman literary agent, named 'la Macht', was 'a real shit'; she had been unkind about Sartre's friend Dolores Vanetti, who had been trying hard (and successfully) to find journalistic commissions for Beauvoir. 'La Macht' had even accused her of dishonesty.

Beauvoir and Dolores met at the Sherry Netherlands Hotel at ten in the evening, after the French visitor had escaped from a boring dinner with Lévi-Strauss and his wife, saying she was tired. Beauvoir assumed that Dolores would tell Sartre all the details about their meeting, but she gave him her impressions when she wrote on January 30th: 'I found her exactly as I had supposed her to be, I like her very much and I was very happy because at one and the same time I understood your feelings, I could touch them, I praised you for having them – and I didn't feel in the slightest way embarrassed.' She had said similar things during the *drôle de guerre* when she was temporarily conducting a 'charm offensive' towards Wanda. She wanted at all costs to keep Sartre as her partner, and in order to do so she felt that she had to accept everything that he said, wrote and did.

Soon after her first meeting with Beauvoir Dolores gave a cocktail party in her own apartment and Beauvoir was accompanied there by Lévi-Strauss. Meeting Sartre's current 'contingent' passion on her home ground was disturbing for Beauvoir: 'I felt quite emotional as I entered this apartment where you lived for such a long time, seeing Calder's bird, and the view, and so many people you talked to me about . . .' Of the hostess she spoke again with praise and also with that vain curiosity she often felt about other people's opinions of herself: 'Dolores was as

---

delightful as a little Annamite idol, and really charming with me, I would very much like to know what she really thought.'

This was not their last meeting. Dolores was about to join the irresistible man in France, and Beauvoir went to say goodbye to her. The session was not too easy 'because we were separating without in fact having known each other, and we had no regrets nor any future plans'. Again she tried to see Sartre's point of view: 'I find her really delightful and very *sympathique*,' even if she was 'just a little too much *bonne femme*, as Bost says, for my own taste' – (not intellectual enough, presumably?) – 'but if one is a male, and what's more, motivated by an imperialist passion for generosity, one cannot meet a more appropriate person'. Beauvoir showed some generosity, if some irony, too.

Beauvoir could not get away from Sartre and did not want to. She returned to her hotel and a letter from Sartre. She felt close to him: 'I read it and slept for an hour clasping it to my heart.' She continued to see the sights he had recommended and one day when she opened the *New York Times* 'there was your photograph smiling at me – a photograph I didn't know. That shook me, my love.' There was no escaping France's intellectual pin-up, and at Vassar, where she lectured, his photograph was on the wall and the students were rehearsing, with much excitement, a production of *Les Mouches*.

Her thoughts rarely left Sartre and there was plenty to tell him, especially her reactions on seeing 'Sammy's Follies' on the Bowery, where she was taken by Gerassi, again on the recommendation of Sartre and Bost. In her edition of *Lettres à Sartre*, Sylvie Le Bon de Beauvoir, Beauvoir's adopted daughter, has described this place as 'a bar with performances by elderly actresses, singers and dancers, aged between sixty and eighty'. Beauvoir found the place wonderful, especially the audience. She felt as she had felt when seeing the sordid districts of Naples in 1933, but now she looked a little deeper. 'In one sense it's disgusting, but it's the extreme limit of all the sordid side of N.Y. and America, and as such it becomes poetic and in reality it's less revolting than the real reasons which allow such a thing to exist.' There was much to be said about it, and she asked Sartre to keep her letters 'which will be my only souvenir from here and I want absolutely to recover them again'. She often borrowed back her own letters when she came to write out descriptions of her travels and other experiences.

At the end of February she left New York temporarily for New London and Washington, then she left again and was not back until mid-April, after a trip which took her over half the continent and in fact led to a major development in her emotional life. First of all she was in Rochester, Buffalo – after seeing the Niagara Falls – and then Chicago, where the consul had reserved a room for her in 'a splendid hotel'. After visiting the museum and seeing the sights, on foot and by taxi, she made a crucial telephone call to a friend of Richard Wright and of Mary Guggenheim whom she had met in New York. All she knew about this friend was that he was called Nelson Algren and was a writer. 'Chicago wasn't awful,' she wrote to Sartre a few days later. 'On the contrary I liked Chicago a lot, perhaps it's because I very much liked the man I saw it with.' It had taken three attempts by Beauvoir and a further one a few hours later, with the help of an American woman, before the two of them succeeded in talking on the telephone. In the end he understood who she was and agreed to meet her at her hotel at nine o'clock that evening.

She continued her letter to Sartre with a brief portrait of Algren. 'He's a typical American with a wooden face and an inexpressive body, who began by travelling across America on freight trains and as a *pin-boy*, the one who collects the skittles in the bowling alleys. Then he wrote, had some success, now he's been living on a contract for two years and after that he'll start to earn his living any old how.' Obviously this was only a fraction of the Algren story so far. He was a year younger than she was, born in Detroit but had spent nearly all his life in Chicago. He was of Swedish-German-Jewish origin and with some financial help from his sister had struggled through a course at the Illinois School of Journalism. The 'success' that Beauvoir mentioned was probably the publication of *Someone in Boots* in 1935 and *Never Come Morning* seven years later. He had spent time in jail when he was young, accused of stealing (he said he merely 'borrowed') a typewriter. He had worked for the Chicago Board of Health as a venereal disease controller from 1941 to 1942, the year in which *Never Come Morning* was published. He had edited the *New Anvil Magazine*, and his life story so far could have been described as a realistic novel in itself; he may have impressed Beauvoir because he had lived through it, not merely imagined it, and knew the *bas-fonds* of American cities, not merely looked at them.

Beauvoir compared his work to that of Saroyan and Damon Runyon, but he is better considered as the third member, along with Richard Wright and James T. Farrell, of the so-called 'Chicago school'. Beauvoir told Sartre that he was 'more or less Communist, naturally. I found him *très sympathique* and intelligent and human, as they can be when they're good specimens.' He was tall, blond, macho, and he soon understood what Beauvoir would most enjoy in Chicago: aspects of the urban 'picturesque'. He took her 'to the Chicago Bowery, to a dance-hall like Sammy's (in New York) but even more lewd and less commercial, a little night-spot where magnificent women took their clothes off and danced in an obscene way while people looked at them with total indifference, to a negro night club and a little Polish bar'. The two of them were obviously taken with each other: 'He put me in a taxi, kissing me in a clumsy, serious and concentrated way.' She had hoped to spend the next day with him but unfortunately the French officials had made other plans for her, including luncheon at the Alliance Française and dinner with the consul. She was furious but could not refuse. When she was driven back to Algren's apartment in the afternoon the officials were scandalized when she asked them to stop the car in such a low-class district. She was happy to find that Algren lived more or less as she did in Paris, 'in the little room of a poor intellectual'. She had to leave again for her official dinner, to the regret of both of them: 'He asked me so insistently to come back to Chicago and kissed me with such feeling as I left in a taxi that I felt emotional myself.'

It was the opening of a new chapter, but it could not be written yet, for Beauvoir was setting off on a different, prearranged adventure. After three nights and two days in the train she arrived at Westwood, near Beverly Hills, where she was going to stay with her young friend Nathalie, Mrs Ivan Moffatt. Her first thrill was a typical Hollywood story of great enthusiasm followed by total lack of interest. 'I'm wild with excitement,' Beauvoir told Sartre, 'for it's possible that Capra will make a film of the 'Immortal Man' [*Tous les hommes sont mortels*] with Claude Rains and Greta Garbo.' Ivan Moffatt was to write a treatment, the producer George Stevens seemed to like both the idea and the author. She worked out that she would earn herself 30,000 dollars. 'Doesn't that make you feel dizzy? You and I would live in America for a year . . .' She was not entirely in the clouds: 'I know very well that many of these things collapse, I've no illusions, but just the idea amuses me.' The project, not surprisingly, went no further. It has been suggested that Stevens was later so intimidated by Beauvoir that he gave up the idea of filming the novel, which in any case would have been a difficult and very expensive enterprise.

Despite her travels in the west and south with Nathalie and her husband it was a letter from Sartre, after three weeks without one, that thrilled her. She found it at Houston at the end of March and began to look forward to seeing him again. She complained that Bost had not written, she was displeased with him. Nathalie was with her for three days in New York, where she was now busier than ever with articles, meetings and invitations. By the end of her stay she had met, in various cities and universities, many famous writers, painters, actors and composers, mostly Europeans: Carlo Levi, Marcel Duchamp, Kurt Weill, Luise Rainer, Miró, Le Corbusier, Tanguy, Darius Milhaud and a talkative Charlie Chaplin. When she met Chaplin an American official whom she disliked made a speech asking her 'to recognize Chaplin as an existentialist; it was grotesque and embarrassing'. She tended to dislike officials of any nationality for, after all, they were representatives of the bourgeois establishment. She went to see the elderly poet Saint-John Perse in Georgetown, Washington, who touched her forehead and said it was 'so French'. She did not know what to say to this perceptive man when he interrupted a conversation on general topics to ask her 'What has made you so humane? Has life hurt you?'

The elderly French (and bourgeois) playwright Henri Bernstein had sought her out to tell her how much he had appreciated her novel *Tous les hommes sont mortels*. However, she was not interested in praise from people she did not care for and dismissed him – he was over eighty at the time – as an 'old horror'. Her favourite people in the U.S. were not the celebrities or the dreary academics, they were Richard Wright and his family, including their little daughter Julia, one of the rare children she liked. She wondered why Ellen Wright had dedicated herself to domestic life when she could have continued her work as an editor, but it does not seem to have occurred to her that this dedication may well have contributed to Julia's happy charm. Beauvoir never learnt much about the mother–daughter relationship. She was sad however that the social and political climate of the U.S. did not help the Wrights, who eventually left New York for Paris, where Ellen Wright later became Beauvoir's literary agent. Theirs was a mixed marriage, unpopular in the 1940s.

There was plenty to enjoy in the U.S., including the whisky, for Beauvoir found it did not taste of iodine, as it did in France, and she drank so much of it that her prowess was admired. At one party she also smoked six marijuana cigarettes which had no effect on her, so 'out of fury' she drank more than half a bottle of whisky and then felt more cheerful but not drunk. Her knowledge of the U.S. in the end was more or less limited to her meetings with intellectuals, who told her that she had not read the most worthwhile American authors: Steinbeck and Dos Passos were all very well but she must read older, classic writers such as Thoreau and Melville, Whitman and Hawthorne. At least she had read Faulkner but remained devoted to Dashiel Hammett, taking him more seriously than his fellow Americans. She met James T. Farrell but wrote him off as a bore.

'A thing I noticed immediately in America was that men and women seldom like each other.' In the pages Beauvoir wrote about women in *L'Amérique au jour le jour* she anticipated many themes she was to take up in depth in *The Second Sex*. In fact she had few good words for American women, whom earlier she had thought to be 'free'. Not at all. In fact, they were preoccupied with 'fishing for husbands, the art of snaring men', and keeping them 'in subjection'. 'In Europe,' she thought, 'women understand much better that the moment to assert their feminine claims is past; they try to prove their worth in politics, in art and science or merely in their lives'. Was that true in 1948? It was in some ways an aspiration, hardly a general fact, and even forty years later the assertion of 'feminine claims' has hardly been silenced. Beauvoir observed and recorded stray facts which add up to a general attitude of criticism: men were often obsessed by the frigidity of their wives, and as lovers they revealed an 'inferiority complex vis-à-vis Europeans and negroes'. Women were full of frustration, doubts and bitterness, but was it not their own fault? They were on the defensive and caught in a dilemma: 'The wish to dominate their men and rule them must seem incompatible with the animal desire for self-immolation which is latent in them.' Beauvoir was obviously taking notes for the large-scale study that was already in her head. As for women in power, she did not get on too well with them. The prestigious Blanche, wife of the publisher Alfred Knopf, became *l'abominable Knopf*, because she wanted Beauvoir to do some surgery on her novel, *L'Invitée*, which the firm had bought. She wanted her to cut the book 'line by line, adjective by adjective: I don't want to, or she'll have to pay me 200 dollars.' Blanche Knopf talked also about not publishing Beauvoir any more – but that was a mere threat.

Beauvoir was introduced to 'a young American novelist, bright hope of the *Partisan Review*, called Mary McCarthy; she's very beautiful and seems intelligent, and without any charm or interest apart from the documentary one – as such she fascinated me'. She could have written pages about this typical American intellectual. 'She has a very insignificant husband (the third without counting two official lovers).' Mary McCarthy had her say about Beauvoir in 1952, when she read an old copy of *L'Amérique au jour le jour*, the year before it was published in the U.S. She entitled her essay 'Mlle. Gulliver en Amérique', a phrase which sums up her demolition of the woman she called 'the leading French *femme savante*'. Like an inhabitant of Lilliput or Brobdingnag, looking at his own country as described by Swift, the American reader would find it 'all wrong, schematized, rationalized, like a scale model under glass'.

Beauvoir had seen the U.S. as a 'masculine world' in which women remained 'dependent and relative', and though her ideas on the subject were still half-formulated, she did not want women to live that way in future, anywhere. She had told *The New Yorker* about her next writing, which was to be 'a very serious book about women'. She had found that American women saw things differently from Frenchwomen but, she added, crucially, 'You'll have to wait for my book to find out how, or how I think how. It can't be explained in a few words.' Eventually her 'very serious book', in its original edition, contained a thousand or so pages.

A week after Beauvoir left the U.S. the *New York Times* of May 25th published an article which summed up her reactions to the way Americans lived, worked and thought. It was entitled 'An Existentialist looks at America'. While admiring much of American civilization, 'this magnificent triumph of man', she asked herself, as an existentialist, whether it provided men with 'valid reasons for living' and whether it justified their existence. Forty years later some of her remarks seem either unfathomable or plainly comic: she found 'much poetry in the drug stores and the ten-cent stores: the abundance and variety of the industrial products displayed all pointed to a magnificent and immediate taste for the transformation of mere things into instruments adapted to human purposes'. She went on, however, to give her deeply serious assessment of the American dilemma. She discerned among many people a 'great inner emptiness' for 'most Americans are afraid of themselves. Their optimism is wholly external.' She believed they were unsure of themselves because they did not trust their individual judgments or personal feelings. She also found that neither discussion of ideas nor self-examination was popular and that Americans were horrified at the idea of feeling guilty. The principles of existentialism would save them, she implied, and of course at this moment she could not see the world in any other way. After saying early during her visit that she had found young people to be aimless, she now thought they could acquire a sense of purpose, for she had faith in their hidden aspirations:

> For me the hope of America . . . lies in the uneasy hearts of the ex-GIs, and in the hearts of thousands of young people. The future of America lies in the consciousness of its youth, suddenly become aware of what the Spanish philosopher Unamuno called 'the tragic sense of life', and the responsibilities incumbent on a great country, if the immense reality that is America is addressed to serving man's mind and freedom as well as his body it may well become a civilization comparable to Athens and Rome. If not, it will remain a fact among other facts, in a world it will not have helped to justify.

In the hope presumably of emphasizing the writer's admonishments, severe, but not without optimism, the editor had flanked the article with a drawing of five men and one woman, who towered over vague outlines of a dam, two factories and a large automobile. The young people look upward, their gaze fixed on an existentialist future, their general attitude reminiscent of a Hollywood poster and a Stakhanovite exhortation from the U.S.S.R. Who would have guessed that this serious writer was more preoccupied at the time with affairs of the heart than with any popularization of the existentialist way of thought?

Towards the end of her stay in the U.S., at the end of April Beauvoir wrote excitedly to Sartre that she had received a long and tender letter from him, and she could hardly live through the following ten days which now separated them. Even though she knew Sartre was with Dolores he was still more important than anyone else. He had told her that, emotionally, things were 'stationary' with Dolores, whom he was taking to Italy on a farewell trip. Beauvoir became lyrical: '*Voyez-vous*, more than the Liberation, more than the trip to New York, each time it's you who are the most astonishing and the strongest and the deepest and the truest presence of my life.' Though New York had 'never seemed so marvellous', when she thought about this presence she began to sleep better. She thought it would be a good idea to meet in Paris at the Hôtel de la Louisiane.

Then she received a shock. Sartre telegraphed in early May asking her to postpone her return by a week. He and Dolores wanted to spend extra time together, or very probably Dolores had willed it. Beauvoir, the faithful 'wife', gave way at once, and had great difficulty in changing her plane reservation, 'but it's you who asked for it', and she did not argue, for 'It was intolerable for me to come back sooner than you wanted.' She saw everyone she could, literally begging for the change to be made, and eventually she succeeded. At the same time she also urged Sartre to arrange for them to have a long and undisturbed time together. The situation had changed for the worse, she was obviously deeply upset, she felt too *nerveuse* to write good letters, 'I sleep four hours per night and I don't eat and I drink like a fish.' However, she told Sartre how she would fill in the extra time: 'On Saturday I'm going to Chicago by plane for three days for a change. The man I liked there has been begging me for two months to come back and I think it will be all right.' By the end of this letter she had recovered enough to tell Sartre that she was 'rolling in money', had bought herself a 'magnificent white coat', would he please tell Bost that she was looking forward to seeing him again and she thought about him 'more than he deserved': he had not been a good correspondent.

Beauvoir must have felt hurt that Dolores had kept her away from Sartre, and that he had not given priority to his Castor. Curiosity about Algren supplied her with a motive for some harmless emotional revenge, and later, as she remembered her feelings at the time – or at least some of them – she made an old-fashioned remark. She had had enough of tourism and now 'I wanted to walk about on the arm of a man who would be, temporarily, mine'. She had admitted to one or two casually contingent lovers in New York but seemed to sense that Algren would be something more, and he was. They reached 'the intoxication of deep understanding', became lovers and flew back to New York together. She decided that she was 'the only person' who understood Algren, who had already been divorced from two wives. She thought that he was a 'good person', he had a social conscience which he had expressed in his life and in his books so far. He also supplied the missing ingredient in her relationship with Sartre: enjoyable, emotional sexuality. Although she knew this with Bost there had always been the complication of Olga's presence in the background. Algren was on his own. She tried to make various things clear to him: he was of course free to have 'contingent' loves if he wished; she could do the same. She loved him deeply but she loved Paris more – she would have to go back because all her life and work were there. Algren said he understood.

On May 18th, wearing a beautiful silver ring which he had given her, she left the country in tears and began to write to him the same day, using the same language that she and Sartre had used for so long in their letters: she saw herself back in Chicago, with Algren, as his 'loving wife'. Was there to be another 'trio', a variant on the original one, consisting now of Beauvoir, Sartre and Algren and complicated by the expanse of the Atlantic ocean?

While flying back over the Atlantic Beauvoir made some mental and emotional adjustment as she thought about her new 'husband' and her original one. No doubt that word, in English as in French, was only used in letters, and in France at least it was irrelevant otherwise. If, in Paris, Beauvoir was tired, depressed and confused she had only herself to blame. She had wanted total experience in her relationship with men and in 1947–48 she needed two of them at least in order to achieve it: the cerebral, theoretical Sartre and the emotional, physical Algren, whose intelligence and experience had always kept him in touch with reality. Having committed herself to two men she now had to manage them, and if neither was easy Algren was at least thousands of miles away. Sartre needed Beauvoir's help with his attempts to cope with *Les Temps modernes* and work out a political stance for himself, but much more so with the dilemma of his personal life, for which, like her, he had only himself to blame. In New York, in 1946 he had been virtually imprisoned in Dolores' apartment in order to prevent gossip, and though he wanted her badly enough he had told Beauvoir that she loved him so much it frightened him. He was still frightened, and when Dolores did not hurry back to New York he began to feel henpecked. He could only run away, so that is what he did, accompanied by Beauvoir.

The two of them moved out to the west of the city, some eighteen miles away to a village near Port-Royal, called Saint-Rémy-les-Chevreuse, where they were not physically pursued by Dolores and could both work. Sartre would go into Paris some evenings in order to see her, but she spoilt her chances of emotional success by pestering him with telephone calls. The frustrated woman could not understand the unfathomable depths of the Sartre–Beauvoir relationship, and the partners' younger friends, the 'children' in this 'chosen' family, obviously did not enlighten her. They did not want the cosy situation changed, for what would happen to them? In the end Dolores went back to New York, temporarily defeated, while Beauvoir began to organize three things: her account of the American trip, her holiday with Sartre, which was to be in Scandinavia, and, most important of all, her return to Chicago.

While travelling in Denmark, Sweden and Lapland with Sartre, she worried: what was going to happen in these complex relationships? What would happen in Chicago? She was there for a fortnight in the early autumn, and all was well, although once more she had to explain that Paris was her intellectual home and she would have to return. Once more too Algren at least appeared to accept the situation. When not making love they discussed American literature and Beauvoir's books, the one she was writing and the one she planned to write, the 'very serious book about women'.

Women, she well knew, fascinated Sartre just as much as ideas and theories, but though he could deal with these latter, he could not manage his so-called love-affairs and he hoped his partner would do that for him. She was used to a triangle situation in her personal life, and she later made a serious attempt to explain how she and that 'village Don Juan' saw such situations. Was it possible, she asked herself, to achieve any reconciliation between 'fidelity and freedom'? If a couple allowed each other 'passing sexual liaisons', that was not true freedom, and she explained that she and Sartre were 'more ambitious; it has been our wish to experience "contingent loves"; but there is one question we have deliberately avoided: How would the third person feel about our arrangement?' Olga, Wanda, Louise Védrine, Bost: they, especially Védrine, may have had unhappy times, but there had been no tragedy. 'It often happened,' Beauvoir went on, 'that the third person accommodated himself [in English it might be safer to add 'or herself', or use a plural construction] to it without difficulty; our union left plenty of room for loving friendships and rapidly passing affairs. But if the protagonists wanted more, then conflicts would break out.' Fortunately no one could break up the home, for there was no home.

In Chicago, in the autumn of 1947, she agreed to make a third visit to the U.S. the following year. She and Algren would go to Guatemala and Mexico together; they would spend an epistolary winter planning the trip.

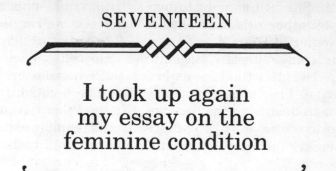

SEVENTEEN

I took up again
my essay on the
feminine condition

By 1948 Beauvoir was hard at work on *Le Deuxième Sexe* (as yet untitled). Five extracts from *L'Amérique au jour le jour* had appeared in *Les Temps modernes*, she accompanied Sartre to Berlin for the première of *Les Mouches* and spent a holiday with him at Ramatuelle in the south. She had worked so fast on *Le Deuxième Sexe* that part of it was published in *Les Temps modernes* in May, the month when she left France on the much-longed-for two-month travelling holiday with Algren.

She had obviously discovered true and satisfying sexuality for the first time in her life, and now that she was forty she was determined to make the best of it. She began to worry about birth control, although she had been told when young that she was unlikely to conceive. Even if this was true, she was nevertheless not going to take any chances. The problem was solved for her in New York where Stépha Gerassi arranged for her to consult a French-speaking woman physician. Then she left for Chicago and with Algren proceeded via Cincinnati and New Orleans to the Yucatan peninsula of Mexico.

If Beauvoir wrote about herself most of her life she wrote about herself and Algren in three phases – in her letters to Sartre, in her memoirs and in her novel *Les Mandarins*. She was also prepared to talk about him, when questioned, until the end of her existence. Her letters to Sartre are the most lively record, because she wrote about events and moods almost as they occurred; she needed – still

– to tell him everything and there was no reason for her to obscure the truth. She had listened to him when he talked about Olga, Wanda and other girls and he had read her letters about Bost. Her travels with Algren in May, June and July 1948 through Mexico and Guatemala literally thrilled her, especially since Mexico proved to be better than she expected; there was plenty of urban picturesque. The tourists saw everything they could, from the ruined sacred cities to the frescoes of Diego Ribera. Algren was also keen to see a Danny Kaye film; Kaye, she explained to Sartre, was a 'remarkable American comic' but he acted in 'rather stupid films'.

Beauvoir was impressed by Mexico City but she encountered an unexpected problem. She could not easily cash travellers' cheques in her own name because the hotels knew her as Mrs Algren. She found a solution: 'We're registered under the name of Mr and Mrs de Beauvoir, which means that you [Sartre] can write to me under the name of Mrs de Beauvoir.' She was invited to become Mrs Algren but predictably refused. Although she addressed Algren in her letters as 'my little husband' it did not occur to her to alter her situation in real life.

She had asked the Gerassis in New York to arrange her return to France in mid-July and although impelled to leave she was obviously torn between the two men in her life, needing them for different reasons. 'I'm beginning to want to see you again very much, *vous autre ma vie*,' she told Sartre, 'but at the same time I'm full of anguish when I think of the coming separation.' Her next sentence brings out clearly the difference between the two men and her response to them: 'When I leave you I don't leave you, but with Algren everything is presence.' She needed the cerebral Sartre and the physical, emotional Algren: but how to have both?

On her return to France Beauvoir found that if she belonged to Paris she no longer felt that she belonged to Saint-Germain-des-Prés. The word 'existentialism' was now identified with a crowd of young people who cared in no way about philosophy or thought of any kind. Wearing their black trousers and pullovers, unaware that the Italian fascists had adopted this 'uniform', they were merely in search of a new kind of bohemianism. They found it when Le Tabou opened, a basement *boîte* run by the publicity-minded Anne-Marie Cazalis, who had recently won a poetry prize, and her close friend Juliette Gréco, destined to become a successful singer with a highly individual style. Sartre wrote songs for her and she became particularly fond of Beauvoir, remembering her with affection and admiration forty years later. Gréco found her beautiful, she had 'disturbing' beauty, a Madonna-like face, and she was particularly impressed by the way Beauvoir had left the bourgeoisie for a life that was outside class from all points of view.

As the gap widened between the thinkers and the long-haired night-club dancers, the right-wing press, seeking an opportunity to attack any aspect, however remote, of what they saw as an outbreak of left-wing subversion, looked round for a scapegoat, and it was easy enough to choose Sartre. The production of his play *Huis clos* in 1944 had been regarded as the true beginning of the Saint-Germain vogue, and as soon as that vogue became 'picturesque' Sartre and his friends were seen as responsible for the excessive aspects of the new local colour. A former philosophy teacher who promoted black American novelists such as Richard Wright, who loved jazz, was a novelty on the Paris scene. He was too successful; he and his friends, including Beauvoir, had to be destroyed. They were soon endowed with the worst qualities of their worst hangers-on, the descendants of the unwashed teenage *zazous* of the Occupation years. For the sensation-minded press, French and foreign, existentialism became 'excrementalism'. The impression was given that the two 'leaders' of this time-wasting group virtually lived in the noisy smoke-laden Tabou, whereas Beauvoir herself said that they only ever went there twice. However, she still spent enough time in the *quartier* to attract attention. Scraps of old film show a smiling Beauvoir walking, or rather striding, along in purposeful fashion, her well-rouged lips parted in a splendid smile. In the destructive press campaign against the 'existentialists' she was accused of swearing with such a disgusting vocabulary that lorry-drivers were shocked. So much for the price of fame, and though literary fame meant a good deal to Beauvoir she refused to be the victim of journalistic voyeurs; she no longer enjoyed living in public. Beauvoir was in any case preoccupied with two interrelated aspects of her own life, the deeply emotional relationship with Algren, and her current book, *Le Deuxième Sexe*. Most of the material for the book lay in her own life so far. The general idea had been in her mind ever since she had discussed it with Colette Audry in Rouen much earlier. As a child she had lived in a predominantly feminine world – one sister, a much-loved maid in the Beauvoir household, segregated education, mostly with women teachers, and her deep friendship with Zaza. Her father retreated from the family and was unfaithful to his wife. By the time she was a student she was already a 'person', she enjoyed equality with her fellow men students and was hardly aware of her femininity until René Maheu was attracted to that very quality.

The war had made her much more conscious of problems peculiar to women, and though she still did not see much of life outside the lycée classrooms, the cafés and the hotel bedrooms, she met no girl or woman without problems they would have to solve on their own. She herself had been a soldier's 'wife', she had even been, briefly, that despised, old-fashioned creature, a housewife. She had 'mothered' Olga and Nathalie in her own resolutely non-maternal way, she had also loved Nathalie and Védrine physically and allowed them to rely on her. After her father's death in 1941 she had seen her widowed mother lead a different, constructive, undomestic, unsubjugated life, studying, working in a library, travelling, seeking out old friends and finding new ones.

Although Beauvoir related all these situations to herself she had never considered them in the abstract. The autobiographical background to her book might have become merely narcissistic if it had not been backed by the person who influenced everything she wrote, namely Sartre, who happened to be a person fascinated by women. He pointed out to her that she had been brought up specifically as a girl. Sartre, who was deeply concerned already with the problems of persecuted minorities – Jews, blacks, homosexuals – may not have noticed that women, whom he loved so much, were not a minority, they made up half the population. It may not have occurred to him either that they were oppressed, for he only met those who were 'free'. Michelle Vian, for instance, his friend Boris's wife, felt 'free' to love him. He was not too pleased when Wanda decided to flirt with Camus, and he complained to Beauvoir: 'Am I not much better?' He seemed to be asking for reassurance, as though *he* were oppressed. And perhaps he looked forward to learning more about women than he already knew. In a recorded conversation many years after the publication of *Le Deuxième Sexe* Sartre agreed that he had 'accepted' the book, but Beauvoir reminded him that it did not change him in any way. Since he was then in his mid-forties, and more particularly because he was Sartre, that was hardly surprising.

Those who have not read *Le Deuxième Sexe* are inclined to think that it covers some practical topics such as women's suffrage, but Beauvoir was little concerned with such practical problems. They could be left in the hands of old campaigners such as Louise Weiss, whom Beauvoir considered bourgeois and not very intelligent. On July 15th, 1945, Louise Weiss had written a long and impassioned letter to *Les Nouvelles Epîtres* urging women to vote in the national elections as they had already done, for the first time, locally. She concluded her letter with a glance at feminist history: 'With your voting paper you must carry on the tradition of Joan of Arc, Madame de Rambouillet, the splendid Frondeuses, Jacqueline Pascal and Théroigne de Méricourt who . . . during the Convention period, would call out beneath the galleries of the Palais-Royal: "We have the right to mount the scaffold. Let us be given the right to vote." ' All this may sound simplistic at the end of the twentieth century, but it proves the social backwardness of France in 1945. Although she set out its history Beauvoir was not interested in women's suffrage. The process of voting implied the acceptance of the existing social order, which was, to her way of thinking, conventional, bourgeois and man-made.

The book therefore is extra-political. Intellectual and literary as it is, the roots of the book are emotional, despite Beauvoir's perpetual efforts to present facts in an objective manner. There is an energetic anger, directed not only towards men, the jailers of women in man-made institutions, but also, as the book proceeds, at women themselves. According to the author the fighters among them have never made any valid progress because they have been fighting for the wrong things. How could women have been so short-sighted? Why blame men? These are just some of the underlying themes which make the book so radical and so radically different from nearly all the campaigning efforts that had preceded it, especially during the last hundred years. Beauvoir was concerned with the great myth of femininity, all that had caused and perpetuated it, all that it implied. The myth must be first analysed, then destroyed, making way for a replacement that would be realistic yet imaginative.

Beauvoir seems to be using an unspoken slogan, an adaptation of Rousseau's dramatic words at the beginning of *Du Contrat social*: 'Woman is born free and everywhere she is in chains.' All her life so far the author had been writing a succession of books about one woman, herself. She set out now to write about Woman, all women, but she had not changed her method as much as she had thought. Fortunately, she could not prevent herself from writing a personal study, for if she had tried to produce an impersonal work, how dull it might have been. She had originally had no intention of attempting such a far-reaching book, but she found herself overwhelmed by the whole subject, she became fascinated intellectually and of course emotionally, for the thesis she was working through was one which had already influenced her entire life so far.

She made a determined effort to present her case in a scientific way. Book I was to deal with *Facts and Myths*, the facts subdivided into 'Destiny' and 'History'. The opening 'Data of Biology' (Chapter 1) would probably dissuade many women and men from reading further, for man reacts to woman with 'uneasy hostility'. 'A vast, round ovum engulfs and castrates the agile spermatozoon; the monstrous and swollen termite queen rules over the enslaved male.' This whole chapter smacks of library research and the translator, who was a biologist, adds several explanatory and corrective footnotes. The chapter ends, as many others do, with the assertion that the material under examination does not explain the vital question: 'Why is woman the *Other*?' After some forthright analyses of Freud's principal theories, and some references to Adler, Chapter 2, 'The Psychoanalytic View', makes the author's personal attitude clear: 'I shall place woman in a world of values and give her behaviour a dimension of liberty.' By the last paragraph of the chapter the 'I' has become plural. 'We shall study woman in an existentialist perspective with due regard to her total situation.' It took Beauvoir a few more pages to understand that through the existentialist perspective 'the biological and economic condition of the primitive horde must have led to male supremacy'.

There are five chapters in Part II and the last, 'Since the French Revolution, The Job and the Vote', is the most intriguing, for it has an international dimension and indicates many problems that have not been solved by the end of the twentieth century: as more and more women enter public life, what happens to family life? How far has feminism been 'an instrument in the hands of politicians'? Great queens were 'neither male nor female – they were sovereigns' and Beauvoir believed that 'the women who have accomplished works comparable to those of men are those exalted by the power of social institutions'. Beauvoir has convincing answers to most of these questions and presents endless controversial assertions without wasting a moment on attempts at objectivity or even complete factual evidence. The emotional evidence is enough: 'The proportion of queens who had great reigns is infinitely above that of great kings.' Within religion Catherine of Siena and St Theresa of Avila were 'sainted souls; the life they led, secular and mystic, their acts and their writings rose to heights that few men have ever reached'. One might timidly ask 'What about Saint John of the Cross?' but indeed that would be timid and a waste of time. Reading *Le Deuxième Sexe* is like falling in love: you respond emotionally, you accept, you do not carp. Any grey hairs, any wrinkles, any squint only become obvious later.

Part III, *Myths*, is important, for Beauvoir is concerned throughout the book with demystification, the destruction of all those myths handed down through the generations, the myths that make up that feminine image so popular still, so indestructible in the world of advertising. Indeed, without the myths and the image that world would probably collapse. It had taken Beauvoir longer than most people to see and face reality; now she insisted that everyone, women and men, should face all of it all the time. She now lived, thought and wrote with the zeal of a convert, and after her slow start she raced ahead into the front rank of imaginative thinkers. She was not a scientific thinker, she was too impatient, and she could never be objective about her own would-be objectivity.

In the first part of this section, 'Dreams, Fears, Idols', Beauvoir uses much impressive rhetoric to prove that woman, with her 'double and deceptive visage', is 'all that man desires and all that

361

he does not attain'. She is associated with magic but once she has been integrated into the family and in society, her magic is dissipated rather than transformed: 'Since the rise of chivalric love it is a commonplace that marriage kills love.' As for the unfortunate mother and her symbolism within Christianity, for instance, she appears to personify disgust behind all the respect she is supposed to earn. There is also a paragraph about the mother-in-law, a 'secondary myth', which allows men to express all the hate they really feel about the birth and inevitable ageing of their wives, for they, the men, will age and die too. The stepmother is obviously an image of hate too. Marriage is really no use to either man or woman, for both, not merely woman, are enslaved.

If it can be assumed that most readers of *Le Deuxième Sexe* are women, this is a particularly depressing chapter, as it aims to destroy anything of value that they may have thought they were contributing to men or to the world; but they must learn reality. Beauvoir is more specifically entertaining, if still destructive, when she moves on to illustrate her theory through the work of five writers. She obviously enjoyed herself in various ways, combining her skills as literary critic and her new-found experience as sociologist. The choice of Henri de Montherlant[1] allows her the maximum energy of attack for there is no aspect of womanhood that he does not detest, with the exception of female athletes, for 'by the independent exercising of the body they can win a spirit, a soul' (Montherlant had studied Nietzsche). Beauvoir was particularly up to date in the choice of this author for his play, *Le Maître de Santiago*, had been produced in 1947 and his four-volume series of novels, *Les Jeunes Filles*, which came out just before the war, was currently being translated, bringing him international fame. Many women hated him. Montherlant, who was bitter and humourless, may have attacked women, but he earned no praise from Beauvoir for he does nothing to deflate the 'eternal feminine myth', he merely turns women into monsters. But in this essentially personal book Beauvoir's attack is so fierce that the reader can even feel not *Pitié pour les femmes*,

[1] Henri de Montherlant (1896–1972): novelist and dramatist. His early works

as the second volume of his tetralogy was entitled, but almost *pitié pour Montherlant*. For once the reader can equate Beauvoir with a feminine image – Hippolyta, Queen of the Amazons.

As for 'D. H. Lawrence or Phallic Pride', any non-British analysis of this author is fascinating, even if Beauvoir's conclusion is unsurprising: 'woman is not evil, she is even good – but subordinated'. In 'Claudel and the Handmaid of the Lord' Beauvoir shows how the dramatic poet apparently exalts woman but in reality 'does no more than express poetically the Catholic tradition in a slightly modernized form', and woman is left with 'the lot which the bourgeoisie has always assigned to her', she must devote herself to 'children, husband, home, estate, Country, Church'.

Beauvoir had been enthusiastic about surrealism when she was young, but in analysing 'Breton or Poetry' she does not rate the surrealist leader very highly as far as his attitude to women is concerned. He is not too far from Claudel, for woman is still 'Other', despite the glory with which he endows her; she is 'the key to the beyond. Truth, Beauty, Poetry – she is All: once more all under the form of the Other. All except herself.' André Breton sees her in relation to man, indispensable, but never existing in her own right.

Of Beauvoir's five male authors Stendhal predictably comes off best; he almost wins her approval, for he sees women with some degree of realism, although they have to help his heroes fulfil their destiny. All heroines as described by these authors, in different ways, have to do that, and of course this role is of no help to women at all. Perhaps, if she had had time, Beauvoir might have sought out a few women novelists and described what they had done with Woman. She was to quote several in the course of the book, but as she denied femininity as such, presumably a contribution by women novelists would have been meaningless in this context.

Woman, then, hardly escapes from myth into reality in this selected fiction. There is a paradoxical conclusion: women are seen as 'truly romantic' when men regard them as 'fellow creatures', as in the unromantic eighteenth century and the twentieth.

exalt manly sports and show fascist tendencies. His works include *Les Célibataires*, *Les Jeunes Filles* and *Le Maître de Santiago*.

Beauvoir cites *Les Liaisons dangereuses*, *Le Rouge et le noir* and *A Farewell to Arms*. She obviously saw herself as a 'fellow creature' to Sartre and others, no doubt 'without mystery' too, like the heroines of these novels. Like Sartre she believed in 'transparency', which is close presumably to demythification. But is everyone capable of 'transparency', and if they achieve it, do they enjoy it and does it help them? Beauvoir insists that heroines without mystery, women without mystery, would not be 'less engaging'. The destruction of myth does not mean the destruction of sexual attraction, 'It is not to do away with poetry, love, adventure, happiness, dreaming. It is simply to ask that behaviour, sentiment, passion be founded upon truth.' If Beauvoir considered her request to be simple, many of her readers would still find it demanding even after half a century of thinking about it.

By the start of Book II, *Woman's Life Today*, Beauvoir assumes that she has proved her point, opening with the most quoted sentence she ever wrote: 'One is not born, but rather becomes, a woman.' She goes on to say that 'No biological, psychological, or economic fate determines the figure that the human female presents in society; it is civilization as a whole that produces this creature, intermediate between male and eunuch, which is described as feminine.' She then examines 'The Formative Years' of this unhappy product. The little girl does not enjoy life very much, she envies her brother, not only because he has a penis but for all his other advantages. Then she has the shock-horror experience of menstruation. By the end of this chapter the little girl is no longer little but the world is a grim place. She had already felt inferior and deprived, but 'the lack of a penis has now become defilement and transgression'. If she does not accept her femininity she cannot grow up. 'So she goes onward towards the future, wounded, shameful, culpable.' It seems remarkable that she goes on living at all.

This immediate future, described in the chapter 'The Young Girl', obviously preoccupies the author deeply. She cites case-histories from technical writers but most of all she quotes various novelists who had influenced her personally when she was young: Louisa M. Alcott, George Eliot, Rosamond Lehmann, and of course Margaret Kennedy, whose *Constant Nymph* Beauvoir seems to have admired more than one might have expected. She also quotes with great relevance from the journal of Marie Bashkirtseff,[1] one of the most revealing documents ever written by a young girl. Beauvoir dwells on the young girl's tendency to day-dreaming and the way in which she can lose herself in the delights of the countryside; in this context she quotes Colette, whom she did not much appreciate as writer or woman, and also Mary Webb, who was surprisingly popular in France for a time. She may have remembered her own youthful happiness at Meyrignac, but unfortunately Beauvoir sees these reveries in the countryside as yet another flight from reality.

Next come thirty or so pages about 'Sexual Initiation'. Beauvoir considers that this crucially important event is 'relatively simple' for a man and that 'women's eroticism' is much more complex, which is surely true. She incorporates within it not a manual of sexual practice but a kind of descant in psychological terms above the description of all that is involved in the physiological aspects of the sexual act. No sentence she wrote could ever be denounced as obscene, but could her earnest attempt to describe the normal heterosexual act make irreverent readers think it highly comic? 'Feminine sex desire is the soft throbbing of a mollusc. Whereas man is impetuous, woman is only impatient; her expectation can become ardent without ceasing to be passive.' Whereas man is compared to 'the eagle and the hawk', 'woman lies in wait like the carnivorous plant, the bog, in which insects and children are swallowed up. She is absorption, suction, humus . . . a passive influx, insinuating and viscous: thus, at least, she vaguely feels herself to be.'

Does she? The irreverent reader will surely laugh. Beauvoir was writing this a few years after World War II, when the Kinsey Report, which she quotes, had at least brought serious discussion of sexual problems out of the psychiatrist's consulting room. Not many women had attempted to write even for the intelligent general public about this crucial area of life, although people have always felt more curious about sex than about anything else. Beauvoir writes convincingly about the problems of women's

[1] Marie Bashkirtseff (1860–84): a Russian-born diarist and painter whose *Journal* of adolescence, written in French and published posthumously, attained great popularity.

masochism and frigidity, quoting Stekel's classic study, and also literary sources. Women can escape these unhappy states, she believes, and the solution can be found not in the 'refinements of technique but rather, on the foundation of the moment's erotic charm, a mutual generosity of body and soul'. Does she mean, simply, love? Beauvoir seems to believe that women, despite all their difficulties, in fact because of them, lead a fuller and more dramatic sex-life than men. The 'deceptive privileges' earned by man's aggressive role and by 'the lonely satisfaction of the orgasm' make him hesitate 'to see himself fully as flesh. Woman lives her love in more genuine fashion.'

Unfortunately however, she does not want to desert the sensuous feminine world for the 'hard and rough' male universe. Heterosexual activity is not enough: 'Her hands still long for contact with soft, smooth flesh: the adolescent boy, a woman, flowers, fur, the child, a whole region within her remains unoccupied and longs to possess a treasure like that which she gives the male.' Do women really want so much? Surely these continued desires must be due to a capacity for love which is greater than that possessed by men? Beauvoir has seemingly denied the existence of 'femininity', which has always traditionally been regarded as possessing precisely this virtue. She understands very well where this capacity will lead. 'This explains the fact that in many women there subsists a tendency towards homosexuality more or less marked.' Colette had often touched on the subject and Beauvoir herself had experienced it. Taking the tendency one stage further, Beauvoir writes next about 'The Lesbian'.

This Chapter 4, which closes the section *The Formative Years*, contains many insights and the demolition of many long-standing received ideas. Beauvoir regards the division of lesbians into 'masculine' and 'feminine' types as 'rather arbitrary', for the true lesbian does not want to copy any male attitudes, she wants to make the most of femininity, to enjoy it to the full. There is a differentiation here between heterosexual and lesbian love which may seem controversial. 'Between man and woman love is an act; each torn from self becomes other . . .' but 'Between women love is contemplative; caresses are intended less to gain possession of the other than gradually to re-create the self through her; separateness is abolished, there is no struggle, no victory, no defeat.' Not every lesbian or bisexual woman would agree. Colette, however, whom Beauvoir quotes repeatedly throughout *Le Deuxième Sexe*, emphasized in *Ces plaisirs* ... that a woman lover enjoys caressing a body 'whose secrets are known to her, and whose preferences her own body indicates to her'. When Beauvoir wrote her book few serious studies about lesbianism were available, although there was plenty of pornographic material. She herself knew intense love for women, although she had denied any lesbianism in her relationship with Zaza, for example; while living through heterosexual relationships she had known and loved women – although she denied eroticism – and many of them had loved her. She had read carefully the few women writers who had attempted to interpret the subject, from Colette to Radclyffe Hall and Renée Vivien, the poet. She had observed the behaviour of such women as Madame de Staël and George Sand, who thought they loved men, but dominated and mothered them.

This is one of the most provocative chapters in the book, and has dated only in minor ways, even if a great amount of serious material has since been published. Beauvoir concludes that homosexual love is 'no more a perversion deliberately indulged in than it is a curse of fate. It is an attitude *chosen in a certain situation* – that is, at once motivated and freely adopted.' It is one of the ways in which women try to solve their 'feminine condition' and their erotic situation. It can go wrong, like any other type of behaviour, and lead to unhappiness, or it can lead to 'lucidity, generosity and freedom'.

In Part V of her book Beauvoir places women in varying 'situations', beginning with the married woman and the mother. The fact that she had no experience of either state should not mean that she might not write discerningly about them, but in fact, she fails to do so. She hardly admits that many wives and mothers enjoy a good part of their existence, even if they grumble. Who does not? A later generation of femininists would relish her description of the housewife's day, French in some ways, but universal in others, for cooking is said to be creative whereas housework is not, as everyone knows. In 1949 married women could still avoid housework-hysteria, for they had servants, who, strangely enough, are more manageable than machines. However, Beauvoir's horror of marriage, which she believes to exclude

367

love, may have become contagious enough over the years and prevented unhappiness among women by keeping them single. As for motherhood, she was infinitely more interested in contraception and abortion than in the production and rearing of children. There is a negative quality about these chapters, an indication that there were limits to Beauvoir's understanding of women, mainly because she was not in touch with ordinary people, and within her own circle there were no 'ordinary', ménages of any kind. She asserts that 'marriage does not generally involve physical love', making her sound old-fashioned as though thinking of middle-class arranged marriages. At its best, she says, marriage can only work when the partners reach a compromise.

Beauvoir is obviously more perceptive when she writes about women on the fringe of society; she discusses prostitutes with understanding and, despite her own atheism, writes compellingly about mystics, especially St Theresa of Avila. Without her early fervent Christianity, and her fear of *tiédeur*, she could probably not have been able to contemplate this passage.

There is no *tiédeur*, no half-heartedness anywhere in *Le Deuxième Sexe*. In 1992 it can sound old-fashioned, especially perhaps in Parts VI and VII, *Justifications* and *Towards Liberation*, for obviously, after forty years, a chapter on 'The Independent Woman' must have dated. However, the problems have not gone away, and probably never will. Beauvoir decided not to pronounce on what will happen to women when they find emancipation through reaching the same situation as men, but she knew the future would be exciting.

After so much destruction of myths she becomes lyrical during the last few pages. 'Feminine charm', she says, is likely to be relegated to the 'attics of time', men will not want women to succeed in this sacrifice of the old mythical 'femininity', some aspects of 'sexual adventure' will vanish in the world of tomorrow, but 'love, happiness, poetry, dream,' will not be banished.

She closes with the theory she held for a long time. With the end of hypocrisy the slavery of half the human race will end too, and at last 'the human couple will finds its true form'. She quotes Marx, noting his use of italics: 'The direct, natural, necessary relation of human creatures is *the relation of man to woman* . . . the relation of man to woman is the most natural relation of human being to human being.' Beauvoir believed he was right. 'It is for man,' she concludes, 'to establish the reign of liberty in the midst of the world of the given. To gain the supreme victory, it is necessary . . . that by and through their natural differentiation men and women unequivocally affirm their brotherhood.' In 1949 this expressed the supreme reality which Beauvoir had now worked out for herself. Sartre after all, had become a kind of brother-figure by now.

The book has been compared to the Bible by later critics, described as the book everyone – at least every woman – owns but never reads. The novelist Raymond Radiguet believed that the Bible 'is more concerned with the future than with the past', and in this context *Le Deuxième Sexe* was and still is, just such a book. At least half its readers will hate half of it, but like atheists, they will continue to discuss with passion the religion it offers.

Later in life Beauvoir was to criticize some aspects of the work; it was too long, there were repetitions. There was no organized bibliography, and to take a mere two years for such a work was surely not long enough. Academic critics have spent much time pointing out the contradictions, obscurities and begged questions, without ever destroying the legend that Beauvoir had liberated women. She herself said that she would always fight for the book.

While writing the book Beauvoir herself experienced endless surprises. Once she had decided to research the whole subject thoroughly her naiveté equalled her intelligence and per-severance; she admitted that she had suddenly discovered, at the age of forty, an aspect of the world that was obvious but unseen. Neither had she realized that her book would shock. Had she forgotten that France was a Catholic country, that the middle class was regaining ground lost during the war, that the government of France was far from radical? The first volume of the book was published in June of 1949 and three extracts had already appeared in *Les Temps modernes*. The chapter on 'Sexual Initiation' was chosen for the May issue, followed in succeeding months by those on the lesbian and the mother. Beauvoir seemed surprised at the speed with which the magazine sold and when Volume I of the book itself appeared 20,000 copies were sold in one week. She was accused of being 'unsatisfied, frigid, priapic, nymphomaniac, lesbian'. She had had endless abortions, she was a 'clandestine mother'. She said that she understood these sex maniacs very well – it was more entertaining for these members of the 'first sex' to write about her like this than to add their graffiti on lavatory walls. The magazine *Paris-Match* was delighted to defend the scandalous book in its usual controversial style.

Since she had written a personal book Beauvoir could surely expect a personal response, and she got it. Albert Camus revealed himself as Mediterranean and macho, while François Mauriac took the most hurtful attitude of all, writing to a member of *Les Temps modernes* staff: 'I now know everything about your boss's vagina.' The reaction from men in France proved that Beauvoir had treated the 'first sex' far too well; perhaps they were feeling nervous, aware that they were in danger of losing their supremacy. They forgot that Beauvoir had not spared women in this analysis, pointing out how far many of them had invited and even enjoyed their abject status, and if they sometimes thought they wanted more independence, in practice they avoided it.

Beauvoir herself could not avoid notoriety. She was stared at and pointed out in cafés. The Catholic church naturally placed the book on the Index. If the two volumes had appeared in any other country the reaction might have been less violent, but France was the country of austere heroines such as Joan of Arc, beautiful and intelligent women who had influenced kings, great entertainers at all levels from Sarah Bernhardt to Mistinguett, occasional women of action, like Charlotte Corday, Frenchwomen who made elegant clothes for themselves and some, like Gabrielle Chanel, who designed them for the whole world; there had been heroines of the Resistance, and there were endless loving wives and mothers. However, France was socially backward and the efforts made by women to improve their situation had been timid. They had concentrated on the fringes of the problem, whereas Beauvoir attacked it at the centre. She was writing ahead of her time, and although radical she was never hysterical, and claimed that her 'objectivity' irritated people. She was *not* objective, there were some things she forgot to say and she found it necessary to add them to her memoirs later. 'Have I ever said I did not enjoy being a woman?' she wrote. As in Sartre's novels, there is not much sign of 'the Joy of Sex'. It could exist, but women had not yet learned how to find it: they would not find it until they had found themselves. While writing the book Beauvoir was celebrating the fact that she herself had found it. The whole rapid emotional movement behind the book was probably the result of that unexpected meeting with Nelson Algren in 1947.

The production of *The Second Sex* was a drama in itself and is not yet over. Britain and the U.S. had to wait four years for a translation, carried out in the U.S., edited and abridged, and later questioned in various ways. When Blanche Knopf brought the book back to New York from Paris in 1949 she seems to have understood only the noun in the French title and no doubt hoped for a good seller on this evidence alone. The firm of Alfred Knopf, seeking expert advice, chose Howard M. Parshley, a Harvard doctor of science and chairman of the zoology department at Smith College, Northampton, Massachusetts. He was well known for his sound popularization of scientific theory and had written in 1933 *The Science of Human Reproduction*. He seemed well qualified for the task and it is to his credit that he commended the book highly and undertook the translation. He found himself working harder than he had expected for he had to correct and explain many of the author's amateur notions about biology. He corresponded with her but she replied slowly to his queries and was not interested in meeting him during her visits to the U.S. in 1950 and 1951: those trips were dedicated to Algren. Parshley had assumed from the somewhat vague correspondence with the author that he was empowered to carry out minor adaptations. The work took him two years and during that time the unfortunate translator had to stop temporarily during 1950 due to a heart attack. He recovered sufficiently to carry on, enhance the book with some additional chapter headings and an invaluable index, which the two-volume French edition did not possess. The author had never contemplated adding a bibliography, which was a serious omission.

The Knopf organization did not want to lose their profits through expensive translation costs of a very long, highly-priced book. Parshley therefore was ordered to make cuts, which he found difficult. He resisted the temptation to 'water down' or annotate Beauvoir's remarks about the family and 'conjugal love', which he could not support and, not wishing to break up the closely reasoned arguments, he decided he would sacrifice history. Who, he thought, could possibly be interested in those unknown names of early women writers whom nobody would ever read? He excised many of them. How could the elderly professor have foreseen the rise of feminism in the 1960s and the inclusion of women's studies in the academic syllabus at many centres? He couldn't. In his preface to the translated work he described it as 'slightly abridged' but did not indicate where the abridgements had been made. He earned enough money from his labours to buy a secondhand Buick, and died in 1953, a year after publication and far too soon to parry the attacks of Dr Margaret Simons of Southern Illinois University. In 1983 she disputed his rendering of various philosophical terms and so deplored the deletions – ten per cent of the original, she claimed – that she hoped for a new and complete translation. The author, who had originally found the translation 'excellent' and never examined it, was now distressed, but after all the main thrust of the book was not affected and it had been a worldwide success, even if many foreign translations were in fact based on Parshley's work.

When the translated version of the book appeared in Britain the reaction of the serious press was on the whole good, the work was regarded as 'objective', there was 'pleasantly little of the earnestness that makes sociological books often so spiritually indigestible' (*The New Statesman*). Beauvoir was referred to as a 'twentieth century Mary Wollstonecraft' (*Time and Tide*), and *The Manchester Guardian* thought that the book avoided 'hysterical propaganda' and might well 'become a classic'. The reviewer also praised the author's 'analytic detachment'. *The Times Literary Supplement* pointed out that the author was a novelist 'and the value of her work owes a great deal to the penetrating power of her imagination'. The poet and novelist Stevie Smith, writing in *The Spectator*, responded in an emotional way to this emotional book. She found that Beauvoir did not really like women 'and it is soon clear that she does not like being a woman'. Smith was a few years older than Beauvoir and this reaction was shared by many women of her generation, not because they were old-fashioned, but because they enjoyed their 'condition', dealt with any problems in their own individual way and could not see Woman as an abstraction.

Beauvoir was pleased with the American reception of the book and believed that the critics were fairer than the 'bitchy' French. However, some of them, unaware perhaps of social conditions in France, found certain aspects of the book difficult to accept: *Time Magazine* (February 23rd, 1953) thought that 'even the inmate of a harem' would find *The Second Sex* out of date. The book was regarded as so important by others that the *Saturday Review of Literature* (February 21st, 1953) appointed a panel of sex specialists in the relevant field to consider it. The anthropologist Margaret Mead gained the impression, taken up by many other critics later, that only masculine values seemed to count, and that the book was very French. She found that 'theoretically the book violates every canon of science and disinterested scholarship in its partisan selectivity, but as a piece of writing it provides a rare, exasperating, but unfailingly interesting experience'. However, Mead found that society had indeed 'wasted women's individual gifts', therefore accepting much of Beauvoir's theory. Phyllis McGinley, that witty satirist whose profession was given in the *Review* as 'housewife', was made aware of her 'enslavement', which she had never noticed before, and found much lack of logic. Other reviewers saw the book as a 'call to action', but McGinley, regretting that the author knew so little about American women, wished she had had a *plan*. No doubt she was thinking of some practical primer which would tell the 'enslaved' women what to do, a step-by-step approach to changing their world and the world in general. This was the last thing that Beauvoir had been aiming to do when she wrote the book. Each individual woman must work her life out for herself, as she had done.

EIGHTEEN

I had to talk
about us

Beauvoir was making notes for a fourth novel and life was very full in other ways. The readers of *Le Deuxième Sexe* had no idea that the author herself was moving through the most romantic love-affair of her life with a man who lived thousands of miles away in Chicago. In June 1949, the month when the first volume of *Le Deuxième Sexe* was published, Nelson Algren came to Paris. He stayed with Beauvoir in the small apartment in the rue de la Bûcherie where she had moved the previous year, at last feeling the need for a home, after spending most of her life in hotel rooms. Algren, who knew nothing of France beyond a brief stay there as a G.I., must have seemed somewhat out of context. Conversation with Sartre was difficult because Beauvoir was too impatient to act as a conscientious interpreter, but superficially at least they got on well. Algren was fascinated by Olga and Michelle Vian and later he corresponded with both of them.

Beauvoir and her friends showed him the sights of Paris from the museums and art galleries to the dog cemetery at Clichy and the Saint-Germain-des-Prés clubs. She later took him to Italy, Tunis, Algiers and Morocco, and they 'had never got on better together'. Although they looked forward to meeting in Chicago in 1950 Beauvoir had some misgivings: how long could this intense emotional relationship continue? Inevitably it had become epistolary, kept alive by the sentimental correspondence which had been flying across the Atlantic ever since 1947. Algren kept

Beauvoir's letters and after his death they were acquired, along with his library, by the Ohio State University Library. They are now being edited by Beauvoir's adopted daughter Sylvie Le Bon de Beauvoir for publication in France. The letters are repetitive tear-jerkers but express Beauvoir's mood at the time. The woman who wrote them seemed as far away as possible from the author of *The Second Sex* who had tried to be scientific and objective about women: no wonder she had failed. Beauvoir was as emotional and prone to tears all her life as any heroine of romantic fiction, and when she wrote to Algren she might have been eighteen, not forty-two. In these letters she calls Algren her husband, she remembers his kisses, she longs to be in his arms.

She left Paris with Sartre in the early summer of 1950 for a trip through Black Africa, visiting Gao, Tamanrasset, crossing the Sahara and returning through Algeria and Morocco. It was not a good trip for Sartre, who had two bouts of fever and was disappointed that the group known as the 'Révolution Démocratique Africaine' failed to contact him. The French government, pursuing its usual repressive colonial policy, had done its best to exterminate them, but they obviously did not see Sartre as their saviour, and the French Communist party had not encouraged any rapprochement. Beauvoir's health stood up well to the trip and she later wrote a good account of it. After spending an evening in one hotel bar drinking with a group of men, she seemed surprised that the hotel owner came to her room during the night and propositioned her. From Meknès in Morocco she wrote to her old friend Simone Jolivet and told her in detail about the lepers in Bamako (Gao), adding some local colour about the 'fetichists' who were accused of killing their parents with poisoned thorns and then eating them.

In July Beauvoir left Paris to travel via New York for a two-month stay with Algren. His novel of 1949, *The Man with the Golden Arm*, about drug addiction had won him the National Book Award in 1950, allowing him to buy a house at Gary, situated at the southern end of Lake Michigan. The couple had to wait in Chicago until early August when the house, called Miller, would be free, and Beauvoir quickly realized that the emotional atmosphere in Algren's Wabansia Street apartment was no longer that of 1949, as she had in fact suspected and feared: 'I didn't need twenty-four hours to learn,' she wrote to Sartre, 'that things had changed – just as I had predicted already that night when I kept you up so late.' When she asked Algren to explain why he was no longer the passionate lover, he did so. 'In fact it's what I had felt through his letters and the rhythm of our story: he's very pleased to see me, but with the resigned impression that I arrive just in order to leave again, that we'll never have anything more than these arrivals and departures, and that's given him a detachment that amounts practically to indifference . . . I think these are the last months we'll ever spend together. Moreover he says that he's incapable of loving a woman ever again.'

Although she was 'rather upset', she was not too surprised: 'I knew that this episode was due to end, and soon; it has died from within, because Algren had realized that it was already dead, petrified.' She was resigned, not uncheerful, she hoped that after all the 'explanations' she would be able to spend 'three very good months'. There was one important consolation: 'Don't worry about me,' she told Sartre, 'because I know that in three months we shall be together again, and that you are my life.' The emotional Beauvoir had accepted Algren as the complement to Sartre but it was clear that the American had no chance of survival in the long term: 'I can't be sorry that this affair is dead,' Beauvoir continued to Sartre, 'because its death was implied in the life that I've chosen and that you give me.'

Conveniently, Sartre, in France, was in the process of liquidating Dolores, who had been a distinct danger for she was very possessive and he did not know what to do with her. However, he replied to Beauvoir quickly with two letters, which she said gave her great support. She then became, if late in the day, full of common sense: 'I think it's really stupid that we have both embroiled ourselves in a whole lot of problems when we were so happy together.' She presumably forgot that various dimensions were missing from that happiness, for Sartre needed several women close to him at the same time while she had obviously needed physical sex in addition to professed emotional warmth and intellectual companionship. 'The good thing is that we shall both be free again within three months since dependence on each other means dependence on nobody.' In writing that she came close to describing the indescribable nature of the Beauvoir–Sartre relationship. Secretly she wondered if she ought to be jealous and asked Algren for more explanations of his changed attitude. There was no other woman in his life but he had recently met his ex-wife, Amanda Kontowicz, again in Hollywood. She worked in the film industry. When she had suggested that they should live together again, 'he refused and got out of it by giving her a car.' Then he had had a brief affair with a Japanese girl, telling her to have no expectations and now he was (understandably) through with women. 'I felt very relieved,' wrote Beauvoir, 'I say that for your information, to learn that he had not fallen in love with another woman, that the change had happened within our relationship and not from the outside.' They passed a 'tender' night together, then she had a high temperature, due to the emotional upset and her mixing of stimulants and whisky, then they tried sleeping together again and it was a disaster. She intended to 'get on top of' the episode, to 'liquidate' it and she seemed to have no regrets. 'I'm glad this has happened the way it has. With a little luck it will end pleasantly.' She assured Sartre they would have a good life in future and a happy old age.

Sartre was still more important than anyone. He represented all she truly cared about. 'If I could press a switch, I'd go back to France.' She would have liked to be with Sartre at Madame Morel's villa at Juan-le-Pins, where he had now gone. She hated the political atmosphere in the U.S., she hated the Korean war, she had been afraid all summer of a third world war. However, Nathalie was coming to Gary in September and she wanted to work hard at her novel. Her life in Gary was 'absurd', she thought: 'I have the impression that I'm held here by old desires while the novelty and the romanticism of my life are with you, *mon petit compagnon de vingt ans.*'

What a lot she had to learn, and what a pity she had left her own sentimental education until so late in life. Her emotional naiveté was nothing short of endearing. She was learning with surprise that passion can die a sudden death; she could not quite understand how it had happened. She and Algren could no longer sleep together. They had tried, but 'he was impotent and I was frigid. In one sense,' she told Sartre, 'this helps to end a story in which sexuality was very important. For we had parted [i.e. the previous year] in a highly feverish state and as soon as I arrived in Chicago everything was dead from this point of view. Perhaps you understand, you who are *du côté masculin.*' Perhaps he did, in his fashion. She became depressed, for one day she nearly drowned in the lake. She was not a good swimmer and took a long time to recover her confidence. The collapse of her passionate love- affair had upset her deeply.

Nathalie Sorokine Moffat's arrival at Miller upset her too, for the girl was now tired of her husband and involved in group sex with two homosexual friends. She also told endless dirty stories. Beauvoir thought she had not matured. Algren and his friends found her very lesbian, but Beauvoir denied this, despite the girl's extravagant displays of affection toward her. Nathalie had had a 'ridiculous and failed experience with a professional lesbian, that's all'. Did Beauvoir remember that it was she who had given Nathalie some early initiation into the mysteries of sex? She found her young friend had remained 'infantile' from this point of view. Algren did not care for her. The whole situation was so uncomfortable that Beauvoir asked Sartre to send her, by air mail, some more stimulants and some earplugs. She also hoped he would have a pleasant time with Michelle Vian. In the meantime she visited Chicago again and came down to earth: 'Places from my past [i.e. from 1947 and 1948], where earthly existence had remained very vague and mysterious, took on an everyday air in the streets of the town; Chicago became real and lost its enchanted air.' It was a sad end to the euphoria of the last two years and all those tender letters full of kisses and the imprint of her lips on the writing paper. She longed to be back in Paris: 'This conjugal life that I lead here is particularly absurd because it implies eternity . . .' She wished she and Algren could have been travelling, as they had done the previous year: 'A journey would not have had this absurd side to it.'

The stay at Gary came to an end and Beauvoir returned to Paris at the end of September 1950. Sadness over what was obviously the end of her love-affair alternated with a concentration on work. She finished her first draft of the novel that was to be *Les Mandarins* and felt she could now show it to Sartre. During the summer and early autumn of 1950 she lived through part of that novel, an emotional story as it developed, with a large-scale sub-plot which she wove into the book, changing it in fact very little. Sartre explained to Beauvoir all that he saw as unsatisfactory in her book and she realized how much work she still had to do. The writing of this novel would be as long-drawn-out as that of *L'Invitée*. When Algren invited her to Gary in the autumn of 1951 she again had to ask Sartre's advice: should she go? Characteristically he replied 'Why not?' She knew by now that Algren was indeed about to re-marry his ex-wife but as she had previously said about the end of the trio with Sartre and Olga, 'friendship triumphed', though only for a time, because Algren was not interested in friendship with a woman, especially a woman whom he had once loved.

While in the U.S. Beauvoir worked on her essay about the Marquis de Sade. She had become interested in him a little earlier when she had been asked to write a preface to his *Justine* and a reading of all his work made her aware of his attempts to deal with the problem of the Other. He was an extremist, as she herself had always claimed to be, and his writing may well have reminded her of her earlier interest, shared with Sartre, in 'monsters'. Her essay, published in *Les Temps modernes* (December 1951 and January 1952) is stimulating, and as 'disturbing' as she had found Sade to be. If it has been criticized as disorganized and full of unsourced quotations there is at least one explanation: she wrote a good deal of it while in the U.S., presumably without complete reference material and while working her way through the potential difficulties of 'friendship' with Algren.

In fact life at Miller in the autumn of 1951 was 'excellent', she told Sartre. Algren was in a good temper and she had a room of her own where she could work, and indeed she worked six hours a day. She admitted she was distracted by the 'scourge' of television, which fascinated her, although it was 'nearly always bad'. Algren's book *Chicago: City on the Make* had appeared and she found it very good. 'On the other hand he has vaguely begun a novel which exactly repeats the others, less well,' and she told him that she thought 'he really should renew himself'. To be fair, he was not satisied with the book himself, but in the end *A Walk on the Wild Side* was published with success in 1956 and Hemingway said of it, 'This is a man writing.' Beauvoir re-read her own novel and found it 'terribly stale'. Probably she could not easily carry out the necessary revision work until she was more detached from Algren and back in France, the principal scene of the book.

Her few published letters of 1951 to Sartre are low-key; possibly she felt her emotional states would not interest him greatly. She was to revive her memories later, both in her novel and her memoirs, knowing that her experiences would interest all the devotees, mainly women, whom she had drawn to herself ever since the publication of *The Second Sex*. When she had first met Algren in 1947 she had wanted a man who would be 'temporarily' her own. Four years later Algren had decided he wanted 'a woman and a house' of his own, but he wanted them permanently. He wanted the woman in his life to be with him, naturally enough, and not with another man thousands of miles away. Beauvoir, after crying for at least a day and a night, knew it was all over.

But life was not over, although she prolonged the elegies and the misery, convinced that she would never again sleep close to 'the warmth of a body'. If Algren had earlier bought off his ex-wife temporarily with the gift of a car Beauvoir could now afford to console herself in the same way: back in France she bought a Simca Aronde and drove round the north of France and into Belgium. Algren re-married his ex-wife in 1953, they were divorced again in 1955.

Most of the Beauvoir–Algren story was included in her 1954 novel *Les Mandarins* as an enlarged sub-plot, and more detail appeared in her letters to Sartre and in her memoirs, where she quoted some of Algren's letters to her. Since the story was so important to her she wanted her later readers to understand how and why she had acquired a lover and then parted from him. The novel, however, had a much wider scope than her own personal history and eventually told its interlocked stories in some 700 pages. The author, having spent four years on the book – 1949–1953, twice as long as she had spent on *Le Deuxième Sexe* – said that she hated the *roman à clé*, but her first novel had been close to one, her second contained many of her own experiences, while the third, more original in many ways, had been a failure. She had now spent these emotional years struggling with a vast novel into which she intended to put 'everything of myself: my relationships with life, death, time, literature, love, friendship, travel; I wanted also to depict other people and most of all to tell that feverish and disappointing story: the post-war years'. Surely few mid-twentieth century authors could have had more ambitious ideas and amazingly this one more or less succeeded. It could be said that she had tried to include 'everything of herself' in most of what she had written so far and she genuinely believed in the universality of her own experience. The value of *Les Mandarins* is that it conveyed a wider experience, that of a small, but potentially influential group of people at a crucial moment of history.

The 'key' to the book remains herself but for the first and last time in her fiction she constructed round that self a complex story in which several characters are at least half-recognizable and the rest are spokesmen, symbols, without losing their human reality. Anne Dubreuilh, whom she admitted to be very much herself, is an analyst married to a writer, Robert Dubreuilh. Beauvoir made him into a Sartre-like figure by describing him as a wonderful teacher twenty years older than herself, all of which destined him to great respect. In their teenage daughter, Nadine, she recreated the daughter-figure she had had in Nathalie Sorokine, saying that she wanted to take her revenge for the girl's aggressive behaviour in the past. Henri Perron, editor of the left-wing newspaper *L'Espoir*, is in some ways slightly reminiscent of Camus as editor of *Combat*. One obvious follow-up to *Le Deuxième Sexe* is the character of Paule, who, on Beauvoir's admission, gave her a good deal of trouble. Paule is the all-for-love masochistic woman who has given up everything for Henri, and, when he no longer loves her, she is driven into mental illness and has to be rescued by Anne.

Why should a novel about a group of intellectuals, writers and journalists in Paris just after World War II have any relevance for the general reader fifty years later? For one crucial reason at least: the book reflected a chapter of history, for if the shooting war was over new wars of ideas were breaking out in France and in other countries. Could the intellectuals somehow find a compromise between Communism and capitalism? They wanted to commit themselves to creative, progressive liberalism, even genuine socialism, but how? In her novel Beauvoir concentrates on a quarrel between Dubreuilh and Henri: should the paper *L'Espoir* publish the horrifying news about the labour camps in the

U.S.S.R.? If the paper does so it will be seen as destroying all hope for a socialist future. If it does not, then it is guilty of suppressing the truth. These problems, highly topical in the immediate post-war years, are still relevant at the end of the twentieth century, when the map of Europe is being redrawn and western-style democracies have still not come to terms with totalitarian states such as China. At the same time socialism is passing through a radical transformation and its future is unclear.

Beauvoir's attitude to politics before and even during the war had been negative, and when she at last saw that politics mattered she had merely thought what Sartre thought. Now she had developed sufficient skill as a novelist to conduct argument through her characters without seeming didactic and she had broken up the discussion of ideology with a reasonably well integrated sub-plot, the emotional adventures of Anne. Later readers know that Anne's romance with 'Lewis Brogan' is her own romance, and if some find it is given a 'Library of Love' treatment this is because Beauvoir felt that way at the time. She used conventional vocabulary for instance to describe the lovers' reunion after long separation: 'I closed my eyes. A man's body was once more weighing on me, heavy with all its confidence and all its desire . . . No, he hadn't changed, nor had I, nor had our love . . .' Beauvoir maintained, as she had done with *L'Invitée*, that she had changed and adapted the real-life story, but it was still very close to what had really happened. Beauvoir obviously needed a Brogan figure in her life, and if Algren had not appeared she would no doubt have found someone else. The book was dedicated to him, but when he read the English translation in 1957 he was not pleased. He had cared enough for Beauvoir to want at least some private memories but he was not allowed to have them; he had to accept 'transparency', and he did not like it. Algren believed in most of the sexual myths which had always profited the 'first sex', and he was hardly the partner whom the post-*Second-Sex* woman could regard as a true 'brother'. Though he did not write a novel about his experiences with Beauvoir, later he was to say exactly what he thought about the woman who had called him her 'little husband'.

The Paris scene was changing fast. In 1951 Cocteau had written in his journal: '*Les existentialistes*. Never did one see a term move so far away from what it expresses. Doing nothing and drinking in little cellars is to be existentialist.' In fact the vogue was virtually over, apart from the hangers-on, the tourist and export trades and, as Cocteau added, 'Sartre is completely unresponsible for this phenomenon. . . . He hates idleness.' Nobody was ever less idle than Sartre; since the end of the war he had published novels and literary criticism, had plays produced, liquidated Dolores, discovered Jean Genet, worked constantly on *Les Temps modernes* and begun his endless and unsatisfactory involvement with politics. Where he wrote and worked, Beauvoir usually followed and inevitably met a new range of people. They included a young politically-minded journalist named Claude Lanzmann who had joined *Les Temps modernes*.

One day Lanzmann invited Beauvoir to come to the cinema with him and she responded like any young girl receiving a man's advances for the first time: she burst into tears. Soon they were lovers. His appearance in her life was exciting: he was seventeen years younger than she was, highly intelligent, committed to the left wing and deeply aware of his Jewish condition, he was irreverent, he was potentially creative and totally free. He moved into the small apartment in the rue de la Bûcherie where there was just room for two people to live and work.

In Beauvoir Lanzmann found what Algren had found in 1947, a deeply emotional woman. In 1978, more than twenty years after their first encounter, the two of them came together to discuss their relationship in the documentary film of Beauvoir's life made by Josée Dayan and Malka Ribowska. Lanzmann said that when he first saw her, he had admired her beauty. 'I found you very beautiful, your face was smooth, I wanted to see what lay behind that kind of impassivity.' At first, he added, this is what had intrigued him. Beauvoir then reminded him of what he had discovered, that she was much less 'impassive' than he had previously thought. He had been struck by the paradox of her nature: her energetic enthusiasm for life that contrasted so violently with her irrational fear of death and the deep feelings that led her so often to tears. Lanzmann's cheerful presence, his realistic approach to social and political problems, helped to dispel Beauvoir's anxieties. She began to enjoy life as much as she had done before the unhappiness of the break with Algren and under his influence she became more seriously interested in politics. She never lost touch with Sartre, who was moving closer to the Communist line and was writing more on political themes. Beauvoir was not always happy about this trend. She wanted to follow him but could not always bring herself to do so. However, as Lanzmann's influence grew stronger she began to think more about political and social issues, and she decided that 'literature was no longer sacred' to her.

However, she still cared enough about her own writing to feel nervous about the reception of *Les Mandarins*, due for publication in October 1954. Sartre had perpetually criticized it, and without encouragement from Lanzmann and Bost she might never have finished it. Would it be a failure? While waiting for its appearance she wrote a novella about a subject which had always haunted her, the death of Zaza, but when Sartre said it was no good she abandoned it. This was her last attempt to present the story as fiction, but by no means the end of it.

When *Les Mandarins* won the Prix Goncourt Beauvoir was pleased to know that she would at last reach a wider public. As the rain was coming through her roof she was also pleased to earn some money, and the following year she was able to buy the studio apartment in the rue Schoelcher, adjoining the Montparnasse Cemetery, where she lived for the rest of her life. At least 40,000 copies of the novel were sold in one month but for Beauvoir success with the public still meant *readers*, people who would respond to the book and write letters to her; she was not much interested in public appearances or personal contact. In 1950 for instance she had been invited to give a talk on the status of women at a club which had had been opened by a self-educated newsagent. She recorded the fact that it was the first time in her life that she had encountered *un public populaire*, a working-class public. For someone so conscious of her break with the bourgeoisie the admission is revealing, especially as Beauvoir was forty-two at the time. She was obviously still writing for the intellectuals, who, as she knew, had an essentially bourgeois education behind them.

She refused most of the journalistic publicity offered to her in 1954 but agreed to give one single interview: she wanted *L'Humanité-Dimanche* (the Communist newspaper) to know that she was not anti-Communist. The journalist, J.-F. Rolland, an old friend, found, like many later interviewers, that it was hard work keeping up with Beauvoir's rapid replies, but he liked her; she was 'frank, direct, sincere'. The ex-philosophy teacher was no austere, bespectacled bluestocking. 'Philosophy has in no way detracted from her graceful regular features and her smile.'

She expressed her disgust with right-wing journalistic methods and her appreciation of the way in which left-wing critics, including the Communist Claude Roy, had understood her book, for left-wing intellectuals, she believed, should work alongside the Communists, despite all that separated them. When the interviewer mentioned that her heroine Anne seemed apolitical, Beauvoir replied that Anne, like herself, was not qualified for active political work, but that 'her life and thought were dominated by the principles that dictated [the] actions' of her politically committed friends. To be apolitical was to be reactionary, Beauvoir added, proving how far she had travelled since the 1930s, when she hardly even read a newspaper.

She defended her presentation of the Communist character Lachaume, who was disinterested and dedicated, and added that she had kept to her own experience, while the subject of Communism would have needed another whole book. She explained also why Anne, in a moment of crisis, chose life, not suicide. Her heroine had been tempted to believe that the inevitability of death removed the meaning from existence, but when she realizes the importance to her husband and Henri of life and action, and the link this forms between them, she recovers her own interest in life. The 1954 interview ended with Beauvoir's statement that she would write no more novels for the time being. When the interviewer reminded her that many 'mandarins', but not hers, believed in the current policies of the newly elected Prime Minister, Pierre Mendès-France, she condemned the attitude of the government towards North Africa and German rearmament, along with their hypocritical economic policy.

True to her word, there was no new novel until 1966, but in the twelve intervening years Beauvoir, whose fame had now spread all over the world, never stopped writing, and also travelling, her main preoccupation being the support of any oppressed individuals and groups, combined with a detestation of the Gaullist régime.

Lanzmann's young presence brought Beauvoir a great deal of happiness, and liberation. She particularly appreciated in his spontaneous approach to life a contrast to Sartre's attitude. If 'Poulou' in some ways never grew up, there was nothing obviously 'young' about his thought or his writing. Beauvoir compared her two recent lovers: Lanzmann belonged to another generation, she said, just as Algren had belonged to another continent, and she believed that with each man this 'foreign' quality 'kept a balance within our relationship'. Through Lanzmann she also came to understand *la realité juive*, something which made her more conscious in future of any racial discrimination she encountered. She had become aware of this problem during the war, but only to a limited extent. On the personal level Lanzmann helped Beauvoir with one of her near-insuperable problems, the fear of death. He was still young enough to have no regrets for the past, so many things in life were new for him that 'he threw an unexpected light on all of them for me. Thanks to him,' she remembered later, 'a thousand things were restored to me: joys, astonishments, anxieties, laughter and the freshness of the world.' The break-up with Algren, her worries about the onset of old age (she was not yet forty-five), all became unimportant: 'I leapt back into happiness. The war was receding. I immured myself in the gaiety of my private life.' She wondered if her relationship with Sartre would survive her new love-affair, but all was well, 'thanks to Lanzmann, Sartre and my own vigilance'.

Beauvoir and Lanzmann were lovers for about seven years and he remained a friend. In the 1978 documentary film made by Josée Dayan and Malka Ribowska there is a discussion between her and Sartre which contains no new themes, followed by a moving scene between Beauvoir and Lanzmann, moving because in a relaxed, unemotional way they talk of all passion spent, thinking not merely of their own relationship, but Beauvoir's feeling that her writing life was over, even though her new-found idleness was busy and 'committed' in its way and contained no indifference. Thanks to Lanzmann's past help in calming her fear of death she could now face the situation before her – the inevitable loss of her close friends. During this discussion Lanzmann, in the film, looks at her with concentrated under-standing and admiration but, sadly, she does not look at him. At least they address each other as *tu*, a contrast to the lifetime *vouvoiement* with Sartre.

Fiction was banished from Beauvoir's writing life for more than a decade, but this decade was nonetheless busy. She wrote on literary and philosophical subjects, which were important to her because she spoke now from her position as a 'mandarin'. In April 1955 Maurice Merleau-Ponty, her old friend from days at the Sorbonne, had published his important book, *Les Aventures de la dialectique*, of which an entire third examined the beliefs of Sartre, especially as set out in the series of articles for *Les Temps modernes* entitled 'Les Communistes et la paix'. Merleau-Ponty found plenty to criticize in Sartre's theory of Marxism and revolution, supporting his views with serious analysis and argument which in fact seemed to undermine the centre of Sartre's thinking. Sartre himself took no counter-action but Beauvoir flew to his defence in the May–June issue. Whether Sartre read her piece in advance is not clear. Entitling her article 'Merleau-Ponty ou le pseudo-sartrisme' she maintained that Merleau-Ponty had misconstrued what Sartre had said; it was the kind of article which has earned her hostility in the academic world, for she seemed to have forgotten one important thing. In 1945, when reviewing *La Phénoménologie de la perception* she had found it 'convincing' and believed that the author held more or less the same views as Sartre on various important points. However, in 1955, in her defence of Sartre, Beauvoir wrote that 'Merleau-Ponty has never understood Sartre'. In fact the article is fierce (Sartre's word was 'sharp'), reads well, but unfortunately shows, on Beauvoir's part, either a lack of logic or a change in her own attitude to Merleau-Ponty's earlier book. If she intended to be 'la grande Sartreuse' on a serious level it would have been better to have remained impartial or explained her change of heart. The interpretation she gave of Merleau-Ponty's attitude to Sartre revealed what mattered most to her: her conviction that Sartre could not possibly be wrong.

In the autumn of that year Beauvoir and Sartre were invited by the government of the People's Republic of China to visit the country, and she even found time to write a book of 480 pages about the trip, *La Longue Marche* (*The Long March*), published in 1957. Although it soon went out of date and became history it is well worth a glance for, despite her insistence that she never accepted the Communist line, she did not find much wrong with China. Her chapter on the family is particularly interesting, for she links its new development to socialism in general and a new status for women. Sh takes up once again the compelling, if over-simplified style of *Le Deuxième Sexe*:

> The social factor possesses an economic dimension; but productivity depends on the human factor; the march towards socialism implies the emancipation of the individual, the affirmation of his right to dispose of his own fate. Marriage and maternity have become free. Love is regarded as a 'progressist' value. . . . The path towards collectivisation is also that which endows women with human dignity and young people with liberty.

Although the Chinese were not yet limited to one child per family Beauvoir was impressed by the importance given to birth control in their social programme and by the fact that abortion, when found necessary, was not illegal. She ended her book by saying that in China the revolution had a special 'colour' of its own and did not seem dominated by Marxist prejudice. Thirty years later, when a documentary film was based on *Le Deuxième Sexe*, the scenes showing Chinese women at work were some of the more memorable. The viewer could feel that Beauvoir was impressed by the progress these women had made since the time of *The Good Earth* (by Pearl Buck)[1] and felt that the rest of the world should be impressed also. She said too that she had never seen women who were as well balanced as the women doctors at work whom she met in China. Their country needed them as professional workers, and the establishment of the minimal family unit, she implied, was a rational solution for China and for the individual. Memories of the 1955 visit stayed with her a long time.

Her increased political awareness was now focused on the situation in Algeria which upset her so deeply that whole sections of the relevant memoirs, *La Force des choses* (*Force of Circumstance*) (1963) become one long moan. The foreigner tends to

[1] Pearl S. Buck (1892–1973): American author brought up in China, where her

forget that the Algerian war, although undeclared, went on for nearly eight years and France could not be proud of it. The reality is brought home occasionally when a headstone in a French village cemetery commemorates the death of a young soldier killed in the Guerre d'Algérie. Although Beauvoir always denied that she was a woman of action she took part in street demonstrations against the policies of de Gaulle and worked, as did so many intellectuals, in the hope of defeating a 'Yes' vote for the General in the 1958 referendum.[1] But the majority of French people supported him and Beauvoir reacted to the news of his victory in her usual way: she burst into tears. She was horrified to find herself so opposed to her own country's policies but remained emotional, making no attempt to consider events objectively.

By the end of 1958 she might well have decided that she was truly getting old at fifty for Sartre was ill, due to overwork and reliance on stimulants. Sadly, she and Lanzmann were drifting apart, and though she knew their separation was inevitable, even a good thing for both of them, she still found it hard. Perhaps she was somewhat consoled to learn that it was hard for him too. She was convinced that they would continue as friends, and that is what happened.

When the first volume of her memoirs appeared that same year, 1958, she did not realize how far her readership would suddenly increase, especially among women. She was surprised in some ways by her success and characteristically she saw it as a kind of failure, for she thought that many readers had merely identified with the 'good' little girl growing up in the bourgeois family, and had failed to grasp her real ambition in writing about her early life. She had intended a severe exposé and criticism of bourgeois life, but if this is obvious to her later readers, who have read all her work and considered her life in perspective, it was not obvious at the time. The new readers were interested, as Lanzmann had been, in what went on behind that smooth face, the face that had

parents were missionaries. Of her many novels about China the best-known, *The Good Earth* (1931), won the Pulitzer Prize.
[1] The 'Yes' vote: The referendum of September 1958 was to consider a proposed new constitution which transferred effective legislative power from the elected Assembly to the President. The new constitution was accepted by a majority of about eighty per cent of the voters.

been so much photographed in the early days of Saint-Germain. Sartre had approved of her plan to write the book and before the end of the following year she had finished the second volume, convinced that readers of this new one would understand her true purpose in writing it and be 'on her side'.

Despite the time and emotional energy she devoted to political problems she was now writing more articles and prefaces dealing with the problems encountered by women or stirred up in some way by their behaviour. Her long, specially commissioned article for *Esquire* in August 1959 about Brigitte Bardot was a case in point. Superficially it is impossible to imagine two more deeply contrasted women, but Beauvoir found some unexpectedly relevant things to say. After the romanticism of the war years eroticism had returned to the cinema but there had to be a new image of woman. This woman had to be very young, practically a nymphet à la Nabokov; the reason why so many women quickly became jealous of Bardot was evident to Beauvoir. Bardot was, or seemed, completely 'natural', any old-fashioned vamp image was absent; this new and desirable girl seemed to despise men. Her behaviour implied sexual equality, which did not help her reputation in France. Beauvoir realized she would change, but hoped she would not be led astray by an urge to become popular. This article was not published in France until 1972, when Bardot had moved into a different sphere. Strangely, she became as devoted to the case of the oppressed as was Beauvoir herself, only, in Bardot's case, the oppressed were not people, not women, but animals, a race of no particular interest to Beauvoir.

During the same year, 1959, Beauvoir was asked by the film director André Cayatte, best known perhaps for *Nous sommes tous des assassins*, to write a script for a film about divorce. She received so much correspondence on the subject from unhappy women that she was tempted to go ahead, but did not feel she had the freedom she wanted. She could not place her people in a realistic social context because she would not be able to mention the Algerian war, for instance. The war so coloured her view of the world that she could not imagine life without it. Cayatte had wanted two independent stories, one showing the woman's side of the problem, one the man's. Beauvoir did not favour this polarity, she saw the life of a married couple as a 'single two-sided story', all her episodes were 'ambiguous', the links between them were 'multiple and vague'. Cayatte found her approach 'confused' and the project was dropped.

A few months later Beauvoir made a more important contribution to social life by prefacing a book on family planning by Dr Marie-Andrée Lagroua Weill-Hallé, who had struggled against the law and medical obscurantism for a long time. The pioneering books of Dr Marie Stopes, which began to appear in Britain before 1920, had soon been translated into many languages, including French, but who had read them? Beauvoir was to write and talk much more on the subject within the next few years.

When in 1949 she had embarked on *Les Mandarins* Beauvoir had said that she wanted to write about 'us', her group of intellectual friends and colleagues. That group was becoming smaller much too soon. Boris Vian had died in 1959, aged only thirty-nine, overwhelmed it appears by a bad film adaptation of one of his novels, and his death was regarded as the symbolic end to the Saint-Germain-des-Prés era. Camus was killed in a car crash in 1960, and though he had already parted company intellectually from many of his former friends, he was still in mid-career. Beauvoir and Sartre, the surviving 'mandarins', now well known internationally through their books and through the ever-controversial *Les Temps modernes*, became ambassadors, not for official French culture or foreign policy, which were usually anathema to them, but for the ideas they themselves had pioneered, 'alternative' ideas. When they were invited in 1960 to Castro's Cuba Beauvoir reacted with all the enthusiasm she had felt in China. The travelling partners spent three days with Castro himself and Beauvoir felt happier than she had felt for years. She was ready to give interviews about Cuba and wrote at least one article about her trip.

Beauvoir's fifty-third year, 1960, was a hectic one. She had hardly expected Nelson Algren to appear in Paris again, but appear he did, and stayed in the rue Schoelcher. The two of them established a kind of modus vivendi, relationships were edgy but bearable. Beauvoir agreed to make a visit to Spain with him but in Paris she always gave priority to any articles, interviews and journeys which involved Sartre, such as a trip to Yugoslavia at the invitation of the writers' union. At the same time she completed the second volume of her memoirs, *La Force de l'âge* (*The Prime of Life*), which described her life from the early days with Sartre in 1929, through the teaching years of the 1930s and World War II, the Occupation and then the Liberation in 1944. Dedicated to Sartre, it is the best of the four-volume set of memoirs for it includes not only her own story but the background to the years so crucial in French history, the moral decline of the 1930s against the background of right-wing extremism and Sartre's 'conversion', followed by her own, to some kind of political commitment. She wrote subjectively, as always, and her reactions were typical of the Montparnasse intellectuals, the 'mandarins', the group she referred to as 'us'. She also wrote at excessive length about how she began, revised and eventually completed her first two novels, recollections of great interest to any professional novelist and to anyone intent on detailed analysis of her work. Although she also wrote about her young friends Bianca Bienenfeld ('Louise Védrine') and Nathalie Sorokine she was discreetly and understandably silent about her complex emotional life with them. This was not revealed to the public until the publication of her letters and the complete *Journal de guerre* in 1990.

Algren could not claim a great amount of her attention in 1960, even though he seems to have been hopeful, after his third divorce, that they might have returned to at least a memory of their earlier relationship. But Beauvoir was preoccupied with her long-delayed entry into public affairs, which she still approached as a writer rather than an activist. She was writing on controversial topics, and if some of them seemed to concern women first, they were also topics which involved everyone.

Dr Weill-Hallé wrote a second book, *La Grand' Peur d'Aimer*, again on the subject of birth-control, an issue which Beauvoir saw as one of the keys to the liberation of women. This time Beauvoir was prepared for a more active role in the campaign, for she attended the press conference when the book came out. She found that the hundred or so people present were old-fashioned, much more ready to talk about 'happy motherhood' than contraception, unable to face the word 'abortion', while sex itself was not mentioned. It is always a shock to Protestant readers outside France to realize that birth-control was so little understood or practised there and another shock perhaps to learn that the

Communists had opposed its spread because it would 'weaken the proletariat by depriving it of children'. The same Communists had not taken kindly to *Le Deuxième Sexe*. In an interview in March 1960 Beauvoir had already stated that women had not yet become human beings, it was even time, she thought, that *Le Deuxième Sexe* should be written again. Women had obviously only just begun to undertake their 'long march' and Beauvoir was always the first to point out one of her principal messages: women must take responsibility for themselves, their own bodies and their own lives.

She herself now took responsibility for the life of another woman: Djamila Boupacha, a twenty-two-year-old Algerian girl, the victim of terrifying torture in 1959 at the hands of the police and the military. She had been accused of planting a bomb, had confessed to it under torture and later recanted. She was not only subjected to the better-known forms of torture by various kinds of electric shock, she was tortured as a woman by soldiers who pushed a beer bottle into her vagina. Beauvoir was appalled by the cruelty of this case, which seemed to symbolize the whole horror of war and the whole cruelty of men towards women. When she wrote to *Le Monde* about it, on June 3rd, 1960, she made her most valid point: 'The Djamila Boupacha affair is the concern of every person in France.' All copies of the paper were immediately confiscated in Algeria. Within six months a Djamila Boupacha Committee had been set up with Beauvoir as its president, one of the earliest episodes in the new phase of her life. She, the theorist, who liked to describe herself as an intellectual and not a woman of action, could perhaps have said, 'One is not born, but rather becomes a woman of action.' The appalling incident, which involved the girl's father and all her family, was described in detail in the book written by the famous woman lawyer who took up the girl's case, Gisèle Halimi. Beauvoir contributed a forthright preface. The book was published in France in 1962 and caused such a stir that it appeared both in Britain and the U.S. in the same year. Two young women novelists, Françoise Mallet-Joris and Françoise Sagan, contributed to the twelve testimonies at the end of the book, while the British edition included an impressive drawing by Picasso. A few months earlier the Evian agreement between France and Algeria had led to an amnesty for

393

Moslem political prisoners – but Djamila Boupacha's torturers were given immunity at the same time.

Between the beginning and end of this case Beauvoir had been drawn into most aspects of Sartre's political life, spending two months with him in Brazil, engaged again in alternative culture, especially after they had signed the Manifesto of the 121 people who supported dissident, even violent action against official French policy towards Algeria. When this was published in *Les Temps modernes* the issue was confiscated and Sartre in particular was in physical danger during the next two years, forced to move out of his home when threatened by plastic bombs. One exploded in the hall at 42 rue Bonaparte where he and his mother shared an apartment, and the day after Beauvoir and Gisèle Halimi had attended the signing session for the book about Djamila Boupacha she was threatened too. However, no bomb exploded. This campaign and Halimi's book, with the preface by Beauvoir, had been her first active participation in politics.

She continued to participate, but in a more literary capacity, a few months after the Algerian war had ended in 1962 by going to Moscow with Sartre, invited by the Union of Soviet Writers. She had believed that there was a thaw in the political relations between France and the U.S.S.R., although this was not evident when they unexpectedly found themselves attacked as representatives of western capitalism.

Beauvoir had now adopted the habit of accompanying Sartre to Rome every year in the late summer or early autumn, but in 1963 her holiday was cut short. Her mother had had an accident and was in hospital, so Beauvoir returned to Paris; finding her mother in an apparently stable condition, and knowing that her sister was there, she left again for Prague where she and Sartre had been invited by the Writers' Union. Once again, however, she was called back. Her mother died in November and by the end of the year Beauvoir began to write her account of this illness and death, *Une mort très douce (A Very Easy Death)*. The following May parts of it appeared already in *Les Temps modernes*. Her mother's death led to some of the most personal and emotional of all Beauvoir's personal and emotional writing. With the naiveté of the intellectual she had told her sister years earlier that she did not expect to be moved by her mother's death. She had not wept when her father died, and later gave him a mere few sentences in her memoirs. Now she was not only tearful but near-hysterical.

She seems to have been naive too about doctors, nurses and clinics, for she had been so rarely ill herself. She found it necessary to set out endless physiological and medical details in her usual meticulous way, for it was her belief that everything must be described in order to be understood. Despite the emotional shock she did not lose her analytical attitude; she disapproved for instance when her mother spoke with the bourgeois voice of her class, and speculated as to why the woman who had been so devout in the past did not want to see a priest. Beauvoir at once became deeply involved with her own personal problems, especially when she wrote 'I do not know what faith is', presumably forgetting her teenage fervour and continuing to ignore that rewarding dimension to existence, the spiritual life, which need not be inseparable from organized religion. She also transferred her own feelings to her mother, believing that like herself she loved life too much to show any yearning for immortality.

Beauvoir used this memoir to describe her mother's early and often frustrated life, which had coloured her own attitude to marriage permanently. She also meditated on the relationship between herself and the woman who had projected the unhappiness of her married life into a domineering attitude towards her children. Beauvoir seemed to feel guilty, as so many daughters do, for having failed to understand her mother. If she was tempted to discuss the wider implications of this illness and death it was grief, one imagines, that stopped her, thereby keeping the book on a level of emotional unity. She did not begin to speculate as to whether doctors and relatives should tell the truth to people dying of cancer, she did not talk about mercy killing. For once in her life Beauvoir restrained her flow of words. Instead, there was a flow of tears, the book was a *cri écrit*, a written cry, to borrow Cocteau's title of 1925.

The death of a mother can only happen once, and is very often traumatic. In France people still give this book to bereaved daughters in the hope that a shared experience can mitigate their loss. In Britain, on a different level, *Une mort très douce* has figured on the list of set books for examinations in French literature taken by students at the age of seventeen to eighteen.

Since Beauvoir wrote it a good deal of research has been carried out into mother–daughter relationships, and in the field of feminist studies there has been speculation on one strange fact: Beauvoir reported in her book that in her dreams her mother had appeared to her 'blended with Sartre'. The implications which could be read into that association are endless and mysterious. Like all Beauvoir's memorable writing the book caused great controversy, which always led to the escalation of sales. It has been alleged that if Beauvoir had truly loved her mother she would not have written or published the book, while other critics have said that she wrote it out of guilt, realizing that after all she *did* love her mother, but had expressed that love too late. For Beauvoir the expression of anything that mattered to her meant the written expression. Later she explained more fully how important this was to her: she had not 'thought of writing *Une mort très douce*. At those times when my life has been hard to me, jotting down words on paper – even if no one is to read what I have written – has given me the same comfort that prayer gives to the believer.' She did not see this comfort as something to be kept to herself: 'By means of language I transcend my particular case and enter into communication with the whole of mankind.'

Twenty years of incessant writing had not destroyed the emotional base of her work, and few situations could be more emotional than this one. At the same time Beauvoir was compelled to write the book for another reason: her own fear of death that still pursued her so relentlessly. She had seen death in all its horror at her mother's bedside, like a medieval image, 'the Death of the dance of death, with its bantering grin . . . a scythe in its hand . . .' This short book brings the average reader closer to Beauvoir than any other piece she wrote. It was ostensibly about someone else, but it was immensely revealing about herself, her capacity for emotion and the way in which she unconsciously subdued the emotional side of her nature through cerebral analysis. Fortunately her self-defence could falter, or even, as here, fail. The result was a moving book.

1964 brought more travel, early thoughts about a new novel and in particular two prefaces. The first of these was her only piece of writing supposedly addressed to children, an introduction to the seventeenth-century fairy-tales of Charles Perrault for a British edition. She told the children that in far-off days oppressed peasants who worked hard in the fields liked to imagine a world where the *grands seigneurs* would fall on hard times. Gilles de Rais, who, according to legend, wickedly killed hundreds of people in the fifteenth century, was not found out until much later because these people were poor and nobody cared about them. But Gilles de Rais, in stories handed down by the fireside, became Bluebeard. There was a lesson to be learned: be like Cinderella, believe in miracles. 'You must have faith, something which appears impossible may not be so at all.' She gave the children, and indirectly their parents, some moral, almost existentialist advice: 'Hope, take action, help yourself, and then heaven will help you.' There was no God or god in that supranormal world, but some kind of heaven, some ideal realm, was allowed to exist. Only Beauvoir could have written for children like this, and she did not tell them that Perrault himself had been a *grand seigneur*. He was in fact so 'grand' that he thought it preferable to publish the stories not under his own name, but under that of his young son instead.

It was a far cry from fairy-tales to the author of *La Bâtarde*. Beauvoir had known the unhappy, hopelessly unlucky Violette Leduc since 1945 and through her Leduc became an author. She had been in love with Beauvoir ever since meeting her. As an unloved daughter she had had a grim start to life but like Beauvoir she was able to write about herself and still fascinate her readers, even if the writing was far from comfortable. After reading *L'Asphyxie* Beauvoir at once recommended it to Camus; it was published in 1946 but without success. After three more books *La Bâtarde* appeared in 1965 with a long preface by Beauvoir, and it became a classic. The book had many qualities likely to attract her: the transparency, the total freedom she and Sartre had sought, while in addition everything was either ecstasy or tragedy, and it unleashed a flood of femininity. Passages from *Thérèse et Isabelle*, so deeply lesbian that the publishers Gallimard were frightened of it, were incorporated in *La Bâtarde*, described later by the *New York Times* as 'the book that scorched France'. There was little intellectual rapport between Beauvoir and Leduc, whom she had transformed into a literary figure, but she appreciated sincerely all the best qualities about her, her 'moral candour' and her care for the oppressed: 'All forms of distress,' she wrote, 'find an echo within her.' Leduc became a symbol of the emotional liberation of the 1960s. All Leduc's books were translated into English but forty years later they had become mere curiosities in Britain. However, American feminists have always been fascinated by Leduc and her love for Beauvoir, which was firmly resisted. Leduc was unique and eccentric, her work was intense and humourless but shot through with poetry. She was fascinated by money, something mentioned by Beauvoir in her preface. Eighteen months after Beauvoir's death some of the letters she received from Leduc between 1945 and 1956 were published in *Les Temps modernes*. They were full of gratitude and admiring, hopeless, masochistic love, but despite all this, maybe out of pique, she was still capable of cheating her friend over the price of some antique chairs. Yet of all the women who approached Beauvoir with their problems, Leduc was the one who wrote those problems most deeply into literature, with Beauvoir's help.

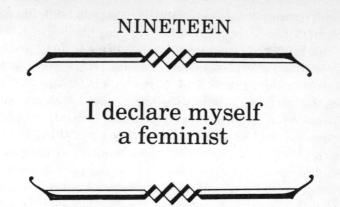

NINETEEN

I declare myself
a feminist

By her mid sixties Beauvoir had moved on from *Le Deuxième Sexe*, for she had studied social developments in France and abroad. In 1972 she made her position clear: 'When I speak of feminism I mean the fact of struggling for specifically feminine claims at the same time as carrying on the class-war: and I declare myself a feminist.' At the same time she had always denied 'the existence of a feminine nature', for she was concerned with society as a whole. She was determined not to go down to history as a 'feminist writer', for she believed this label diminished her interests and achievements. Although she had in principle agreed to the publication of her feminist writings in volume form she then decided against it and the book, although announced, never appeared. She preferred to continue with her near-political writing, which was nearly always controversial. Most progressive people begin life as revolutionaries and gradually become sedentary analysts, but in Beauvoir's case, paradoxically, the process was reversed. It had taken her thirty years or so to emerge from 'pure' literature, with an admixture of philosophy, into committed writing; a long time before she could say, as she did after meeting Claude Lanzmann, that 'literature was no longer sacred' to her. Yet writing, more journalistic now than 'literary', was her weapon of attack and defence, an edged tool she had sharpened over the years, and she never missed an opportunity to defend, through writing, the freedom of the individual. She continued to compose prefaces of increasing political importance and it was she who in 1966 introduced Jean-François Steiner's book about life in the concentration camps, *Treblinka*, supporting the author through the bitter controversy which followed, during which he was even accused of anti-semitism. However, he won the Prix de la Résistance and Beauvoir's support was vindicated.

Despite the 'rest' from fiction she had promised herself after *Les Mandarins* she had not intended it to be her last novel. Since 1954 however a great deal had happened in the world of literature, and more especially in the world of fiction. The older novel-reading public had forgotten the war, the younger readers had not known it. Sartre was not writing novels, he was preoccupied with the theatre, his political commitments and his vast book about Flaubert. Something new must surely follow the existentialist vogue and the result was the 'new novel'. Alain Robbe-Grillet had published *Les Gommes* as far back as 1953, Michel Butor, Claude Simon and Marguerite Duras followed with a long list of titles, although to label these writers as a group was dangerous, for each novelist had his or her individual style, especially Nathalie Sarraute, of Russian origin and as radical in her approach to fiction as Beauvoir had been to the problems of women in *Le Deuxième Sexe*. The new novelists received hard words from the author of *L'Invitée* and *Les Mandarins*: 'Sometimes, with the intention of saying nothing, they mask the absence of content with formal convolutions in a pastiche of Faulkner or Joyce, who both invented hitherto unheard-of ways to say something new.' Perhaps the hardest of all concerned her belief that 'one of the constant factors of this whole school of writing is boredom; it takes all the savour, all the fire out of life, its impulse towards the future.' With hindsight, it must be admitted that much of her criticism remains valid. She attacked Sarraute in particular.

Beauvoir had met Sarraute during the attempted intellectual resistance during the Occupation and had noted that she would talk only about literature, and passionately so. Beauvoir quoted Sarraute's description of how, when she sat down at her desk, 'I leave politics, current events, the world, outside the door; I become a different person.' Beauvoir then demolished this attitude, asking how anyone could fail 'to put the whole of oneself into the act that for a writer is the most important of all – writing'. She had obviously forgotten – something she was prone to do – her own earlier attitude, her apathy about politics and current affairs. Beauvoir had some personal reasons for her antipathy to Sarraute: Sartre had found her early work interesting and had written a preface to *Portrait d'un homme inconnu* in 1947, classifying it as an *anti-roman*. If Beauvoir was not jealous of pretty girls she did her best to keep creative women, especially writers, away from Sartre.

Individual titles from the 'new novel' era can still be readable, but there are not too many of them. The best of the novels by Duras, early and late, do not belong to the group at all. She has emerged as one of the most provocative writers since the end of the war, addressing herself also to the theatre and cinema, as well as to feminism. The other development of the post-war era was the appearance of young women writers. If young men like Cocteau or Raymond Radiguet[1] had been sensationally successful earlier in the century, young women had still been too busy with traditionally feminine occupations and if they wrote, as part of their *ouvrage de dames*, the results did not interest commercial publishers or literary critics. However, from 1950, which brought the remarkable *Rempart des béguines* from Françoise Mallet (as she then was), and 1954, which saw the publication of Françoise Sagan's *Bonjour Tristesse* (as well as *Les Mandarins*), young women writers formed the success story of the age; even if they did not produce 'literature', their books were short and readable, they were prolific and although not 'committed' in the technical sense, many of them were known to hold sound liberal views, far from those professed by many of the people they wrote about.

As she saw herself approaching sixty, Beauvoir had begun to write a novel about old age but abandoned it in the end as an unsuitable theme for fiction. Something of this abandoned novel may have survived into *Les Belles Images*, for it is a story of three generations, occupying, fortunately for the reader, only 200 or so pages. Published in 1966 it has always had, like most of Beauvoir's work, obsessive admirers and detractors. If no two of

[1] Raymond Radiguet (1903–23): died at the age of twenty, having written two brilliant novels of psychological analysis, the first, *Le Diable au corps* (1923), a study of adolescence forced into maturity by the events of war, and *Le Bal du Comte d'Orgel*, which was published posthumously.

her novels are alike, this one was hardly recognizable as a follow-up to *Les Mandarins*. The surface of its world is as far removed from Saint-Germain-des-Prés or Montparnasse as can be imagined. The characters are not merely bourgeois, they belong to the new, powerful, technocratic society which was taking over the world and embodied more of a sudden change in old-fashioned France than in most other countries.

Yet beneath that surface the whole of Beauvoir is evident, preoccupied as ever with moral and social issues: the hypocrisy of the advertising world, the behaviour of women, the way they are treated by men and the problems they encounter when they try to combine a professional career with bringing up children. Laurence, who is in her early thirties, works in advertising and finds it hard to explain to her elder daughter, who is not yet eleven, why there should be unhappiness and poverty in the world, especially as her own work is so little concerned with the truth. At the same time her own elegant careerist mother Dominique collapses into hysteria when her lover deserts her. Dominique owes her career to some other man and now, left alone, the world is an empty place for her; she is another version of Paule in *Les Mandarins*, she has not escaped from the traditional old-style feminine values. In fact she renews contact with her separated husband, of whom Laurence is very fond. Father and daughter go on holiday in Greece, but Laurence is more impressed by the poverty of the country – as Beauvoir had once been – than with the delights of archaeology. Laurence has to take all the strains of family life. Her husband contributes only optimistic noises to the insolvable problem of their daughter's education while Laurence herself gives up her lover and become anorexic, even suicidal. Beauvoir offers no real solution to a set of problems that on one level might figure in the lonely hearts column but have still not lost their relevance. Perhaps Laurence's basic problem is the complex relationship with her father, which naturally colours all her relationships with other men. Was Beauvoir remembering her own father in some indirect way?

Beauvoir was accused of having attempted to enter the world of Françoise Sagan, a world she detested, but even if she could avoid it personally the behaviour of this kind of society, with its new conformism, which Beauvoir attempts to emphasize, was affecting society as a whole. It was morally wrong, thought Beauvoir, and destructive, to run life as one might run an advertising agency, presenting everything through *les belles images*, pretty pictures, rather than through reality. The pressures of this kind of existence were causing stress among women and this in turn was affecting the development of children, particularly of course girls. It is a pity of course that the author did not choose to develop her characters and her themes more deeply, but she was obviously intent now on making her points through brevity. It is a pity too that her detractors did not look a little more closely for the sub-text, which is certainly there. Beauvoir was no longer interested in emphasizing the obvious 'messages' that she had formerly used in fiction. She now wanted her readers to do a little more thinking themselves, she had moved on faster than they had. However, if the messages were less direct, the novel was still very successful.

She immediately undertook her last fiction, the two stories and one monologue which make up *La Femme rompue* (*The Woman Destroyed*). Late in 1967 an *édition de luxe* with impressive etchings by Hélène de Beauvoir appeared, followed by the commercial edition early in 1968. The stories have been condemned as fit only for *Elle*, the well-known women's magazine in which they were serialized, and at the same time praised as a highly significant continuation of the novelist's work, especially by feminists. They illustrate the basic themes of *Le Deuxième Sexe*: marriage is a trap, and if women are ill-treated by their husbands, especially as they grow older, it is entirely their own fault. If, like Dominique in *Les Belles Images*, these women have not created an independent life of their own, then they are lost. Obviously these heroines are expected to earn our pity, but the stories lack depth and it has to be admitted that many more 'commercial' novelists have dealt with these problems more frequently and more impressively. In 1968 the stories had a sensational success in France, for thousands of women there, who were trying to face up to their unsatisfactory lives, had been treating the author as a marriage guidance counsellor ever since the publication of *Le Deuxième Sexe*. Letters, not meetings, had always been Beauvoir's preferred way of making contact with women readers; letters taught her how women of different types lived and tried to cope with their problems. She studied these letters and replied when she could.

The third piece in *La Femme rompue*, sandwiched between the two stories, is entitled 'Monologue', and is a tour de force, the first-person tale of a foul-mouthed, angry woman who has alienated all her family and driven her daughter to suicide. Murielle, the speaker, may be cruel and on the verge of insanity but is infinitely more interesting than the naive moaning heroines of the other two stories. 'Monologue' is unique in Beauvoir's work and shows that if she had decided when younger to write more for the theatre, she might have done so with success. Though this trio of women are not presented in as much detail as Anne in *Les Mandarins*, or Françoise in *L'Invitée*, they make a certain symbolic impact, especially Murielle. As for the men in these stories, they are no more than mere two-dimensional macho stereotypes and make one think that Beauvoir herself did not find them particularly interesting.

The season of riot and would-be revolution in Paris in 1968 has been commemorated and much pondered over twenty-five years later, even if no analyst has come to any positive conclusions about it. Beauvoir and Sartre knew about student unrest all over the world but had to admit they had not anticipated the French student revolt. Early in May Beauvoir and Sartre, who did not want to feel left out of the stirring developments at Nanterre and the Sorbonne, asked Alain Geismar, one of the student sympathisers, to explain the whole situation to them. He was summoned to Beauvoir's apartment at two a.m. and the meeting lasted some two hours. Later Geismar said that he had the feeling, despite the obvious sympathy of the older couple, that even though they listened to him carefully they did not really understand what was happening. However, they did what they could. Sartre spoke to the students and Beauvoir wrote an excellent and colourful account of the events. She joined in the street demonstrations, although obviously not in the violence. Sartre also conducted a good interview for *Le Nouvel Observateur* with Dany Cohn-Bendit, spokesman for the students, talking as little as possible, like a good journalist, and asking the right questions.

However, participation from him and Beauvoir could only be limited, for the world had moved on. Despite their years as teachers and their continued interest in all socio-political problems their attempts to teach their beliefs through intervention in current scandals now had only a symbolic significance. In 1972 Pierre Gaxotte, best known as a historian, re-wrote an early novel, borrowing a title from Voltaire, although not daring to write a pastiche. In *Le Nouvel Ingénu* a Huron Indian comes to Paris in the hope of seeing Sartre, whose fame in Dallas, Houston and Oklahoma was overtaken only by that of Brigitte Bardot and Monsieur de Gaulle. He meets, at Le Flore, *un monsieur triste*, who gives him sad news.

> Monsieur Sartre has not frequented for many years the establishments that constitute the fame of this *quartier*, which was his kingdom. And, in 1968, there were great upheavals round the Sorbonne and the Odéon. Young people from the better districts built barricades and fought the police. Monsieur Sartre was on their side, but his fame collapsed in these disturbances. He has been dethroned by a Monsieur Marcuse who was teaching somewhere in your continent. At present Monsieur Sartre, in order to avoid becoming a museum piece, is trying to cobble together seditious articles which are not much read and organize minor revolts which subside into banality.

Unkind, only partly accurate, but Sartre was used to it. It was unfair to suggest that he was becoming a 'museum piece', but though his vast and varied output and his constant interventions in political and social problems kept him in the news, his career had never proceeded in a straight line. Beauvoir's development, if slow, had shown a much more logical and unified progress. Sartre had suffered from being much talked about but less read than he had hoped. His early key book *L'Etre et le néant* did not appear in English (*Being and Nothingness*) until 1958, although of course it was known to specialists. When Mary Warnock prefaced it she wrote: 'But the time has come to consider existentialism as part of the history of philosophy, not as a means of salvation nor as a doctrine of commitment. And, as for Sartre himself, we must realize that he is no longer an existentialist at all.' However, the partners continued their examples of political commitment, limited, since they refused to work through any party machine, to

405

controversial articles and emotional appeals. They hoped to receive emotional and even active response in return.

In 1969 *Le Deuxième Sexe* was twenty years old. The authoritative Belgian writer Suzanne Lilar (mother of the novelist Françoise Mallet-Joris) chose to attack Beauvoir as someone who wished to 'neutralize' women, and there were various controversial articles in the press, but Beauvoir, in accordance with her usual policy, remained aloof. She realized how influential her book had become, for the feminist movement was now catching up with it, but she had become 'more cautious' about the condition of women; she found they still lived subjugated lives, and they had acquired little new freedom. She would have liked to write an updated *Deuxième Sexe*, but she had little time, for she gave herself entirely to social and political interests, and if she usually followed Sartre here her life still proved the type of independence she had hoped women would achieve. In 1966 for instance she had been appointed as the only woman member of the tribunal set up by Bertrand Russell to enquire whether the United States, during the Vietnam war, had been guilty of crimes against humanity. She was conscientious in her attendance at the tribunal sessions but again, aloof. Lawrence Daly, a member of the executive of the National Union of Mineworkers in Britain, and the only delegate from Britain, remembered that Sartre dominated the proceedings and that Beauvoir quietly directed him when she found it necessary. Although she spoke English she made virtually no contact with the other members of the tribunal.

1970 was a busy year for the partners, especially for Beauvoir. She had begun to write about ageing in the same way as she had earlier written about the condition of women and in this year she published *La Vieillesse* ('Old Age'), for she wanted to break the silence that surrounded this unmentionable subject. Indeed she received the response she had expected. Old people, writing to her, 'had proved . . . to me that their state is even darker and more wretched than my descriptions'. Again she saw no cause for optimism and it cannot be said that the book is successful *as a book*. She had tried to use the same method as she had used for writing about women, but the result is more like an anthology, full of odd but unproved or even irrelevant fact. She herself later found it unsatisfactory.

More important that year was the affair of the newspaper, *La Cause du peuple*. Sartre could not resist the appeals from younger people who needed him to help in their opposition to the right-wing repressive government. In 1970 the government banned that section of the Maoist movement known as 'La Gauche Prolétarienne', and looked for a way to suppress the group's newspaper *La Cause du peuple*. They approached the problem indirectly by arresting the editors and also sent thirty people to prison for selling the paper. The paper itself was not banned, but how could it be sold? Sartre and Beauvoir decided that they could help. Sartre would now be the editor of the paper, and he, Beauvoir and their friends would sell it in the streets, drawing attention to the gross unfairness of the arrests. Few biographies of either partner are without those touching photographs of the elderly couple walking along the pavement and handing out leaflets or the paper itself. It was Beauvoir rather than Sartre who organized the demonstration by the disparate band of intellectuals. The purpose was to invite arrest and prove that they, as 'personalities', did not receive the same harsh treatment as the unknown editors and newsvendors. When they were photographed through the barred windows of the police van and questioned at the station they felt they had made their point. After identity checks they were released. According to legend, De Gaulle once said that 'one does not arrest Voltaire'.

Later, Beauvoir herself agreed to become director of another newspaper in trouble, *L'Idiot international*, whose editor had been arrested. This publication represented no party, but according to Beauvoir it intended to publicize 'voices constantly on the increase which are "the expression of an emerging world" . . . the tangible proof that a new political force is there, which wants to change life and hope'. The paper intended for instance to expose accidents at work which in fact were not accidents at all, they were more like 'legalized crimes'. These were the terms in which Beauvoir wrote to *Le Monde* and she made her position quite clear: 'Let us make no mistake: those in authority tolerate only news which is of use to them, [they] refuse the newspapers which reveal suffering and revolt the right to information.' She went boldly forward: 'Despite punishments and legal action I say along with my comrades on *L'Idiot international*, we shall pursue through the fight for a free press the fight for liberty.' There were further anti-establishment attacks during her directorship but she was not arrested. Once again she had been regarded as a privileged person, the authorities refusing to accept that she personally had anything to do with this provocation. The same authorities, she maintained, only wanted to attack the paper because it had 'made the mistake of re-awakening the deep fear experienced by the bourgeoisie since May 1968'. Her directorship lasted into 1971, but she then found that she was no longer in agreement with the editors who were, she thought, merely expressing their own views. They had become negative, disorganized and uncertain, no different from the leftists in general, incapable of bringing about any unity of action.

Beauvoir believed totally and sincerely in the freedom of the press, but she was not well equipped to take her views further than short-lived annoyances to the government. Although she did not share what François Mauriac called Monsieur Sartre's 'thirst for martyrdom' and knew when to retire from the action, she never became a truly political person. It is hard to learn the techniques of political manoeuvring in middle age, and she approached public life as she approached writing: she remained emotional. She was sad to find that after a few years of euphoria Cuba, for instance, was no longer a socialist dream state. Who, apart from amateur observers such as Beauvoir and Sartre, could have imagined it would last, even if they could have said earlier, like Wordsworth contemplating the first days of the French revolution, 'Bliss was it in that dawn to be alive . . .'?

True socialism was something that Beauvoir continually sought, and feminism was to be part of it. If she could not yet find both dimensions at the same time she continually looked for them, especially when travelling, and made the best of what she found, realizing that women's problems outside France were sometimes more complex than she had expected. While touring Japan in 1966 and giving excellent talks about women's conditions she had gone down to the docks and talked to women: they were handling merchandise as if they were men. In Israel, the following year, she had found that women working in the kibbutzim were highly emancipated but sometimes tried too hard to carry out work more suited to men. She also realized that they had not yet worked out the ideal way to bring up children in these circumstances.

In the 1970s Beauvoir showed more independence of mind than Sartre, whose confused involvement with the Maoists was not a political success. After 1968 there were new themes in the air, a growing interest in ecology, linked with anti-nuclear protest, while in the more personal field came the defence of gay rights and, most important of all to Beauvoir, the women's movement. It needed to grow fast in France, as in Italy, for the conservatism of the Catholic church, supported strongly by the traditionally-minded bourgeosie, had been of no help to women. Beauvoir was not taken in by President Giscard d'Estaing's attempts to placate women, believing that the State Secretariat set up in 1974 for the Status of Women could be of no practical help either, just as she later condemned the International Women's Year as equally useless, for too many of the delegates merely represented the views of the oppressive male-dominated governments.

The 1970s were Beauvoir's most active years as a feminist and have naturally been much written about. She had said on the outbreak of war, 'I changed'; now she could say she had 'evolved'. She became active within feminism for the same personal emotional reasons as she had become active – after her fashion – in the political field, but her activity within feminism was more practical because womanhood is a condition, whereas politics is a profession, for which she had not been trained.

Beauvoir was determined to work for the personal liberation of women, and as a start she believed that they must liberate their bodies. When, in 1970, the government was considering a bill that would legalize abortion, the Mouvement de la Libération des Femmes (M.L.F.) urgently wanted the bill to be strengthened. Beauvoir was asked to sign a short letter for publication in *Le Nouvel Observateur*. Each signatory would state that she had had an abortion and demanded that every woman who wanted one should have the legal freedom to proceed. Each year, the letter claimed, a million women had abortions in France, in secrecy and often in dangerous conditions. As the lawyer Gisèle Halimi was to say later, it was wrong that it should be 'the knitting needle for some and the nursing home for others'. The letter was described as

the 'Manifesto of the 343' because of the number of signatures
added. One of the signatories, Hélène de Beauvoir, said in 1987
that neither she nor her sister had in fact undergone an abortion
but, like many other of the women, they had signed the letter out
of 'solidarity'. Soon after the publication of the 'abortion
manifesto', late in 1970, Beauvoir took part in the women's march
organized by the M.L.F. as part of the demand for 'freedom of
maternity, contraception and abortion'.

In 1972 Beauvoir became president of the society known as
'Choisir', set up by Gisèle Halimi with the aim of promoting
knowledge about and availability of contraception, to complement
a law of 1967 which had already improved the situation. The
problem remained because so few women, a mere seven per cent,
used safe and scientific methods of contraception. Beauvoir
appeared as witness in the much-publicized 'Bobigny' case of
November 1972 when a girl, Marie-Claire Chevalier, was in
trouble for having had an abortion. Since she herself was only
seventeen she could not be prosecuted, but her mother, who was
unmarried, had to take the responsibility and was charged with
procuring the abortion. When asked during the trial whether she
herself had had an abortion Beauvoir replied 'Yes. That was a
long time ago.' The association 'Choisir' took care to publicize all
the details of the case, although the proceedings were supposed to
be in camera.

Beauvoir's activism continued. From the end of 1973 a new
feature was introduced into *Les Temps modernes*, entitled 'Le
sexisme ordinaire', which was to print or reprint any stories of
discrimination against women. Beauvoir herself wrote a short
piece introducing the column, stating that 'sexist insults will be
considered as a crime'. Readers, women and men, were invited to
contribute and if women themselves were responsible for any of
these insults the magazine would not hesitate to denounce them,
for the sexism of certain women was 'just as virulent' as that
of men.

Early in 1974 Beauvoir accepted the presidency of the 'Ligue du
Droit des Femmes', which had been formed at the request of the
M.L.F. Its purpose was to end all discrimination against women in
speech and in documents, including any published by the government. Although feminism was in the air, there was no progress

without continual struggle, for when the Ligue tried to collect signatures in order to put forward a candidate in the presidential elections of that year they failed to find sufficient support.

Beauvoir later look up a point of French law of particular concern to women: was it fair that a child born to a married woman could be recognized only by the woman's husband while the natural father had no right to paternity? There was a great deal of work to be done in France concerning relationships within the family and Beauvoir realized that she herself would never get to the end of it.

The following year Beauvoir accepted the Jerusalem Prize, the first she had accepted since the Prix Goncourt in 1954, for, like Sartre, she was not interested in official awards, so often given to mediocrities. The Jerusalem Prize is awarded to writers who have promoted the concept of individual liberty, and previous winners had been highly eminent: they included Bertrand Russell, Ignazio Silone, Borges, Ionesco. Beauvoir received the prize at the Palais des Nations in Paris where her speech was a great success. Characteristically however she later wrote to *Le Monde* to correct a statement made by a journalist; she had *not* said that Jerusalem should belong definitely to Israel. She had hoped that 'when peace was restored to the Middle East the two communities, Arab and Jewish, would find a political solution allowing the physical unity of Jerusalem to be preserved'.

The 1970s continued for Beauvoir with activities, usually shared with Sartre and other leading intellectuals, which comprised the championship of anyone in difficulties caused by political repression. Her more strictly feminist action, still in many ways literary action, was bound up with her continual support for the principles of true socialism, as distinguished from the pseudo-socialism of the many French left-wing parties. But what of personal life, her personal life, her 'chosen' family, the small circle of people close to herself and Sartre? Now that she had become an international figure did she share the problems common to all women with a successful career? How much personal time was she ready to give to individuals, those not part of her professional life and the constant fight in support of her principles?

TWENTY

I am committed to
looking reality
in the face

Near the end of *Tout compte fait* (*All Said and Done*), the last
volume of her memoirs, published in 1972, Beauvoir wrote: 'Yet I
am committed to looking reality in the face and speaking about it
without pretence: and who dares to say that it is a pleasant sight?'
She was thinking of the plight of old people and also of tragedies
that had occurred in Biafra and Bengal: she added of the latter
that they took her 'by surprise'. There were unpleasant surprises
in store for her much nearer to home.

As she looked at the small group of people around her – Sartre
himself, Olga and Bost, Nathalie and even Algren in the U.S. –
she may have realized that the 'chosen' family and the 'extended'
family were as capable of causing trouble as the natural or
biological family. In 1950 she had written cheerfully to Sartre
saying that they would surely enjoy 'a happy old age'. But it never
happened; there were too many people, too many projects in the
way. Sartre had never stopped falling in love. In 1955 he had been
fascinated by Claude Lanzmann's beautiful sister, an actress who
used the stage name of Evelyne Rey. His play *Les Séquestrés
d'Altona*, performed in 1959, included parts for her and for
Wanda, who was still in his life. In 1946 he had met the Algerian
student Arlette El-Kaim, they became lovers and she remained
close to him, despite his continuing adventures with other women.
In Brazil he had fallen so madly in love with a girl called Cristina
that he had suggested marriage. Since the girl was a virgin and a

412

member of a traditional and bourgeois family he had no choice. However, this crisis passed, after Beauvoir had been concerned about how Arlette would react. She did not seem worried about her own position. A little later a young Jewish girl, Liliane Siegel, in need of moral support and spurred on by all that Beauvoir had written about Sartre, approached him directly. He helped her greatly, they became close but at first she had to remain '*la clandestine*', hidden, illegal as it were, for Wanda, Michelle Vian and Arlette were not to know about her. Only le Castor would know, for she knew everything. Liliane found her exceptionally kind and helpful.

Beauvoir was still close to Sartre and the hours allotted to her in his timetable were more or less sacred. However, that time could not be too long, for he was deeply preoccupied with the writing of his vast two-volume work on Flaubert (published in 1971) and his political interventions. As the *littérateur* and the thinker within him fought for more time to spend on writing he had systematic-ally ruined his health by increasing dependence on stimulating drugs to which, for good measure, he added alcohol. During 1970 he began to die, and Beauvoir, experienced already in describing illness and death, started a journal that would record his decline and fall. She had developed an alarming skill in this field, consoling herself with a clinical account of her mother's death and perhaps carrying out an unconscious revenge when she recounted the appalling end of Simone Jolivet – a chronic and lonely alcoholic since Dullin's death – Sartre's one-time mistress and the first woman to call out her jealousy when she was young.

There had been another tragedy, for Nathalie Sorokine, who had meant a good deal to Beauvoir in 1940 and afterwards, died young in 1967. She had always been eccentric and unpredictable, now she had divorced her first husband, re-married, had a son, but was overtaken by illness. It was a sad end for someone still relatively young, but Beauvoir dealt with her sadness in her usual way, by writing about the girl's death as though conducting a pathological examination. Her other young friend, Védrine had divorced her husband and never lost her forlorn love for Beauvoir.

Fortunately for Beauvoir another young woman, almost thirty years younger than herself, had in the meantime brought her immense happiness. She had first encountered Sylvie Le Bon, then a philosophy student, in 1960. Their contact had been by letter, Beauvoir's preferred way of meeting people, but although they met, the contact remained intermittent for several years. Sylvie had been able to console Beauvoir to some extent after the death of her mother. The girl became a philosophy teacher and by coincidence taught in the girls' lycée in Rouen to which Beauvoir had been appointed in 1932. Gradually their friendship became close, warm and rewarding, an essential part of their lives, and lasted until Beauvoir's death. Sylvie meant as much to her older friend as Zaza had meant when they were both schoolgirls and students. All her life Beauvoir had mourned Zaza, and despite all the women friends she had acquired, no one succeeded her, until now. This relationship inevitably intrigued the voyeurs who would later question both Beauvoir and Sylvie with crude persistence about its exact nature: were they lesbians, were they mother and daughter? No, Beauvoir replied, this was *autre chose*, something else, and later she settled the question finally with the ultimate definition: the relationship, with its emotional and intellectual centre, was similar to the one she had enjoyed with Sartre.

Was Beauvoir now slightly more distant from Sartre? He had begun to behave in ways that indeed surprised her. In 1965 he had decided that he would adopt Arlette El-Kaim as his daughter, and the unusual aspect to this was that he did not consult Beauvoir first. Bost had been detailed to break the news to her and to say that she was not pleased is an understatement. How would this affect her own privileged position? In the end she accepted both the adoption and, at least for the time being, Arlette herself. She even, with Lanzmann, acted as sponsor to the legal proceedings. Sartre still could do no wrong.

However, Beauvoir was obviously determined to prove that only she, after a close relationship lasting half a century, could occupy the place at Sartre's side. They had maintained the habit of spending a holiday in Rome together in the late summer, and while there she made a point of recording several long and intriguing conversations with Sartre, questioning him about his early life, his relationships with women, his philosophical, literary and political thought. She was in fact compiling the material for a biography of the man, the kind of biography only she could write because only she could ask such intimate questions. At the same time the recordings brought out, through prompting from her, a good deal about their own personal relationship. He may not have realized how many notes she was taking about the decline of his own health; it might not have occurred to him that such details would be of interest to anyone. They certainly interested Beauvoir, the expert now in decribing decline, decadence and deterioration. Would anyone be interested to hear about Sartre's incontinence, his worsening eyesight, his problems with balance, with walking? Yes, Beauvoir knew very well that all she wrote about Sartre would eventually reach the public, all those thousands of people to whom his name symbolized a revolt against bourgeois values a form of honourable dissidence.

As Sartre became gradually blind and immobile he was helped by Beauvoir and Arlette, and often too by other women friends, including Michelle Vian and Françoise Sagan, with whom he shared a birthday and an age gap of thirty years. Not all his friends understood that certain medication should not be combined with alcohol, and some of them would secretly bring him bottles. He had to accept that he could not see to eat and that food had to be cut up for him. He could not read and had to be read to.

As life changed and Sartre could no longer write, Beauvoir was indeed forced to look reality in the face; despite her own lifelong fear of death she had to accept the fact that Sartre would die, and there seemed every possibility that he might die before she did. She did not realize how vulnerable she was. Her relationship with Sartre may have been at a higher level than mere marriage, but like the 'chosen' family, it could be problematic. There had been no registrar, no ring, but 'transparency', already destroyed by the surprise adoption of Arlette, could come to an end just as a marriage can end, often because one partner takes too much for granted. Unfortunately this is what happened to Beauvoir. She had always maintained that the intellectual side of her long partnership with Sartre was the side she valued most, but though she followed him ideologically in most ways she had been partaking independently in feminist activity and seen less of his latest developments. Sartre described himself as a feminist but there was little question of him taking any part in *her* work in this field. Despite his declining health he was still fascinated by new ideas and inevitably they were usually put to him by young people, whom he had met through his association with the Maoists.

Notable among these was an Egyptian Jew named Benny Lévy, who called himself Pierre Victor. He had left his country, studied philosophy at the Ecole Normale Supérieure, had been active in 'La Gauche Prolétarienne' but was in difficulties because he was a stateless person. Sartre realized he could help him and when in 1973 he appointed him as his secretary the young man was at once given French nationality. At first Beauvoir was pleased that Sartre had an intelligent assistant; it was Arlette who worried lest Lévy should acquire too much power. Then came another surprise. Arlette and Lévy came closer to each other, recognizing their common Jewish origins, and began to study Hebrew together. Gradually the two young people began to form a kind of united front, the direction of Sartre's thought began to change, and the longstanding *huis clos* with Beauvoir was broken. Lévy taped several lengthy conversations with Sartre which appeared to show that the older thinker had revised many of the earlier opinions which had influenced an entire generation.

The tapes were transcribed into articles in dialogue form and were to be published in *Le Nouvel Observateur*. Beauvoir heard of this and asked to see the transcripts. After a good deal of trouble she was allowed to do so and was at once convinced that Sartre had been manipulated by Lévy into saying things he did not believe or mean. She had not been a party to these new ideas: surely, inevitably, Sartre would have shared them with her? But he hadn't. When friends, including Lanzmann, tried to influence the magazine's decision to publish, Sartre himself telephoned the editor: he knew precisely what he had said during the recordings and wanted no changes to the proposed articles. He maintained that his older friends did not understand the new direction of his thought: 'it eludes them all, including Simone de Beauvoir'. It was the cruellest thing he ever said about her. Superficially the two of them assumed a form of understanding, but it was a distant one. Even Sartre was upset at her disagreement, something which hardly ever happened. She cried, but that happened often.

The first two of these articles appeared in *Le Nouvel Observateur* in March 1980. By the time the third appeared, on March 24th, Sartre had been taken to hospital. On April 13th he sank into a coma and two days later he died. Beauvoir, Arlette and others had taken turns at his bedside and Arlette had been the last person with him. When Beauvoir heard the news Sylvie at once drove her to the hospital. She telephoned her friends Lanzmann, Bost and others, since Arlette had not done so. They were allowed to spend the night in the hospital room, fortified by whisky. Beauvoir wanted to get into bed with all that remained of Sartre, but was warned of the danger of gangrene. So she lay down on the bed and the others left her alone. Finally a nurse threw a sheet over the body and the last mourner reluctantly went away.

What could happen to her now? Only drugs made it possible for her to attend the funeral, where she was so badly jostled that the famous turban became untied, a moment not missed by the press photographers. Her sister Hélène and Sylvie were naturally concerned about her health and it took her some two years to recover. She had suffered from arthritis for a long time, now she was understandably seriously depressed, and there were painful problems about the ownership of Sartre's papers, effects and copyrights. Mercifully Sylvie was at hand and probably saved her life, taking her to Scandinavia and to various places in France, never leaving her alone. Beauvoir decided to adopt her, for her sister, living near Strasbourg, was too far away, and after all, not much younger. Sylvie accepted the adoption for practical purposes, although she knew their personal relationship was not in need of any 'official' recognition. Beauvoir recovered from Sartre's death and in fact prolonged his life by publishing, in 1981, *La Cérémonie des adieux* (*Adieux: A Farewell to Sartre*), the story of his last ten years. The book displeased Arlette and divided the public. Beauvoir's approach was in some ways so objective that it became subjective, and although she described it as 'a book about Sartre' it was also a book about herself. The publication by Beauvoir of two volumes of Sartre's letters in 1983 also fascinated the public, who were mostly unaware of the many unpleasant situations that had developed between Beauvoir and Arlette during the editorial work. The letters too were in a sense a book about Beauvoir, for they showed more than anything else what she had meant to the now vanished Sartre ever since their early life together.

Beauvoir gradually returned to a life of her own, which was in a sense the first time she had been alone since 1929. The presence of Sylvie meant that she was not isolated and at last she found herself working on the two aspects of life, now combined, that interested her most. This was due to the election of the socialist François Mitterrand as President in 1981. He set up, under the control of Yvette Roudy, a 'Commission Femme et Culture', and Beauvoir, who had supported Mitterrand, agreed to accept the honorary chairmanship. It looked as though many of the long-distance objectives of *The Second Sex*, which had been only hinted at, might even be realized in the end.

The fame of that book had soared to such an extent that its thirty-year anniversary had been celebrated with a Commemorative Conference on Feminist Theory at the Loeb Student Center of New York University in September 1979.

Beauvoir's writing and persona always fascinated women writers. Although she stated that feminists had radicalized her she did not allow them to take her over. She behaved within feminism as within politics. Her support was essentially personal and independent, and she was no supporter of fanatical or excessive behaviour. She had often described herself as extremist, but she was not so in everything, at least now. She was opposed to the feminist faction which favoured a wholly feminine culture, a kind of enlightened gynaeceum. She was not in favour of excluding men from personal relationships and she was not impressed by those who wanted to reform the language by the elimination of gender. This latter idea seemed to her élitist and would limit communication. Other things were more important, at least for the time being. Beauvoir gave priority to the education of girls, militant action against rape and the problem of battered wives. In 1982 she gave her name to the Centre Audiovisuel Simone de Beauvoir, set up under the presidency of the actress Delphine Seyrig, by the Association 'Les Muses s'Amusent', with financial assistance from various government departments. The centre maintained an audiovisual library of material of interest to women, available to individuals or educational groups. With the election of a right-wing government in 1986 official assistance was reduced and the centre was forced to move from Montparnasse to a smaller, cheaper office.

1983 brought Beauvoir the Danish Sonning Prize for the ensemble of her work, and she used the money for a trip to the U.S. with Sylvie, remaining incognito except for a visit to the farm of Kate Millett, the feminist writer, near Poughkeepsie, New York state. A film of part of this visit, showing Beauvoir in a white dress, looking relaxed and happy, was included in a four-hour documentary film based partly on *The Second Sex*. It is one of the few successful sections in it, apart from the brief moment of humour supplied unexpectedly enough by Norman Mailer (although it is not clear whether the film-makers intended this effect), who described how his wife, having read *The Second Sex*, left him. Unfortunately the film was not sufficiently original in itself, only serving to prove that Beauvoir's medium was writing, and the kind of writing that cannot be translated easily into the visual medium.

This film was shown in 1985 at a colloquium on Simone de Beauvoir at the Maison Française of Columbia University. Yvette Roudy, described now as a minister delegate from the Ministère des Droits de la Femme, outlined the main points in Beauvoir's life and work. She had gambled on happiness, 'the happiness that each one of us can build by building from within himself or herself'. Roudy made several perceptive points, emphasizing that Beauvoir's 'fortune lies perhaps in her not being a feminist at first'. She had had to discover everything about herself. She was the woman who 'lit the magic lantern, for it is thanks to her that we are discovering the deep-seated reasons why women's freedom has been curtailed'. Beauvoir's ideas had influenced all the leading American writers on feminism in the 1960s but the French had to wait for the upheavals of 1968 before feminist ideas were taken seriously. It was Beauvoir who had pioneered these ideas and Yvette Roudy explained how far they had influenced her personally and in her work as a minister delegate. During this seminar Kate Millett, whose *Sexual Politics* had been deeply influenced by Beauvoir, gave an appreciative paper on Beauvoir as a writer of autobiography.

The poster announcing this meeting reproduced a photograph

of Beauvoir which shows her as severe and remote. Why did she, so emotional in fact, seem so aloof, so distant, as though not wishing to communicate except through her writing? Over the years many people had noticed her attitude. Tennessee Williams had observed her in Cuba, several years earlier. Sartre was 'very warm and charming', but 'Miss de Beauvoir was rather an icy lady'. There was some conversation but 'Miss de Beauvoir continued to be icy'. On another occasion Claude Lévi-Strauss invited Beauvoir to meet his eminent colleague Dr Margaret Mead, but he was dismayed to find that the two women did not really meet at all, they remained at opposite ends of the room, each surrounded by her own coterie. The painter Jan Le Witt, meeting Beauvoir in Tel Aviv, had a similar experience. This social coolness was not hostility, Beauvoir was simply not interested in small talk. Sometimes even close friends found her distant and obstinate: she did not suffer fools gladly, she did not believe in half-measures and with her there never were any.

On the personal level there was more unhappiness. Nelson Algren died in 1981, and in a sense it could have been Beauvoir's fault. The translation of *Les Mandarins* had upset him deeply, and her second volume of memoirs, which appeared in English in 1962, had been even more hurtful. He could not understand why, if she had cared for him, and indeed even if she hadn't, it was necessary to tell the whole world the details of their relationship. It was true that he had given permission for the publication of some letters, but he had been reluctant about it. His death has become a classic sad story, a novel in itself. Algren had been elected a member of the American Academy of Art and Letters and had invited friends to a celebration. The day before the party he gave an interview to W. J. Weatherby, a British journalist who was then writing for *The Times*, during which he took the opportunity to attack Beauvoir. He had no good words for 'transparency': 'Hell, love letters should be private. I've been in whorehouses all over the world and the woman there always closes the door.' Beauvoir, 'this woman', not only opened the door but 'called in the public and the press . . .' He became very angry and some time later died of a heart attack. His body was found by the first guest to come to his party the next day. He was seventy-two. Beauvoir later attempted to contradict years of emotional letter-writing and memories of a happy sexual life by suddenly saying she had not cared for Algren and the whole story had been fabricated. It sounded to the world as though Algren might have been right when he alleged that she 'must have been awfully hard up for something to write about'. During this last stage of her life Beauvoir was given to self-contradiction and what might have been conscious 'forgetfulness', a reminder that it is nearly always better to read and re-read an author rather than listen to gossip or believe sudden denials. Beauvoir was so much the writer and her life and experiences supplied so much of her subject matter that she may well have believed what she wrote rather than what had actually happened.

Another sadness was the death of Olga in 1983. She had quarrelled with Beauvoir over the publication of Sartre's letters and the references in them to herself and her sister Wanda. The novel *L'Invitée*, which contained the story of the trio made up of Sartre, Beauvoir and Olga, had been published forty years earlier, but Olga had not forgotten it. The quarrel was not mended before Olga's death, hastened probably by the neglect of her own health. As for Wanda, she had vandalized Arlette's apartment as a protest against Sartre's adoption and before that she had cut up the first volume of Beauvoir's memoirs with a kitchen knife. Though these women and several others had received much generous support from Beauvoir and Sartre over the years this had not put them in a grateful mood.

So what was left? The dedicated companionship of Sylvie, who kept an eye on Beauvoir's health and tried to reduce her drinking. Beauvoir had developed cirrhosis of the liver and could walk only with difficulty. She could no longer embark on any concentrated writing, but she undertook the preface to a short book by an American whom Lanzmann had met. The author remained anonymous, calling himself 'Alan'. The book told the factual, desperate love story of an unhappy man, a sculptor, who owned an art shop and fell in love with a young Moroccan navvy, Milhoud, whom he had met by chance in Belleville, the working-class *faubourg*, where Garric, Beauvoir's teacher at the Institut Sainte-Marie, had lived. Alan's enemy was Milhoud's family, for they insisted that Milhoud return to North Africa, marry and settle down. No American publisher, and no major French publisher, would accept this book. Eventually a small house took it on and Beauvoir was asked to preface it. The title was simply *Milhoud*. The author of *The Second Sex*, always interested in any problems of sexuality, presumably read with fascination Alan's description of how and why he became a homosexual. His mother had hated sex, she had not wanted a child. As a result Alan decided 'to accept the sperm of other men and stop the cycle of procreation. I felt pity for women and in becoming homosexual I was protecting them from male violence.' Before the book was published the author had died of AIDS. Beauvoir had always said that she liked to be *'dans le feu de la vie'*, in the thick of things, as she had been when she wrote *Les Mandarins*. This last preface, which was not published until after her death, proved that she had never lost interest in the problems of sexuality and always responded to the loneliness of the unhappy individual.

Envoi

Her own death came with unexpected suddenness. Towards the end of March, 1986 Beauvoir entered the Hôpital Cochin in Montparnasse, suffering from stomach pains, thought at first to be caused by appendicitis. She was found to have pulmonary oedema and exploratory surgery proved that the liver damage was serious. The surgery was followed by pneumonia and intensive care. Beauvoir then appeared to be out of danger, so much so that her sister, in consultation with Sylvie, decided she could fly to the U.S. where some of her paintings were being exhibited at Stanford University. But Hélène soon heard from Sylvie that Beauvoir had been returned to intensive care. She seemed to make progress but had a further relapse and died during the afternoon of April 14th. The coincidence was remarkable: Sartre, in 1980, had died on April 15th and the cause of his death, if more complicated, was almost identical. Sartre had been nearly seventy-five, Beauvoir was seventy-eight.

Sartre, after death, had been dressed in a maroon corduroy suit, completed by a tie with an abstract design. Beauvoir was dressed in a long red bathrobe and a matching red turban. Algren's silver ring remained on her finger. Hélène, Sylvie, her cousins from Meyrignac, and her remaining friends came to pay their respects. On April 19th some five thousand people joined the family cortège and walked to the Montparnasse Cemetery. Several personalities from the former socialist government – Yvette Roudy, Laurent

Fabius, Jack Lang – attended. The coffin, bearing the initial B, was lowered into the grave that Beauvoir was to share with Sartre. Claude Lanzmann read a passage from *La Force des choses* and quoted Beauvoir's own words about Sartre from the preface to *La Cérémonie des adieux*: 'My death will not reunite us.' Women sang a verse from a hymn of the M.L.F.

There was a great range of tributes. Jacques Chirac, in his capacity as Mayor of Paris, showed respect but perhaps also a feeling of relief. Beauvoir's death, he said, indicated the end of an era. Her committed literature was 'representative of certain currents of ideas which once made their mark on our society'. He clearly hoped that all such ideas belonged to the past and had now been swept away for good.

Tributes from left-wing leaders and commentators were understandably warmer and more personal. Even the inimitable and untranslatable *Canard enchainé* paid attention. Georges Marchais, general secretary of the Communist party, paid homage to the woman who would always be 'a witness to a great moment in the progressive thought of our country'. The communist newspaper *L'Humanité* published a serious account of Beauvoir's life and added a short revealing article by Michel Boué, who when younger had often watched Beauvoir and Sartre lunching, in silence, at La Coupole. 'I was fascinated by this outrageous couple who master-minded an entire generation and consumed, with a hearty appetite, *nourritures terrestres* like you and me.' He had often seen Beauvoir at the opera, where she wore a bandeau of silver lamé and never left her seat during the intervals. He remembered her for another important reason: it was his reading of her early memoirs which had led him towards the left wing and the Communist party. These books, more than *La Nausée* and *L'Etre et le néant*, had taught him commitment. Without Le Castor he would not have been writing for *L'Humanité*, and he thanked her.

A contrasting point of view appeared in the right-wing *Figaro-Magazine*. Here Georges Suffert concentrated on the human story. 'Was Simone de Beauvoir a philosopher? No. Not essentially. Nor was she militant. What remains of her is not action or ideas: she was unaware of too much. It is her passion, for life and for a man. A woman's destiny, in the end.' It was a romantic, traditionalist point of view which would have angered her, but it contained a grain of truth. If she had not truly loved Sartre how could she have forgiven him so much? She tried to love other people, Algren, even Bost or Lanzmann, but Sartre was never out of the picture. As *Le Figaro* said, 'He was her teacher, her father and her lover.' Naturally this relationship was examined in detail by many writers and she at last received the credit she had barely won during her lifetime, for she had always remained in the background. Sartre said once that he owed her everything; the praise she never sought but heard with secret pleasure. He had been incapable of judging the length of his articles, for instance, and it was Beauvoir who knew how to edit them to the precise length required. She was the perfect editorial 'wife', the 'wife' who never cooked him a meal or sewed on a button, for such domesticity was against her principles. As the two of them grew older she had discreetly managed him more and more. Sir Angus Wilson remembered the constant sound of her voice as they travelled together on a coach during one of Khrushchev's organized cultural trips in the U.S.S.R. She could always be heard saying 'Sartre and I, we . . .' Sartre did not attempt to speak for himself and seemed relieved that she spared him the effort.

Few women writers ever received so many tributes. Hélène de Beauvoir spoke movingly of her sister, recalling their early life together and the different ways in which they both became independently feminist. Warm words from the feminists were predictable but were no less sincere for that. Many younger women spoke of her as their spiritual 'mother', a compensation in one way for Beauvoir's failure to understand what motherhood was all about. She seemed to be frightened of it, just as she seemed uncomprehending about marriage, thinking of it only in a bourgeois context and inevitably concerned with money. Women who could have been her grandchildren regarded themselves as her 'daughters' and developed an urge to talk about themselves. Without Beauvoir, they thought, they would have lived unhappy lives.

Journalists were fascinated by her. Why, asked *Libération*, had she insisted so obsessively on wearing that turban? She had nothing to hide. Was it an Amazon's helmet, a symbol of discipline? A protection against the disorders of the world?

Perhaps the wearing of it had been an unconscious attempt to minimize her femininity, to remind others that they were dealing with an individual, not 'merely' with a woman. Six months after her death a new milliner opened in the rue Vivienne in Paris and the star headgear of his show was a 'Simone de Beauvoir turban', made of a kind of raffia.

Just as Jean Cocteau had died a few hours after his friend Edith Piaf in 1963, Beauvoir's death was followed almost immediately by that of Jean Genet, and attractive photographs of the two of them together were published. This second death renewed speculation about Beauvoir's bisexuality. Genet for instance had once said of her relationship with Sartre that she was the man of the couple and Sartre was the woman. Beauvoir had confirmed that Genet was aware of one aspect of their behaviour: Sartre was more 'sensitive', she thought, she was more 'brusque'. At the same time she had reminded her questioner that Genet 'did not like women too much'.

'No bourgeois mother would have found any cause for complaint', wrote a woman journalist in 1960. 'Madame de Beauvoir is wearing a blouse that has been ironed with care; she is as fresh as a rose, her face is smooth and clear, she wears a discreet perfume, she is really perfect.' Fortunately she was never perfect, she was human. Twenty-five years later, when I visited her in the rue Schoelcher studio apartment that was more of a décor perhaps than a home, filled with tourist trophies varying from a huge bullfight poster to small carved wooden figures, she was no less 'perfect' in her own way. There was a welcoming dignity about her, a kind of sympathetic grandeur that impressed without ever intimidating. She was the 'perfect' symbol of an intellectual tradition that she had inherited and carried a stage further.

She looked to me frailer and less tall than one might have expected. In her trouser suit and its matching purple turban she was still essentially feminine. Her voice was dry and rapid, her red-nailed hands impatient and restless.

In the process of talk about British novelists – the conversation turned to George Eliot and Doris Lessing – Beauvoir expressed, without any didactic effort, the points which were so important to her: she wanted to see real socialism, she wanted a higher standard of education for everyone. Most of all, when talking of her own writing, she insisted that feminist issues made up only part of her work. The absence of real socialism had led her to take positive action within the women's movement. She had come to feminism late, just as she had come to politics late, and to active feminism later still. Beauvoir, it has been said, took the hysteria out of feminism, even if she conjured up no humour to take its place. Her escape from bourgeois escapism had taken her into the real world and into an enviable classlessness, and she saw the route to feminism, the longest revolution of all, as the second stage of her journey.

What do women want? Freud did not know. Beauvoir knew what *she* wanted: she wanted everything, and she had more than most women – most people – because she broke through restrictions and took what she wanted. She wanted independence, she wanted love, she wanted intellectual attainment. She extended her wants to the whole world, she wanted justice and freedom for everyone. At the end of her third volume of memoirs she had confused her readers by saying that she had been 'cheated'. Later she had to explain that the cheating came from bourgeois society, which was based on false values. She saw marriage as a trap, but sadly she was caught in it herself. She thought she was independent within her unmarried marriage but she had not realized that intellectual infidelity could hurt her so much. She had been the over-trusting intellectual 'wife' and, ironically, if she had not given so much time to women and their problems, she might have remained closer to the changing ideas of Sartre at the end of his life.

Her own ideas, developed more from her own experience than from anything else, will live longer than those of Sartre because they are more meaningful to ordinary people. Anyone who is not afraid of emotional reality can learn from them. Her close relationships with women for instance had taught her a good deal and she was not afraid to say so. In 1982 for instance she told the German feminist Alice Schwarzer about the friendships with women that she had enjoyed all her life, they had been 'even physical', but never 'erotic'. She believed that 'every woman is a bit ... homosexual. Quite simply, because women are more desirable than men'. Many women would agree with her, but not many women over the age of seventy would have spoken out on the subject. Beauvoir had a great capacity for love, she had lived through its splendours and miseries, she had loved both men and women. Her novels are out of fashion at the time of writing, but there is a great deal to be learned from *L'Invitée* and *Les Mandarins*, even if their settings seem restricted. The four volumes of memoirs, despite their longueurs, are classics. It is a mistake to remember Beauvoir only through *Le Deuxième Sexe* or *La Femme rompue*, without taking into account her early fiction and its complex, ambitious themes.

François Mauriac, musing about the state of literature in 1957, decided that after a writer's death 'the books died and the authors remained'. Readers transferred their curiosity from the books to the people who wrote them. But later, he said, there followed a second and more important stage: 'The life recedes and the work remains.' Few women readers fail to respond to Beauvoir's books, even if they criticize them as narcissistic, or out of date. They remain alive, for that 'magic lantern' lit by Beauvoir has never grown dim. It shines even for men.

Sartre, when he was young, had once told Beauvoir that he wanted to be 'Spinoza and Stendhal'. One decade or so after his death many critics, especially in France, have found him too close to Heidegger, who in his turn was too close to the Nazis. His plays continue to have international success and there has even been a play about his near-last days in 1980, shared with Beauvoir against a background of Pergolesi's *Stabat Mater*. Seven years after his death it was possible, outside the Café de Flore, to buy pictures of him, even if those most likely to read him could not afford to order coffee there. There is no need for any nostalgic pictures of Beauvoir because the problems she addressed are still current, still unsolved, and they involve men as much as women: over-population, birth control, abortion, divorce, the abuse of privilege, racial discrimination, nationalism. And 'real socialism': can it ever be achieved, or will the world regress into materialism and uncaring social confrontation?

Beauvoir's personal problems, her blind spots, indecisions and failures offer, paradoxically, a hope for everyone, for she came to terms with them. Her later experiences within her personal life – her break with Algren, the rift with Sartre – justify that mysterious observation by Saint-John Perse in 1947: 'What makes you so humane? Has life hurt you?'

When she was a little girl she had insisted that she was not a 'child', like other children, she did not want to be a member of a group, a race, or like other people. *J'étais moi*, she insisted, and repeated the phrase years later. 'I was myself.' She was unique.

BIBLIOGRAPHY

I Works by Simone de Beauvoir

1 Fiction

L'Invitée, Gallimard, Paris, 1943
   She Came to Stay, Secker & Warburg and Lindsay Drummond,
      London, 1949
   She Came to Stay, World Publishing, Cleveland, 1954
Le Sang des autres, Gallimard, Paris, 1945
   The Blood of Others, Secker & Warburg and Lindsay
      Drummond, London, 1948
   The Blood of Others, Knopf, New York, 1948
Tous les hommes sont mortels, Gallimard, Paris, 1946
   All Men are Mortal, World Publishing, Cleveland, 1955
Les Mandarins, Gallimard, Paris, 1954
   The Mandarins, World Publishing, Cleveland, 1956
   The Mandarins, Collins, London, 1957
Les Belles Images, Gallimard, Paris, 1966
   Les Belles Images, Collins, London 1968
   Les Belles Images, Putnam, New York, 1968
La Femme rompue (Stories), Gallimard, Paris, 1969
   The Woman Destroyed, Collins, London, 1969
   The Woman Destroyed, Putnam, New York, 1969
   Broken Woman (Monologue), Translated and performed by
      Diana Quick, BBC Radio 3; January 17th, 1989
Quand prime le spirituel, Gallimard, Paris, 1979

When Things of the Spirit Come First, André Deutsch, London,
1982
When Things of the Spirit Come First, Pantheon, New York,
1982

2 Drama

Les Bouches inutiles, Gallimard, Paris, 1945
Who Shall Die?, River Press, Florissant, Missouri, 1983

3 Essays

Pyrrhus et Cinéas, Gallimard, Paris, 1944
Pour une morale de l'ambiguité, Gallimard, Paris 1944
The Ethics of Ambiguity, Philosophical Library, New York, 1948
L'Existentialisme et la sagesse des nations, Nagel, Paris, 1948
L'Amérique au jour le jour, Morihien, Paris, 1948
   America Day by Day, Duckworth, London, 1952
   America Day by Day, Grove Press, New York, 1953
Le Deuxième Sexe, I, II, Gallimard, Paris, 1949
   The Second Sex, Jonathan Cape, London, 1953
   The Second Sex, Knopf, New York, 1953
Privilèges ('Faut-il brûler Sade?' 'La pensée de droite aujourd'hui'
   'Merleau-Ponty ou le pseudo-sartrisme'), Gallimard, Paris,
   1955
   Must we Burn de Sade?, Peter Nevill, London, 1953
   Must we Burn de Sade?, Grove Press, New York, 1955
La Longue Marche, Gallimard, Paris, 1957
   The Long March, André Deutsch, London, 1958
   The Long March, World Publishing, Cleveland, 1958
Djamila Boupacha (with Gisèle Halimi), Gallimard, Paris, 1962
   Djamila Boupacha (with Gisèle Halimi), Weidenfeld & Nicolson,
   London, 1962
   Djamila Boupacha(with Gisèle Halimi), Macmillan, New York,
   1962
La Vieillesse, Gallimard, Paris, 1970
   Old Age, André Deutsch, London, 1972
   The Coming of Age, Putnam, New York, 1972

4 Autobiography and Memoirs

Mémoires d'une jeune fille rangée, Gallimard, Paris, 1958
   Memoirs of a Dutiful Daughter, André Deutsch and Weidenfeld
   & Nicolson, London, 1959

Memoirs of a Dutiful Daughter, World Publishing, Cleveland, 1959
La Force de l'âge, Gallimard, Paris, 1960
  The Prime of Life, World Publishing, Cleveland, 1962
  The Prime of Life, André Deutsch and Weidenfeld & Nicolson,
    London, 1965
La Force des choses, Gallimard, Paris, 1964
  Force of Circumstance, André Deutsch and Weidenfeld &
    Nicolson, London, 1965
  Force of Circumstance, Putnam, New York, 1965
Une mort très douce, Gallimard, Paris, 1964
  A Very Easy Death, André Deutsch and Weidenfeld & Nicolson,
    London, 1966
  A Very Easy Death, Putnam, New York, 1966
Tout compte fait, Gallimard, Paris, 1972
  All Said and Done, André Deutsch and Weidenfeld & Nicolson,
    London, 1972
  All Said and Done, Putnam, New York, 1974

5 Biography

*La Cérémonie des adieux: suivi de Entretiens avec Jean-Paul
    Sartre août–septembre 1974*, Gallimard, Paris, 1981
Adieux: A Farewell to Sartre, André Deutsch, London, 1984
  Adieux: A Farewell to Sartre, Putnam, New York, 1984
Journal de guerre, Septembre 1939–Janvier 1941, Edition
    présentée, établie et annotée par Sylvie Le Bon de Beauvoir,
    Gallimard, Paris, 1990
Lettres à Sartre, I, *1930–1939*; II, *1940–1963*, Edition présentée,
    établie et annotée par Sylvie Le Bon de Beauvoir, Gallimard,
    Paris, 1990

6 As Editor

Lettres au Castor et à quelques autres, I & II, Jean-Paul Sartre,
    Gallimard, Paris, 1983

7 Articles, Lecture Texts

'Brigitte Bardot and the Lolita Syndrome', *Esquire*, New York,
    August 1959
'Brigitte Bardot and the Lolita Syndrome', André Deutsch and
    Weidenfeld & Nicolson, London, 1960
'Mon expérience d'écrivain' and 'La femme et la création', lectures
    given in Japan, October 11th, 1966
(Note: these articles and texts appear in *Les Ecrits de Simone de
    Beauvoir*, ed. C. Francis and F. Gontier, Gallimard, Paris, 1979)

8 Prefaces (In chronological order)

Le Planning familial, Dr Marie-Andrée Labroua Weill-Hallé,
   Maloine, Paris, 1959
La Grand'peur d'aimer, Dr Marie-Andrée Lagroua Weill-Hallé,
   Julliard-Séquana, Paris, 1960
Djamila Boupacha (Listed as joint author with Gisèle Halimi.
   Beauvoir wrote only the Preface), Gallimard, Paris, 1962
Bluebeard and Other Fairy Tales, Charles Perrault, Collier-
   Macmillan, London, 1964
La Bâtarde, Violette Leduc, Gallimard, Paris, 1964
   La Bâtarde, Violette Leduc, Peter Owen, London, 1965
   La Bâtarde, Violette Leduc, Farrar Straus & Giroux Inc., New
   York, 1965
James Joyce in Paris: His Final Years, Gisèle Freund and V. B.
   Carleton, Harcourt Brace & World Inc, New York, 1965
Tréblinka, Jean-François Steiner, Fayard, Paris, 1966
Majorité sexuelle de la femme, Dr E. & Dr P. Kronhausen,
   Bûchet-Chastel, Paris, 1966
Simone de Beauvoir ou le refus de l'indifférence, L. Gagnebin,
   Fischbacher, Paris, 1968
Avortement: une loi en procès – L'Affaire de Bobigny, Association
   Choisir, Gallimard, Paris, 1973
Divorce en France, Claire Cayron, Denoël-Gonthier, Paris, 1974
Les Femmes s'entêtent, Gallimard, Paris, 1975 (Republication in
   book form of the special number with the same title, *Les
   Temps modernes, avril–mai*, 1974)
Regards féminins, Anne Ophir, Denoël-Gonthier, Paris, 1976
Histoires du M.L.F., Anne Tristan & Annie de Pisan, Calmann-
   Lévy, Paris, 1977
History (*La Storia*), Elsa Morante, Franklin Library Book Club,
   New York, 1977
Milhoud, Anon., Alinéa, Paris, 1986

II

1 Books about Simone de Beauvoir

Appignanesi, Lisa, 'Simone de Beauvoir' (*Lives of Modern Women*),
   Penguin, Harmondsworth, 1988
Ascher, Carole, *Simone de Beauvoir, A Life of Freedom*, Beacon
   Press, Boston, 1981 and Harvester Press, Brighton, 1981
Audet, Jean R., *Simone de Beauvoir face à la mort*, Lausanne,
   1979

Bibliography

Bair, Deirdre, *Simone de Beauvoir: A Biography*, Jonathan Cape, London, 1990

Bieber, Konrad, *Simone de Beauvoir*, Twayne, Boston, 1975

Burdman, Ralph (Trans. Jean-Louis Roux), *Tête-à-Tête*, Play in 2 acts, Editions du Boréal, Montreal, 1988

Cayron, Claire, *La Nature chez Simone de Beauvoir*, Gallimard, Paris, 1973

Dayan, Josée, & Ribowska, Malka, *Simone de Beauvoir*, film: scenario, Gallimard, Paris, 1979

d'Eaubonne, Françoise, *Une femme nommée Castor: Mon amie Simone de Beauvoir*, Encre, Paris, 1986

Evans, Mary, *Simone de Beauvoir, A Feminist Mandarin*, Tavistock, London, 1985

Forster, Penny & Sutton, Imogen (Eds), *Daughters of de Beauvoir*, The Women's Press, London, 1989

Francis, Claude & Niepce, Jeanine, *Simone de Beauvoir et le cours du monde*, Klincksieck, Paris, 1978

Francis, Claude & Gontier, Fernande, *Les Ecrits de Simone de Beauvoir*, Gallimard, Paris, 1979

Francis, Claude & Gontier, Fernande, *Simone de Beauvoir: une vie*, Librairie Académique, Perrin, Paris, 1985

Francis, Claude & Gontier, Fernande, *Simone de Beauvoir*, St Martin's Press, New York, 1987 and Sidgwick & Jackson, London, 1987

Gagnebin, Laurent, *Simone de Beauvoir ou le refus de l'indifférence. Préface de Simone de Beauvoir*, Editions Fischbacher, Paris, 1968

Henry, A. M., *Simone de Beauvoir ou l'échec d'une chrétienté*, Fayard, Paris, 1961

Jeanson, Francis, *Simone de Beauvoir ou l'entreprise de vivre. Avec deux conversations avec Simone de Beauvoir*, Editions du Seuil, Paris, 1966

Julienne-Caffié, Serge, *Simone de Beauvoir*, Gallimard, Paris, 1966

Keefe, Terry, *Simone de Beauvoir – A Study of Her Writings*, Harrap, London, 1983

Marchessault, Jovette, *La Terre est trop courte, Violette Leduc*, Les Editions de la Pleine Lune, Montreal, 1982

Okely, Judith, *Simone de Beauvoir*, Pioneers of Modern Feminism, Virago, London, 1986

Schwarzer, Alice, *Simone de Beauvoir Today*, Chatto & Windus and The Hogarth Press, London 1984

Whitmarsh, Anne, *Simone de Beauvoir and the Limits of Commitment*, Cambridge University Press, Cambridge, 1981

Periodical 'Simone de Beauvoir: Witness to a Century', *Yale French Studies*, No. 72, New Haven, 1986

2 Other books consulted

Ardagh, John, *France in the 1980s*, Secker & Warburg, London, 1982

Ardagh, John, *France Today* (a new and revised edition of *France in the 1980s*), Penguin, Harmondsworth 1990

Beauvoir, Hélène de, *Souvenirs Recueillis par Marcelle Routier*, Librairie Séguier, Paris, 1987

Bourges, Hervé, *The Student Révolt* (*La Revolte étudiante*) Panther, London, 1968

Cau, Jean, *Croquis de mémoire*, Julliard, Paris, 1985

Chapsal, Madeleine, *Les Ecrivains en personne*, Julliard, Paris, 1960

Cobb, Richard, *Promenades*, Oxford University Press, Oxford, 1980

Cobban, Alfred, *A History of Modern France*, Vol.3., Penguin, Harmondsworth 1984

Coe, Richard N., *When the Grass was Taller. Autobiography and the Experience of Childhood*, Yale University Press, New Haven, 1984 and London, 1985

Cohen-Solal, Annie, *Sartre 1905–1980*, Gallimard, Paris, 1985 *Sartre 1905–1980*, Heinemann, London, 1986

Cruickshank, John. (ed.), 1, *The Novelist as Philosopher. Studies in French Fiction, 1935–1960*, OUP, London, 1962

Cruickshank, John, *French Literature and its Background 6*, *The Twentieth Century*, OUP, London, 1970

Drew, Bettina, *Nelson Algren: A Life on the Wild Side*, Bloomsbury, London, 1991

Fitch, Noël Riley, *Sylvia Beach and the Lost Generation*, W. W. Norton & Co., New York, 1983 and Souvenir Press, London, 1984

Frank, Bernard, *Les Rats*, La Table Ronde, Paris, 1953

Friedan, Betty, *The Feminine Mystique*, W. W. Norton & Co., New York, 1963 and Penguin, Harmondsworth 1965

Gaxotte, Pierre, *Le Nouvel Ingénu*, Fayard, Paris, 1972

Giroud, Françoise, *Si je mens . . . Conversations avec Claude Glayman*, Stock, Paris, 1972

Gréco, Juliette, *Jujube*, Stock, Paris, 1982

Gurney, Jason, *Crusade in Spain*, Faber & Faber Ltd, London, 1974

Halimi, Gisèle, *La Cause des femmes, Propos recueillis par Marie Cardinal*, Grasset, Paris 1973

Halimi, Gisèle, *Propos recueillis par Marie Cardinal*, Stock, Paris 1973

Bibliography

Hayman, Ronald, *Writing Against. A Biography of Sartre*, Weidenfeld & Nicolson, London, 1986

Huddleston, Sisley, *In and about Paris*, Methuen, London, 1927

Huddleston, Sisley, *Back to Montparnasse*, Harrap, London, 1931

Jardin, Pascal, *La guerre à neuf ans*, Bernard Grasset, Paris, 1971

Jardin, Pascal, *Guerre après guerre*, Bernard Grasset, Paris, 1973

Johnson, Paul, *Intellectuals*, Weidenfeld & Nicolson, London, 1988

Kirsner, Douglas, *The Schizoid World of Jean-Paul Sartre and R. D. Laing*, University of Queensland Press, 1976

Le Boterf, Hervé, *La Vie parisienne pendant l'Occupation*, I & II, Editions France Empire, Paris, 1974, 1975

Lévy, Louis, *The Truth about France*, Penguin Special, Harmondsworth, 1941

Lilar, Suzanne, *Aspects of Love in Western Society*, Thames & Hudson, London, 1965

Lottman, Herbert, *The Left Bank. Writers in Paris from the Popular Front to the Cold War*, Heinemann, London, 1982

Macquarrie, John, *Existentialism*, Penguin, Harmondsworth, 1973

Madsen, Axel, *Hearts and Minds. The Common Journey of Simone de Beauvoir and Sartre*, Wm. Morrow, New York, 1977

Marks, Elaine, and de Courtivron, Isabelle (Eds), *New French Feminisms*, Harvester Press, Brighton, 1981

McClelland, J. A. (Ed.), *The French Right from de Maistre to Maurras*, Cape, London, 1970

Millett, Kate, *Sexual Politics*, Rupert Hart-Davis, London, 1971

Mitchell, Juliet, *Psychoanalysis and Feminism*, Penguin, Harmondsworth, 1974

Mitchell, Juliet, & Ann Oakley (eds), *The Rights and Wrongs of Women*, esp. pp. 351–78, 'Simone de Beauvoir' by Margaret Walters, Penguin, Harmondsworth, 1976

Mouloudji, Marcel, *Un Garçon sans importance*, Gallimard, Paris, 1971

Nadeau, Maurice, *Le Roman français depuis la guerre. Nouvelle édition revue et augmentée*, Gallimard, Paris, 1970

Parturier, Françoise, *Lettre ouverte aux femmes*, Albin Michel, Paris, 1974

Peyre, Henri, *The French Novel Today*, OUP, New York, 1967

Rabil, Albert Jr, *Merleau-Ponty. Existentialist of the Social World*, Columbia University Press, New York & London, 1967

Reader, Keith A., *Intellectuals and the French Left in France since 1968*, Macmillan, London, 1987

Richards, Janet Radcliffe, *The Sceptical Feminist. A Philosophical Enquiry*, Routledge & Kegan Paul, London, 1980 and Pelican, Harmondsworth, 1982

Rudorff, Raymond, *The Myth of France*, Hamish Hamilton, London, 1970

Russell, Bertrand, *War Crimes in Vietnam*, Allen & Unwin, London, 1967

Sagan, Françoise, *Réponses 1954–1974*, J.-J. Pauvert, Paris, 1974

Sagan, Françoise, *With Fondest Regards* (*Avec mon meilleur souvenir*), W. H. Allen, London, 1986

Sartre, Jean-Paul, *Les Carnets de la drôle de guerre, novembre 1939–mars 1940*, Gallimard, Paris, 1983

Sartre, Jean-Paul, *Lettres au Castor*, I & II, Gallimard, Paris, 1983

Sartre, Jean-Paul, *Les Mots*, Gallimard, Paris, 1964
  Words, Hamish Hamilton, London, 1964

Sartre, Jean-Paul, *Existentialism and Humanism* (Translated and introduced by Philip Mairet), Methuen, London, 1948

Sartre in the Seventies. Interviews & Essays, André Deutsch, London, 1978

Shattuck, Roger, *The Innocent Eye. On Modern Literature and the Arts*, Farrar, Straus & Giroux, New York, 1984

Siegel, Liliane, *La Clandestine*, Maren Sell et Cie, Paris, 1988

Spender, Stephen, *World within World*, Hamish Hamilton, London, 1951

Spender, Stephen, *Engaged in Writing & The Fool and the Princess*, Hamish Hamilton, London, 1958

Thorez, Maurice, *France Today and the People's Front*, Gollancz, London, 1936

Tint, Herbert, *France since 1918*, 2nd Edition, Batsford Academic, London, 1980

Vian, Boris, *Chroniques du menteur*, Christian Bourgois, Paris, 1974

Webster, Paul and Powell, Nicholas, *Saint-Germain-des-Prés*, Constable, London, 1984

Articles

Michèle Le Doeuff, 'Sartre l'unique sujet parlant', *Esprit*, Mai 1984

Nancy Huston, 'Les Enfants de Simone de Beauvoir', *Lettre Internationale*, No. 11, hiver 86–87

NOTES

All translations used in the quotes are by the author, unless otherwise indicated.

INTRODUCTION

Page
1: a kind of vanity: Transcript: *Simone de Beauvoir*, film de Josée Dayan et Malka Ribowska, Gallimard, 1979.
2: Mrs Sartre and all the little Sartres: Patrick Marnham, *The Independent*, April 15th, 1987.

1: I WAS A GOOD LITTLE GIRL

5: good little girl: *Mémoires d'une jeune fille rangée*, Gallimard, 1958.
10: *Mesdemoiselles: Souvenirs*, Hélène de Beauvoir, Séguier/Garamond, 1987.
11: If any individual: *La Force de l'âge*, Gallimard, 1960, Prologue.
11: The apartment was red: *Mémoires d'une jeune fille rangée*.
12: a feeling of constant security: ibid. All further quotes in this chapter, unless otherwise indicated, are taken from *Mémoires d'une jeune fille rangée*.
22: I had enough: *Souvenirs*, Hélène de Beauvoir.
22: If she said: ibid.
22: We are waiting: ibid.
23: she composed: Interview with François Jonquet, Paris, 1986.

2: I SAW MYSELF AS A CHARACTER IN A NOVEL

27: the brave Zouave: *Souvenirs*, Hélène de Beauvoir.
28: I could not tolerate: *Mémoires d'une jeune fille rangée*.
My grandmother succeeded: ibid. All further quotes in this

chapter, unless otherwise indicated, are taken from
Mémoires d'une jeune fille rangée.

31: Catholico-sadico-masochistico: *Souvenirs*, Hélène de Beauvoir.
33: To dispel mystification: *Tout compte fait*, Gallimard, 1972.
38: violent passion for Zaza: Interview with François Jonquet, Paris, 1986.
41: It would have been preferable: *Souvenirs*, Hélène de Beauvoir.
41: At the Cours Désir: ibid.
42: good little racists: ibid.
44: Give me the strength: Quoted by Jean-Pierre Barou, *Le Monde*, May 30th 1986.

3: I WAS NO LONGER ALONE

51: If I could succeed in making myself noticed: This and all quotes in the first part of this chapter, unless otherwise indicated, are taken from *Mémoires d'une jeune fille rangée*.
66: Families! I hate you: *Les Nourritures terrestres*, André Gide, Gallimard, 1917.
68: He wears glasses and he's very ugly: *Souvenirs*, Hélène de Beauvoir.
69: I didn't want to: Film transcript: *Simone de Beauvoir.*
75: allergic to chlorophyll: *La Force de l'âge*, Gallimard, 1960.
76: without enthusiasm: ibid.
77: see a sheet of blank paper: *Lettres au Castor et à quelques autres, I,* Gallimard, 1983.
77: Only one man is alive for me: ibid.
78: unpleasant and even crude: 'Sartre et les femmes', interview, Catherine Chaîne, quoted by Annie Cohen-Solal in *Sartre*, Gallimard, 1985.
79: I love you tenderly: *Lettres au Castor, I.*
80: contingent: *La Force de l'âge.*
82: quite grotesque: ibid.
82: thought all the time: *Mémoires d'une jeune fille rangée.*
82: all is well if the body: *La Force de l'âge.*
82: the slightest disturbance: ibid.
82: classic relationships implied: *La Cérémonie des Adieux, suivi d' Entretiens avec Jean-Paul Sartre, 1974*, Gallimard, 1981.
83: But the sexual act: ibid.
83: feverish caresses and love-making: *La Force de l'âge.*
83: too shy to go up to a hotel bedroom: ibid. All further quotes in this chapter are taken from *La Force de l'âge.*

4: I HAD TO TAKE DECISIONS

89: We would meet in the morning: This and all quotes in this chapter, unless otherwise indicated, are taken from *La Force de l'âge*.

102: Sartre a father?: *With Fondest Regards*, Françoise Sagan, Alison and Busby, 1988.

110: *O partie de moi-même: Lettres au Castor, I.*

5: I SANK INTO PROVINCIAL BOREDOM

116: divertissement of a coup d'état: This and all quotes in this chapter, unless otherwise indicated, are taken from *La Force de l'âge*.

122: It was not a murder . . . but a revolution: *Paris was Yesterday*, Janet Flanner, Angus and Robertson, 1973.

128: a kind of 'debagging' of public figures: *Penguin Companion to Literature*, 19. A.R. (Angus Ross).

144: We were divided: *World within World*, Stephen Spender, Hamish Hamilton, 1951.

6: I REFUSED TO FACE REALITY

145: She talked to me about Baudelaire: *La Force de l'âge*.

145: We were threatened . . . by an enormous lady: Film transcript: *Simone de Beauvoir*

146: Because I was shy: ibid.

146: I was rather fierce: ibid.

146: She didn't like us: ibid.

146: No, I was rather élitist: ibid.

147: Roumanian and Polish Jews: *La Force de l'âge*. All further quotes in this chapter, unless otherwise indicated, are taken from *La Force de l'âge*.

149: went straight to essentials: *Mémoires d'une jeune fille rangée*.

150: The time required for the excitation: Dorland, *Illustrated Medical Dictionary*, 1960.

152: At twenty-eight I was unknown: *Les Carnets de la drôle de guerre*, J.-P. Sartre Gallimard, 1983.

152: We were tired: ibid.

153: I was beginning to lose my hair: ibid.

153: dreams, hypnotic images: ibid.

158: Pretty women should not be allowed to study: *Quand prime le spirituel*, Gallimard, 1979.

159: and even intimidated: Film transcript: *Simone de Beauvoir*. I thought that if anyone dedicated themselves: ibid.

161: I was at my lowest ebb: *Les Carnets de la drôle de guerre*. And then le Castor and I: ibid.

162: I began to doubt: ibid.

162: Her face was largely hidden: *L'Age de raison*, Sartre,

Gallimard, 1945; *The Age of Reason* (Trans. Eric
Sutton), Hamish Hamilton, 1947.
163: very capricious: *Souvenirs*, Hélène de Beauvoir.
    too natural: ibid.
165: art seemed very useless: *Les Carnets de la drôle de guerre*.
166: Have you sometimes been rebuffed: *Entretiens avec
    J.-P. Sartre*.
    167: When a woman is intelligent: Film transcript: *Simone de
    Beauvoir*.
167: That book about women: ibid.

7: I CHANGED
169: disturbed: *La Force de l'âge*.
170: in a carefree mood: ibid. All quotes in this chapter, unless
    otherwise indicated, are taken from *La Force de l'âge*.
171: A passage is missing: *Lettres au Castor, I*.
174: I have never been elegant: Conversation with author, 1985.
    purely feminine values: *Entretiens avec J.-P. Sartre*.
176: There is no place . . . Montparnasse: *Back to Montparnasse*,
    Sisley Huddleston, Harrap, 1931.
176: Montparnasse does not intend: ibid.
179: It was the end of my passion: *Les Carnets de la drôle de
    guerre*.
180: for things are still idyllic: *Lettres au Castor, I*.
180: totally present in flesh and blood: ibid.
180: postillion-style cap: ibid.
181: He even made me write: *Souvenirs*, Hélène de Beauvoir.
181: Oh, Poupette: ibid.
182: She didn't hate me: *Lettres au Castor, I*.
182: with a comfortable sadness: ibid.
182: stories rather than protestations of love: ibid.
182: If it lasts: ibid.
182: *les états d'âme*: ibid.
183: hypocritical little man: ibid.
183: I was very moved: ibid.
183: yes, *bon* Castor: ibid.
184: a little too full of nature: ibid.
184: brains of a dragonfly: ibid.
186: That would have cost us 1500 francs: ibid.

8: I HAVE LOTS TO TELL YOU
189: lots to tell: *Lettres à Sartre, I, 1930–1939*, Gallimard, 1990.
189: politically extreme: *La Force de l'âge*.
190: The future . . . had detached itself: ibid.

190: I was thinking about my childhood: ibid.

190: Since Sartre was detained in Paris: ibid.

190: absurd little globe-trotter: *Lettres au Castor, I*.

191: *les vicissitudes de la galanterie*: ibid.

191: Mysteries, eternal feminine: ibid.

191: ever since the Olga business: ibid.

191: unfortunately we are free: ibid.

191: liked touching: *Simone de Beauvoir Today: Conversations, 1972–82*, Alice Schwarzer, Chatto and Windus, The Hogarth Press, 1984.

192: Let's move on: *Lettres au Castor, I*.

192: They entertained me greatly: *Lettres à Sartre, I*.

192: his role as an impartial monk: ibid.

192: the first time I've been to bed: *Lettres au Castor, I*.

193: I've always wanted to be with a man: ibid.

193: You must realize, *mon charmant* Castor: ibid.

194: *Mon doux petit mari*: *Lettres à Sartre, I*.

194: passionate letters from Védrine: ibid.

194: something very pleasant has happened: ibid.

195: just like that: *Simone de Beauvoir*, Claude Francis and Fernande Gontier, Sidgwick and Jackson, 1987.

195: I don't think I'll ever love: *L'Invitée*, Gallimard, 1943.

196: Our relationship has become so deep: ibid.

196: My love, I have your long letter: *Lettres au Castor, I*.

196: In Casablanca the European quarter bored us: *La Force de l'âge*.

197: When I'm with you: *Lettres à Sartre, I*.

197: to becoming a second-rate nation: *Lettres au Castor, I*.

198: rejoiced . . . without scruples: *La Force de l'âge*.

9: I COMMITTED MYSELF TO LITERATURE

199: splendour of new worlds: This and all quotes in this chapter, unless otherwise indicated, are taken from *La Force de l'âge*.

203: a friend of mine with whom Sartre began a liaison: *Lettres au Castor, I*.

203–4: talked to me at length about Bost: *Lettres à Sartre, I*.

204: *Mon amour*: *Lettres au Castor, I*.

204: has provided excellent circumstances: *Lettres à Sartre, I*.

205: Only, if she refuses: *Lettres au Castor, I*.

205: As I don't want you to suffer: ibid.

206: I must love her: ibid.

206: You know I'd told her: ibid.

207: He made a few advances: *Lettres à Sartre, I*.

207: even read avidly: *Lettres au Castor, I*.

207: parents are like knives: ibid.
208: *Ma chère petite flamme*: ibid.
210: very humble compared to the complicated: ibid.
211: really didn't think there would be a war: ibid.
211: mobilization is not war: ibid.
213: I'm not too sorry for *le bon* Castor: ibid.

10: I DON'T KNOW HOW TO DEAL WITH THIS WAR

216: The bourgeoisie don't want war: *Le Sursis*, J.-P. Sartre, Gallimard, 1945.
216: That makes me feel almost calm: This and all further quotes in this chapter, unless otherwise indicated, are taken from *Journal de guerre, Septembre 1939 – Janvier 1941*, Gallimard, 1990.
217: The wonderful behaviour of the government: *Journals, 1889–1949*, André Gide, Penguin, 1977.
217: Yes, all that might well disappear: ibid.
218: What a delight to have your address: *Lettres à Sartre, I*.
218: Atrocious state of mind: ibid.
218: physical liberation: ibid.
218: talking to each other: ibid.
218: It's a strange life of leisure: ibid.
219: It will be good for him: ibid.
219: I asked [Olga]: ibid.
219: there's a deep frivolity in her: ibid
219: For me . . . you are more solid: ibid
220: I'm sorry the Café de Flore is closed: ibid.
221: evolutionism, and mechanism and animals: *Lettres à Sartre, I*.
221: I never told you enough how much I loved you: ibid.
222: a sister with a bone complaint: *La Force de l'âge*.
222: My dear love: *Lettres au Castor, I*.
222: You have made me such a beautiful life: *Lettres à Sartre, I*.
222–3: My heart was empty: *La Force de l'âge*.
223: I offered only feeble resistance: ibid.
223–4: And that's why you refuse to see me: ibid.
224: The need she had of me: ibid.
224: She drew me on to the bed: *Lettres à Sartre, I*.
224: if Védrine did not exist: ibid.
224: When I see all these failures: ibid.
224: I find that so far it's a success: ibid.
225: I'm glad you're becoming fond: *Lettres au Castor, I*.
225: All these questions pierced me: ibid.
225: So you're rather in love: ibid.

225: Le Dôme is still lively: *Journal de guerre* and *Lettres à Sartre, I.*

225: This morning there were lots of familiar faces: *Lettres à Sartre, I.*

225: a smoke-laden room full of people: ibid.

226: in one sense *against* someone: ibid.

226: I am the only one . . . whom you don't overestimate: ibid.

226: You're a fine philosopher: ibid.

230: a time-bomb, dislocating my calm: *Les Carnets de la drôle de guerre.*

230: we loved each other so much: *Lettres au Castor, I.*

230: *petit chef du budget*: ibid.

231: passionate night: *Lettres à Sartre, I.*

231: she must live out our absence: ibid.

232: I think he is safer with me: ibid.

233: *Que de femmes sur mes pauvres bras*: ibid.

233: loved her as passionately as if she were a man: ibid.

234: you are my daily bread: ibid.

234: a black pullover which revealed her neck: ibid.

234–5: slowly the passion . . . it's your choice: ibid.

235: her cossack hat, a blouse with a tie: ibid.

236: she looked after him with devotion: ibid.

236: to transform Poupette into a slave-wife: ibid.

236: that [Lionel] was perfect: ibid.

236: made one with his life: ibid.

237: in a curiously negative way: *La Force de l'âge.*

11: I WANTED TO WORK

238: We began to kiss: This and all quotes in this chapter, unless otherwise indicated, are taken from *Journal de guerre.*

239: She asked if I went to bed: *Lettres à Sartre, II, 1940–1963,* Gallimard, 1990.

239: Do you know what's happening to me?: ibid.

239: I've dressed in my best: ibid.

239: more interesting than Wanda: ibid.

239: very well that you feel affection for this: ibid.

240: She is far from living only for you: ibid.

241: which interested her very much: ibid.

241: posing like a star: ibid.

241: in addition to the usual body smell of a redhead: ibid.

242: His new morality: *La Force de l'âge.*

244: I am calm: ibid.

245: strange social event in dirty grey: *Les Carnets de la drôle de guerre.*

245: How beautiful it was: *Lettres au Castor, II*.

247: luxurious and warm: *Lettres à Sartre, I*.

247: I loved Wanda very much: *Lettres au Castor, II*.
thinking of you happily: ibid.

248: Only excellent things: *Les Carnets de la drôle de guerre*.

248: During my leave you noticed: *Lettres au Castor, II*.

248: I wasn't much aware of the war there: *Les Carnets de la drôle de guerre*.

248: It was a city of men without features: ibid.

249: Yes, Paris seemed to be like a family vault: ibid.

250: I found you physically attractive: *Lettres au Castor, II*.

250: Why did I need that girl?: ibid.

251: You know very well . . . that I'd trample on: ibid.

251: Oh my love: *Lettres à Sartre, II*.

252: more than I cling to anything: *Lettres au Castor, II*.

252: You must blame me when I deserve it: ibid.

252–3: There is no pain: *The Unquiet Grave*, Palinurus (Cyril Connolly), Horizon, 1944.

253: the only thing which it hasn't been necessary to change: *Lettres au Castor, II*.

253: It brings the possibility of freedom: *Lettres à Sartre, II*.

253–4: I have reproached the two of us: ibid.

254: I'm ashamed of letters so much shorter: ibid.

255: only comfort: ibid.

256: this could well decide: *Lettres au Castor, II*.

256: serious and weighty conversations: ibid.

257: In describing the world: *La Force de l'âge*.

257: What transcendence is possible: ibid.

257: even this enclosed existence: ibid.

257: in principle I was right: ibid.

258: I did not feel I had the right to publish: *Lettres au Castor, I*, Preface.

258: They were transcriptions of day-to-day life: *Entretiens avec J.-P. Sartre*.

12: I FELT RATHER EMOTIONAL

261: Have you seen: This and all quotes in the first part of the chapter, unless otherwise indicated, are taken from *Lettres au Castor, II*.

262: *pas assez gentilles*: *Lettres à Sartre, II*.

263: *ma charmante vermine*: ibid.

264: I sat down . . . and began to cry: *La Force de l'âge*.

265: That meant . . . it was all over: ibid.

265: I imagined with anguish the arrival of the Germans: ibid.

266: her pretty red dress: *Journal de guerre*.

266: the war, about a possible defeat: ibid.

266: I felt the German advance as a personal threat: This and all further quotes in this chapter, unless otherwise indicated, are taken from *La Force de l'âge*.

270–1: I'm a prisoner: *Lettres au Castor, II*.

271: This letter matters hugely: *Journal de guerre*.

271: and I've always told you, as long as there are the two of us: *Lettres au Castor, II*.

271: If I find you again: ibid.

271: behind the statue of Balzac: ibid.

271: They don't bite: ibid.

273: a brief moment of intellectual warmth: *Lettres à Sartre, II*.

276: My love: *Lettres au Castor, II*.

277: This afternoon with Bost: *Lettres à Sartre, II*.

277: Moreover, she hates me: ibid.

277: At this moment I'm aware: ibid.

279: No, the Germans did not walk: Sartre in *La France Libre*, 1945, later in *Situations*, III, 18, 1949.

285: You and I . . . should write as one speaks: *Lettres au Castor, 11*

13: I WAS SATISFIED WITH MYSELF

286: I had an unpleasant surprise: This and all quotes in this chapter, unless otherwise indicated, are taken from *La Force de l'âge*.

288: The idea . . . will be given to you: *Lettres au Castor, II*.

292: At last Eugénie Leguen appeared: *Un Garçon sans importance*, Marcel Mouloudji, Gallimard, 1971.

295: Are you an existentialist: *La Force des choses*, Gallimard, 1963.

295: the relationship between individual experience: ibid.

295: *L'Invitée* would appear: ibid.

296: your little book . . . an excellent novel: *Lettres au Castor, II*.

298: Her old jacket was hanging: *L'Invitée*.

299: She felt Xavière's lovely warm breasts: ibid.

300: I would hate to be a Marie Laurencin: ibid.

14: I WAS OLD, I WAS THIRTY-SIX

307: to burn like a flame: *Mémoires d'une jeune fille rangée*.

308: the world had grown wider: This and all further quotes in this chapter, unless otherwise indicated, are taken from *La Force de l'âge*.

310: self-creating being . . . acts of pure decision: Anthony Quinton quoted in *Fontana Dictionary of Modern Thought*, 1977.

315: We fight for liberty: *Les Bouches inutiles*, Gallimard, 1945.
315: each of us is alone: ibid.
319: It was over . . . Paris was liberated: *La Force des choses*.
319: A life of action . . . dread of death: 'On the Fear of Death',
   Essay XXIII, *Table Talk*, William Hazlitt, 1821–22, 1824.

15: I WAS PUSHED INTO THE LIMELIGHT
322: those researchers into the human spirit: Cyril Connolly in
   Horizon, Vol XI No. 65, May 1945.
323: about the whole ambience of the Flore: ibid.
323: Flaubert and Goncourt responsible: ibid.
325: anyone who uses words to tell lies: This and all further
   quotes in this chapter, unless otherwise indicated, are taken
   from *La Force des choses*.
326: with the violence of her stormy nature: *Lettres au Castor, II*.
331–2: She disturbed me and filled me with remorse: *Lettres à
   Sartre, II*.
332: She's the only person to whom we've . . . done harm: ibid.
336: they had twined garlands of flowers: *Tous les hommes sont
   mortels*, Gallimard, 1946.
336: If that is true: ibid.
336: Now I am in love and I can suffer: ibid.
337–8: Some time later . . . I read it once more: Letter to author
   from the Queen of Denmark's Lord Chamberlain, quoting
   her words, September 17th, 1987.
338: juvenile work: ibid.

16: I WANTED TO WRITE ABOUT MYSELF
340: nihilist, miserabilist, frivolous: *Pour une morale l'ambiguité*,
   Gallimard, 1947.
340: maxims of Kant: ibid.
341: Do you remember . . . this room: This and all further quotes
   in this chapter, unless otherwise indicated, are taken from
   Lettres à Sartre, II.
342: the female intellectual counterpart of J.-P. Sartre: *New
   Yorker*, February 22nd, 1947.
342: deep blue with a large green pattern: *La Force des choses*.
348: A thing I noticed: *L'Amérique au jour le jour*, Monhien, 1948.
348: fishing for husbands: ibid.
348: In Europe . . . women understand: ibid.
348–9: inferiority complex vis-à-vis Europeans: ibid.
349: *On the Contrary*, Mary McCarthy, Weidenfeld and Nicolson
   1980.
349: a very serious book about women: *New Yorker*, February
   22nd, 1947.

350: this magnificent triumph of man: *New York Times*, May 25th, 1947.
352: I wanted to walk about: *La Force des choses*.
354: fidelity and freedom: ibid.
354: It often happened: ibid.

17: I TOOK UP AGAIN MY ESSAY ON THE FEMININE CONDITION

All quotes in this chapter, unless otherwise indicated, are taken from the Parshley translation of *Le Deuxième sexe*.
356: remarkable American comic: *Lettres à Sartre, II*.
356: I'm beginning to want to see you again: ibid.
358: Am I not much better: *Lettres au Castor, II*.
359: accepted: *Entretiens avec J.-P. Sartre*.
359: With your voting paper: *Les Nouvelles Epitres, 1945–1946*, presentées par *Le Monde illustré*.
369–70: unsatisfied, frigid: *La Force des choses*.
370: I now know everything: ibid.
370: Have I ever said: ibid.
373: theoretically the book violates: *Saturday Review*, February 21st, 1953. housewife: ibid.

18: I HAD TO TALK ABOUT US

374: had never got on better: *La Force des choses*.
375–6: I didn't need twenty-four hours to learn: This and all further quotes in this chapter, unless otherwise indicated, are taken from *Lettres à Sartre, II*.
379: This is a man writing: Hemingway, quoted by Bettina Drew in *Nelson Algren: A Life on the Wild Side*, Bloomsbury, 1990.
380: everything of myself: *La Force des choses*.
382: I closed my eyes: *Les Mandarins*, Gallimard, 1954.
382–3: *Les existentialistes*: *Le Passé Défini, Journal I, 1951–52*, Jean Cocteau, Gallimard, 1983.
383: I found you very beautiful: Film transcript: *Simone de Beauvoir*.
384: literature was no longer sacred: *La Force des choses*.
385: frank, direct, sincere: J. F. Rolland in *L'Humanité-Dimanche*, April 19th, 1986.
385: her life and thought were dominated: ibid.
386: kept a balance within our relationship: *La Force des choses*.
386: he threw an unexpected light: ibid.
387: Merleau-Ponty has never understood Sartre: 'Merleau-Ponty et le pseudo-sartisme', in *Privilèges*, Gallimard, 1955.

388: the social factor possesses: *La Longue marche*, Gallimard, 1957.

390: single two-sided story: *La Force des choses*.

393: The Djamila Boupacha affair: *Le Monde*, June 3rd, 1960.

395: I do not know what faith is: *Une mort très douce*, Gallimard, 1964.

396: thought of writing *Une mort très douce*: ibid.

396: the death of the dance of death: ibid.

397: You must have faith: Introduction to *Bluebeard and Other Fairy Tales* by Charles Perrault, Collier-Macmillan, 1964.

397: the book that scorched France: Undated quote for a 1965 book blurb, *New York Times*.

398: All forms of distress: Foreword to *La Bâtarde*, Dell, 1966.

19: I DECLARE MYSELF A FEMINIST

399: when I speak of feminism: *Tout compte fait*.

399: literature was no longer sacred: *La Force des choses*.

400: Sometimes with the intention of saying nothing: ibid.

400: one of the constant factors of this whole school: ibid.

400: I leave politics, current events: ibid.

405: Monsieur Sartre has not frequented: *Le Nouvel ingénu*, Pierre Gaxotte, Fayard, 1972.

405: But the time has come: Mary Warnock's Introduction to *Being and Nothingness,* Methuen, 1957.

406: had proved . . . to me that their state: *Tout compte fait*.

407: voices constantly on the increase: *Le Monde*, October 19th, 1970.

408: thirst for martyrdom: François Mauriac in *Figaro Littéraire*, June 15th–21st, 1970.

409: the knitting needle for some (Halimi): La Cause des Femmes, Grasset, 1973.

410: Yes. That was a long time ago: Beauvoir's evidence during the Bobigny affair. Association 'Choisir': *Avortement: une loi en procès. L'affaire de Bobigny*. Gallimard, 1973.

410: sexist insults will be considered as a crime: *Les Temps modernes*.

411: when peace was restored to the Middle East: *Le Monde*, May 3rd, 1975.

20: I AM COMMITTED TO LOOKING REALITY IN THE FACE

412: Yet I am committed: *Tout compte fait*.

412: a happy old age: *Lettres à Sartre*.

416: it eludes them all: Quoted by Annie Cohen-Solal in *Sartre*.

417: a book about Sartre: *La Cérémonie des adieux*, Gallimard, 1981.

419: the happiness that each one of us can build: 'Simone de Beauvoir's Gamble', Seminar on Simone de Beauvoir, Columbia University, New York, 4th–6th April, 1985.

420: very warm and charming: *Memoirs*, Tennessee Williams, W. H. Allen, 1976.

420: Hell, love letters should be private: Interview with W. J. Weatherby, *The Times*, May 10th, 1981.

422: to accept the sperm of other men: Quoted by Antoine Spire, *Le Matin*, April 29th, 1986.

422: *dans le feu de la vie*: Interview with Pierre Viansson-Ponté, *Le Monde*, January 10th–11th, 1978.

ENVOI

424: representative of certain currents: Jacques Chirac, quoted in *Libération*, April 15th, 1986.

424: a witness to a great moment: Georges Marchais in ibid.

424: I was fascinated: *L'Humanité*, April 15th, 1986.

424: Was Simone de Beauvoir a philosopher: *Figaro-Magazine*, April 19th, 1986.

425: He was her teacher, her father, and her lover: ibid.

425: Sartre and I, we . . . (Sir Angus Wilson): postcard to the author, 21.8.1986

426: did not like women: *Simone de Beauvoir Today*, Alice Schwarzer.

426: No bourgeois mother: *France-Observateur*, March 1960.

427: every woman is a bit . . .: *Simone de Beauvoir Today*, Alice Schwarzer.

428: books died and the authors remained: *Les Ecrivains en personne*, Madeleine Chapsal, 1960.

428: Spinoza and Stendhal: *La Cérémonie des adieux*.

INDEX

Index